Selected Papers from CEES 2021, the first International Conference on Construction, Energy, Environment and Sustainability (Coimbra, 2021), on the topic of Sustainable Construction Materials and Technologies

Selected Papers from CEES 2021, the first International Conference on Construction, Energy, Environment and Sustainability (Coimbra, 2021), on the topic of Sustainable Construction Materials and Technologies

Guest Editor

Enrico Zacchei

Basel • Beijing • Wuhan • Barcelona • Belgrade • Novi Sad • Cluj • Manchester

Guest Editor
Enrico Zacchei
Department of Mechanical
Engineering
University of Salamanca
(USAL)
Salamanca
Spain

Editorial Office
MDPI AG
Grosspeteranlage 5
4052 Basel, Switzerland

This is a reprint of the Special Issue, published open access by the journal *Infrastructures* (ISSN 2412-3811), freely accessible at: https://www.mdpi.com/journal/infrastructures/special_issues/ CEES_conference.

For citation purposes, cite each article independently as indicated on the article page online and as indicated below:

Lastname, A.A.; Lastname, B.B. Article Title. *Journal Name* **Year**, *Volume Number*, Page Range.

ISBN 978-3-7258-4056-4 (Hbk)
ISBN 978-3-7258-4055-7 (PDF)
https://doi.org/10.3390/books978-3-7258-4055-7

Contents

About the Editor

Enrico Zacchei

Enrico Zacchei is a Senior Structural Engineer, Researcher, and Adjunct Professor. Prof. Zacchei has been a Consultant for "Special Projects and Activities" at the Maua Institute of Technology (IMT), Brazil, Visiting Professor at the Department of Civil Engineering of the University State of São Paulo (UNESP), Brazil, and Visiting Researcher at the Institute of Mechanics, Materials and Civil Engineering (IMMC) of the Catholic University of Louvain (UCL), Belgium, in Structures.

Prof. Zacchei has a PhD from the University of Salamanca (USAL), Spain, in co-tutorship with the Polytechnic School of the University of São Paulo (USP), Brazil, a Second PhD from the University State of São Paulo (UNESP), Brazil, and Master and Bachelor degrees in Civil Engineering—Structures, from the University of Roma Tre (Uniroma 3), Italy, and has undertaken 10 specialization courses at USP and UNESP. Prof. Zacchei has received 10 grants/scholarships, 4 of which for stays at R&D centers: USP (2.5 years); UNESP (8 months) under ministerial scholarship "CAPES"; School of Industrial Engineering of the University of Malaga (UMA), Spain (9 months); UCL (3 months) under "WBI excellence scholarship". Prof. Zacchei has als received two prizes.

Prof. Zacchei has 9 years of technical experience in national/international companies and institutes (Italy, Brazil, Portugal) and 7 years of scientific experience. Prof. Zacchei has been a member of 10 technical projects (5 large projects) and 13 funded research projects (10 more than 500k euro) and Coordinator of 4 projects. Prof. Zacchei has more than 40 papers published in high-impact journals (JCR, Scopus) and more than 25 participations/presentations at conferences (8 as Invited/Keynote Speaker).

Prof. Zacchei has been a member of the working group "Seismic behaviour of dams: World relevant cases", ITCOLD, Italy, a member of the research group "CERIS-Coimbra" and "Experimental dynamic analysis of structures", USP, an Editor for JCR Journals (*Infrastructures, Frontiers in Built Environment*), a Reviewer for more than 15 JCR journals, and a technical-scientific committee member (9) and organizer of mini-symposia (3) for congresses/events.

Preface

The construction sector's carbon emissions drive innovation in sustainable materials and systems. As industries modernize, digital transformation becomes essential. This 2022 Special Issue (SI) highlights sustainable technologies, stressing multidisciplinary collaboration to enhance efficiency, meet environmental standards, and support the United Nations sustainable development goals (SDGs) for "peace and prosperity for people and the planet".

The published papers align with some SDGs, including "clean water and sanitation" (SDG 6), "affordable and clean energy" (7), "industry, innovation and infrastructure" (9), "sustainable cities and communities" (11), "responsible consumption and production" (12), "climate action" (13), "life below water" (14), and "partnership for the goals" (17). The 12 papers in this Special Issue are summarized as follows (Paper: Methodology and analysis type - Number of references - SDGs):

Alves et al.: Numerical and analytical analyses. Case study - 16 figures and 1 table - 69 - 11.

Cintura et al.: Analytical and experimental analyses - 11 figure and 10 tables - 88 - 9, 12.

Ferreira et al.: Analytical and experimental analyses. Case studies - 12 figures and 3 tables - 55 - 11, 14.

Figueiredo et al.: Numerical and experimental analyses - 12 figures and 2 tables - 32 - 7, 12.

Franco et al.: Bibliographic review and bibliometric analyses - 5 figures and 4 tables - 110 - 9, 12.

Goidea et al.: Experimental analyses - 5 figures - 26 - None.

Lima et al.: Analytic analyses - 11 figures and 12 tables - 68 - 9, 17.

Lourenço et al.: Experimental analyses - 7 figures and 3 tables - 21 - 12, 13.

Meireis et al.: Numerical analyses - 12 figures - 29 - 7, 9, 12.

Pérez et al.: Experimental analyses. Case study - 7 figures and 1 table - 48 - 11.

Ranesi et al.: Experimental and numerical analyses - 10 figures and 2 tables - 68 - None.

Zacchei and Colacicco: Numerical and analytical analyses - 6 figures and 3 tables - 35 - 6, 7.

The SDGs were retrieved from the new "impact" section in the Scopus database, which links papers to SDGs based on research relevance. Around 650 references highlight the depth of research. In total, 53 authors have participated, involving 7 different countries (Portugal, Spain, Italy, Germany, Sweden, Switzerland, Brazil), indicating the intent to create a multidisciplinary, holistic, and international SI. The SDGs and their percentage of occurrence were as follows: None (9%), 6 (5%), 7 (14%), 9 (19%), 11 (14%), 12 (24%), 13 (5%), 14 (5%), and 17 (5%). This could indicate the contribution to achieving some of the main SDGs (obviously in a minimal form). The most frequent SDGs are 7, 9, 11, and 12. Note that as SDG 9 aligns directly with engineering disciplines and thus with "sustainable construction materials and technologies", it is interesting to note that other SDGs can still be addressed within the engineering topics.

Enrico Zacchei
Guest Editor

Article

Analysis of the Optical Response of Opaque Urban Envelope Materials: The Case of Madrid [†]

Gloria Pérez [1,*], Fernando Martín-Consuegra [1], Fernando de Frutos [1], Arturo Martínez [1,2], Ignacio Oteiza [1], Borja Frutos [1] and Carmen Alonso [1]

[1]   Instituto de Ciencias de la Construccion Eduardo Torroja (IETCC), CSIC, 28033 Madrid, Spain
[2]   Departamento de Construcción y Tecnología Arquitectónicas, ETSAM, Universidad Politécnica de Madrid, 28040 Madrid, Spain
*   Correspondence: gperezaq@ietcc.csic.es
†   This paper was presented at the CEES 2021, the First International Conference on Construction, Energy, Environment and Sustainability in Coimbra, Portugal. It has been modified for publishing in the journal.

Abstract: The optical response of opaque materials in an urban envelope plays an important role in a city's energy exchange with the environment as it defines the absorption of radiation and emission of heat. In the present work, the most common surfaces of the finishing materials of pavement and walls in the city of Madrid (Spain) were identified, and their reflectance was measured in situ to determine their solar absorptance and color coordinates. Most of the selected pavement showed a relatively high solar absorptance in the range of 0.87 to 0.60, while in vertical surfaces, the range was 0.85 to 0.29. The variations of the color coordinates obtained for pavement were 27.1, 11.4, and 6.7 for ΔL^*, Δa^*, and Δb^*, respectively. Significantly higher values were obtained in the case of vertical surfaces (47.5, 20.5, and 23.6, respectively). The results were included into a database intended to be the seed for a catalogue of the experimental thermo-optical properties of opaque envelope materials in Madrid. The catalogue will be useful for the analysis of the stimuli generated by the urban environment for citizens and for achieving more reliable results from energy simulation tools in the search for strategies to improve urban comfort and sustainability.

Keywords: optical properties; urban envelope; opaque materials; energy refurbishment; urban heat island

1. Introduction

In the context of an increasingly urgent energy transition, the management of solar radiation in urban environments is the subject of a growing number of studies [1]. The need for the distributed generation of renewable energy directly at places where high consumption occurs has led to the proliferation of studies aimed at quantifying incident solar radiation in urban landscapes [2–6]. However, the needs of inefficient cities with high consumption cannot be met by renewable energy potential alone. Energy demand must be drastically reduced through retrofitting so that these renewable installations can be reasonably sized [7–9]. In solving this complex equation, less attention is being paid to outdoor comfort and the influence of the microclimate on the energy efficiency of urban fabrics [10]. A complete bioclimatic analysis of a building, aimed at the rational use of natural resources, must take into account not only the characteristics of the environment [11], but also the influence of the buildings on the microclimate [12]. Land surface temperature has already been positively correlated with urban density and floor area ratio [13]. Further, a building's frontal area density has an effect on the physiologically equivalent temperature, thermal comfort, and air quality at the pedestrian level above the sidewalk [14]. Solar obstructions caused by urban morphology are fundamental, but so is the configuration of public spaces, including vegetation and the optical characteristics of the materials that conform to them [15]. The passive cooling of outdoor urban spaces has also been addressed

Infrastructures **2022**, *7*, 116. https://doi.org/10.3390/infrastructures7090116   https://www.mdpi.com/journal/infrastructures

through comparative studies that aimed to investigate the suitability of materials in order to contribute to lower ambient temperatures and fight the urban heat island effect [16].

Improving the quality of the outdoor environment of our cities has been identified as a priority challenge at the European level. High-quality urban spaces—such as well-designed streets, footpaths, squares, and parks—provide the structure that enables cities to come to life and encourages and accommodates diverse activities [17]. The optical response of opaque surface materials has a major impact on this challenge [18]. On the one hand, this response regulates the reflection and absorption of solar radiation, thus conditioning the impact of solar heating on the urban microclimate and on a building's energy efficiency [19,20]. Recent research has shown how substituting high-emission thermal terrestrial materials with low-emission ones plays a key role in modifying the outdoor microclimate [21].

However, research on urban coatings must be assessed to consider the potential relationship between the environmental quality and thermal sensation in outdoor spaces [22]. The optical response in the visible part of the spectrum, related to different textures and colors, generates multiple stimuli in citizens, affecting their well-being. Therefore, some strategies for the mitigation of the urban heat island (UHI) effect can lead to considerable benefits in terms of temperature and energy but could also determine a penalization of the well-being of pedestrians [23]. The bio-meteorological observations of a solar reflective coating to investigate its thermal performance from a pedestrian perspective has shown that the surface temperature of coated asphalt concrete was lower than that of regular asphalt concrete, but this effect could increase the mean radiant temperature [24]. Similar research has already been carried out to evaluate the stimuli created by green spaces, finding relations between the reduction in anxiety and psychological distress [25].

A recent synthetic review of methods has identified six research gaps in the use of cool pavements for UHI mitigation. These are the lack of research on how permeable pavement affects building energy consumption and greenhouse gas emissions when used for UHI mitigation; the lack of research to quantify the relationship between cool pavements, surface and air temperatures, and human thermal comfort at multiple spatial scales; the lack of research on the durability of cool pavements; the need to fully evaluate numerical simulations against detailed field experiments; the lack of research on the life cycle assessments (LCA) of cool pavements; and the improper use of terminology for pavement-related strategies in research [26].

Previous works have analyzed the effect of the surface finish of buildings on their energy exchange with the environment as a basis for mitigation strategies for the urban heat island effect [27,28] and for improving the energy performance of buildings, with special attention to their renovation [29]. These works have shown that the use of multi-functional and innovative materials in building envelopes can provide radical improvements in the energy efficiency and economic value of new and refurbished buildings, while improving outdoor thermal comfort. In addition, the benefits of the solar resources to the public must be addressed. Due to the dynamic shadowing effects present on building surfaces, quantifying these phenomena is essential for predicting solar radiation availability that can significantly affect the potential for solar energy use [1]. As a continuation of these works, it is necessary to extend this knowledge outside of buildings to study the configuration of the urban space, and to assess the influence that the surroundings have on the buildings and that the buildings have among themselves and on the environment [28,30]. Frameworks for evaluating building energy performance and outdoor thermal comfort are being developed for the holistic assessment of the urban environment [31].

A monitoring campaign of the energy performance and indoor environment quality of dwellings located in inefficient and deprived residential areas in city outskirts is being carried out in Madrid (Spain) [32,33]. The areas are socioeconomically vulnerable, containing a high proportion of dwellings without thermal insulation and having high energy needs. The present work aims to take the focus away from the interior of the buildings to analyze the exterior spaces. This will make it possible to assess the influence of the outdoor environment on the thermal performance of buildings and to reach innovative and integral conclusions for the rehabilitation of neighborhoods that include the improvement of the thermal performance of buildings, harnessing the solar potential, and improving the quality of the outdoor environment [34].

Some studies point to the disparity between the results of predictive microclimate models and in situ measurements obtained by monitoring climatic parameters in urban environments [35]. The precise characterization of the optical properties of urban finishing materials would allow for obtaining more accurate models than those currently used.

2. Objectives

The specific objective of this work is to carry out an inventory that includes the experimental optical properties of the most common opaque surface finishes in the urban areas of the outskirts of the city of Madrid. Both pavements and vertical surfaces are considered in this analysis. This catalogue will be useful for deepening the knowledge of the optical characteristics of these materials and their effects on the energy performance of buildings and on outdoor comfort. In addition, the use of the experimental optical parameters will provide more realistic results from energy simulation studies. This, in turn, will allow for the elaboration of more efficient proposals for the improvement of urban spaces aimed at reducing the urban heat island effect and achieving more sustainable cities.

3. Materials and Methods

The work was carried out in two campaigns that consisted of field visits to selected neighborhoods.

3.1. First Campaign

The first step of the analysis consisted of a visual identification of the opaque materials conforming the horizontal and vertical surfaces of the urban landscape. Visits were made to eight neighborhoods along the city of Madrid: Picazo, Orcasitas, Orcasur, Fuencarral, Villaverde Bajo, Simancas, Tetuan, and Montecarmelo. Before starting the visits, a route was traced in each neighborhood to register the materials in the buildings and the urban spaces representative of the area whose identification allowed a general material characterization.

Through a walking tour, the finishing materials present along the way were photographed, including the vertical and horizontal finishes accessible from the pedestrian level. The aim was to capture the variety of combinations of textures and colors present during the tour.

In addition to the fact that the classification sought to distinguish and locate the materials in the urban environment, an attempt was made to anticipate their potential impacts on urban environment through the assignment of a descriptive reference to each photographed material. In the case of vertical finishes, the reference indicated the vertical placement within the façade or wall. This information is of interest as, although there is a greater variety of coatings in the lower parts of buildings, most of the time, they represent a low percentage of the envelope. The categories were as follows: cladding covering the total or most of the vertical element surface (TVS), cladding covering only the lower part (LVS), or cladding covering only the higher part (HVS). In the case of horizontal finishes, the reference categorizes the materials according to the specific use: sidewalks (SDW), driveways (DRW), or landscaped areas (LND). Correlative numbers were added to the reference to differentiate the materials of the same category.

Each of the photographed materials was geo-located using maps and street views on the Google maps ® system to facilitate future consultation. In the case of restricted areas for street views, general photographs of the surroundings were taken instead.

The images of the materials were included in information sheets, which in this first phase contained the assigned reference, location (neighborhood/street), estimated frequency of use of the finishing in the studied neighborhood, and perceptible morpho-material characteristics. The latter were determined through an evaluation of the finishes through the eyes of trained personnel and refers to surface material, color, tone, aging level, texture, and size of the unitary element, if applicable. In the case of vertical finishes, the estimated wall height (expressed as building levels) and orientation were also collected.

3.2. Second Campaign

The second campaign consisted of recording the optical properties of the materials identified in the first campaign as the most frequently occurring finishes in the sample, as well as those with the largest surface area. In situ measurement of the reflectance was carried out at representative and accessible urban elements. The reflectance was recorded in the 350 to 1700 nm wavelength range (covering 95% of the total solar energy) with a Stellarnet handheld fiber optic equipment fitted with a reflectance probe. The equipment consists of a tungsten halogen lamp with a color-equalizing filter, a miniature spectrometer covering the wavelength range between 350 and 1080 nm (model BLK-C-SR), and another spectrometer covering an overlapping range from 900 to 1700 nm (model Dwarf Star). These elements were connected through a fiber optic reflectance probe in which seven illumination fibers were installed around a central reading fiber. The measuring system allowed for an adequate signal-to-noise ratio with low measuring times. The probe was placed using a suitable accessory at a fixed distance from the measuring surface and was at a 90° angle. This was the most suitable configuration for the majority of the materials at the urban envelope that showed appreciable surface roughness. The system was calibrated previous to the measurement of each sample by blocking the light from the lamp to define the 0% reflectance signal and by measuring a Spectralon standard to define the 100% reflectance signal.

The solar and visible absorptance values were calculated from the mean spectrum of three measurements in each case. In addition, the three color coordinates defined in the CIELAB 1976 space, corresponding to the CIE 1964 Standard Observer and D65 Illuminant, were calculated for each sample from the mean reflectance spectrum in the visible range (380–780 nm). The L* coordinate indicated lightness, with values of 0 for black and 100 for white. The a* coordinate could have values of between −90 and +90, with negative values for green and positive values for red. Finally, the b* coordinate may also have had values of between −90 and +90, and negative was for blue, and positive was for yellow.

4. Results

4.1. First Campaign: Identification of Materials

Figure 1 shows representative images of the tasks carried out in the first campaign to identify the finishing materials in the selected neighborhoods. In the left, a map is depicted of the route taken to go through the different urban morphologies and open urban spaces encountered within the Picazo neighborhood. In the right image, the information collected at a specific area of the neighborhood is shown. This includes geo-localization and a street view picture of the area and the detailed location and image of three different vertical finishing materials that are properly identified by the assigned reference.

The results from the different neighborhoods of the city were compiled for the selection and classification of the materials more frequently used or used in larger surfaces. Table 1 is representative of the results compiled for the case of vertical finishes in the Picazo neighborhood. The data from the first campaign correspond to the groups named "General data" and "Morpho-material characteristics".

Table 1. Representative information sheet obtained from the experimental campaigns.

Neighborhood	Picazo
Date of data collection	18 January 2022
Campaign	1—Identification

Table 1. *Cont.*

Neighborhood	Picazo
VERTICAL FINISHING MATERIALS	
A. GENERAL DATA	
Reference	**TVS-5**
Image	
Location	García Llamas 16
Wall height	3 to 5
Wall orientation	South-east
Frequency of use	>50%
B.1. MORFO-MATERIAL CHARACTERISTICS	
Surface material	Brick
Color	Orange
Tone	Mean
Ageing level	Mean
Texture	Mean
Unit size (cm)	4×9
B.2.OPTO-THERMAL PARAMETERS	
Solar absorptance	0.495
Visible absorptance	0.657
Color coordinates (L*/a*/b*)	60.6/20.0/26.8
Infrared emissivity	Pending

Figure 1. Images of the tasks carried out in the first campaign in the Picazo neighborhood. **Left**: definition of the route. **Right**: geolocation and close-ups of the materials. Image created from Google earth Studio and Google Maps.

4.2. Second Campaign: Optical Characterization of Materials

The second campaign, dedicated to the in situ measurement of the finishes identified as most representative, gave rise to the results detailed as follows. Figure 2 collects the images of the twenty materials selected for the horizontal finishes. H1 to H15 correspond to finishes at the sidewalks. H1 to H3 are the most frequently used grey concrete tiles at different degradation stages and H4 and H7 are brand new pavers, in grey and pink colors, used in urban refurbishment actions in the neighborhoods. H5, H6, and H8–H11 are reddish pavement elements with different material compositions, surface patterns, and degradation stages, respectively. Specifically, H8 corresponds to a pink paver in a degraded stage at an area which was intended to be repaired with H7 pavers. H12 and H13 correspond to similar elements within the same urban area in a slightly used black-colored stage and in a degraded grey-colored stage, respectively. H14 corresponds to the prefabricated curb most present in the sample and H15 to tiles of exposed aggregate concrete. H16 to H20 correspond to the following frequent materials used in driveways: asphalt in two different degradation stages, concrete paving sets, and white paint to identify crosswalks and granite slabs, respectively.

Figure 2. Horizontal surface finishes.

Twenty finishing materials were selected from the surfaces of vertical urban-facing elements (see Figure 3). V1 corresponds to calcareous stone cladding with a smooth surface, V2 to ceramic tiles with a semi-rough surface and common terracotta color, V3 and V4 to concrete blocks painted with two different light colors, V5 to white paint on rough plastering, and V6 and V7 to different continuous cement mortar wall coatings. One of the most common finishing materials in the facades found in the sample from Madrid was the facing brick. V8 to V14 are the cases selected from the wide range of colors and textures found in this type of building facade surface in the neighborhoods analyzed in this work. V15 is an exposed aggregate concrete cladding and V16 to V18 are representative of the wide variety of mortar claddings found in the facades, most of them in light or reddish colors. Finally, V19 is a pre-cast concrete white element and V20 is a granite slab.

The experimental optical response of each of the surface finishes collected in Figures 2 and 3 were measured in situ in the representative and accessible urban elements and the resulting opto-thermal parameters were added to the information sheet (see Table 1). Figure 4 shows the collected the solar absorptance values of the 40 materials under analysis, calculated from the experimental solar reflectance. The lowest value of this parameter in the case of pavements was equal to 0.270 and corresponded to sample H19, the white-painted areas identifying crosswalks in driveways (see Figure 2). Apart from this sample, all the horizontal finish materials showed a solar absorptance of between 0.87 and 0.60. In general, the results indicated that the most usual pavements of Madrid give rise to a high absorption of solar energy.

Figure 3. Vertical surface finishes.

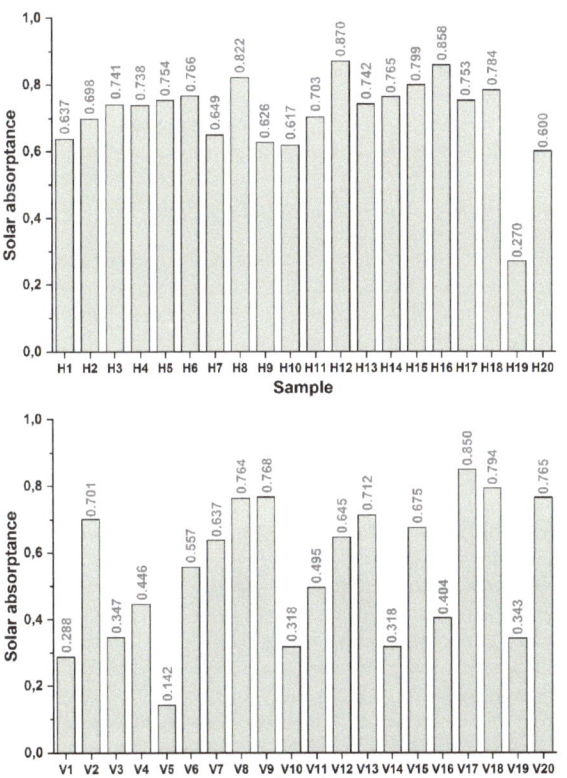

Figure 4. Solar absorptance of the materials analyzed in situ. **Top**: horizontal surface finishes. **Bottom**: vertical surface finishes.

In more detail, the grey-colored cementitious pavements included in Figure 2 (samples H1 to H4, H14, and H18) showed solar absorptance values ranging from 0.64 to 0.78. There is a wide variety for the optical properties of cement and concrete samples in the literature, depending on the use of grey or white Portland cement and on the type of aggregates included in the concrete formulation [36–39]. For matrices based on grey cement, Levinson and Akbari [36] reported solar absorptance values in the range of 0.48–0.81. More recently, Sanjuan et al. [39] studied commercial pavements and obtained solar absorptance values ranging between 0.69 and 0.72 for paving materials made with dark grey Portland cement and fine siliceous aggregates. These values are in good agreement with the experimental results of the present work, taking into account that an increase in absorptance is expected by the weathering effect and the accumulation of dirt in the in-use materials analyzed [36]. Accordingly, within the reddish horizontal finishes (from H5 to H11), higher values of α_s are measured for the samples showing higher aging (H5, H6, and H8). On the contrary, a decrease in solar absorptance is observed between the new black element H12 (0.87) and the corresponding aged sample H13 (0.74). The effect of aging on the optical response of the horizontal finishes will be further described below.

Regarding the asphalt finishes, the solar absorptance obtained for sample H16 (0.86) is in good agreement with the values between 0.8 and 0.9 reported in [40] for in-use asphalt. The lower value of 0.75 obtained in the present work for the more-degraded asphalt represented by sample H17 is also coherent with the values reported for roads subject to long aging, in which the binder has almost disappeared and the surface is mainly composed of aggregates.

On the other hand, the lowest solar absorptance value for vertical finish materials was 0.142, measured in the white paint on rough plastering (V5 in Figure 3). However, a wide range of solar absorptance values was obtained for the rest of the samples, ranging from 0.850 to 0.288. This variation indicates that typical facades may be found in Madrid favoring the absorption or the reflection of the solar radiation incident on the buildings. A similar variety was reported in reference [41] for the optical response of 80 vertical claddings available in the market, including the most-used materials, as well as the new tendencies found in the city of Mendoza (Argentina). These results suggest that the choice of façade materials is not, in general, defined by the thermal effect expected by their solar response at the specific climatic conditions of the city.

The CIELab color coordinates calculated from the reflectance spectra of the finish materials are shown in Figures 5 and 6. The coordinate L^* shows a variation, ΔL^*, of 27.1 for the horizontal surfaces, with the same exception of H19 as before. This value is significantly lower than the ΔL^* of 47.5 shown by the vertical surfaces. Regarding the a^* and b^* coordinates, a clearly higher dispersion was also observed in the façade finishes as compared to the pavements in Figure 6. The difference is more significant, taking into account the different scales used in the two graphs. Quantitatively, the variation of a^*/b^* is 11.4/6.7 in horizontal finishes and 20.5/23.6 in vertical ones.

The quantitative results of the colorimetric characterization were coherent with the appearance of the samples. Horizontal finish surfaces may be divided in two groups, as indicated in Figure 6 (left): one group corresponds to the white-, black-, and grey-colored pavements (H1–H4 and H12–H20 in Figure 2) that show lower a^* values, from 0.1 (H19) to 2.4 (H14). The other group collects the reddish-colored pavements (H5–H11 in Figure 2) with higher a^* values of between 6.7 for H5 and 17.1 for H7. The color contrast between the groups is used to capture the attention of the citizens, indicating proposed pathways or a proximity to risk elements, such as a driveway. The same intention of capturing attention is assumed for the black (H12) pavement with a significantly lower b^* value than the rest of pavements in the low-a^* group and for the white paint (H19) with the highest L^* value.

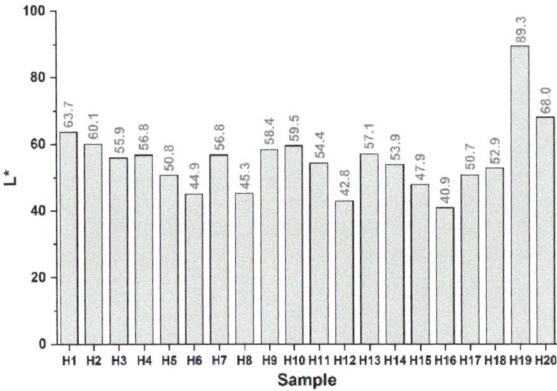

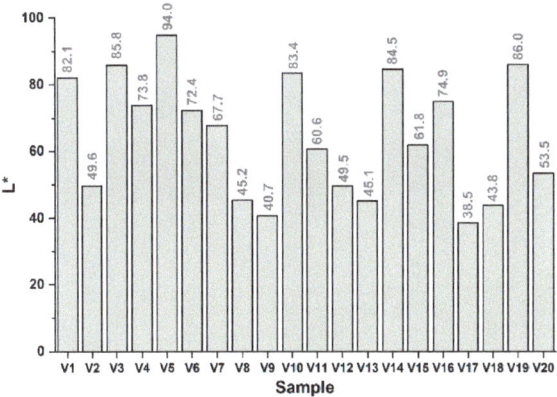

Figure 5. Color coordinate L* of the materials analyzed in situ. **Top**: horizontal surface finishes. **Bottom**: vertical surface finishes.

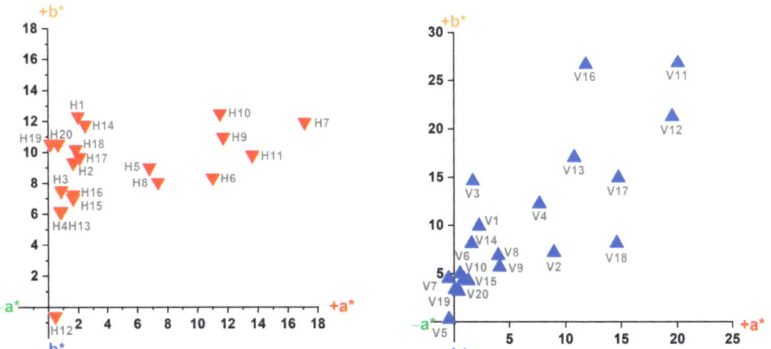

Figure 6. Color coordinates a* and b* of the materials analyzed in situ. **Left**: horizontal surface finishes. **Right**: vertical surface finishes.

A similar differentiation is applicable for the vertical finishes, although with a significantly higher dispersion within each group, as observed in Figure 6 (right). The wide variety of colorimetric responses of facade materials is probably determined by aesthetic aspects and gives rise, to a large extent, to the wide variety of solar absorptance values noted in Figure 4.

As previously noted, an interesting result from the characterization of the surface urban materials refers to the aging effect on their optical response. Figure 7 shows the mean reflectance spectra of four of the measured pavements representing different aging stages. In the case of the pink pavement named as H7 in its brand-new stage, a clear decrease in the reflectance is observed upon aging (sample H8) in the whole solar wavelength range, which gives rise to the significant increase in solar absorptance from 0.65 to 0.82 (Figure 4). This variation will increase the heating of the pavement surface by solar radiation and is coherent with previous works on the effect of weathering, soiling, and abrasion on the solar response of cement-based materials [36]. Regarding the visible range (wavelengths from 380 to 780 nm), the decrease in reflectance with aging accounts for the decrease in the L^* coordinate from 56.8 for H7 to 45.3 for H8. A change in the shape of the reflectance spectrum is also observed for wavelengths higher than 616 nm. This change gives rise to the variation of the b^* and, especially, the a^* coordinates that takes a significantly higher value in the new H7 sample related to the reflectance maximum at 750 nm, which is not present in the aged stage (H8). The results are coherent with the appearance of the surfaces shown in Figure 2.

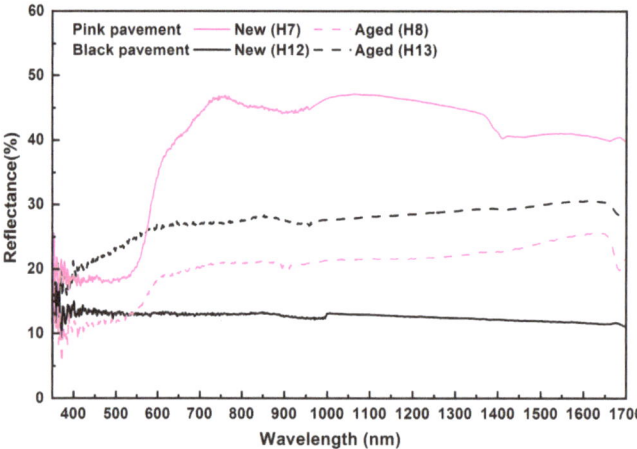

Figure 7. Mean reflectance spectra of the different horizontal surface finishes shown in Figure 2.

A different behavior of the black pavement upon aging is derived from the optical characterization of the H12 (new) and H13 (aged) samples. The new pavement shows a low and nearly constant reflectance along the solar spectral range that accounts for the high solar absorptance (0.87), the low L^* value (42.8), and the a^* and b^* values close to zero, indicating that no color predominates in the black surface. Upon aging, the reflectance of the surface clearly increases at all the wavelengths, giving rise to the decrease in the solar absorptance down to 0.74, the increase in the L^* value up to 57.1, and the coherently lighter appearance of the surface (Figure 2). The spectral curve is still flat, except for a smooth decrease in reflectance for decreasing wavelengths in the visible range, below 590 nm, that accounts for the slight increase in the b^* coordinate. The change in α_s observed in this case is similar to that previously reported for the aging effect in asphalt pavements [40].

Further analysis is necessary to separate the contribution to the changes observed in the optical response of the urban materials which is due to aging from the possible contributions of other effects, such as the composition of the samples.

5. Discussion

Papers characterizing the optical properties of urban materials are mainly devoted to the analysis of innovative materials to support the interest of their development and application [42–44]. However, urban surface finishes in the outskirts of big cities usually implement conventional materials whose optical properties are scarcely studied. In addition, in most of the works considering these conventional materials [36–39,41], the optical characterization is performed at a laboratory level on new samples or those weathered under controlled conditions, which gives rise to a lower degradation as compared to the in-use samples analyzed in the present work. An exception is, for instance, the work by Sen and Roesler [40], which studied the optical properties of asphalt samples from real roads in different degradation stages and concluded an increase in the effect with aging time.

This type of controlled experiment is necessary to properly define the materials available in the market or in development within energy simulation tools and to predict the effect of their aging in studies of comfort and energy efficiency, both at the building or urban scale. However, in order to obtain a reliable proposal for the refurbishment of urban areas, it is also necessary to perform an in situ characterization of the in-use materials, such as the ones presented in this work. The results will be necessary for the challenging quantitative analysis of the solar energy balance obtained for in-use materials and different retrofitting options. In Qin's review on the development of cool pavements to mitigate the urban heat island effect, held in 2015, it was concluded that the influence of cool pavements on the air temperature in the urban canopy layer is unknown, and that the impact of cool pavements on the thermal conditions of adjacent buildings and pedestrians remains unknown [45]. In fact, works approaching this research gap are very scarce. In [46], a modeling approach was proposed for a detailed analysis of the impact of different pavements and meteorological conditions (wind, sun, and rain) on the absorption and storage of heat and moisture in urban environments, concluding that albedo influences pavement surface temperature in both dry and wet conditions. Remote sensing was used in [47] to assess the cooling effects of city-scale efforts to reduce the urban heat island effect, concluding that Chicago's new reflective surfaces since 1995 produced a noticeable impact on the citywide albedo, raising it by approximately 0.016, while the citywide normalized difference vegetation index (NDVI) increase was approximately 0.007. This finding, along with counts of pixels with increased albedo and NDVI, suggest that the reflective strategies influenced a larger area of the city than the vegetative methods.

In this context, the use of experimental optical properties of surface finishes in the assessment of the initial state of the urban area to be refurbished will allow for better estimating the potential improvement in urban comfort or energy demand from retrofitting actions. Moreover, those parameters related to the interaction of materials with the visible parts of the solar spectrum (visible reflectance, color coordinates, and roughness) will be useful for the analysis of the stimuli generated by the urban environment on citizens. The adequate analysis and management of these stimuli has proven to be necessary to improve the well-being of citizens. Finally, the results will also be of interest for the calibration of aircraft and spacecraft spectroscopic data used for the classification of materials at the urban scale [48].

6. Conclusions

This work presents the optical characterization of opaque surface finish materials in use in Madrid, representing a large European city. The parameters related to the interaction of solar radiation with those materials that affect the city's sustainability are defined and collected in a format useful for future consultation. The experimental results obtained from the in situ measurements in the city of Madrid indicate that most of the materials used in pavements favor glare reduction, as well as solar heating. A wide variety of responses are obtained in the case of facade materials, likely determined by aesthetic aspects that are related to the visual perception of citizens more so than to the thermal implications.

Different lines of action are planned to complete the experimental analysis of the optical response of opaque surface finishes in the city of Madrid. On the one hand, the characterization of the urban materials presented in this work should be completed by the in situ measurement of their emissivity in order to complete the knowledge of their thermo-optical response. On the other hand, the inventory of urban materials in use in the city of Madrid should be completed with the selection and characterization of the most usual materials in roofs. In this case, the in situ characterization may require other approaches, such as the use of drones.

In future research, a quantitative analysis of the solar energy balance obtained for the in-use materials and different retrofitting options will be addressed, including the possible aging effects. The analysis will be based on combining urban outdoor and building indoor energy modeling, and outdoor environmental quality monitoring of the stressed areas of the city under analysis. Finally, the effects of vehicles typically parked and driving along the roads will be considered in future projects, as the solar absorption at their metal surfaces and their shading in parking areas may also affect the solar energy balance.

Author Contributions: Conceptualization, G.P. and F.M.-C.; methodology, F.M.-C. and A.M.; software, F.d.F.; validation, G.P., F.M.-C. and A.M.; formal analysis, G.P., A.M. and F.d.F.; investigation, G.P., F.M.-C., F.d.F., A.M., B.F. and C.A.; data curation, G.P., F.d.F. and A.M.; writing—original draft preparation, G.P., F.M.-C. and A.M.; writing—review and editing, F.d.F., B.F. and C.A.; visualization, G.P., F.d.F. and A.M.; supervision, I.O.; project administration, G.P. and I.O.; funding acquisition, G.P. and I.O. All authors have read and agreed to the published version of the manuscript.

Funding: This research is part of Grant PID2020-114873RB-C31 funded by MCIN/AEI/10.13039/501100011033 and Grant BIA2017-83231-C2-1-R funded by MCIN/AEI/10.13039/501100011033.

Institutional Review Board Statement: Not applicable.

Informed Consent Statement: Not applicable.

Data Availability Statement: The data presented in this study are available on request from the corresponding author.

Acknowledgments: Arturo Martínez acknowledges the support provided by the Consejo Nacional de Ciencia y Tecnología (CONACYT) and the Fundación Nacional de Bellas Artes (FINBA) given through its doctorate scholarship program. The authors acknowledge the support from Grant INCGLO0008 funded by the CSIC under the Lincglobal 2021 Program.

Conflicts of Interest: The authors declare no conflict of interest.

References

1. Freitas, S.; Catita, C.; Redweik, P.; Brito, M. Modelling solar potential in the urban environment: State-of-the-art review. *Renew. Sustain. Energy Rev.* **2015**, *41*, 915–931. [CrossRef]
2. Redweik, P.; Catita, C.; Brito, M. Solar energy potential on roofs and facades in an urban landscape. *Sol. Energy* **2013**, *97*, 332–341. [CrossRef]
3. Sarralde, J.J.; Quinn, D.J.; Wiesmann, D.; Steemers, K. Solar energy and urban morphology: Scenarios for increasing the renewable energy potential of neighbourhoods in London. *Renew. Energy* **2015**, *73*, 10–17. [CrossRef]
4. Shi, Z.; Fonseca, J.A.; Schlueter, A. A parametric method using vernacular urban block typologies for investigating interactions between solar energy use and urban design. *Renew. Energy* **2020**, *165*, 823–841. [CrossRef]
5. Takebayashi, H.; Ishii, E.; Moriyama, M.; Sakaki, A.; Nakajima, S.; Ueda, H. Study to examine the potential for solar energy utilization based on the relationship between urban morphology and solar radiation gain on building rooftops and wall surfaces. *Sol. Energy* **2015**, *119*, 362–369. [CrossRef]
6. Wegertseder, P.; Lund, P.; Mikkola, J.; Alvarado, R.G. Combining solar resource mapping and energy system integration methods for realistic valuation of urban solar energy potential. *Sol. Energy* **2016**, *135*, 325–336. [CrossRef]
7. Bertoldi, P.; Economidou, M.; Palermo, V.; Boza-Kiss, B.; Todeschi, V. How to finance energy renovation of residential buildings: Review of current and emerging financing instruments in the EU. *WIREs Rev. Energy Environ.* **2020**, *10*, e384. [CrossRef]
8. Martín-Consuegra, F.; Hernández Aja, A.; Oteiza, I.; Alonso, C. Energy needs and vulnerability estimation at an urban scale for residential neighbourhoods heating in Madrid (Spain). In Proceedings of the PLEA 2016 Los Angeles—32th Interna-tional Conference on Passive and Low Energy Architecture, Los Angeles, CA, USA, 24 October 2016; pp. 1413–1419.

9. Helge Sigurd Næss-Schmidt. Multiple Benefits of Investing in Energy Efficient Renovation of Buildings. Copenhagen Economics. 2012. Available online: https://copenhageneconomics.com/publication/multiple-benefits-of-investing-in-energy-efficient-renovation-of-buildings/ (accessed on 7 July 2022).
10. Anderson, J.E.; Wulfhorst, G.; Lang, W. Energy analysis of the built environment—A review and outlook. *Renew. Sustain. Energy Rev.* **2015**, *44*, 149–158. [CrossRef]
11. Ascione, F.; Bellia, L.; Mazzei, P.; Minichiello, F. Solar gain and building envelope: The surface factor. *Build. Res. Inf.* **2010**, *38*, 187–205. [CrossRef]
12. Fabbri, K.; Gaspari, J.; Bartoletti, S.; Antonini, E. Effect of facade reflectance on outdoor microclimate: An Italian case study. *Sustain. Cities Soc.* **2020**, *54*, 101984. [CrossRef]
13. Yang, J.; Ren, J.; Sun, D.; Xiao, X.; Xia, J.C.; Jin, C.; Li, X. Understanding land surface temperature impact factors based on local climate zones. *Sustain. Cities Soc.* **2021**, *69*, 102818. [CrossRef]
14. Li, Z.; Zhang, H.; Wen, C.-Y.; Yang, A.-S.; Juan, Y.-H. Effects of frontal area density on outdoor thermal comfort and air quality. *Build. Environ.* **2020**, *180*, 107028. [CrossRef]
15. Alchapar, N.L.; Correa, E.N. Optothermal properties of façade coatings. Effects of environmental exposure over solar reflective index. *J. Build. Eng.* **2020**, *32*, 101536. [CrossRef]
16. Doulos, L.; Santamouris, M.; Livada, I. Passive cooling of outdoor urban spaces. The role of materials. *Sol. Energy* **2004**, *77*, 231–249. [CrossRef]
17. Hanafi, I.; El Araby, M.; Al Hagla, K.; El Sayary, S. Human Social Behavior in Public Urban Spaces: Towards Higher Quality Cities. *Spaces Flows Int. J. Urban Extra Urban Stud.* **2013**, *3*, 23–35. [CrossRef]
18. Santamouris, M. Recent progress on urban overheating and heat island research. Integrated assessment of the energy, environmental, vulnerability and health impact. Synergies with the global climate change. *Energy Build.* **2020**, *207*, 109482. [CrossRef]
19. Ko, Y.; Radke, J.D. The Effect of Urban Form and Residential Cooling Energy Use in Sacramento, California. *Environ. Plan. B Plan. Des.* **2014**, *41*, 573–593. [CrossRef]
20. Berardi, U.; Garai, M.; Morselli, T. Preparation and assessment of the potential energy savings of thermochromic and cool coatings considering inter-building effects. *Sol. Energy* **2020**, *209*, 493–504. [CrossRef]
21. Atwa, S.; Ibrahim, M.G.; Murata, R. Evaluation of plantation design methodology to improve the human thermal comfort in hot-arid climatic responsive open spaces. *Sustain. Cities Soc.* **2020**, *59*, 102198. [CrossRef]
22. Lau, K.K.-L.; Tan, Z.; Morakinyo, T.E.; Ren, C. Environmental Perception and Outdoor Thermal Comfort in High-Density Cities. In *Outdoor Thermal Comfort in Urban Environment: Assessments and Applications in Urban Planning and Design, Springer Briefs in Architectural Design and Technology*; Lau, K.K.-L., Tan, Z., Morakinyo, T.E., Ren, C., Eds.; Springer: Singapore, 2021; pp. 51–65. [CrossRef]
23. Falasca, S.; Ciancio, V.; Salata, F.; Golasi, I.; Rosso, F.; Curci, G. High albedo materials to counteract heat waves in cities: An assessment of meteorology, buildings energy needs and pedestrian thermal comfort. *Build. Environ.* **2019**, *163*, 106242. [CrossRef]
24. Middel, A.; Turner, V.K.; Schneider, F.A.; Zhang, Y.; Stiller, M. Solar reflective pavements—A policy panacea to heat mitigation? *Environ. Res. Lett.* **2020**, *15*, 064016. [CrossRef]
25. Kondo, M.C.; Triguero-Mas, M.; Donaire-Gonzalez, D.; Seto, E.; Valentín, A.; Hurst, G.; Carrasco-Turigas, G.; Masterson, D.; Ambròs, A.; Ellis, N.; et al. Momentary mood response to natural outdoor environments in four European cities. *Environ. Int.* **2019**, *134*, 105237. [CrossRef] [PubMed]
26. Wang, C.; Wang, Z.-H.; Kaloush, K.E.; Shacat, J. Cool pavements for urban heat island mitigation: A synthetic review. *Renew. Sustain. Energy Rev.* **2021**, *146*, 111171. [CrossRef]
27. Santamouris, M. Cooling the cities—A review of reflective and green roof mitigation technologies to fight heat island and improve comfort in urban environments. *Sol. Energy* **2012**, *103*, 682–703. [CrossRef]
28. Urrutia, N.; Grijalba, O.; Hernández Aja, A. A case-based urban microclimate variety classification procedure: Finishing materials and shading in urban design. *J. Urban Environ. Eng.* **2020**, *14*, 42–51. [CrossRef]
29. Alonso, C.; Martín-Consuegra, F.; Oteiza, I.; Asensio, E.; Pérez, G.; Martínez, I.; Frutos, B. Effect of façade surface finish on building energy rehabilitation. *Sol. Energy* **2017**, *146*, 470–483. [CrossRef]
30. Irmak, M.A.; Yilmaz, S.; Dursun, D. Effect of different pavements on human thermal comfort conditions. *Atmósfera* **2017**, *30*, 355–366. [CrossRef]
31. Mirzabeigi, S.; Razkenari, M. Design optimization of urban typologies: A framework for evaluating building energy performance and outdoor thermal comfort. *Sustain. Cities Soc.* **2022**, *76*, 103515. [CrossRef]
32. Frutos, F.; Martin-Consuegra, F.; Oteiza, I.; Alonso, C.; Frutos, B.; Galeano, J. Energy efficiency and comfort on a deprived neighbourhood in Madrid (Spain). In *Planning Post Carbon Cities. Proceedings of the 35th PLEA Conference on Passive and Low Energy Architecture*; Rodríguez Álvarez, J., Soares Gonçalves, J.C., Eds.; University of A Coruña: A Coruña, Spain, 2020. [CrossRef]
33. Martín-Consuegra, F.; de Frutos, F.; Oteiza, I.; Alonso, C.; Frutos, B. Minimal Monitoring of Improvements in Energy Performance after Envelope Renovation in Subsidized Single Family Housing in Madrid. *Sustainability* **2020**, *13*, 235. [CrossRef]
34. Santos, T.; Gomes, N.; Freire, S.; Brito, M.; Santos, L.; Tenedório, J. Applications of solar mapping in the urban environment. *Appl. Geogr.* **2014**, *51*, 48–57. [CrossRef]

35. Acero, J.A.; Herranz-Pascual, K. A comparison of thermal comfort conditions in four urban spaces by means of measurements and modelling techniques. *Build. Environ.* **2015**, *93*, 245–257. [CrossRef]
36. Levinson, R.; Akbari, H. Solar Reflectance of Cool Paving Materials Effects of Composition and Exposure on Albedo of Con-crete. *Cem. Concr. Res.* **2002**, *32*, 2001–2002. [CrossRef]
37. Takebayashi, H.; Moriyama, M. Study on Surface Heat Budget of Various Pavements for Urban Heat Island Mitigation. *Adv. Mater. Sci. Eng.* **2012**, *2012*, 523051. [CrossRef]
38. Lin, Y.; Ichinose, T. Experimental evaluation of mitigation of thermal effects by "Katsuren travertine" paving material. *Energy Build.* **2014**, *81*, 253–261. [CrossRef]
39. Sanjuán, M.Á.; Morales, Á.; Zaragoza, A. Precast Concrete Pavements of High Albedo to Achieve the Net "Zero-Emissions" Commitments. *Appl Sci.* **2022**, *12*, 1955. [CrossRef]
40. Sen, S.; Roesler, J. Thermal and optical characterization of asphalt field cores for microscale urban heat island analysis. *Constr. Build. Mater.* **2019**, *217*, 600–611. [CrossRef]
41. Alchapar, N.; Correa, E.N.; Cantón, M.A. Classification of building materials used in the urban envelopes according to their capacity for mitigation of the urban heat island in semiarid zones. *Energy Build.* **2014**, *69*, 22–32. [CrossRef]
42. Karlessi, T.; Santamouris, M.; Apostolakis, K.; Synnefa, A.; Livada, I. Development and testing of thermochromic coatings for buildings and urban structures. *Sol. Energy* **2009**, *83*, 538–551. [CrossRef]
43. Zinzi, M. Characterisation and assessment of near infrared reflective paintings for building facade applications. *Energy Build.* **2016**, *114*, 206–213. [CrossRef]
44. Perez, G.; Sirvent, P.; Sanchez-Garcia, J.A.; Guerrero, A. Improved methodology for the characterization of thermochromic coatings for adaptive façades. *Sol. Energy* **2021**, *230*, 409–420. [CrossRef]
45. Qin, Y. A review on the development of cool pavements to mitigate urban heat island effect. *Renew. Sustain. Energy Rev.* **2015**, *52*, 445–459. [CrossRef]
46. Ferrari, A.; Kubilay, A.; Derome, D.; Carmeliet, J. The use of permeable and reflective pavements as a potential strategy for urban heat island mitigation. *Urban Clim.* **2019**, *31*, 100534. [CrossRef]
47. Mackey, C.W.; Lee, X.; Smith, R.B. Remotely sensing the cooling effects of city scale efforts to reduce urban heat island. *Build. Environ.* **2011**, *49*, 348–358. [CrossRef]
48. Ramzi, A.I. Towards Construction of Spectral Library of Urban Surface Materials Based on Spectroscopy. *J. Al Azhar Univ. Eng. Sect.* **2016**, *11*, 33–43. [CrossRef]

 *infrastructures*

Article

Improved Cementitious Tile Adhesives' Workability and Mechanical Performance with the Use of Recycled Materials

Ana Lourenço [1,*], Luís Silva [2], Vera Fernandes [2] and Pedro Sequeira [2]

[1] Departamento Engenharia Civil, Universidade de Aveiro, 3810-193 Aveiro, Portugal
[2] Saint-Gobain Weber Portugal, 3780-055 Aveiro, Portugal
[*] Correspondence: ana.ministro@ua.pt

Abstract: The impact that construction has on sustainability as a relevant consumer of materials is well known, especially with regard to cement, which contributes to high CO_2 emissions. It is well known that in tile adhesives, cement add positive technical contributes, supporting tensile adhesion, especially after water immersion and freeze–thaw cycles. On the other hand, it is also known that that it is possible to replace Portland cement with alternative sources, such as blast furnace slag, fly and bottom ashes, or other pozzolanic materials. Even so, other materials can be also used to contribute to additional performance. This work intends to prove that using recycled materials or by-products is not just a potential way to replace existing materials, improving environmental sustainability, but also contributes additional value to mortars, such as cement-based tile adhesives. Different recycled waste materials are introduced to a cement-based tile adhesive and the evaluation of properties according to EN 12004 is conducted. The results show how the introduction of recycled rubber can contribute to improve the workability of a tile adhesive, acting as a lightweight aggregate. Moreover, it can contribute to reducing the dynamic elasticity modulus; thus, it has a potential contribution to reduce global tensions in tiling systems, and the adhesion results are maintained by the introduction of slag, another recycled material. The weight reduction reduces mortar consumption, one of the main targets to support indicated strategy and justify a more sustainable performance. The results indicate that the introduction of rubber and slag provide good technical and mechanical performance for the mortars, as well as excellent workability.

Keywords: tile adhesive; residues valorization; circular economy; sustainability

1. Introduction

Building construction presents an important economic axis for any country. However, the industry is also a relevant material consumer, with potential negative impacts on environmental sustainability. For instance, aggregates (as the main component of many construction materials) as mortars can represent annual consumptions of 8 ton/habitant/year just in the European Union, which is only overcome by water consumption. Consequently, it is fundamental to find alternative processes to decrease or prevent such negative potential impacts. The potential use of recycled aggregates or the use of materials with reduced consumption per surface area are possibilities to support this strategy. Additionally, cement represents great potential for harm due to its high consumption and respective CO_2 emissions, considering that each produced ton of Portland cement contributes, in general, 0.8 ton of CO_2. Thus a strategy to reduce this in construction building materials is required [1–4].

Cement-based tile adhesives, according to EN 12004, consist of a mix of cement, redispersible polymer (usually ethylene, vinyl acetate, or vinyl versate co-polymer), aggregates as silica sand, and specific adjuvants as cellulose ether, starch ether or accelerators to present good workability or improve the reactivity of the system. According to EN 12004 or ISO 13007-1, cementitious adhesives should comply with the C1 fundamental characteristics reported in Table 1, meaning a minimal adhesion value of 0.5 MPa under several curing conditions. Additional characteristics for C2 tile adhesives (improved performance) are also presented in the same table, requiring a minimal adhesion value of 1MPa. Concerning mechanical performance, an additional requirement can also be applied, named transverse deformation, which consists of the deflection recorded at the center when a beam of hardened adhesive is subjected to three-point loading [3,5,6].

Table 1. Summary of specifications for cementitious adhesives, including fundamental and special characteristics [5,6].

Characteristic	Property	Requirement
C1—Normal cementitious adhesives (fundamental characteristics)	Tensile adhesion: Initial After water immersion After heat ageing After freeze–thaw cycle	$\geq$0.5 MPa
	Open time (tensile adhesion)	$\geq$0.5 MPa (after not more than 20 min)
C2—Improved cementitious adhesives (additional characteristics)	Tensile adhesion: Initial After water immersion After heat ageing After freeze–thaw cycle	$\geq$1.0 MPa
S—Transverse deformation	Deformable adhesive (S1)	$\geq$2.5 mm, <5 mm
	Highly deformable adhesives (S2)	$\geq$5 mm

Recent works have presented the stress distribution generated by thermal expansion in a ceramic bonding system through the use of finite element modeling, in which a thermal source induces a temperature variation carried out incrementally in the simulation. A temperature gradient is assumed from the exposed face, crossing the element interface until it reaches the internal mass of the ceramic adhesive interface. Using the same numerical model, this research led to the evaluation of thermal equivalent stresses according to the von Mises criterion, adopting different elastic modulus combinations for tile adhesive and joint grout. The results indicate that such a relation has an impact on tension, both at adhesive and support levels, and conditioning the decision related to the joint width between tiles and with supports such as EPS, render and concrete. This also means that, in addition to adhesion and transverse deformation by EN 12004, additional mechanical considerations of tile adhesives, as the dynamic elastic modulus, can contribute to the better performance of the products [7,8].

According to EN 15804 and ISO 14025, sustainability goals and scopes for mortar should include the functional unit used, the product's description, application and the boundaries of the analyzed system. Additionally, an Inventory Analysis is considered, where energy, water, used resources, the emission of pollutants into the air, and waste production are quantified. Finally, an Impact Assessment is performed where the inputs and outputs of the system are translated into potential environmental impact and divided into different categories.

Considering the existing results of the Life Cycle Assessment for different categories, measure per functional area of 1kg of produced tile adhesive (class C2S), and phases A1–A3, Table 2 shows typical values for CO_2 emission coming from different existing sources. In addition, Figure 1 also shows the main responsible impact per category. According to Figure 1, ordinary Portland cement (OPC) and redispersible polymer resin (RDP) represent the components with major impact in all categories, except ADP. Focusing on GWP (global warming performance, expressed in kg CO_2 emission per kg of final product), any particular action that can contribute to reducing OPC and RDP dosage represents an important contribution to achieve a better performance on such a level, since these represent more than 50% of CO_2 emissions for tile adhesives [9,10].

Table 2. Impact evaluation for C2S tile adhesives according to different sources (modules A1–A3).

Category/Functional Unity		Source 1 [9]	Source 2 [9]	Source 3 [10]
GWP	kg CO_2 equ./kg of powder	0.511	0.556	0.530

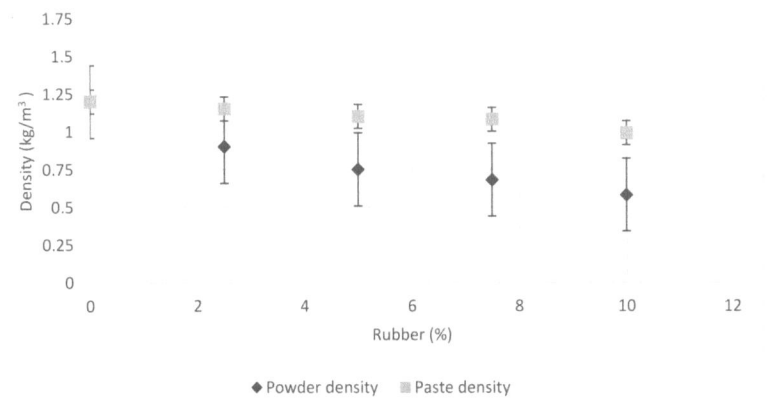

◆ Powder density ▦ Paste density

Figure 1. Powder and paste density of a C2S tile adhesive as a function of recycled rubber content.

Concerning tile adhesive mortars, a fundamental requirement is the ability of the mortar to be easy to apply, a property that is usually based on empirical evaluation, even if some rheological measures can be performed and linked to specific properties of the mortar, such as the fresh density and fine texture materials, providing smooth textures.

When considering the three previous questions, (a) relevant CO_2 emissions values, highly impacted by Portland cement and polymer resin, (b) technical performance including a focus on additional properties such as Young modulus, and (c) improvement in workability to make the daily use easier for application, a combined arrangement of raw materials is considered in order to provide improvements for the three conditions. Additionally, the introduction of recycled materials is understood as a main part of the solution, considering that:

1. The high use of redispersible polymer, to ensure adhesion level after heat storage conditions and transverse deformation, can be partially replaced by lightweight aggregates that can reduce the Young modulus of the mortar and ensure tension accommodation, for instance, as a result of temperature differentiation [11];
2. Then, considering the need to include lightweight aggregates, recycled rubber can be used as a predilection material due to its low density and fine grain size. Vulcanized rubber is extensively used in many industrial sectors due to its good physical, mechanical and dynamic properties, as well as excellent durability, outstanding abrasive resistance and relatively low cost. Unfortunately, most post-consumer rubber-derived products are still discarded as waste, buried in landfills, or incinerated. Such materials require many years to degrade naturally due to (i) their complex cross-linked composition, and (ii) the additives used during manufacturing to extend the lifespan of rubber. Extensive research has investigated the use of end-of-life rubber as binders (e.g., elastomers, bitumen) or as conglomerates (cement, gypsums) to produce innovative composites in construction. To improve the properties of composites made with recycled rubber, the surface of rubber has been treated with different costly processes

to work on the Interfacial Transition Zone (ITZ). However, the results available in the literature are inconsistent and many technical and practical aspects remain unsolved, thus preventing the cost-effective use of rubber in the construction industry [12,13];

3. On the other hand, considering the introduction of lightweight aggregates, it is expected that more binder will be needed to maintain technical performances such as tensile adhesion, which can be contradictory to the intention to decrease CO_2 emissions via reducing the Portland cement dosage. To overcome this question, mineral binder dosage can be completed by using another recycled material such as ground granulated blast slag (GGBS). This material is obtained by quenching molten iron slag (a by-product of iron and steel-making) from a blast furnace in water or steam to produce a glassy, granular product that is then dried and ground into a fine powder. GGBS has to be rapidly quenched in large volumes of water, as quenching optimizes the cementitious properties, resulting in a material with high CSH (calcium silicate hydrates) referred to as 'GGBFS' or 'slag cement [14–18].

The main goal of this work is to show how the introduction of recycled materials, as rubber and blast furnace slag, can result in tile adhesive with improved mechanical properties and make application work easier for professionals. This research shows an improvement in sustainability levels by introducing recycled materials or by-products as one of the best strategies for the decarbonization of mortars.

2. Experimental Methodology

To develop the tile adhesive mortar we focused on two main materials: recycled rubber and blast furnace slag.

Considering the recycled rubber, the following properties were considered as the starting point to be introduced in tile adhesive mortars [19]:

Characteristics	Requirements
Particle size (d50)	Minimum: 250 μm Maximum: 400 μm
Metal and fiber content	<0.1%
Ash (silica) content	<24%
Specific particle density (by pycnometric method)	1150 kg/m^3
Bulk density (according EN 1097-3)	<400 kg/m^3

Considering blast furnace slag, the following properties were considered [20]:

Characteristics	Requirements
Chemical composition based on a chemical modulus ($\geq$1.2 according to NF EN 206/CN)	$(CaO + MgO)/SiO_2 > 1.25$
Blaine-specific surface area	4450+/−250 cm^2/g
Particle size (d50)	11 μm
Bulk density	800 kg/m^3

The tile adhesive mortar was evaluated according to EN 12004-1:2017 definitions and classification. Properties and test methods were performed following EN 12004-2:2017. Additionally, the dynamic elasticity modulus (EdL) was calculated according to EN 14146 through the fundamental resonance longitudinal vibration given by the following equation (valid to any mold format):

$$Ed_L = 4 \times 10^{-6} \times L^2 \times F_L^2 \times \rho_L \tag{1}$$

expressed in MPa (L in m; ρ_L in kg/m^3; F_L in Hz).

Powder density was evaluated according to EN 459-2:2012; paste density was evaluated according to EN 1015-6; finally, the dry bulk density of hardened mortar was evaluated according to EN 1015-10.

Particularly, for the powder and paste densities and tensile adhesion properties, evaluation was made according to the recycled rubber content as the most relevant source of the aggregate added to the final formulation.

Dynamic elasticity modulus, transversal deformability and open time evaluation were made to the considered optimized formulation including rubber, in comparison with the conventional tile adhesives of the same EN 12004 class classification. The same procedure was completed for the GWP evaluation regarding sustainability impact, taking the Ecoinvent database as the source to specify the most considered components, i.e., Portland cement, polymer resin and recycled rubber [21].

3. Results and Discussion

Phase 1: Recycled rubber introduction to support workability improvement

First, we introduced rubber to understand the impact on mortar workability during its application. Starting from a C2S cement-based tile adhesive (40% of the weight of ordinary Portland cement, type I, 42.5N, 5% redispersible polymer, vinyl acetate-ethylene copolymer), different amounts of rubber powder (0; 2.5; 5; 7.5 and 10%) were added to this mortar in replacement of the equivalent dosage of silica sand.

From the workability perspective, it was noticed that with a higher rubber content a better workability was obtained, in addition to the contribution to powder and paste density, according to the results from Figure 2. In fact, the results showed a continuous reduction in both densities, which suggests that this is an easier product to carry and apply during use. On the other hand, the results in Figure 3 indicate how adhesion level is impacted by rubber introduction. Looking at this trend, it can be noticed that an addition above 7.5% starts to contribute to a relevant decrease in adhesion values, especially after ageing conditions such as water immersion, freeze–thaw cycles, and heat storage.

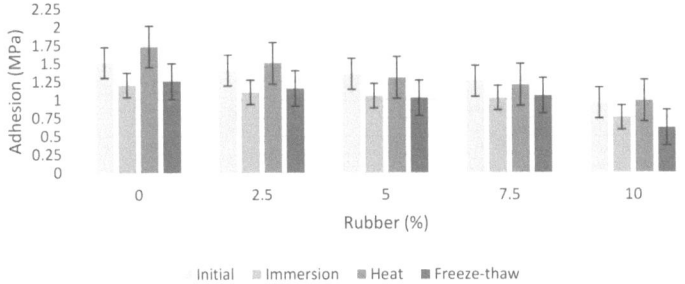

Figure 2. Tensile adhesion according to EN 12004 for a tile adhesive as a function of recycled rubber content.

Phase 2: Adhesion performance improvement by mineral binder content correction

Considering the positive impact of rubber introduction on workability/smooth texture, together with the interesting impact on powder and paste density (making the material easy to work with and to apply), there is a natural concern about the need to adjust binder quantity, such as Portland cement (OPC) or redispersible resin (RDP), in order to maintain good mechanical performance according to EN 12004 (as adhesion and transverse deformation). However, besides a possible cost increase due to potential higher dosages of Portland cement and redispersible resin, an additional concern is a potential negative impact on CO_2 emissions.

To minimize both concerns, two corrective hypotheses are considered:

1. The potential need for more cement can be compensated by the addition of blast furnace slag instead.

Figure 4 presents the adhesion results for a tile adhesive, with a constant content of recycled rubber and different amounts of mineral binder as a combination of ordinary Portland cement and GGBS (slag). As for all lightweight tile adhesives, additional mineral binder is essential to guarantee adhesion. In the present case, to obtain a C2 class (higher than 1 MPa), more than 50% mineral binder content was necessary. Additionally, it is also possible to notice that part of the OPC content can be replaced by slag and still maintain the desired performance.

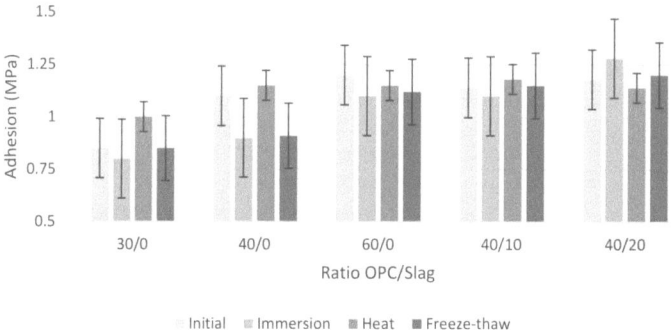

Figure 3. Tensile adhesion according to EN 12004 for a tile adhesive as a function of OPC and GGBS (slag) content, keeping rubber dosage constant.

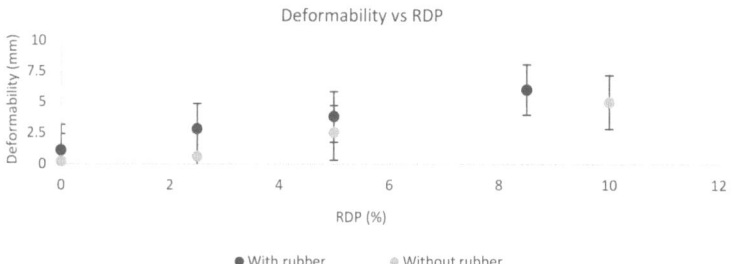

Figure 4. Transverse deformation according to EN 12004 for two tile adhesives, with and without recycle rubber incorporation, as a function RDP content.

2. The potential addition of rubber to compensate for part of the redispersible powder resin as a methodology to achieve desired transversal deformation and lower the dynamic elasticity modulus.

Considering that polymer resin is key to achieving transversal deformation [11], a hypothesis was raised about the possibility to optimize it by using rubber in the formulation. Considering transverse deformation and the elasticity modulus as properties that depend on similar parameters of the tile adhesive structure, it is well known that the impact of rubber introduction to reduce the elasticity modulus value of materials results in softer products, contributing to decreasing the hardened density of the material [12,13]. Taking this into consideration, a study was performed to test different polymer dosages in two tile adhesives: a standard one, without rubber introduction, and a new approach, based on rubber incorporation, following the previous results for workability and adhesion level.

The results are presented in Figures 5–7. Regarding transversal deformation, it is noticed that rubber introduction always results in a higher deformability level, even if a lower polymer resin is used (as compared to between 8.5 and 10% RDP). A similar trend shows that the dynamic elasticity modulus is strongly related to the impact on density decrease as a result of rubber introduction.

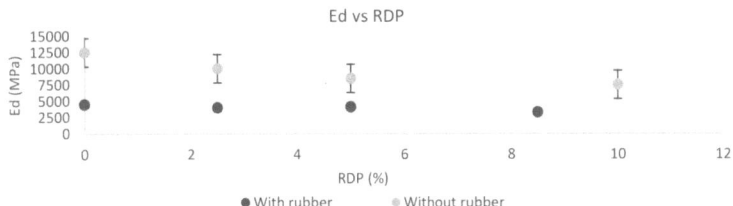

Figure 5. Dynamic elasticity modulus for two tile adhesives with and without recycle rubber incorporation as a function RDP content.

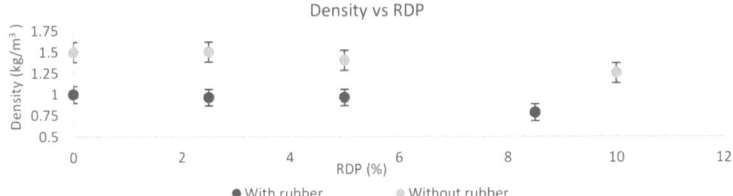

Figure 6. Hardened density for two tile adhesives with and without recycle rubber incorporation as a function of RDP content.

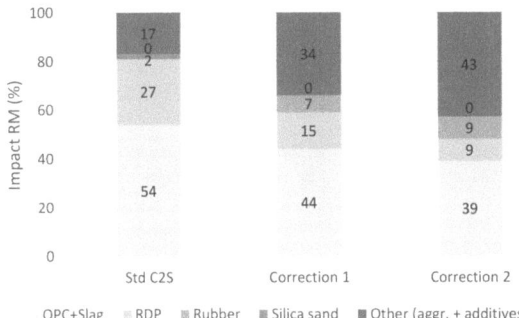

Figure 7. Impact of different components on CO_2 emissions (kg CO_2/kg adhesive) for three tile adhesive (standard version and corrected versions with rubber introduction).

Phase 3: Sustainability impact by measuring GWP (CO_2 emissions)

Considering the possible corrective factors previously indicated, based on the use of the partial replacement of Portland cement by GGBS and polymer resin decreasing as a consequence of recycled rubber introduction, the following work presents the results of the related exercise regarding global warming performance based on CO_2 emissions, with a particular focused on mineral binder, polymer and aggregate impact.

Figure 7 presents the impact of the different combinations promoted by the recycled rubber introduction and, consequently, the additional mineral binder content, but also the possibility to correct this by GGBS introduction plus polymer resin optimization (Correction 1: standard C2S tile adhesive; C2S tile adhesive with rubber introduction plus additional binder introduction to support adhesion. Correction 2: C2S tile adhesive with rubber introduction plus additional binder correction with GGBS and RDP optimization).

Table 3 presents the final results concerning CO2-equivalent emissions expressed in phases A1–A3:

- Weight (kg) of CO_2 per weight (ton) of tile adhesive, following the conventional approach to mortars [9];
- Weight (kg) of CO_2 per surface area (m^2) of the applied surface, following a different approach for the functional unit. It should be considered that rubber introduction contributes to lower powder apparent density, implicating half of the consumption when applied (thus, implicating half of the consumed resources) when compared to conventional tile adhesive.

Table 3. CO_2 emission evaluation for three tile adhesives (standard version and corrected versions with rubber introduction) according to different sources (module A1–A3).

Product Type	Standard C2S	Correction 1	Correction 2
Kg CO_2/ton of powder	589	1095	868
Kg CO_2/m^2 of applied surface	2.65	2.74	2.17

It is particularly relevant that the resulting version with rubber, corrected by GGBS binder introduction and resin polymer optimization, presented 18% less CO_2 emissions than the conventional tile adhesive (considering functional unity and adhesive consumption per m^2 of applied surface). From Figure 7, it can be noticed how Portland cement and polymer resin had a greater impact on sustainability performance.

4. Conclusions

Improvements at the circular economy level, including decreases in the CO_2 emissions of mortars, demand continuous research into new possibilities and combinations of materials. In the particular case of tile adhesive mortars, it has been shown that recycled rubber can contribute positively to sustainability impact, even providing additional features, can add value to customers, for instance, and is related to better and easier workable products.

For the presented case, recycled rubber introduction contributed to lighter versions, reducing mortar consumption and contributing to polymer redispersible optimization, contributing to lowering the CO_2 emissions. Finally, a positive trend in mechanical performance, with changes in transverse deformation and the dynamic elasticity modulus, was also achieved.

On the other hand, such actions can also result in critical consequences that need to be solved. In fact, this introduction demands higher binder content to keep adhesion level, with potential drawbacks related to global warming performance (CO_2 emissions). Thus, the solution to overcoming this challenge consists of the introduction of another recycled material, ground granulated blast-furnace slag, a well-known material to provide good mechanical performance when combined with ordinary Portland cement (OPC).

As a main conclusion, our results clearly indicate the possibility of introducing recycled materials of a content higher than 30% of the weight of the cement-based tile adhesive, contributing to the circular economy and reducing the CO_2 emissions of the applied mortar. This can also offer additional features related to mechanical performance and workability during application. However, the end CO_2 emissions are still far from zero as result of it being very difficult to eliminate redispersable polymer and Portland cement, as the two main contributors, without losing mechanical performance.

Author Contributions: Conceptualization: L.S. and P.S.; methodology: A.L., V.F. and L.S.; software, A.L. and V.F.; validation, L.S., A.L., V.F. and P.S.; formal analysis, L.S. and P.S.; investigation: A.L., V.F., L.S. and P.S.; resources: A.L. and V.F.; data curation, A.L. and V.F.; writing—A.L. and L.S.; writing—review and editing: A.L., V.F., L.S. and P.S.; visualization: L.S.; supervision: L.S.; project administration: L.S. and P.S.; funding acquisition: Not applicable. All authors have read and agreed to the published version of the manuscript.

Funding: The authors received no financial support for the research, authorship, and/or publication of this article.

Institutional Review Board Statement: Not applicable.

Informed Consent Statement: Not applicable.

Data Availability Statement: No applicable.

Conflicts of Interest: The authors declared no potential conflicts of interest with respect to the research, authorship, and/or publication of this article.

References

1. European Commission. *Directorate E-Industry and Environment-Management of Construction and Demolition Waste*; Working document n°1 DG ENV.E.3–4 April 2000; European Commission: Luxembourg, 2000.
2. Azevedo, A.; Alexandre, J.; Marvila, E. Influence of incorporation of glass waste on the rheological properties of adhesive mortar. *Constr. Build. Mater.* **2017**, *148*, 359–368. [CrossRef]
3. Michalak, J. Ceramic Tile Adhesives from the Producer's Perspective: A Literature Review. *Ceramics* **2021**, *4*, 378–390. [CrossRef]
4. Hoffman, D. Allerte aux Pilleurs de Sable, Le Parisien: 19 Août 2013. Available online: https://www.leparisien.fr/week-end/international-alerte-aux-pilleurs-de-sable-19-08-2013-3064795.php (accessed on 11 June 2021).
5. EN 12004-1:2017; Adhesives for Ceramic Tiles—Part 1: Requirements, Assessment and Verification of Constancy of Performance, Classification and Marking. CEN: Brussels, Belgium, 2017.
6. ISO 13007-1:2014; Ceramic Tiles—Grouts and Adhesives, Part 1: Terms, Definitions and Specifications for Adhesives. ISO: Geneva, Switzerland, 2014.
7. Silva, L.; Sequeira, P.; Melo, F.; Lopes, C.V. The evaluation of von Mises stress field in bonded tiling ceramics as function of the elastic modulus of the tile-adhesive and joint grout mortars. *Proc. Inst. Mech. Eng. L J. Mater. Des. Appl.* **2020**, *235*, 413–420. [CrossRef]
8. Lopes, C.M.; Silva, L.; Sequeira, P.; Melo, F. Assessing the thermal degradation of bonded joints in flat ceramic tiles of building facades by numerical and experimental dynamic analysis. *Proc. Inst. Mech. Eng. L J. Mater. Des. Appl.* **2020**, *234*, 1129–1141. [CrossRef]
9. Silva, L.; Sequeira, P.; Soares, L.; Matos, M. Desenvolvimento de Uma DAP Relativa a Uma Argamassa-Cola to Tipo C2S. In Proceedings of the CINCOS 14, Congress of Innovation on Sustainable Construction, Porto, Portugal, 13–14 November 2014.
10. SNMI. *Syndicat National des Mortiers Industriels*; SNMI: Reston, VA, USA, 2007.
11. Jenni, A.; Holzer, L.; Zurbriggen, R.; Herwegh, M. Influence of polymers on microstructure and adhesive strength of cementitious tile adhesive mortars. *Cem. Concr. Res.* **2005**, *35*, 35–50. [CrossRef]
12. Cairns, R.A.; Kew, H.Y.; Kenny, M.J. The Use of Recycled Rubber Tyres in Concrete Construction. In *Sustainable Waste Management and Recycling: Used/Post-Consumer Tyres*; Limbachiya, M., Roberts, J., Eds.; Thomas Telford Ltd.: London, UK, 2004; Volume 3, pp. 135–142. ISBN 0727732862.
13. Medina, N.F.; Garcia, R.; Hajirasouliha, I.; Pilakoutas, K.; Guadagnini, M.; Raffoul, S. Composites with recycled rubber aggregates: Properties and opportunities in construction. *Constr. Build. Mater.* **2018**, *188*, 884–897. [CrossRef]
14. Snellings, R.; Mertens, G.; Elsen, J. Supplementary Cementitious Materials. *Rev. Mineral. Geochem.* **2012**, *74*, 211–278. [CrossRef]
15. Juenger, M.; Winnefeld, F.; Provis, J.; Ideker, J. Advances in alternative cementitious binders. *Cem. Concr. Res.* **2011**, *41*, 1232–1243. [CrossRef]
16. Ramirez, D.E.A.; DE Gutierrez, R.M.; Puertas, F. Alkali-activated Portland blast-furnace slag cement: Mechanical properties and hydration. *Constr. Build. Mater.* **2017**, *140*, 119–128. [CrossRef]
17. Moranville-Regourd, M. *Cements Made from Blast Furnace Slag*, 4th ed.; Elsevier Ltd.: Amsterdam, The Netherlands, 1998; pp. 637–678.
18. Kolani, B.; Lacarrière, L.; Sellier, A.; Escadeillas, G.; Boutillon, L.; Linger, L. Hydration of slag-blended cements. *Cem. Concr. Compos.* **2012**, *34*, 1009–1018. [CrossRef]
19. Tyre Recycled Solutions. *TyreXol™ Product Data Sheet*; Tyre Recycled Solutions: Préverenges, Switzerland, 2020.
20. Ecocem. *Technical Data Sheet Ground Granulated Blast Furnace Slag*; Ecocem: Aix En Provence, France, 2017.
21. Ecoinvent. Available online: https://www.ecoinvent.org/database/access-the-database/access-the-database.html (accessed on 11 June 2021).

Article

The Use of Envi-Met for the Assessment of Nature-Based Solutions' Potential Benefits in Industrial Parks—A Case Study of Argales Industrial Park (Valladolid, Spain)

Felipe Macedo Alves [1], Artur Gonçalves [1,*] and M. Rosario del Caz-Enjuto [2]

[1] Centro de Investigação de Montanha, Instituto Politécnico de Bragança, 5300-253 Bragança, Portugal; felipe.alves@ipb.pt

[2] Departamento de Urbanismo y Representación de la Arquitectura, University of Valladolid, 47002 Valladolid, Spain; charo@arq.uva.es

* Correspondence: ajg@ipb.pt

Abstract: Urbanization causes major changes in environmental systems, including those related with radiation balances and other meteorological conditions because of changes in surfaces and the physical environment. In addition, cities generate specific microclimates as a consequence of the diverse conditions within the urban fabric. Industrial parks represent vast urban areas, often neglected, contributing to the degradation of the urban environment, including poor thermal comfort as a result of soil sealing and low albedo surfaces. Nature-Based Solutions (NBS) can promote the mitigation of the anthropic effects of urbanization using nature as an inspiration. The present study, aimed at estimating the microclimate conditions in a fraction of the Argales industrial park in the city of Valladolid (Spain), with the use of the ENVI-Met software, assesses the current situation and a planned NBS scenario. Base scenario simulation results demonstrate different conditions across the simulations, with higher temperatures on sun-exposed surfaces with low albedo, and lower temperature spots, mostly associated with shadowed areas near existent buildings. After the simulation of the NBS scenario, the results show that, when compared with the base scenario, the projected air temperature changes reach reductions of up to 4.30 °C for the locations where changes are projected from impervious low albedo surfaces to shaded areas in the vicinity of trees and a water body.

Keywords: modeling; ENVI-Met; air temperature; nature-based solutions

1. Introduction

Climate is one of the factors responsible for variations in landscapes, biological diversity, construction methods and typologies, as well as human habits and customs [1]. The relationship of society with its environment can be analyzed by the architecture of the place, which is, in many cases, related to the climatic and geographical environment [2]. In other words, the balance between humans and their habitat, as well as their harmony and adaptation to the environment through social and cultural expressions, is present across generations [3].

Understanding the urban climate is paramount for the development of design solutions to improve local conditions [4], as it should be considered in city planning and in promoting comfortable, salubrious and low-energy-consuming environments [5]. This idea, associated with that of Oke, Mills and Christen [6], correlates humans and vegetation with urban variables that must be considered in the study of urban climate, such as climate scales, physical and physiological bases, solar radiation, wind, humidity and topography [7].

Decades of research demonstrate that cities are almost always warmer than their surroundings because of the phenomenon known as the urban heat island (UHI) [6,8–10].

Infrastructures **2022**, *7*, 85. https://doi.org/10.3390/infrastructures7060085

Assessments of differences in temperature between urban and rural areas contribute to analyses of UHI intensity. Such differences can be attributed to differential heating (from sunrise to sunset) and cooling (from sunset to sunrise) in urban areas [11,12].

The combination of climate change with the aggravated effects of the UHI can be seen as a determining context that should trigger change, thus fostering the implementation of measures that can help to attenuate air temperature in cities [13,14]. Climate change adaptation measures should help to alleviate effects on thermal comfort through adequate urban design policies [15].

In the development of urban sustainable solutions, it is necessary to plan projects that can promote urban transformation, seeking to make urban areas more pleasant to its users [16]. In this context, solutions that seek to mitigate anthropic effects while being inspired in nature are called Nature-Based Solutions (NBSs), and they incorporate natural elements into urban structures and have the premise of regenerating landscapes altered by humans [17–19]. Some examples of NBS are linear parks built around water bodies, such as rivers and streams, creating green corridors along their paths. These can integrate other solutions, consequently bringing synergy to already installed alternatives [20]. Green roofs and walls can also reduce temperatures and increase energy savings [21].

In 2021, the European Union developed a common manual for evaluating the impacts of NBS [16,22], which aims to provide professionals with a comprehensive framework for evaluations and a robust set of indicators and methodologies to assess them in 12 social challenges (Climate Resilience; Water Management; Natural and Climate Hazards; Green Space Management; Biodiversity; Air Quality; Place Regeneration; Knowledge and Social Capacity Building for Sustainable Urban Transformation; Participatory Planning and Governance; Social Justice and Social Cohesion; Health and Well-being; and New Economic Opportunities and Green Jobs). Nonetheless, the multiple benefits of NBS vary according to each alternative, as do their costs and benefits, which must be analyzed individually for each case [16].

In recent years, several relevant projects have approached the introduction of NBS in urban environments, including the following H2020 projects: OPERANDUM, BiodivERsA, CLEARING HOUSE, CLEVER Cities and NATURVATION.

NBS can help respond to various urban challenges, including those presented by brownfields, climate change, urban decay and infrastructure degradation [17,19,23]. Industrial zones take part in the physical and anthropic evolution of the city, entailing interactions between the natural and built environment, which can sometimes lead to the degradation of natural ecosystems [19,24]. To avoid this process, the sustainable rehabilitation of industrial parks tries to improve these urban contexts, facing the endemic problems of these frequently highly artificial urban landscapes [25].

Natural phenomena are often very complex, which makes them difficult to study and understand. One way to address complexity is to apply analysis models that allow the understanding and anticipation of these phenomena, and such is the case of using climate models to assess the impact of urban morphological changes on local meteorological conditions [3,26]. Their projections and results give essential information for the improvement of management and decision making because they investigate the degree to which climate change derives from natural variability, human intervention or combinations thereof [27].

The modeling process requires a theoretical, comprehensive and specific study, with the collection of as much information as possible; therefore, the simulations are close to reality and thus can provide reliable information that can inform efficient decision making [13].

One of the most widely recognized software for urban climate modeling is ENVI-Met, a tridimensional model that simulates the interactions of the surface–vegetation–atmosphere and generates simulations for the microscale dimension [28]. This software allows the investigation and quantification of the effects of urban planning and architecture on outdoor microclimate through simulation [29].

Envi-Met is notable for its ability to model changes in solar radiation by building structures and elements in the surroundings of a given location [30]. This software also estimates the effects of vegetation, including the potential temperature of leaves, considering photosynthesis rates, soil moist content and local evaporation rates [31,32]. One of its main advantages is the fact that it reproduces the main atmospheric processes that affect microclimate, including wind, its turbulence, radiation fluxes, air temperature and relative humidity, using the fundamental laws of thermodynamics and fluids mechanics [33,34]. The simulations consider daily cycles in complex urban structures, including buildings and vegetation in numerous shapes and sizes, from a microclimate perspective [35,36].

ENVI-Met has been used in several studies to simulate near-ground air temperatures and to help understand the impact of the urban form on microclimate [37–40]. This software can be used to simulate scenarios, often testing the benefits of NBSs, and its outputs can be used as a reference for urban design, with the purpose of mitigating the effects of heat islands in urban areas, as well as improving the thermal comfort of users [41–45].

Thus, trying to approach the urban climate through simulation and focusing on the analysis of the public infrastructure in an industrial park, this study aims at estimating microclimate conditions in a section of the Industrial Park of Argales in Valladolid (Spain), assessing the potential benefits of the introduction of NBS and focusing on Climate Resilience, with the help of ENVI-Met Software. This study includes the definition of a base and an NBS scenario, with the definition of 3D models, followed by simulations for equivalent climate conditions.

The study is part of the POCTEP INDNATUR project, developed by a partnership led by the University of Valladolid, along with six other partners, including the Polytechnic Institute of Bragança. The main objective of the project is to promote the improvement of environmental conditions in industrial zones or parks through the implementation of Nature-Based Solutions.

2. Materials and Methods

2.1. Study Area

This study takes place in Valladolid, the capital of the Spanish region of Castilla and Leon. It has approximately 300,000 inhabitants and covers over 200 km^2 [46]. It has a diversified urban fabric [47], with industrial spaces close to the urban core, as is an industrial tradition [48]. The study area is located within the Argales Industrial Park (Figure 1), an area with a high concentration of industrial and commercial buildings, with vast impermeable areas and no public green spaces.

Valladolid has a Csa Climate by the Köppen–Geiger classification, which is a Mediterranean hot summer climate. This climate has moderate temperatures and changeable rainy weather during the winter. Summers are usually hot and dry.

2.2. Location of the Study Area

The size of the study area is one hectare (Figure 2) and is part of the urban redevelopment of the public road and sidewalk infrastructure by the European-funded INTERREG POCTEP INDNATUR project, including a comma-shaped roundabout, in a central area of the Argales Industrial Park near the Pilar Miró Roundabout. This area, until the fall of 2021, included a large open space with paved surfaces in streets and industrial building yards, including asphalt on roads and driveways, cement and stone on sidewalks and derelict land in the center of the roundabout. Buildings include commercial pavilions, with heights ranging from 1.8 m to 7.10 m. The southeast part of the simulation includes a fragment of a dry stream and large derelict land with railway tracks from a nearby train repair facility.

2.3. Modeling

For the modeling of the study area and simulation of microclimate conditions, the ENVI-Met Software was used. This software allows for investigating and quantifying the effects of architecture and urban planning on microclimate [37].

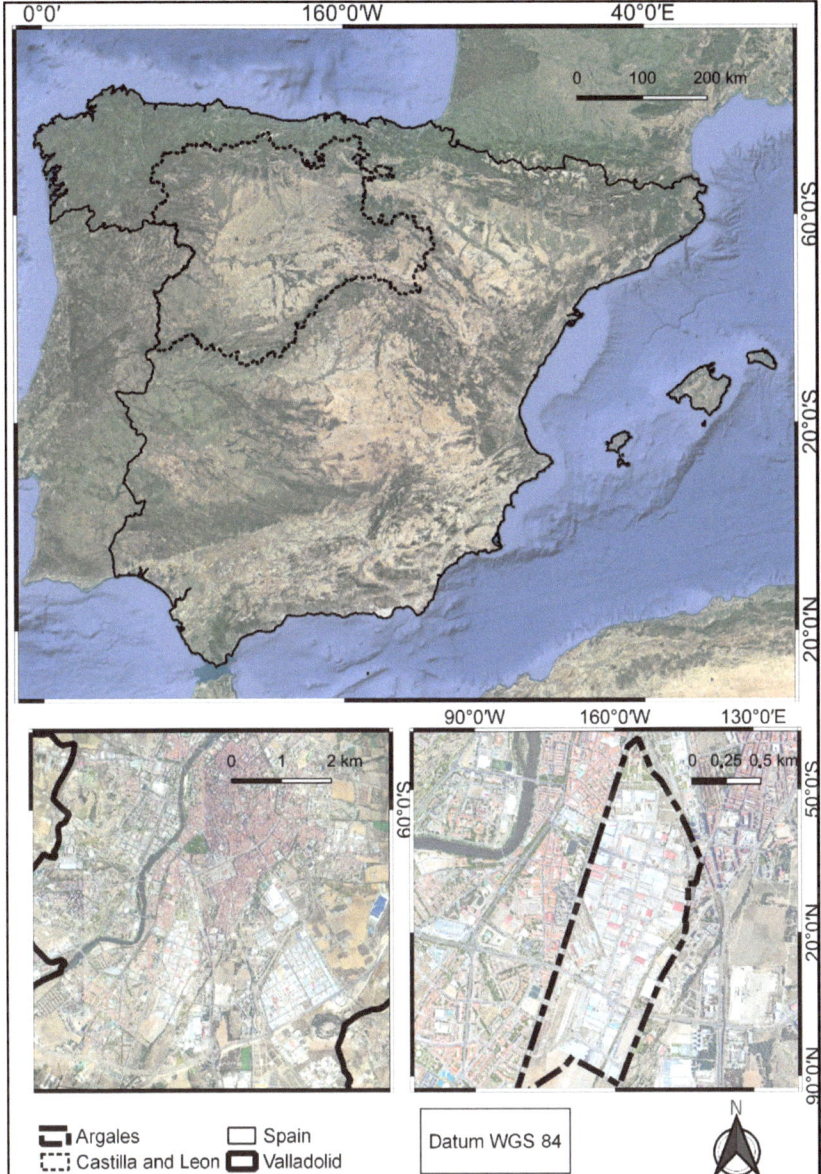

Figure 1. Location map for the Argales region in Valladolid/Spain.

In the digitalization of the area to be modeled, a 1 m × 1 m × 1 m resolution was used, with a total of 100 × 100 × 30 grids. This resolution was chosen to provide a detailed representation of the area [49]. A grid was kept at the edge, avoiding instabilities in the modeling.

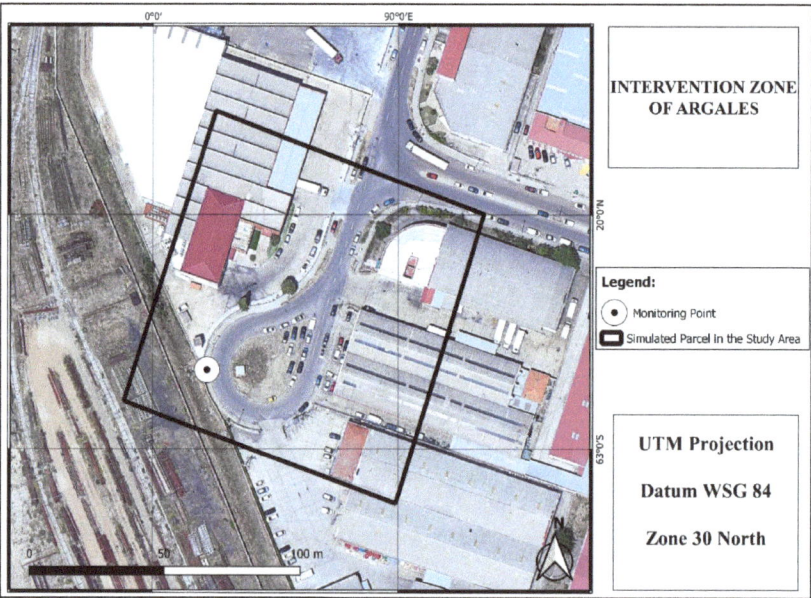

Figure 2. Location of the study area.

The model considers the interactions between three layers: the atmosphere, surface (including the various surface covers, buildings and vegetation) and soil [50]. Meteorological data for the model includes maximum and minimum values for air temperature and relative humidity as well as average wind speed and wind direction.

In this study, two scenarios were modeled. The first is a representation of the study area before any recent intervention, and the second incorporated Nature-Based Solutions, as part of the INDNATUR project. The scenarios are differentiated by the incorporation of vegetation in different strata while keeping the same characteristics of the urban geometry and artificial ground cover materials in other locations. The modeling materials used resemble those found in the study area, and they included: *grass, asphalt, concrete pavement gray* for sidewalks and clay and loam soil for exposed soil areas. For buildings, mostly *concrete walls* were used.

After integrating the 2D model inputs, ENVI-Met provides a 3D representation that allows the visual representation of the study area (Figure 3). With this 3D model validated, and considering the meteorological data input, ENVI-Met simulates the conditions for the given date and meteorological conditions.

Under the framework of the INDNATUR project, a new development was designed to contemplate a major NBS intervention in the study area, including the re-naturalization of the roundabout using vegetation and a water pond and changes in the sidewalks to incorporate porous surfaces and alignment trees. This new project should help to ameliorate the microclimate conditions.

For the NBS project, a new ENVI-Met scenario, designated the NBS scenario, was produced to contemplate the planned changes (Figure 4), considering that the elements were fully developed (adult trees). This new scenario was then modeled considering the same meteorological data and the same day of the year as the base scenario. Finally, these two scenarios were compared to assess the potential impact of the NBS on this case study location.

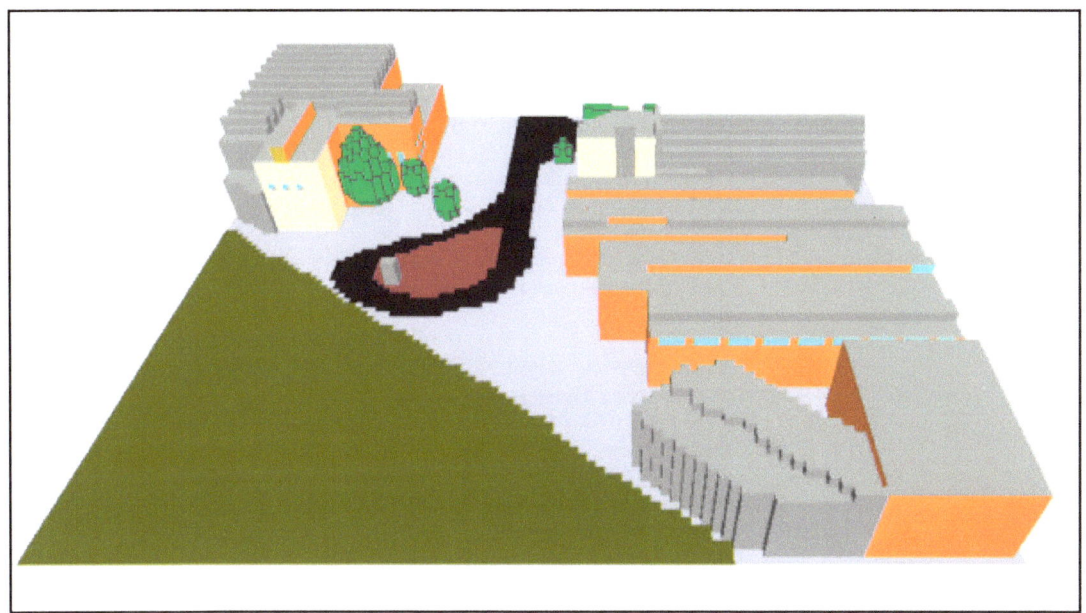

Figure 3. A 3D model of the study area before the INDNATUR Project intervention.

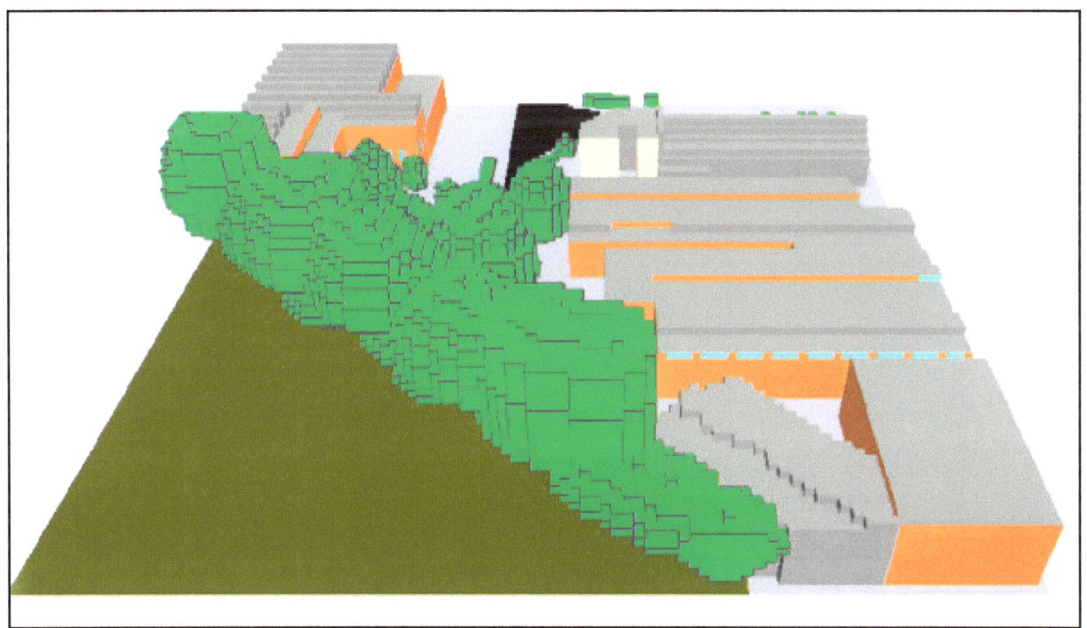

Figure 4. A 3D model of the study area after the INDNATUR Project intervention.

The location of the trees in the Pilar Miró street roundabout was limited by the existence of medium-voltage overhead powerlines, the traffic of heavy vehicles and the need for the proper operation of activities in the industrial area, as well as the existence of infrastructure incompatible with the roots of the trees (Appendix A) (Figure A1). For this location, a solution as natural as possible was designed, with a mixture of shrubby, perennia, and graminae species arranged in irregular groups of 5 to 7 units. In this location, the existence of the powerlines prevented the planting of very large trees. *Acer campestre*, deciduous trees, were planted on the outer edge of Pilar Miró street because they are close to the buildings.

Without facing limitations, the intervention on the dry bed of the Espanta stream included diverse varieties and sizes of evergreen and deciduous trees, which were planted to promote an increase in biodiversity while ensuring a high level of shadows on the nearby sidewalk.

The trees added in the model were consistent with the planted species, and they include *Acer campestre, Cupressus stricta, Eleagnus angustifolia, Populus nigra, Prunus avium, Rhus typhina* and *Sorbus aucuparia*. For grass species, the following were considered: *Calamagrostis acutiflora, Centranthus ruber, Cistus albidus, Cistus salvifolius, Euphorbia characias, Gaura lindheimeri, Lippia nodiflora, Lygeum spartum, Nepeta faassenii, Perovskia atripcifolia, Pistacia lentiscus, Rubus Betty Ashburner, Salix purpurea* Nana, *Teucrium fruticans* and *Verbena banariensis*. A choice was made for the NBS scenario by assuming that trees and grass have the maximum vegetative development.

All planted species were adapted to local climatic conditions and did not present any phytosanitary problems, as they are considered suitable for easy maintenance solutions with low maintenance costs.

2.4. Microclimatic Computer Simulation

The microclimatic computer simulation of the urban environment consists of a simplification of real scenarios that intends to represent the characteristics of the elements that constitute the space [29]; however, it is not a complete representation of the real world because it does not reproduce all its complexity.

This research studies the intra-urban layer by simulating building–urban environment interactions. For this purpose, the simple forcing method was used by considering on-site data collection, including wind speed and direction, air temperature and minimum and maximum relative humidity for the simulated day. With this information, the software simulates the behavior of the climatic parameters for a whole day [51].

2.5. Model Input Data

For an adequate representation of the local environment, it was necessary to collect data to be incorporated into the ENVI-Met simulation. Local spatial data were collected by QGIS 3.10.3 image interpretations of orthophotography and Google Earth, with the identification of land cover and building materials, along with measurements of the height of existing buildings and structures. These features were then validated by fieldwork using laser measurement equipment (STABILA LD 500, Annweiler, Germany). Vegetation data included tree species identification and 3D configuration. Variables such as canopy height and diameter were collected using a telescopic ruler. Surface materials were characterized by local interpretation with the identification of dominant colors and materials.

The computer simulation was performed according to the meteorological data collection period (23–24 June 2021) using two data collection systems: one was fixed (EF), used to collect the air temperature and relative humidity data; and one was mobile, used to collect the average radiant temperature and wind speed data.

The fixed station (FS) has compact data acquisition systems ("mini dataloggers") with air temperature and relative humidity sensors (Gemini Data Loggers, model Tinytag TGP-4500, Chichester, West Sussex, UK). These systems were placed in shelters that protect them from radiation, at a height of 2.5 to 3 m from ground level, facing south so as not to suffer shading from the fixing pole. Their shelters are painted white to reduce the heating effects of the shelters. The mobile station, on the other hand, is a thermal microclimate data logging station—Delta Ohm 32.3, a multifunctional instrument that measures environmental conditions.

The simulated time is equivalent to a little more than a day, with a total of 29 h. Thus, the analyzed data start on 23 June 2021 at 6 h and end on 24 June 2021 at 18 h. Data collected locally were used to define the parameters for the ENVI-Met simulation (Table 1).

Table 1. Setting up climate data for microclimate simulation in ENVI_met®.

	Ta (°C)	RH (%)	WS (m/s)	WindDir (deg)
		Input Data		
Maximum	27.60	88.53	1.4	121.5
Minimum	9.19	22.60		

Ta: Air Temperature; RH: Relative Humidity; WS: Wind Speed; WindDir: Wind Direction.

3. Results and Discussion

3.1. Microclimate Data Validation

3.1.1. Air Temperature

The microclimatic monitoring provided the air temperature profile over a 24 h campaign (Figure 5). These data were used as input to perform the simulations for both the base and the NBS scenario. The results show that data from the simulation overestimate the air temperature when compared to local measurements, and this difference can be justified by the use of the *simple forcing* method, in which the program forces the behavior of the climatic parameters during the day across the simulation area, not only including the data collection location, based on their maximum and minimum values used for the simulation input [52,53]. Nonetheless, the data follow a similar profile to the Pearson correlation between the two datasets, which is strong (0.777).

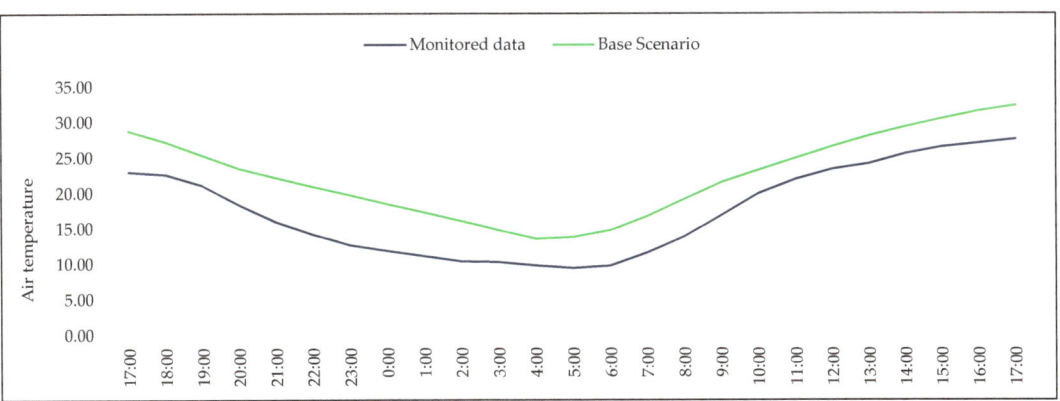

Figure 5. Monitored and simulation air temperature (Base Scenario) at the monitoring location.

3.1.2. Relative Humidity

The relative humidity data from both fixed station and the base scenario simulation are presented in Figure 6. Values from the fixed stations were also used as input for the simulations, as well as for this study's NBS scenario.

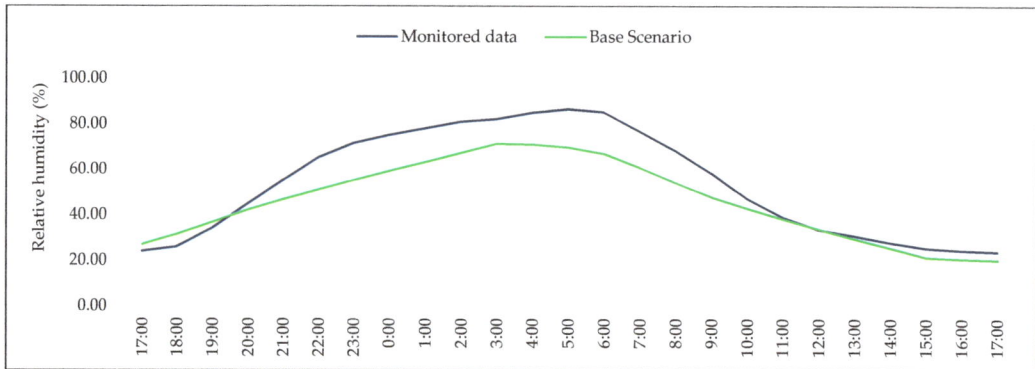

Figure 6. Monitored and simulation relative humidity (Base Scenario) at the monitoring location.

Relative humidity decreases during the day and rises at night, which can be mostly justified by the relation of this variable with the air temperature and pressure of the air; i.e., when the temperature decreases, the maximum amount of water vapor that can be present in the air decreases, and consequently, the relative humidity of the air mass increases. The changes in these two sets are similar, and the data correlation (Pearson) for these two datasets is very strong (0.960). Larger differences were found in the hours of higher relative humidity.

3.1.3. Wind Speed

Wind speed can have a major influence on the behavior of air temperature since it can affect dynamic processes such as convection. Figure 7 presents the variation of data from the two datasets: monitored and simulated (base scenario). The wind speed averages were used in the simulation of the base scenario and the scenario with the NBS.

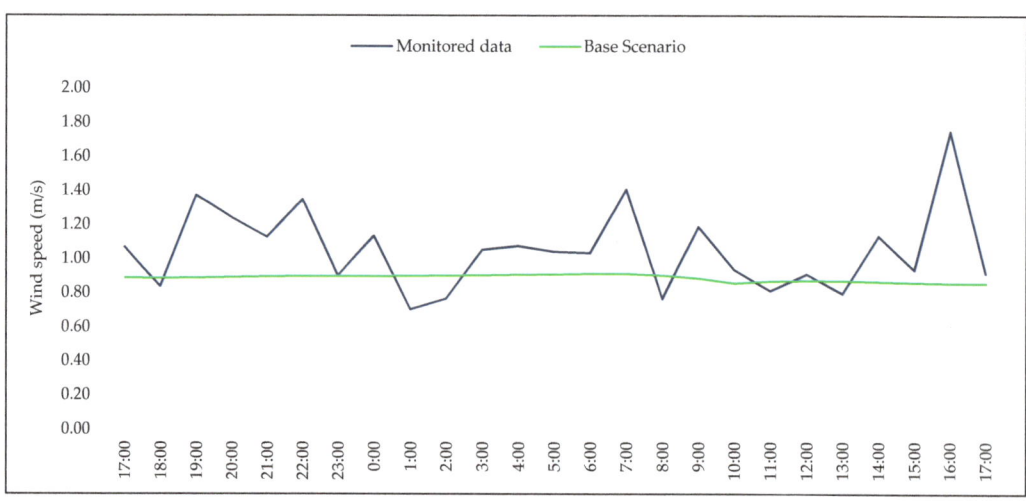

Figure 7. Monitored wind speed between actual and modeled scenarios.

Unlike the other variables, ENVI-Met generates stable values over the whole simulation, thus failing to grasp variations in wind speed across the day. Nonetheless, the data show that only light wind was present throughout the measurement campaign, thus limiting the potential effects of wind on local heat exchange processes.

3.1.4. Mean Radiant Temperature

Mean radiant temperature is a parameter influenced by surfaces' albedo and by the shading from both buildings and trees. Its behavior changes throughout the day as a consequence of the solar radiation load [31]. The analysis between the monitored data and the baseline scenario simulation demonstrates that there was a similar MRT behavior at the pedestrian level (1.5 m above ground) for the measurement period (Figure 8).

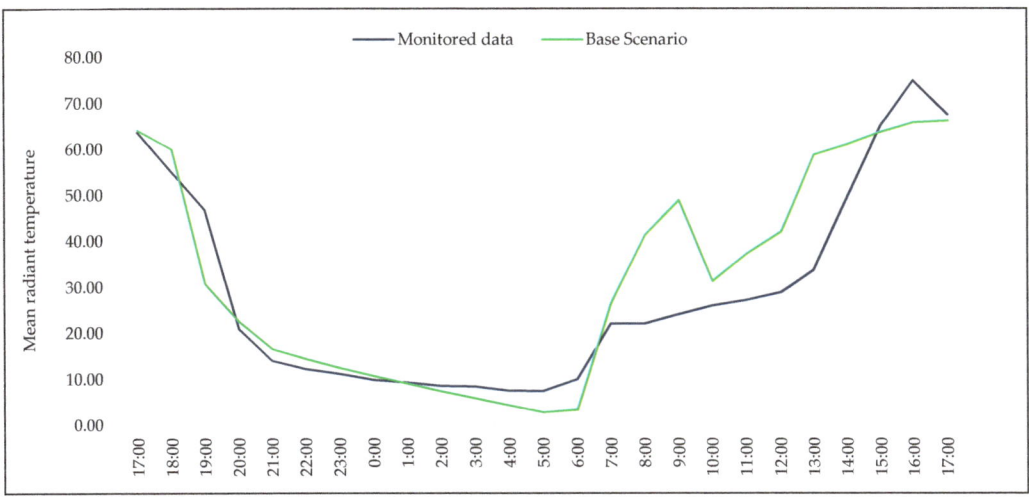

Figure 8. Monitored mean radiant temperature between actual and modeled scenarios.

The results show an overestimation of the MRT during the morning and afternoon periods and show similarities during the night. These differences can be explained due to the model resolution not being accurate in differentiating the shading caused by certain urban elements, as well as changes in cloud cover. Moreover, ENVI-Met may fail to completely traduce the complexity of surface albedos and vegetation properties (e.g., leaf area index), which may also justify the differences between monitored and modeled results [54,55]. Despite the differences in results, the data correlation (Pearson) between the two datasets is strong (0.870).

3.2. Scenarios

3.2.1. Air Temperature

Simulations were performed in ENVI-Met for air temperature (Figure 9). For this parameter, hourly maps were generated for 5 h (just before sunrise, with the lowest air temperature value), 7 h (just after sunrise), 12 h (noon, with the highest solar angle) and 17 h (mid-afternoon). The height considered for reading the model data was 1.2 m.

The simulations (Figure 9) allow us to foresee the influence of urban design on air temperature [45]. The results allow us to identify the potential influence of NBSs as solutions to improve thermal comfort, providing a detailed estimation of the benefits of the introduction of vegetation in a public road infrastructure in an industrial zone.

Overall, the base scenario had ranges of 2.7 °C, 1.4 °C, 8.3 °C and 10.5 °C for the simulated times of 5 h, 7 h, 12 h and 16 h, respectively. For the same periods, the simulations for the NBS scenario foresaw amplitudes of 10.5 °C, 7.1 °C, 4.3 °C and 9.7 °C, respectively.

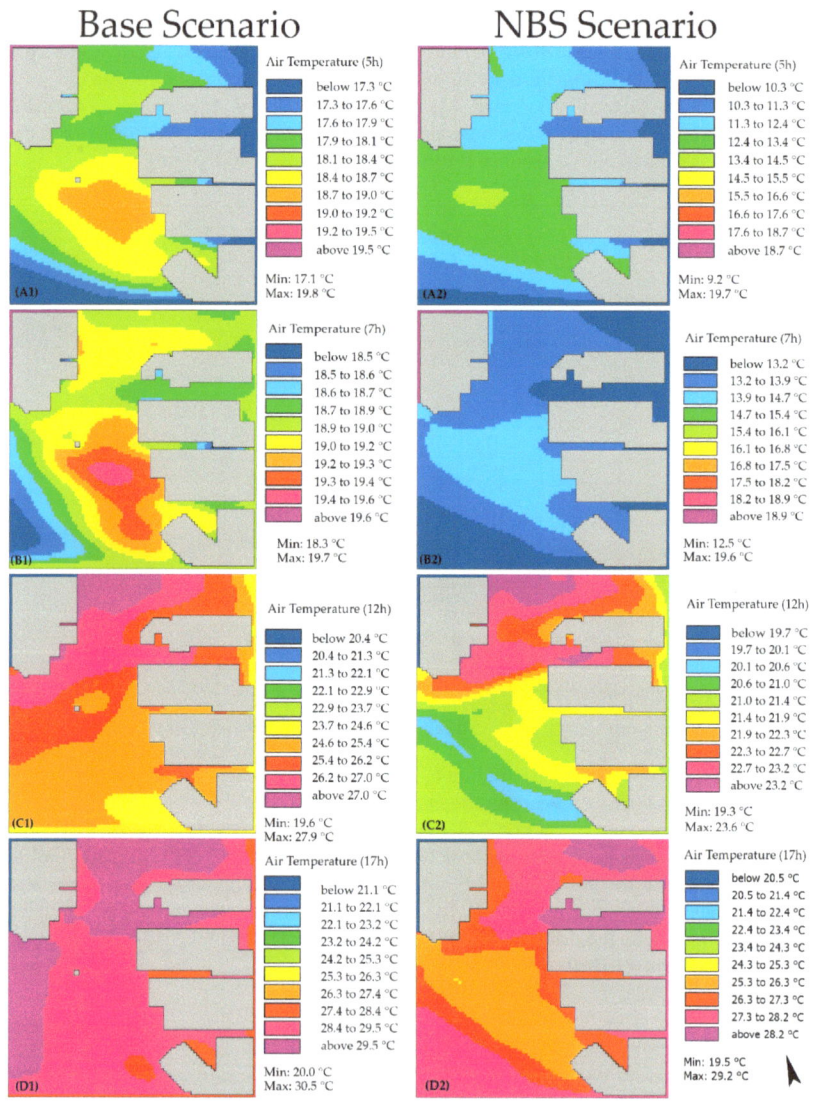

Figure 9. Simulated air temperature for the base and NBS scenarios. Hours: (**A1,A2**), 5 h; (**B1,B2**), 7 h; (**C1,C2**), 12 h; (**D1,D2**), 17 h.

The maps suggest that the highest air temperatures were expected to be reached over asphalt and sidewalks, whereas the lowest air temperatures were simulated over grass surfaces, under trees, and in other shaded locations from both buildings and trees. Before sunrise (5 h), the highest simulated temperatures are between 18.7 °C and 19.8 °C, concentrated in the traffic circle and asphalted area. With a sunrise (7 h), there was an increase in temperature, especially close to low albedo surfaces. For the following hours (12 h and 17 h), air temperature increased considerably, reaching maximum temperatures of 27.9 °C and 30.5 °C for the base and NBS scenarios, respectively.

For the NBS scenario, when compared with the base scenario, lower temperatures extended to the areas where trees were added, thus expanding the original cool areas in the base simulation. The most expressive differences were found at sunrise (7 h) and noon

(12 h). These differences can be explained by the fact that, starting from dawn, trees partially intercepted the sun's rays, causing lower solar incidence. Additionally, trees provide water vapor through transpiration, which helped reduce the air temperature. Grass surfaces also provided additional temperature reductions, especially when irrigated, although this vegetation was less effective than trees in thermal regulation.

The addition of vegetated areas in the NBS scenario contributed to reductions in the heat island effects, as shown in Figure 9A2,B2, with reductions in air temperature over the afternoon periods. This phenomenon can be justified by increases in evapotranspiration, which contributed to increases in relative humidity.

The presence of vegetation in the urban fabric has proven to be efficient in regulating air temperature. The radiant energy received produces a high level of evapotranspiration when combined with good site irrigation, which can help maintain the vegetation's capacity to contribute to local thermal comfort.

For the simulations performed for the base and NBS scenario (Figure 9), there was a smaller temperature reduction for the dawn period when compared with the afternoon period. A similar result can be found in a study by Silva and Shinzato et al. [51,56], which points out that the method used for simulation, *simple forcing*, which does not use many input parameters and forces the climatic behavior, may not generate fully realistic scenarios [28,57–59]. Ketterer and Matzarakis [55] as well as Middel et al. [30] report higher simulated values for daytime air temperature and lower values for nighttime. For this study, ENVI–Met generally tended to underestimate all Ta values. This lack of coincidence between the measured and predicted values was also identified by Tsoka et al. [39], analyzing several papers that used ENVI-Met for simulations for various purposes.

The simulated scenarios demonstrate that, in general, the addition of green areas and nature-based solutions can potentially decrease air temperature, especially in early afternoon hours, where solar incidence is stronger and where surfaces warm throughout the previous hours, and these results are consistent with those of Tsoka et al. and Tsilini et al. [39,43]. In simulations performed in tropical climates, Morakinyo and Lam [44] had similar results, highlighting the importance of tree selection as unique characterization parameters in conjunction with leaf area index (LAI) values, leaf density distribution (LAD) by height and the planting pattern or arrangement, which can affect trees' potential benefits.

3.2.2. Wind Speed

Wind speed simulations (Figure 10) produced little variation throughout the day, as ENVI-Met does not consider relevant variations in wind speed and direction inputs throughout the simulation, offering similar results for each of the periods.

In all periods, lower wind speeds were found near the buildings, whereas open areas exposed to predominant wind had higher wind speeds.

The results suggest that the addition of vegetation in the NBS did not induce considerable changes; however, there was an increase in wind speed in the west direction. This result can be justified because the model was simulated by a single input value of wind speed and direction, southeast of the maps, without providing visible changes throughout the day. These circumstances are, according to Ketterer and Matzarakis [55], related to the modeled values of wind speed, which do not represent the measured data correctly, assuming a constant value.

The ENVI-Met model has been very rarely evaluated for its ability to accurately reproduce diurnal wind speed profiles. Some authors [39,54,60] have suggested that the model is unable to simulate relevant variations in wind speed and direction because of the static nature of the model, which provides little variation from the initial parameters' definition, corresponding to the daily mean values.

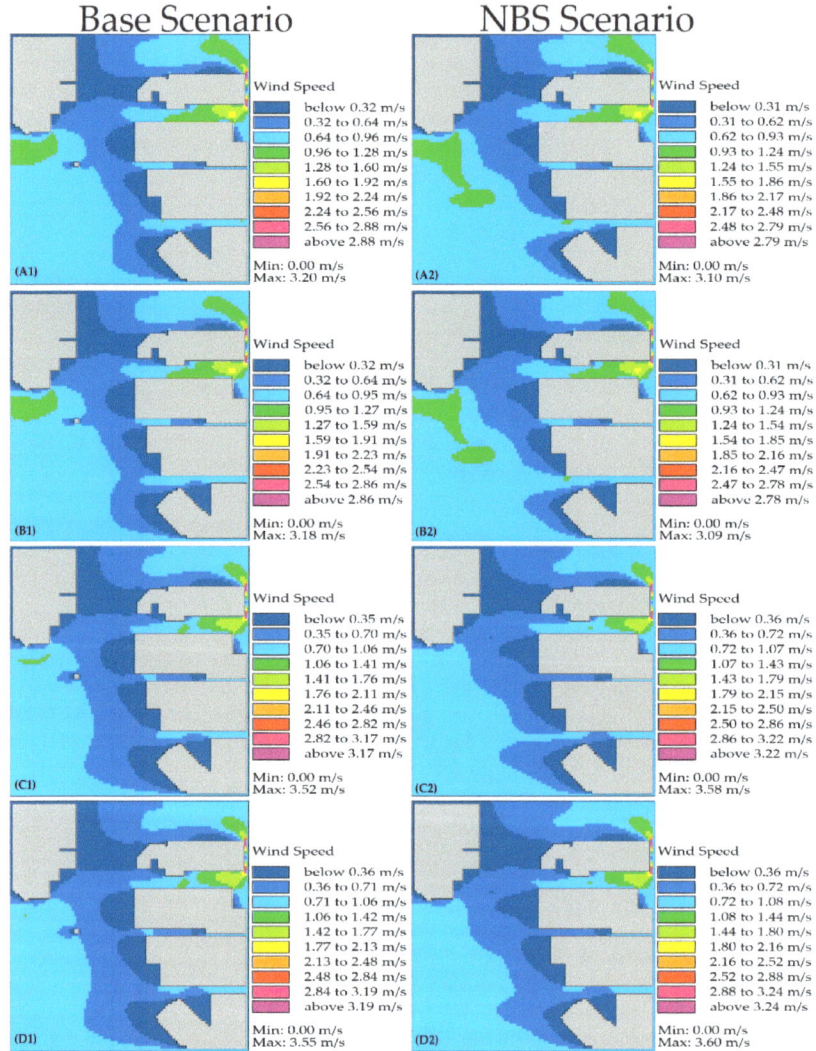

Figure 10. Simulated wind speed for the base scenarios and scenarios with NBS interventions. Hours: (**A1,A2**), 5 h; (**B1,B2**), 7 h; (**C1,C2**), 12 h; (**D1,D2**), 17 h.

3.2.3. Mean Radiant Temperature

In this study, mean radiant temperature (MRT) is the parameter proportionately most affected by the shadows cast by trees and buildings [33]. The simulations (Figure 11) demonstrate how this variable changed at the pedestrian level (1.2 m) for the four simulation periods, for both the base and NBS scenarios.

MRT expresses the effects of direct and reflected shortwave and longwave radiation fluxes at a given location [61]. As expected, solar radiation played an important role in MRT, and higher values can be understood mostly as a consequence of both low albedo on the ground and wall surfaces and sun exposure on those surfaces. Consequently, higher differences were found between sunny and shaded areas, with maximum values on paved surfaces.

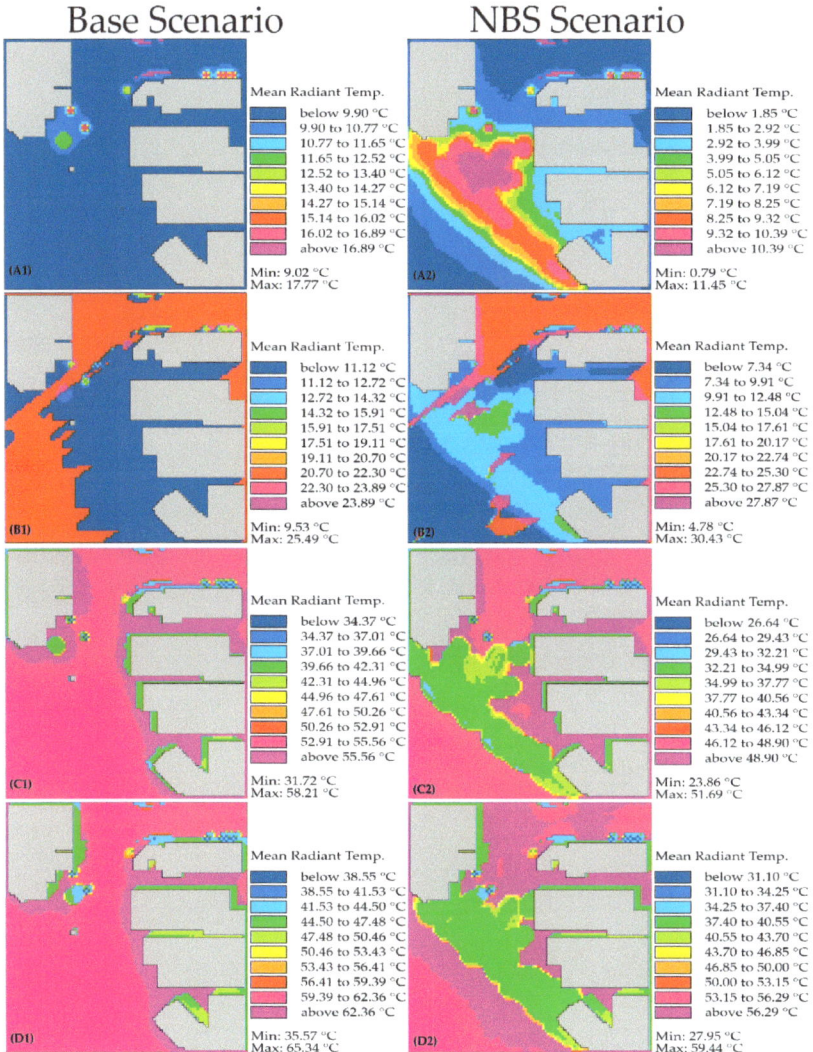

Figure 11. Simulated mean radiant temperature for the base scenarios and scenarios with NBS interventions. Hours: (**A1,A2**), 5 h; (**B1,B2**), 7 h; (**C1,C2**),12 h; (**D1,D2**), 17 h.

Nights are cooler (Figure 11A1,A2) because, during this period, there is no incoming shortwave radiation, i.e., there is an energy deficit, and the surface–atmosphere system cools down through the emission of longwave radiation into space. Both scenarios have low MRTs compared to the others before sunrise; however, in the NBS scenario, there was an increase in the MRT in the center of the area because, with the addition of vegetation, there was an increase in energy dissipated during the night due to its low albedo.

From dawn (Figure 11B1,B2), the sun incidence can be noticed from the northeast side through the red and pink colors. Note that the trees in the central region prevented radiation from direct incidence on most of the study area, reducing the MRT on the opposite side of the simulation.

For the NBS scenario, trees (Figure 11C2,D2) primarily provided solar radiation shielding, preventing direct shortwave radiation. The lawn in the roundabout also acted as an attenuator of reflected radiation, since plants intercept part of the shortwave radiation and integrate it into their physiological processes, such as photosynthesis. Thus, as can be seen in Figure 10, after sunrise, it was expected that the areas with added vegetation, in general, had a lower MRT.

In urban areas, heat transmission by radiation is the most important factor in the energy exchange processes between the human body and its environment. During the night, the simulations show the influence of trees (Figure 11), which can be explained by their energy balance, demonstrating the effectiveness of the software in designing tree models in detail [62].

ENVI-Met provides similar behaviors between air temperature and MRT, especially when considering the spatial variability in the selected spaces [63]. Therefore, the results (Figure 11) are consistent with the characteristics of the urban geometry at each site; however, as suggested by Acero and Herranz-Pascual [54], ENVImet still fails to grasp every aspect from the microscale energy radiation balance (e.g., diffuse/reflected radiation or longwave radiation), which can be explained by the limited options regarding surfaces' albedos and vegetation properties.

3.3. Comparison between Scenarios

3.3.1. Air Temperature

The map (Figure 12) expresses the variation across the modeling space and presents a prediction of the behavior of the study area for the solar noon period, when the differences are most expressive, from the four periods in this study. This first representation compares the simulations between the base scenario and the NBS scenario.

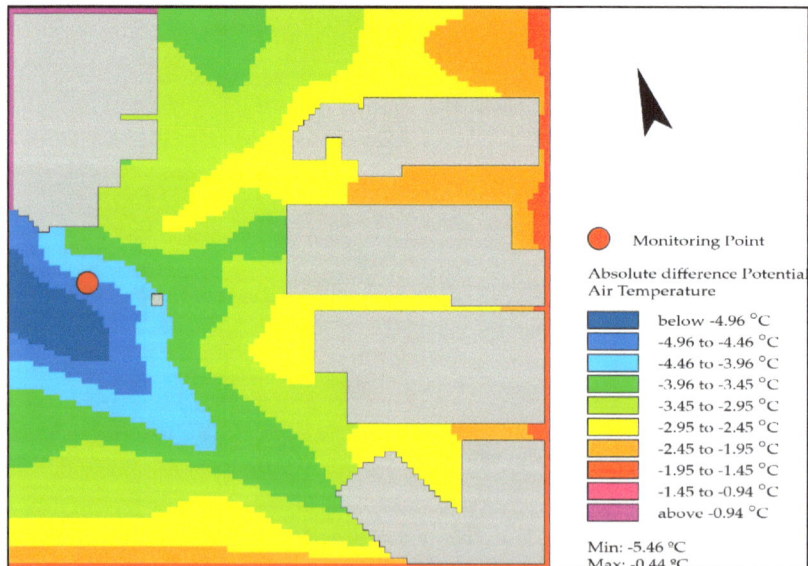

Figure 12. The air temperature difference between the base scenario and NBS scenario at noon.

It is important to note that the places with major temperature reductions were located where the NBS simulation included additional trees and grass, on the dry stream between the roundabout and the railway tracks. In these locations, ENVI-Met estimated reductions of up to 4.96 °C. Inside the traffic circle area, the expected air temperature decrease was smaller though significant, around 3.45 °C to 3.96 °C. The smallest reductions were simulated for shaded areas near the buildings, areas already cooler and those which had no addition of vegetation.

The projected differences in air temperature between scenarios suggest that NBSs, and particularly vegetation introduction, when fully developed, can promote decreases in air temperature, as there were general decreases in temperature in the simulated area. Tsoka et al. [39] report that, in their study, the simulation revealed that ENVI-Met can be considered a useful tool for the definition of heat mitigation strategies with the incorporation of urban vegetation, giving even better results when using combined strategies, such as green roofs.

The curves in Figure 13 represent the hourly variation of air for the two defined scenarios. The curves follow a similar daily variation pattern; however, the incorporation of the NBS in the scenario determined reductions in the simulated air temperature in all periods, although they were more expressive in periods of greater solar incidence.

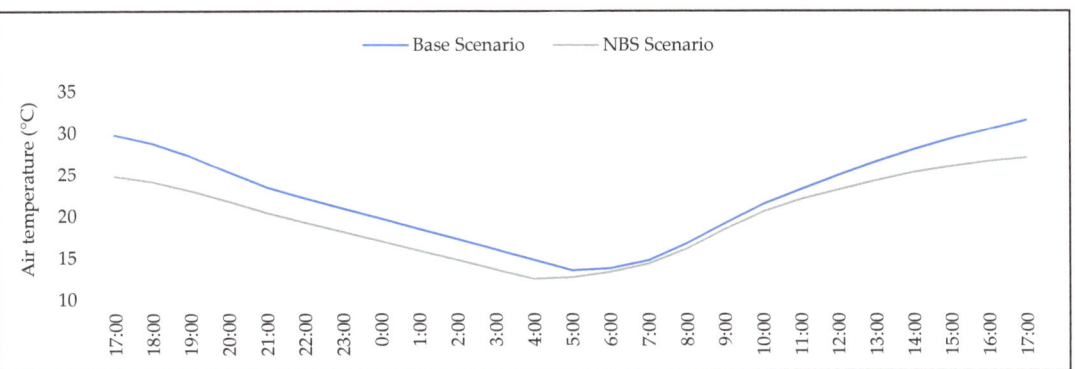

Figure 13. Air temperature profile for the base scenario and NBS scenario for the measurement location.

The incorporation of vegetation in streets and sidewalks determines potential reductions in air temperature. In a period of higher relative humidity (Figure 6), a minimum reduction of 0.94 °C at 5 a.m. and 6 a.m. was identified, with a maximum reduction of 4.95 °C observed in the sunny periods.

3.3.2. Mean Radiant Temperature

The results presented in Figure 14 express the differences between the base scenario and the effects of incorporating vegetation (NBS scenario) on the average radiant temperature, measured at the pedestrian level for the solar noon period.

In general, when observing the differences between the base scenario and the NBS scenario, there was an estimated reduction in MRT in the largest proportion of the map, between −7.28 °C and −4.32 °C, identified in yellow. The greatest reduction was estimated for the central region of the map, visible with the colors in blue tones, followed by colors close to the green, located mostly near the buildings. Only a few small points are shown by orange and pink colors, which identify smaller reductions in MRT.

Looking at the differences in the study area for the noon period, the greatest reductions in MRT were simulated for the areas where there was a major introduction of trees, assuming their full development, with reduction that reached over 19 °C. At these locations, solar radiation was partially absorbed by the leaves, avoiding some reflection to other surfaces [64]. In addition to receiving direct radiation, the vegetation intercepted the radiation coming from horizontal and vertical surfaces.

It is important to mention that, during this simulated period, the area was mostly affected by direct solar radiation, forming a distinctive low temperature in shadow areas near buildings, which is represented by green. In these areas, milder reductions occurred, ranging from 10.25 °C to 7.28 °C.

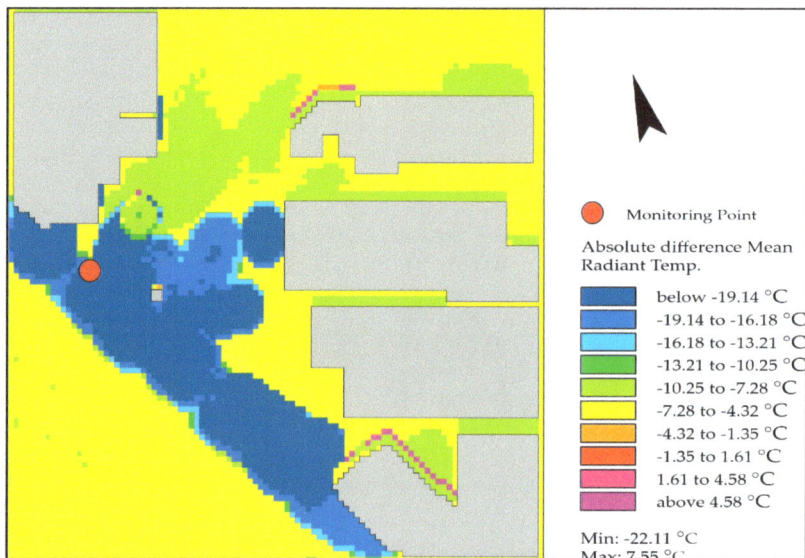

Figure 14. Differences in mean radiant temperature between the base scenario and NBS scenario at noon.

Figure 14 also shows that changes in the surroundings, such as the addition of trees and vegetation; different urban materials with different reflectivity and emissivity; and building configurations (orientations and inclinations), can favor radiative exchanges between building facades and surfaces, causing increases in absorption or reductions in radiation [36].

Differences between the base and the NBS scenario change throughout the study timeframe for the reference location (Figure 15). During the night, differences were small, with slightly higher temperatures in the NBS scenario. This difference can be explained by the lower sky view factor (SVF) near tree canopies, which can reduce the nighttime longwave radiation emissions [54].

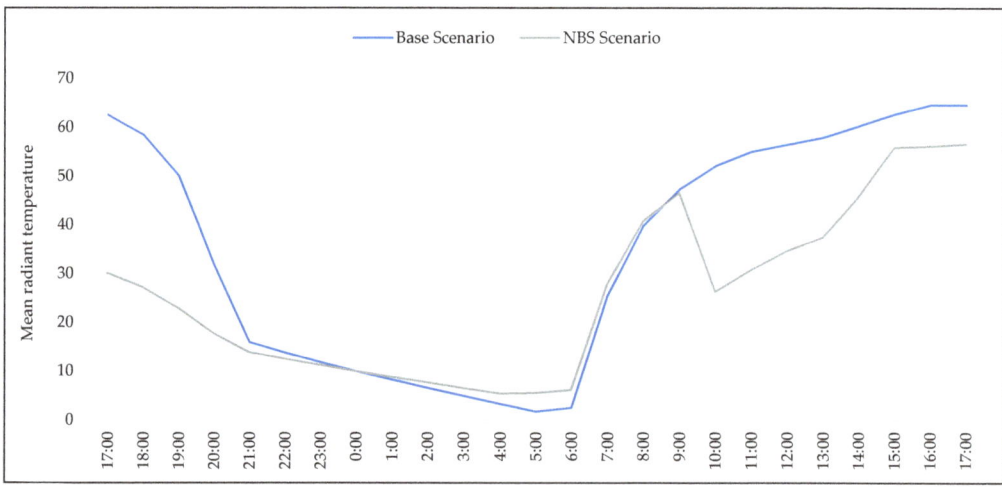

Figure 15. Mean radiant temperature profile for the base scenario and NBS scenario, considering the initial monitoring location.

For the afternoon period, the decreases in both air temperature and MRT were more expressive, suggesting that the changes incorporated for the new scenario provided decreases in air temperature. Successful incorporations of trees were also studied by Ferwati et al. [65].

For sunrise, the reference location in the base scenario was more exposed to solar radiation when compared with the projected NBS scenario, a factor that, combined with the thermal behavior of the vegetated surroundings, explains the lower MRT simulated for this second scenario.

The base scenario overestimated the MRT when compared to the monitored data (Figure 7), mainly in the afternoon period, and this overestimation was also reported by other authors using ENVI-Met [55,63,66,67]. Thus, the results suggest that the calculation of the radiation fluxes may not be entirely accurate and may explain differences in the modeled results.

4. Limitations

As previously suggested in this article, ENVI-Met still has some limitations, such as the ones regarding the thermal behavior of building walls, which can influence microclimate, as a single material is assumed by the model, differing from reality [15]. Additionally, the simulations of air temperature and relative humidity are adjusted by the model during the simulations, whereas wind conditions and cloudiness remain almost unchanged [68].

Another limitation is associated with MRT and the estimation of radiative fluxes, which seems to be slightly inaccurate, even though a strong correlation was found between the modeled and measured data [69]. Finally, anthropogenic heating, vehicles and mechanical cooling systems that can alter thermal conditions are not accounted for in the model [44].

5. Conclusions

This study used climate modeling to estimate the potential benefits of incorporating NBS in the public road infrastructure of an industrial park through ENVI-Met simulation. With the use of this modeling software, it was possible to estimate differentiated patterns in the behavior of air temperature, relative humidity, mean radiant temperature and wind speed for two scenarios: a base and an NBS scenario. When comparing these two scenarios, for a summer day, the results show potential reductions in air temperature as a potential effect of the implementation of an NBS project, including new vegetation elements, changes in land cover and the incorporation of water bodies.

NBS proved to be effective for the particular study, demonstrating that it is possible to transverse cities into greener and more innovative models. This concept has significant potential in climate change mitigation and adaptation in urban areas, and it contributes to the resilience and livability of cities.

The results show a good correlation between the values that were measured and the base scenario in all climatic parameters, with strong to very strong correlations. In a more detailed data comparison, coherent behavior was observed, although with overestimations in the air temperature and MRT. However, for MRT, the values were overestimated by ENVI-Met, mostly in the period from sunrise to noon.

Finally, when comparing the simulation of the current scenario with the new NBS scenario, positive results were obtained for all periods, suggesting that the proposed Nature-Based Solutions may potentially decrease air temperature for the simulation context. Overall, the software was able to estimate air temperature and other variables. Nonetheless, the simulation maps still showed inconsistent results, which can be partially attributed to the limitations of the simulation process.

A possible method for future modeling design is to measure multiple points within a domain and to study other ways to simulate the data using the *full forcing* method to draw the best conclusions and to confirm the quality of ENVI-Met simulations.

Under the INDNATUR Project framework, additional studies and actions will be carried out, including: ENVI-Met simulations for all seasons, with special emphasis on extreme climate circumstances (cold and heat); and validation campaigns, with on-site data collection to validate the simulated results. In addition, as INDNATUR interventions already took place, data will be continuously collected with the help of on-site sensors (air temperature and relative humidity), complemented by monitoring campaigns. This newly acquired data, along with additional modeling (e.g., different times of day), will provide further understanding on the potential benefits of NBS in industrial parks.

Author Contributions: Conceptualization, A.G. and F.M.A.; methodology, A.G. and F.M.A.; software, F.M.A.; validation, A.G. and M.R.d.C.-E.; formal analysis, F.M.A.; investigation, F.M.A.; resources, A.G.; writing—original draft preparation, F.M.A.; writing—review and editing, A.G.; visualization, F.M.A.; supervision, A.G.; project administration, M.R.d.C.-E.; funding acquisition, M.R.d.C.-E. All authors have read and agreed to the published version of the manuscript.

Funding: Interreg V-A Spain-Portugal POCTEP 2014–2020, European Commission, under ERDF (European Regional Development Fund). Project code: 0599_INDNATUR_2_E.

Institutional Review Board Statement: Not applicable.

Informed Consent Statement: Not applicable.

Data Availability Statement: Not applicable.

Acknowledgments: The authors are grateful to the Foundation for Science and Technology (FCT, Portugal) for financial support by national funds FCT/MCTES to CIMO (UIDB/00690/2020). Appreciation must also go to the other INTERREG POCTEP INDNATUR Project partners for the help and support during this study with the provision of means that helped a lot in the research. To the Polytechnic Institute of Bragança and the University of Valladolid that supported the collaboration in the project.

Conflicts of Interest: The authors declare no conflict of interest. The funders had no role in the design of the study; in the collection, analyses or interpretation of data; in the writing of the manuscript; or in the decision to publish the results.

Appendix A

Figure A1. Graphic of the area in which the different plant species are indicated.

References

1. Tourinho, L.; Prevedello, J.A.; Carvalho, B.M.; Rocha, D.S.B.; Vale, M.M. Macroscale Climate Change Predictions Have Little Influence on Landscape-Scale Habitat Suitability. *Perspect. Ecol. Conserv.* **2022**, *20*, 29–37. [CrossRef]
2. Mehryar, S.; Sasson, I.; Surminski, S. Supporting Urban Adaptation to Climate Change: What Role Can Resilience Measurement Tools Play? *Urban Clim.* **2022**, *41*, 101047. [CrossRef]
3. Shi, C.; Guo, N.; Zeng, L.; Wu, F. How Climate Change Is Going to Affect Urban Livability in China. *Clim. Serv.* **2022**, *26*, 100284. [CrossRef]
4. Ray Biswas, R.; Sharma, R.; Gyasi-Agyei, Y. Urban Water Crises: Making Sense of Climate Change Adaptation Barriers and Success Parameters. *Clim. Serv.* **2022**, *27*, 100302. [CrossRef]
5. Ribeiro, H.; Pesquero, C.R.; De Sousa Zanotti Stagliorio Coelho, M. Clima Urbano e Saúde: Uma Revisão Sistematizada Da Literatura Recente. *Estud. Av.* **2016**, *30*, 67–82. [CrossRef]
6. Oke, T.R.; Mills, G.; Christen, A.; Voogt, J.A. *Urban Climates*, 1st ed.; Sheridan Books, Inc.: Cambridge, UK, 2017; ISBN 9781139016476.
7. Stewart, I.D.; Oke, T.R. Local Climate Zones for Urban Temperature Studies. *Bull. Am. Meteorol. Soc.* **2012**, *93*, 1879–1900. [CrossRef]
8. Landsberg, H. *The Urban Climate*; Academic Press: Cambridge, MA, USA, 1981; Volume 53, ISBN 9788578110796.
9. Iain Stewart, G.M. *The Urban Heat Island*, 1st ed.; Elsevier: Amsterdam, The Netherlands, 2021; ISBN 9780128150177.
10. Oke, T.R. *Boundary Layer Climates*, 2nd ed.; Routledge: London, UK, 2002.
11. Gonçalves, A.; Ornellas, G.; Ribeiro, A.C.; Maia, F.; Rocha, A.; Feliciano, M. Urban Cold and Heat Island in the City of Bragança (Portugal). *Climate* **2018**, *6*, 70. [CrossRef]
12. Vahmani, P.; Luo, X.; Jones, A.; Hong, T. Anthropogenic Heating of the Urban Environment: An Investigation of Feedback Dynamics between Urban Micro-Climate and Decomposed Anthropogenic Heating from Buildings. *Build. Environ.* **2022**, *213*, 108841. [CrossRef]
13. Gettelman, A.; Rood, R.B. *Demystifying Climate Models: A Users Guide to Earth System Models*; Springer: Berlin/Heidelberg, Germany, 2016; Volume 2, ISBN 9783662489574.
14. Liu, M.; Lo, K. A Comparative Review of Urban Climate Governance in Chinese and Western Contexts. *Urban Gov.* 2021; in press. [CrossRef]
15. Crank, P.J.; Sailor, D.J.; Ban-Weiss, G.; Taleghani, M. Evaluating the ENVI-Met Microscale Model for Suitability in Analysis of Targeted Urban Heat Mitigation Strategies. *Urban Clim.* **2018**, *26*, 188–197. [CrossRef]
16. Raymond, C.M.; Frantzeskaki, N.; Kabisch, N.; Berry, P.; Breil, M.; Nita, M.R.; Geneletti, D.; Calfapietra, C. A Framework for Assessing and Implementing the Co-Benefits of Nature-Based Solutions in Urban Areas. *Environ. Sci. Policy* **2017**, *77*, 15–24. [CrossRef]
17. European Commission. *Towards an EU Research and Innovation Policy Agenda for Nature-Based Solutions & Re-Naturing Cities: Final Report of the Horizon 2020 Expert Group on "Nature-Based Solutions and Re-Naturing Cities"*; European Commission: Brussels, Belgium, 2015; ISBN 9789279460517.
18. Toxopeus, H.; Kotsila, P.; Conde, M.; Katona, A.; van der Jagt, A.P.N.; Polzin, F. How 'Just' Is Hybrid Governance of Urban Nature-Based Solutions? *Cities* **2020**, *105*, 102839. [CrossRef]
19. Faivre, N.; Fritz, M.; Freitas, T.; de Boissezon, B.; Vandewoestijne, S. Nature-Based Solutions in the EU: Innovating with Nature to Address Social, Economic and Environmental Challenges. *Environ. Res.* **2017**, *159*, 509–518. [CrossRef]
20. Devecchi, A.M.; Chirmici, A.C.; Simonetti, C.; Thiago, B.C. Desenhando Cidades Com Soluções Baseadas Na Natureza. In *Parcerias Estratégicas*; CGEE: Brasília, Brasil, 2020; pp. 217–233. ISBN 1413-9375.
21. Kabisch, N.; Frantzeskaki, N.; Pauleit, S.; Naumann, S.; Davis, M.; Artmann, M.; Haase, D.; Knapp, S.; Korn, H.; Stadler, J.; et al. Nature-Based Solutions to Climate Change Mitigation and Adaptation in Urban Areas: Perspectives on Indicators, Knowledge Gaps, Barriers, and Opportunities for Action. *Ecol. Soc.* **2016**, *21*, 39. [CrossRef]
22. European Commission. *Evaluating the Impact of Nature-Based Solutions: A Handbook for Practitioners*; Dumitru, A., Wendling, L., Eds.; European Commission: Brussels, Belgium, 2021; ISBN 9789276229612.
23. Frantzeskaki, N. Seven Lessons for Planning Nature-Based Solutions in Cities. *Environ. Sci. Policy* **2019**, *93*, 101–111. [CrossRef]
24. Ávila, L.B. Instrumento Multicritério de Análise Para a Implantação de Zonas Industriais: Variáveis Legais, Antrópicas e Naturais. 2018. Available online: http://www.repositorio.jesuita.org.br/handle/UNISINOS/7088 (accessed on 15 April 2022).
25. Presumido, P.H.; Gonçalves, A.; Feliciano, M.; Igrejas, G.; Romero, F. Projeto Rehabind-Qualidade Ambiental Em Áreas Industriais Transfronteiriças-Mirandela e Zamora (Espanha). In *Livro de Atas da Conferência Internacional de Ambiente em Língua Portuguesa, Avaito, Poretugal, 8–10 May 2018*; Universidade de Aveiro: Aveiro, Portugal, 2018; pp. 21–24. ISBN 978-972-789-540-3.
26. González, J.E.; Ramamurthy, P.; Bornstein, R.D.; Chen, F.; Bou-Zeid, E.R.; Ghandehari, M.; Luvall, J.; Mitra, C.; Niyogi, D. Urban Climate and Resiliency: A Synthesis Report of State of the Art and Future Research Directions. *Urban Clim.* **2021**, *38*, 100858. [CrossRef]
27. Geophysical Fluid Dynamics Laboratory. Climate Modeling.
28. Gusson, C.S.; Duarte, D.H.S. Effects of Built Density and Urban Morphology on Urban Microclimate—Calibration of the Model ENVI-Met V4 for the Subtropical Sao Paulo, Brazil. *Procedia Eng.* **2016**, *169*, 2–10. [CrossRef]
29. Daniela Bruse, Michael Bruse, Helge Simon ENVI_MET GmbH 2020.

30. Middel, A.; Häb, K.; Brazel, A.J.; Martin, C.A.; Guhathakurta, S. Impact of Urban Form and Design on Mid-Afternoon Microclimate in Phoenix Local Climate Zones. *Landsc. Urban Plan.* **2014**, *122*, 16–28. [CrossRef]
31. Bruse, M.; Fleer, H. Simulating Surface-Plant-Air Interactions inside Urban Environments with a Three Dimensional Numerical Model. *Environ. Model. Softw.* **1998**, *13*, 373–384. [CrossRef]
32. Bruse, M. *ENVI-Met 3.0: Updated Model Overview*; University of Bochum: Bochum, Germany, 2004; pp. 1–12.
33. Duarte, D.H.S.; Shinzato, P.; dos Santos Gusson, C.; Alves, C.A. The Impact of Vegetation on Urban Microclimate to Counterbalance Built Density in a Subtropical Changing Climate. *Urban Clim.* **2015**, *14*, 224–239. [CrossRef]
34. McRae, I.; Freedman, F.; Rivera, A.; Li, X.; Dou, J.; Cruz, I.; Ren, C.; Dronova, I.; Fraker, H.; Bornstein, R. Integration of the WUDAPT, WRF, and ENVI-Met Models to Simulate Extreme Daytime Temperature Mitigation Strategies in San Jose, California. *Build. Environ.* **2020**, *184*, 107180. [CrossRef]
35. Cárdenas Celis, A.M.; Silva, C.F. Protocolo de Elaboração de Arquivo Climático de Cidades Brasileiras Para o Software ENVI-Met 4.0. *Paranoá Cad. Arquitetura Urban.* **2018**, *22*, 32–50. [CrossRef]
36. Ali-Toudert, F. Exploration of the Thermal Behaviour and Energy Balance of Urban Canyons in Relation to Their Geometrical and Constructive Properties. *Build. Environ.* **2021**, *188*, 107466. [CrossRef]
37. Ali-Toudert, F.; Mayer, H. Numerical Study on the Effects of Aspect Ratio and Orientation of an Urban Street Canyon on Outdoor Thermal Comfort in Hot and Dry Climate. *Build. Environ.* **2006**, *41*, 94–108. [CrossRef]
38. Aslam, A.; Rana, I.A. The Use of Local Climate Zones in the Urban Environment: A Systematic Review of Data Sources, Methods, and Themes. *Urban Clim.* **2022**, *42*, 101120. [CrossRef]
39. Tsoka, S.; Tsikaloudaki, A.; Theodosiou, T. Analyzing the ENVI-Met Microclimate Model's Performance and Assessing Cool Materials and Urban Vegetation Applications–A Review. *Sustain. Cities Soc.* **2018**, *43*, 55–76. [CrossRef]
40. Salata, F.; Golasi, I.; Petitti, D.; de Lieto Vollaro, E.; Coppi, M.; de Lieto Vollaro, A. Relating Microclimate, Human Thermal Comfort and Health during Heat Waves: An Analysis of Heat Island Mitigation Strategies through a Case Study in an Urban Outdoor Environment. *Sustain. Cities Soc.* **2017**, *30*, 79–96. [CrossRef]
41. Maleki, A.; Mahdavi, A.; Design, U. Evaluation of Urban Heat Islands Mitigation Strategies using 3dimentional Urban Microclimate Model Envi-Met. *Asian J. Civ. Eng.* **2016**, *17*, 357–371.
42. Evola, G.; Gagliano, A.; Fichera, A.; Marletta, L.; Martinico, F.; Nocera, F.; Pagano, A. UHI Effects and Strategies to Improve Outdoor Thermal Comfort in Dense and Old Neighbourhoods. *Energy Procedia* **2017**, *134*, 692–701. [CrossRef]
43. Tsilini, V.; Papantoniou, S.; Kolokotsa, D.D.; Maria, E.A. Urban Gardens as a Solution to Energy Poverty and Urban Heat Island. *Sustain. Cities Soc.* **2015**, *14*, 323–333. [CrossRef]
44. Morakinyo, T.E.; Lam, Y.F. Simulation Study on the Impact of Tree-Configuration, Planting Pattern and Wind Condition on Street-Canyon's Micro-Climate and Thermal Comfort. *Build. Environ.* **2016**, *103*, 262–275. [CrossRef]
45. Lobaccaro, G.; Acero, J.A. Comparative Analysis of Green Actions to Improve Outdoor Thermal Comfort inside Typical Urban Street Canyons. *Urban Clim.* **2015**, *14*, 251–267. [CrossRef]
46. CENIE Centro Internacional Sobre o Envelhecimento (CENIE)—Instituto Nacional de Estadística. Available online: https://cenie.eu/pt/observatorio/demografia/valladolid (accessed on 10 May 2022).
47. Instituto Nacional de Estadística (INE) Cifras de Población. Available online: https://www.valladolid.es/es/ciudad/estadisticas/utilidad/servicios/observatorio-urbano-datos-estadisticos-ciudad/datos-estadisticos-temas/informacion-estadistica-ciudad/poblacion/cifras-poblacion (accessed on 13 May 2021).
48. Propuesta de Orden de la Consejería de Empleo e Industria por la Que Se Aprueba el Programa Territorial de Fomento para Medina del Campo y Su Entorno 2021–2024. Available online: https://transparencia.jcyl.es/participacion/Participaci%C3%B3n%20Empleo%20e%20Industria/2021-10-21%20Propuesta%20Orden%20PTF%20MEDINA%20DEL%20CAMPO%20v4.pdf (accessed on 15 February 2022).
49. De Souza, V.S. Mapa Climático Urbano Da Cidade De João Pessoa-Pb. In *Encontro Latino-Americano de Conforto no Ambiente Construído*; Federal University of Paraíba: João Pessoa, Brazil, 2019.
50. Simon, H.; Kissel, L.; Bruse, M. Evaluation of ENVI-Met's Multiple-Node Model and Estimation of Indoor Climate. In Proceedings of the PLEA, Edinburgh, UK, 2–5 July 2017; Volume 2, pp. 2173–2180.
51. E Silva, C.F.; Romero, M.A.B. *Simulação do Clima Urbano do Distrito Federal: Experimentando o ENVI-Met*; Editora da Universidade de Brasília: Brasília, Brasil, 2020.
52. Oke, T.R. The Energetic Basis of the Urban Heat Island. *Q. J. R. Meteorol. Soc.* **1982**, *108*, 1–24. [CrossRef]
53. Mohammad, P.; Aghlmand, S.; Fadaei, A.; Gachkar, S.; Gachkar, D.; Karimi, A. Evaluating the Role of the Albedo of Material and Vegetation Scenarios along the Urban Street Canyon for Improving Pedestrian Thermal Comfort Outdoors. *Urban Clim.* **2021**, *40*, 100993. [CrossRef]
54. Acero, J.A.; Herranz-Puaascl, K. A Comparison of Thermal Comfort Conditions in Four Urban Spaces by Means of Measurements and Modelling Techniques. *Build. Environ.* **2015**, *93*, 245–257. [CrossRef]
55. Ketterer, C.; Matzarakis, A. Human-Biometeorological Assessment of Heat Stress Reduction by Replanning Measures in Stuttgart, Germany. *Landsc. Urban Plan.* **2014**, *122*, 78–88. [CrossRef]
56. Shinzato, P.; Simon, H.; Silva Duarte, D.H.; Bruse, M. Calibration Process and Parametrization of Tropical Plants Using ENVI-Met V4–Sao Paulo Case Study. *Archit. Sci. Rev.* **2019**, *62*, 112–125. [CrossRef]

57. Ouyang, W.; Sinsel, T.; Simon, H.; Morakinyo, T.E.; Liu, H.; Ng, E. Evaluating the Thermal-Radiative Performance of ENVI-Met Model for Green Infrastructure Typologies: Experience from a Subtropical Climate. *Build. Environ.* **2022**, *207*, 108427. [CrossRef]
58. Forouzandeh, A. Prediction of Surface Temperature of Building Surrounding Envelopes Using Holistic Microclimate ENVI-Met Model. *Sustain. Cities Soc.* **2021**, *70*, 102878. [CrossRef]
59. Nasrollahi, N.; Hatami, Z.; Taleghani, M. Development of Outdoor Thermal Comfort Model for Tourists in Urban Historical Areas; A Case Study in Isfahan. *Build. Environ.* **2017**, *125*, 356–372. [CrossRef]
60. Acero, J.A.; Arrizabalaga, J. Evaluating the Performance of ENVI-Met Model in Diurnal Cycles for Different Meteorological Conditions. *Theor. Appl. Climatol.* **2018**, *131*, 455–469. [CrossRef]
61. Salata, F.; Golasi, I.; de Lieto Vollaro, R.; de Lieto Vollaro, A. Urban Microclimate and Outdoor Thermal Comfort. A Proper Procedure to Fit ENVI-Met Simulation Outputs to Experimental Data. *Sustain. Cities Soc.* **2016**, *26*, 318–343. [CrossRef]
62. Perini, K.; Chokhachian, A.; Dong, S.; Auer, T. Modeling and Simulating Urban Outdoor Comfort: Coupling ENVI-Met and TRNSYS by Grasshopper. *Energy Build.* **2017**, *152*, 373–384. [CrossRef]
63. Ali-Toudert, F.; Mayer, H. Thermal Comfort in an East-West Oriented Street Canyon in Freiburg (Germany) under Hot Summer Conditions. *Theor. Appl. Climatol.* **2007**, *87*, 223–237. [CrossRef]
64. Lopez-Cabeza, V.P.; Alzate-Gaviria, S.; Diz-Mellado, E.; Rivera-Gomez, C.; Galan-Marin, C. Albedo Influence on the Microclimate and Thermal Comfort of Courtyards under Mediterranean Hot Summer Climate Conditions. *Sustain. Cities Soc.* **2022**, *81*, 103872. [CrossRef]
65. Ferwati, S.; Skelhorn, C.; Ferwati, S.; Shandas, V.; Makido, Y. Urban Form and Variation in Temperatures. In *Urban Adaptation to Climate Change*; Springer: Berlin/Heidelberg, Germany, 2020.
66. Ali-Toudert, F.; Mayer, H. Effects of Asymmetry, Galleries, Overhanging Façades and Vegetation on Thermal Comfort in Urban Street Canyons. *Sol. Energy* **2007**, *81*, 742–754. [CrossRef]
67. Müller, N.; Kuttler, W.; Barlag, A.B. Counteracting Urban Climate Change: Adaptation Measures and Their Effect on Thermal Comfort. *Theor. Appl. Climatol.* **2014**, *115*, 243–257. [CrossRef]
68. Huttner, S.; Bruse, M. Numerical Modeling of the Urban Climate—a Preview on ENVI-MET 4.0. In Proceedings of the 7th International Conference on Urban Climate ICUC-7, Yokohama, Japan, 29 June–3 July 2009; 2009; pp. 1–4.
69. Lee, H.; Mayer, H.; Chen, L. Contribution of Trees and Grasslands to the Mitigation of Human Heat Stress in a Residential District of Freiburg, Southwest Germany. *Landsc. Urban Plan.* **2016**, *148*, 37–50. [CrossRef]

 *infrastructures*

Article

Direct Method to Design Solar Photovoltaics to Reduce Energy Consumption of Aeration Tanks in Wastewater Treatment Plants

Enrico Zacchei [1,2,*] and Antonio Colacicco [3]

1   Itecons, 3030-289 Coimbra, Portugal
2   University of Coimbra, CERIS, 3004-531 Coimbra, Portugal
3   Environmental Engineer-Freelancer, Luigi Pernier Avenue, 00124 Rome, Italy; antonio_colacicco@hotmail.it
*   Correspondence: enricozacchei@gmail.com

Abstract: Photovoltaic (PV) energy systems are considered good renewable energy technologies due to their high production of clean energy. This paper combines a PV system with wastewater treatment plants (WWTPs), which are usually designed separately. For this, a recent methodology was adopted, which provides direct steps to estimate the peak powers of PV plants (PVPs) by using the airflow of blowers. The goal was to reduce the energy consumption of aeration tanks in WWTPs. Analytical equations and parameters based on the air temperature, solar irradiation, biological kinetic, dissolved oxygen, and mechanical oxygenation are adopted. The key parameter in this methodology is the air temperature variation that represents an approximated temperature in the WWTP's oxidation tanks. It is shown, through the analysis of small WWTPs, that since the temperature changes for each season, there is a peak in the function of the quantity of oxidation, which is high in the summer season. Further, the curve trends of temperature for WWRPs are similar to PVPs. Therefore, it could be possible to design the PV system with the WWTPs well. The results show that the air temperature curves increase in a directly proportional way with the consumption of energy from oxidation blowers; this could induce a more conservative PVP design. Furthermore, the results show that the mean trend of the energy consumption of the analyzed aeration systems reaches about 8.0% at a temperature of 20–25 °C, covering a good part of the oxidation tank consumption.

Keywords: auto-consumption systems; clean energy; oxidation tanks; PVP; WWTP

1. Introduction

Photovoltaic (PVPs) plants are considered good renewable energy technologies since they have a high potential for clean energy productivities [1]. They have various environmental advantages, for instance, in producing low fossil-fuel and CO_2 emissions. Moreover, PVPs are based on auto-consumption due to the free input energy.

This paper aims to develop a smart method for designing PVs by optimizing the auto-consumption of oxidation tanks in wastewater treatment plants (WWTPs). For this, the key design parameters are the air and wastewater temperatures and their correlations. Some parameters that consider the bacteria respiration have also been accounted for in accordance with innovative projects [2,3].

PVPs are treated in the literature at the level of forecasting power generations, where several time series prediction statistical methods and algorithms on artificial intelligence are introduced, investigating the effect of prediction time horizon variation [1] and of the design in extreme conditions, where mathematical models to predict the energy generation of PVPs in hot and humid climatic condition are studied [4]. In [1,4], some parameters were studied that impact the electrical power generation, e.g., the type of solar cells and their conditions, electrical circuits of modules, solar incidence angle, and weather conditions.

Infrastructures **2022**, *7*, 79. https://doi.org/10.3390/infrastructures7060079

In [5], a state-of-the-art PV solar energy generator has been made, showing the ways of obtaining the energy, its advantages and disadvantages, applications, current market, costs, and technologies. Here, the possible applications are shown, e.g., for telecommunications, water pumping, agriculture, water heating, grain drying, water desalination, and space vehicles and satellites.

WWTPs have been treated by considering the aeration energy consumption, where a fuzzy logic supervisory control system for optimizing nitrogen removal has been developed [6], the influence of seasonal temperature fluctuations on raw domestic wastewater composition and collected sludge filterability [7], and the balance of the micropollutant flows, where a simple balancing method using passive samplers over a period has been tested to determine the elimination rates of several common micropollutants of household and industrial sources in full-scale WWTPs of different performances [8].

In [9], a complete review has been shown to provide a technical contribution to the regulations as well as to support stakeholders by recommending possible advanced treatment options, in particular, the removal of contaminants of emerging concern and antibiotics, antibiotic-resistant bacteria, and antibiotic resistance genes.

In [10], some strategies to achieve environmental sustainability for wastewater treatments are presented; in particular, it examines how environmental technology contributes to wastewater improvement in several countries. Annualized information was used and collected from various official sources of information and subsequently processed with various econometric approaches.

As mentioned, this paper combines PVP with a WWTP since solar PV has a great generation potential in WWTPs. It is known that technical, economic, and socio-political factors influence the decision to adopt solar PVs in WWTPs as treated in [11,12].

Some papers that combine PVs with WWTPs have been published. In [13], a direct connection of PV modules to the electrochemical reactor was carried out to reduce the non-renewable primary energy consumption; for this, a solar PV electro-oxidation process for WWTP was modeled; in [14], both plants are combined with each other to design floating PVs installed on, e.g., natural lakes, dams reservoirs, and offshore areas, where a simple and economic design solution in South Australia with optimal orientation and distance among rows was suggested; in [15], where a wastewater-to-hydrogen processor was proposed to maximize the hydrogen and minimize the energy consumption. In [16], the control and planning for energy durations, where the feasibility of using solar PV cells and a battery system as a renewable energy source for driven electrochemical WWTPs were studied; whereas in [17], the feasibility and utility of using an electro-oxidation system directly powered by a PV array for the treatment of wastewater was demonstrated.

More recent papers have carried out a quantitative analysis of the solar energy generated from WWTPs where specific 105 Californian WWTPs were examined, of which 41 installed a solar PV system [18]. In [19], it was shown that the synergy of small and medium WWTPs with PV is of great interest from an energetic/environmental/economic point of view; it was stated that "this synergy is worth exploring and implementing on a large scale for all new WWTP". Therefore, more studies are necessary.

Moreover, in [20], electric energies from PV modules were used to remove aniline in wastewater, showing that this process is feasible, and aniline can be removed in a safer and lower-cost way. In [21], it was highlighted that small and insular communities are sometimes not served by an efficient WWTP, and this was a hazard for both the environment and public health. For this, it was shown that a PV system covers the electricity needs of the apparatus. Thus no external electricity source should be necessary for its use. This coupling could be used to minimize the community's costs.

The motivation of this research is based on some critical analyses published in previous studies [22,23], which should justify the two main hypotheses for this work: (i) the oxidation tanks consume ~30.0% of the total cost of the energy of a WWTP. Thus the use of a PV could cover part of this consumption in a clean way; (ii) for a small treatment plant, the energy consumption is high in the function of the oxygenation in aeration blowers where a PV could be installed.

Further, through the analysis of the Zurich WWTP, in [24], it is shown that the temperature of wastewater in the entrance changes for each season. For a small WWTP, a peak of energy consumption in the summer was verified since when the temperature of the wastewater increases the oxygen consumption, thus the aeration blowers need to work more.

Therefore, through critical analyses, some preliminary data have been collected that, with the relations and parameters on the oxygen consumption and temperature, provide several materials to be used in this work (Section 2.1). Section 2.2 shows the model, where its goal is to provide some analytical relations to design PVPs to reduce the energy consumption of WWTPs since they represent an important part of the "anthropic water cycle" [12]. Finally, in Section 3, analyses and results have been presented in terms of energy consumption of blower's aeration systems with respect to PV plants to evaluate the good and/or optimum performance of the system.

This work could help the sector make decisions over PV investments, especially regarding wastewater utilities, which ultimately lead to more sustainable management practices. Thus, we encourage a further contribution to promoting the integration of renewable energy sources as PVPs, together with WWTPs and their sectors.

This purpose is consistent with goal 7 of the 2030 Agenda [25] in order to "ensure access to affordable, reliable, sustainable and modern energy for all".

2. Materials and Methods

2.1. Materials

2.1.1. Reference Data

The electricity consumption of an "anthropic water cycle", considering the final uses (e.g., agricultural, civil, and industrial uses), ranges between 1.0 and 8.0 kWh/m^3. This consumption of energy includes a percentage, without including the final uses, between 1.0% and 5.0% of the national electricity requirements and between 5% and 20%, including the final uses [22].

The flowchart in Figure 1 shows the process diagram of the water management cycle (water source → water body) from withdrawal (i.e., pumping and transport) to the wastewater disposal, where the water body is re-introduced in accordance with the European directive [26]. It is shown that the "wastewater treatment" phase (yellow box in Figure 1) allows the closing/opening and continuation of this cycle.

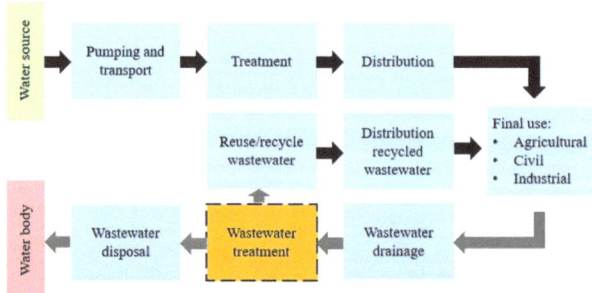

Figure 1. Water management cycle: process diagram (adapted from [22]).

As already mentioned, in urban WWTPs, it is estimated that ~30% of the costs of the management are attributed to energy consumption, even if ~50% can include additional costs of the other treatments, as shown in [22,23].

The electricity consumption of a WWTP with anaerobic sludge digestion is between 0.40 and 0.70 kWh/month in function of the type/size of the studied plant. In general,

WWTPs have an electricity consumption between 10 and 40 kWh/PE per year (PE is the population equivalent estimated as 1 PE $\approx$ 60 gBOD$_5$/d [8], where BOD$_5$ is the biochemical oxygen demand during the day, d), whereas in a WWTP, with digestion of an aerobic-type, the electricity consumption can reach values of 40–70 kWh/PE per year due to the lack of energy to be recovered [23].

The BOD$_5$ parameter includes the biodegradable portion of the organic substances with respect to the chemical oxygen demand (COD) parameter, which measures the global oxidation of (in)organic substances.

The biological oxidation regards the highest percentage of total consumption (e.g., 50–65%), then there are the treatment lines of the sludge, which can reach a consumption of 20%, and, finally, there is the pumping phase, using ~15% [23].

In the WWTPs of urban sludges, a great part of the electricity is used in the oxidation tanks by the aeration process. The percentage incidence of the consumption of the energy, in the function of the operation costs, as well as maintenance costs, are shown in [23], with the following weight: 50% energy, 21% management, 13% chemical, 11% maintenance, 5% others.

In [23], it is shown that the distribution of the electricity in the various steps of traditional WWTPs, in particular, the oxygen aeration in tanks, is the greatest with a value of 55.6%, whereas the lowest value refers to pre-treatment of the wastewater process with a value of 0.4%. Moreover, by analyzing 253 WWTPs, an acceptable agreement between the total consumption of the energy of WWTPs and the volume of sewage flows was shown. In the same way, the impact of the large plants, which have low energy consumption (expressed in m^3) of treated sewages and removed organic substances (in kg), has been highlighted.

Finally, an example of the specific consumption per kg of COD removed (expressed in kWh/kgCOD$_{rem}$) has been shown, which identifies the quality of the water by the variation of treatment classes for WWTPs. For a potential class < 2000 PE corresponds to a mean value of 3.21 kWh/kgCOD$_{rem}$, whereas for >100,000 PE, we have 0.85 kWh/kgCOD$_{rem}$.

All these data represent the input parameters that have incentivized this study.

2.1.2. Oxygen and Temperature Role

In the oxidation tanks, to activate the reactions of biological substances, the presence of dissolved oxygens (DOs) is necessary; thus, its continuous creation to equilibrate the consumption of the carbon-oxidant bacteria respiration is also necessary [2,9,27]. DO is a parameter that allows the control of the biological process in relation to the energy reduction [6,28]; also, the biological oxidation processes are correlated to the temperature, T.

The biological reactions can increase with a temperature between 0 and 40 °C with an estimated optimum T between 25 and 35 °C. However, in the aeration tanks, the latter temperatures are rarely achieved. With a temperature T < 5 °C, the biological activity can strongly decrease [29].

The respiration of the bacteria is quantified by two different coefficients: active breathing, a (Equation (1)), and endogenous respiration, c_T (Equation (2)).

The a-coefficient is correlated to the oxidative reactions as well as synthesis reactions where the microorganisms take energy by their own metabolism and by the creation of new cell synthesis. Further, this coefficient represents the consumption of oxygen for the destruction of the organic substances, which is proportional to the removed substrate of carbonaceous [30].

This a-coefficient varies with respect to the WWTP used, and it can be evaluated by [30]:

$$a = \frac{0.65 \times kg_{O_2}}{kg_{BOD_5}} \tag{1}$$

where kg_{O2} is the mass of the consumption of oxygen (O$_2$), and kg_{BOD5} is the mass of the BOD$_5$ concentration. Both parameters are correlated with each other through the volume of the oxidation reactor, V_{oxi}, by $kg_{BOD5} = V_{oxi} \times BOD_5$.

The other coefficient, i.e., endogenous respiration, is related to the use of the available substrate for critical temperature and demolition of bacteria cells. In this sense, it regards the metabolism of the bacteria. This endogenous respiration coefficient, c_T, can be described by [30,31]:

$$c_T = c_{20} \times 1.084^{T-20} = \left(\frac{0.13 \times kg_{O_2}}{kg_{VSS} \times d} \right) \times 1.084^{T-20} \tag{2}$$

where c_{20} refers to a c value of 20 °C (i.e., $c_{T=20} \rightarrow c_{20}$), and kg_{VSS} is the mass of volatile suspended solids (VSSs).

Therefore, the oxygen consumption can be expressed by [6,30]:

$$R_{o2} = \frac{a \times kg_{BOD_5}}{d} + \frac{c_T \times kg_{Biomass}}{d} \tag{3}$$

where $kg_{Biomass}$ is the biomass (= $V_{oxi} \times VSS$; here approximated by $kg_{Biomass} \approx VSS$ [12]).

If there are no relevant variations of the kg_{BOD_5} during a season, the requirement of oxygen mainly varies due to the function of the T increasing due to Equation (2). Furthermore, in the wastewater, the oxygen concentration depends on Henry's law, which correlates the concentration of O_2 present in the liquid phase with respect to its concentration present in the gas phase [32]. In this study, this correlation indicates that the amount of DO is inversely proportional to the increase in the wastewater temperature. Therefore, to maintain an acceptable aerobic degradation of kg_{BOD_5} with an increasing wastewater T, in the oxygenation tanks, some oxygen "surplus" must be supplied. This implies that the aerator systems could work hard during the hot months to guarantee a sufficient concentration of DO [6,29].

In [7,29], the fluctuation of the wastewater T as a function of time is shown. In [26], the air temperature curve where it is evident that the curves of the high/low temperatures of the wastewater vary, with a maximum value in summer months (i.e., July in the Mediterranean area) is also plotted. These fluctuations of the curves refer to a small plant since they do not fluctuate (i.e., they are quasi-constant) in large plants.

An important phenomenon regards the overlapping of the wastewater temperature curves (high and low) with the curve that shows the maximum air temperature. This overlap happens in small WWTPs, because of the seasonality, which is directly correlated with the irradiation/temperature. Therefore, the adoption of the air temperature values for the design could provide a good estimation regarding the thermal trend of the wastewater overdesign, in favor of safety, the PVPs.

Finally, some aspects should also be mentioned to indicate the increase in the temperature of the wastewater (influent) flow in hot periods, which are associated with high proliferation of organic substances in WWTPs with small and/or medium size. This increase can amplify the total consumption of energy, mainly involving the aeration systems for producing oxygen.

These aspects regard the energy (see two hypotheses in Section 1), chemical–physical, and biological factors. Regarding the chemical–physical factors in the wastewater: (1) the temperature oscillates due to its seasonality, and due to the wastewater flow rate; (2) the increase of the T reduces the solubility of the oxygen. The biological factors include (3) the increasing of the wastewater flow rate and the oxygen requirement of organic substances for the kinetic digestions.

Small WWTPs have greater power consumption than large plants, making them more sensitive to increases in energy cost [33]. Therefore, it is important for small plants to find alternative energy sources to increase resilience to energy cost fluctuations. Solar PV represents a suitable source of energy for small WWTPs for two main reasons: the lack of biogas recovery opportunities and land availability [18].

Table 1 shows the parameters used to carry out the analyses. Some parameters have already been explained, whereas other ones will be explained in Section 2.2.

Table 1. Data used for the analysis.

Parameter	Value
Active breathing coefficient, a	0.65 (Equation (1)) [a]
Biochemical oxygen demand, BOD_5	0.8 kg_{BOD5} [b]
Endogenous respiration coefficient, c_T	0.09–0.19 (Equation (2)) [c]
Volatile suspended solids, VSS	4.0 kg_{VSS} [12]
Correction factor, α	0.80 [30]
Aerators fouling factor, F	0.90 [12]
Correction factor, β	1.0 [30]
Standard aeration efficiency, $SAE_{20°}$	1.55–3.0 kg_{O2}/kWh [34] [d]

[a] Assuming kg_{O2} = kg_{BOD5}. [b] The value is correlated to the sludge loading rate (SLR) by: SLR = BOD_5/VSS = 0.20 [8,12]. [c] With c_{20} = 0.13 and T = 15–25 °C. [d] For clean water at 20 °C, pressure of 101.32 kPa, and DO = 0 mg/L. The SAE value depends on the adopted aeration system.

2.2. Methodology

For estimating the maximum consumption of energy of a selected aeration system, direct analytical equations, recently introduced in [12], have been used. These equations should verify the energy consumption variations of a certain aeration system regarding the oxygen requirements and wastewater temperature in oxidation tanks.

Considering the relations already mentioned in Section 2.1.2, i.e., $kg_{Biomass}$ = V_{oxi} × VSS and kg_{BOD5} = V_{oxi} × BOD_5, Equation (3), by multiplying for d and dividing for V_{oxi}, describes the incremental parameter of R_{02}, I_{RO2}, which estimates the increasing of R_{02} with respect the standard temperature T (i.e., T = 20 °C) in the wastewater. It is defined, as a percentage (%), as:

$$I_{RO2} = \frac{[(a \times BOD_5) + (c_T \times VSS)] - [(a \times BOD_5) + (c_{20} \times VSS)]}{[(a \times BOD_5) + (c_{20} \times VSS)]} \quad (4)$$

An aeration blower should be defined by the oxygen transfer capacity, i.e., the oxygen transfer rate (OTR):

$$OTR = SOTR\left(\alpha \times 1.024^{(T-20)} \times \frac{\beta(C_s - C_L)}{C_s} \times F\right) \quad \text{with} \quad SOTR = \left(1.024^{(T-20)} \times \alpha \times F\right) \quad (5)$$

where C_L is the service oxygen concentration and C_s is the saturated oxygen concentration. Both concentrations are expressed in mg/L, and here, they are assumed to be $C_s = C_L$, neglecting the dynamic component of gas concentration. α, β, and F (i.e., aerator fouling factors) are constants. SOTR is the standard-OTR, which refers to the oxygen measurements in the clean water under standard pressures and temperatures. OTR is expressed in kg_{O2}/h.

From Equation (5), the incremental parameter of SOTR, I_{SOTR} (in %), is:

$$I_{SOTR} = \frac{\left(1.024^{(T-20)} \times \alpha \times F\right) - (\alpha \times F)}{(\alpha \times F)} \quad (6)$$

For measuring the variation of the SAE, I_{SAE}, with respect 20 °C (i.e., SAE_{20}), and by considering Equation (6), Equation (7), expressed in kg_{O2}/kWh, is used:

$$I_{SAE} = SAE_{20} + (SAE_{20} \times I_{SOTR}) \quad (7)$$

Finally, to correlate I_{SAE} with the I_{RO2} (Equation (4)) Equation (8), in %, is used:

$$I_{PRO2} = \frac{1}{I_{SAE}} \times I_{RO2} \quad (8)$$

Equation (8) provides the main output that allows the energy consumption values for different aeration blowers adopted in the oxidation tanks to be plotted.

The general methodology can be described step-by-step as follows: (i) collection of data by database, the literature, and Equations (1)–(3) (see Table 1); (ii) plotting the average monthly energy production curves, E_m (see Section 3); (iii) estimation of I_{RO2} curves by the proposed equation, Equation (8), for 5 aeration systems; (iv) defining the performances of the coupled system (see Section 3).

3. Analyses and Results

The analyses consist of developing the above-mentioned equations for a general case and then for a specific example. The correlation key of the analyses regards the fact that the energy consumption of the aeration blowers should measure the whole energy consumption of the WWTP. This correlation represents an important issue for the whole system in order to maintain the equilibrium of the energy.

In Equations (4) and (6), the following (some) values have been calculated for wastewater T = {15, 20, 25} °C: $I_{R02} = \{-16.6, 0, 24.8\}\%$, and $I_{SOTR} = \{11.2, 0, -12.6\}\%$. Thus, the I_{SAE} (Equation (7)) and I_{PRo2} (Equation (8)) values are obtained for five aeration systems: (1) large bubble ventilation; (2) surface aerators with low speed; (3) surface turbines with downward flow; (4) superficial brushes; and (5) submerged turbines with injector.

Figure 2 shows the results of I_{PRO2} with respect to the wastewater T in the oxidation tanks. These curves are calibrated at T = 20 °C (middle point), which represents, as already mentioned, the standard conditions.

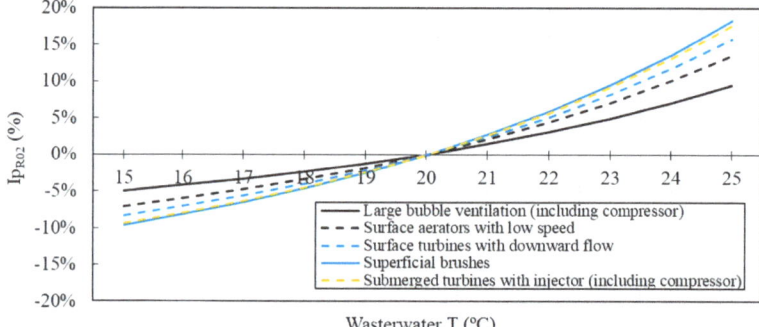

Figure 2. I_{PRO2} values as a function of wastewater T for five aeration systems.

The curves in Figure 2 allow the quantification of not only the aerator technology that can be classified as most energy-efficient but also the increasing of the seasonal consumption of energy of the considered aerator, independently of the influent flow rate of BOD_5.

It is shown that the trend of the I_{PRO2} curves for the five aeration systems ranges between −10% and 18% for 15–25 °C. The "superficial brushes" (blue solid line) systems represent the technologies's more energy intensiveness.

The "large bubble ventilation" (black solid line) is less energy-intensive; in fact, the presence of the bubbles in an aeration system is correlated to the energy generation; in particular, the dimension of the air bubbles affects the airflow and its velocity, as treated in [31].

Wastewater temperature mainly depends on the external air temperature and seasonality; therefore, this temperature could be approximated to the air temperature, as shown in [12]. The idea of using the air temperature curve should be in favor of safety since this curve would overestimate the PV system in terms of power outcomes covering the peaks of energy demands. In fact, in [29], it is shown that between ~8 and 20 °C, the external air temperature curve is higher than the high wastewater temperature curve.

To validate the methodology and the results shown in Figure 2, an example has been carried out. To design the peak powers, in a preliminary way, of a PV system, data (from the period 2007–2016 year retrieved from database [35]) regarding the solar radiations and air temperatures for "Is Arenas" WWTP, Cagliari region, Italy, have been collected. Figure 3 shows the correlated data plotted by blue points highlighting the widespread trends and a high concentration from 300.0 W/m^2 for 15–25 °C.

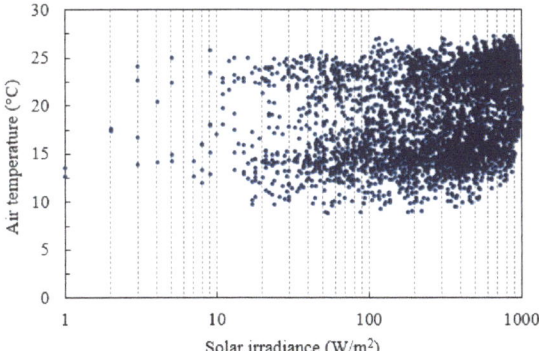

Figure 3. Solar irradiance/air temperature points at "Is Arenas" WWTP (Cagliari, Italy) [35].

Figure 4 shows the solar irradiance and air temperature curve during a day, indicating their possible correlation [15]. The air T curve could be consistent with the daily power outputs of a PVP: it assumes a null value between 7:00 p.m. and 4:00 a.m. and a very low value between 4 and 6 h and 17 and 19 h; therefore, in this example, only the values between 7 and 16 h have been considered.

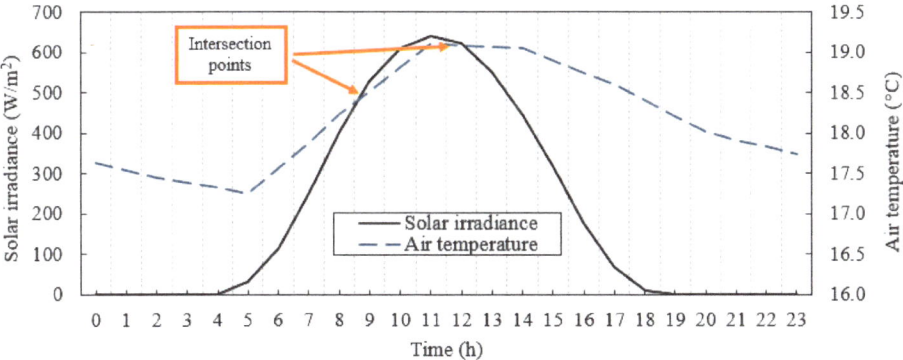

Figure 4. Solar irradiance/air temperature curves over time [35] (adapted from [12]).

By using the estimated global irradiances (Figure 3), a possible estimation of the produced mean energy for PVPs is defined. To verify the overlapping of the production of PV energy with the collected data due to the increasing of the energy consumption of aeration blowers, the following restraints were assumed: (i) the PV production during the months of a PVP has a peak power of 1 kWp; (ii) the energy consumption of WWTPs happen under the standard condition at 20 °C, for the curve fluctuations of the air temperature during the months. Moreover, the used hypothesis is that, during the whole year, $R_{O2} = 150$ kg$_{RO2}$/month (Equation (3)).

Table 2 lists the energy production of PVs by several parameters processed by database [35]. The peak value of the average daily sum of global irradiation received by the modules, $H(i)_d$, is $H(i)_d = 7.28$ kWh/m^2/d, which is consistent with the literature's [4] reference peak.

Table 2. PV energy production values processed by database [35].

Month	E_d (kWh/d)	E_m (kWh/m) (Figures 5 and 6)	$H(i)_d$ (kWh/m²/d)	$H(i)_m$ kWh/m²/m)	$\pm\sigma_m$ (kWh)
1 (January)	3.05	94.57	3.65	113.01	9.44
2	3.62	101.28	4.34	121.58	12.23
3	4.27	132.23	5.21	161.45	11.9
4	4.73	141.80	5.90	177.0	10.24
5	5.05	156.45	6.41	198.65	10.81
6	5.42	162.68	7.04	211.10	4.26
7	5.52	171.09	7.28	225.59	5.55
8	5.44	168.51	7.14	221.44	6.85
9	4.73	142.04	6.10	182.91	5.0
10	4.11	127.39	5.16	160.10	7.57
11	3.20	95.88	3.90	117.13	9.91
12 (December)	2.89	89.50	3.47	107.48	9.46
Mean	4.34	131.95	5.47	166.45	2.40

AOI loss (%)	Spectral effects (%)	Temperature/solar irradiance loss (%)	Combined loss (%)	
−2.65	0.66	−5.93	−20.73	

Note: E_d = Average daily energy production (kWh/d). E_m = Average monthly energy production (kWh/month). $H(i)_d$ = Average daily sum of global irradiation per square meter received by the modules (kWh/m²/d). $H(i)_m$ = Average monthly the solar irradiation sum per square meter received by the modules (kWh/m²/mm). σ_m = Standard deviation of the monthly energy production due to year-to-year variation (kWh). AOI = Angle of incidence.

Figure 5 shows the results in terms of the air temperature and PV energy production, E_m (Table 2), for each month. The air T curve considers the daily thermal variation; thus, it would measure only the seasonal trend (it refers to mean values for a period of 2007–2016 [35]).

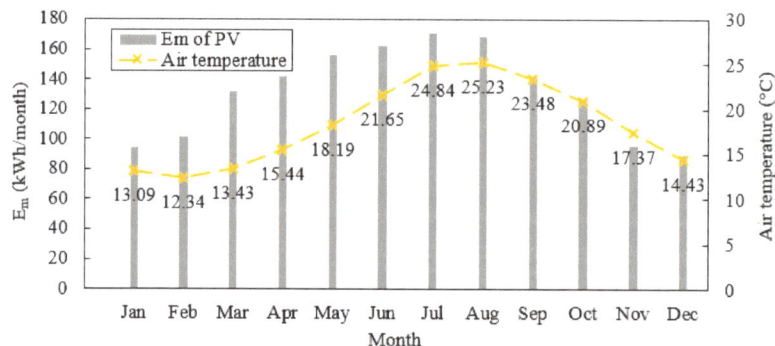

Figure 5. Air temperature curve and mean energy, E_m, of PV histograms [35] (adapted from [12]).

The results shown in Figure 2 should facilitate, in a parallel way, the design of PVPs with aeration systems to estimate a possible power value that optimizes the energy auto-consumption, improving future economic analyses for the investments of PVPs. The E_m histograms, shown in Figures 5 and 6, are proportional to the fluctuations of the air temperature during a season, where, as already mentioned, T is strongly correlated to the solar radiation curves in terms of amplitude and trend.

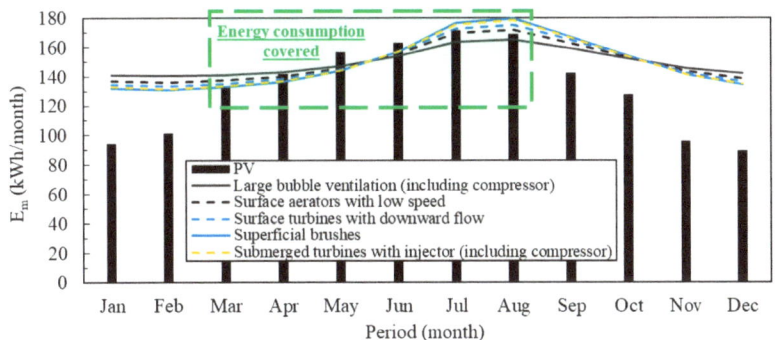

Figure 6. PV energy E_m and I_{PRO2} in WWTP for each aeration system.

By combining these E_m histograms with the I_{PRO2} curves (see Figure 2), plotted in function of the months, new results are obtained, as shown in Figure 6. In this way, the idea to correlate PVs to WWTPs is more evident, i.e., PV E_m histograms $\leftrightarrow$ I_{PRO} curves.

The five curves in Figure 6 indicate a reduction in the energy consumption in the winter months and an increase in the summer months in the Mediterranean area (i.e., from June to August). Thus, if the blower's aeration system is known, it is possible to design an easy way to power the peak of PVPs that maximizes the annual auto-consumption of the oxidation tanks by using only the mean variation of the air temperature over a month. It is also possible to see that the energy consumption curves of the different aerator systems overlap in some points with a PV energy production of 1 kWp. These points indicate the optimum performance of the PV system.

Therefore, when E_m histograms of PV overlap the I_{Ro2} curves, the energy consumption is covered in an optimum way, for example, from March to August (see the green area in Figure 6). For the other cases, the performance is considered good (September–October) or poor (other months, not shown in Table 3). Finally, Table 3 shows the auto-consumption for the five blower systems.

Table 3. Auto-consumption for each aeration system (from March to October).

Month	Auto-Consumption (%) for Aeration Systems					
	Superficial Brushes	Surface Turbines with Downward Flow	Low-Speed Surface Aerators	Large Bubble Ventilation	Submerged Turbines with Injector	Performance
3 (March)	100.0	98.0	96.0	94.0	99.0	
4	100.0	100.0	100.0	99.0	100.0	
5	100.0	100.0	100.0	100.0	100.0	Optimum
6	100.0	100.0	100.0	100.0	100.0	
7	97.0	99.0	100.0	100.0	97.0	
8	94.0	96.0	98.0	100.0	94.0	
9	85.0	86.0	87.0	89.0	85.0	
10 (October)	83.0	83.0	83.0	84.0	83.0	Good
Mean [a]	87.0	87.0	87.0	86.0	87.0	-

[a] The mean is calculated for the whole year (from January to December).

In Table 3, the mean auto-consumption in 1 year is $\geq 86.0\%$ for all systems, whereas the mean auto-consumption in the months ranges between 63.0% and 100.0%, with a spread of 8.0% (i.e., $\Delta I_{PRO2} = 18{-}10 = 8\%$ in August up to 14% by considering other aeration systems as shown in [13]), which should cover a part of 30.0% mentioned in Section 2.1.1.

Considering the energy production for PVs in a year, it is possible to conclude that in summer, spring, and in part of autumn (March to October), the mean auto-consumption oscillates between 83.0% and 100.0%, whereas the mean auto-consumption in winter (from November to February, not shown in Table 3) reduces and oscillates between 63.0% and 77.0%.

4. Conclusions

This work presents a recent method proposed by authors to design PVs to optimize the energy auto-consumption of oxidation tanks in WWTPs. This method consists of providing, in a direct way, analytical equations to quantify the energy generation of PVs only using the air temperature, T, and the standard conditions of WWTPs. We conclude that:

(1) If the air temperature curve increases, the energy consumption in oxidation blowers also increase. Therefore, the designing of PVs should be carried out without a punctual measurement of the energy consumption of the oxidation tanks; however, just considering chemical parameters, e.g., biochemical oxygen demand, BOD_5, volatile suspended solids, VSS, as there are easily recoverable in WWTPs. Thus, by considering the air temperature, the proposed equations should be excellent proxy functions for designing the necessary photovoltaic power and avoiding expensive energy and electric analyses in terms of time and analytical resolutions.

(2) The overlap of the energy consumption curves of the system and photovoltaic production curves should make the calculation of the power sufficient to individuate the maximize the energy auto-consumption. In this sense, the proposed approach would simplify the energy consumption analyses since traditional measurements used for controlling need available data (which, in many cases, can be difficult to retrieve) on WWTPs.

(3) The results show that the mean trend of I_{PRO2} of the five aeration systems reaches a value of ~8.0% of the consumption of energy, with a temperature that varies between 20.0 and 25.0 °C. The consumption curves regarding the "superficial brushes" aeration system represent the technologies's more energy intensiveness.

Author Contributions: Conceptualization, A.C.; methodology, A.C. and E.Z.; software, A.C.; validation, E.Z. and A.C.; formal analysis, A.C.; investigation, E.Z. and A.C.; data curation, A.C. and E.Z.; writing—original draft preparation, E.Z. and A.C.; writing—review and editing, E.Z. and A.C.; supervision, E.Z. and A.C. All authors have read and agreed to the published version of the manuscript.

Funding: This research received no external funding.

Institutional Review Board Statement: Not applicable.

Informed Consent Statement: Not applicable.

Data Availability Statement: Not applicable.

Acknowledgments: The first author thanks the Itecons institute, Coimbra, Portugal, and the University of Coimbra (UC), Portugal, to pay the rights (when applicable) to completely download all papers in the references.

Conflicts of Interest: The authors declare no conflict of interest.

References

1. Sharadga, H.; Hajimirza, S.; Balog, R.S. Time series forecasting of solar power generation for large-scale photovoltaic plants. *Renew. Energy* **2020**, *150*, 797–807. [CrossRef]
2. Nairn, C.; Rodriguez, I.; Segura, Y.; Molina, R.; Gonzalez-Benitez, N.; Molina, M.C.; Simarro, R.; Melero, J.A.; Martinez, F.; Puyol, D. Alkalinity, and not the oxidation state of the organic substrate, is the key factor in domestic wastewater treatment by mixed cultures of purple phototrophic bacteria. *Resources* **2020**, *9*, 88. [CrossRef]
3. Deep Purple Project. Available online: https://deep-purple.eu/ (accessed on 1 June 2021).
4. Chakraborty, S. Reliable energy prediction method for grid connected photovoltaic power plants situated in hot and dry climatic condition. *SN Appl. Sci.* **2020**, *2*, 1–13. [CrossRef]
5. Sampaio, P.G.V.; Gonzalez, M.O.A. Photovoltaic solar energy: Conceptual framework. *Renew. Sustain. Energy Rev.* **2017**, *74*, 590–601. [CrossRef]

6. Serralta, J.; Ribes, J.; Seco, A.; Ferrer, J. A supervisory control system for optimising nitrogen removal and aeration energy consumption in wastewater treatment plants. *Water Sci. Technol.* **2002**, *45*, 309–316. [CrossRef]
7. Krzeminski, P.; Iglesias-Obelleiro, A.; Madebo, G.; Garrido, J.M.; van der Graaf, J.H.J.M.; van Lier, J.B. Impact of temperature on raw wastewater composition and active sludge filterability in full-scale MBR systems for municipal sewage treatment. *J. Membr. Sci.* **2012**, *423-424*, 348–361. [CrossRef]
8. Gallé, T.; Koehler, C.; Plattes, M.; Pittois, D.; Bayerle, M.; Carafa, R.; Christen, A.; Hansen, J. Large-scale determination of micropollutant elimination from municipal wastewater by passive sampling gives new insights in governing parameters and degradation patterns. *Water Res.* **2019**, *160*, 380–393. [CrossRef] [PubMed]
9. Rizzo, L.; Gernjak, W.; Krzeminski, P.; Malato, S.; McArdell, C.S.; Sanchez Perez, J.A.; Schaar, H.; Fatta-Kassinos, D. Best available technologies and treatment trains to address current challenges in urban wastewater reuse for irrigation of corps in EU countries. *Sci. Total Environ.* **2020**, *710*, 1–17. [CrossRef]
10. Khan, S.A.R.; Ponce, P.; Yu, Z.; Golpira, H.; Mathew, M. Environmental technology and wastewater treatment: Strategies to achieve environmental sustainability. *Chemosphere* **2022**, *286*, 1–10. [CrossRef] [PubMed]
11. Strazzabosco, A.; Kenway, S.J.; Lant, P.A. Quantification of renewable electricity generation in the Australian water industry. *J. Clean. Prod.* **2020**, *254*, 120119. [CrossRef]
12. Colacicco, A.; Zacchei, E. Optimization of energy consumptions of oxidation tanks in urban wastewater treatment plants with solar photovoltaic systems. *J. Environ. Manag.* **2020**, *276*, 111353. [CrossRef]
13. Alvarez-Guerra, E.; Dominguez-Ramos, A.; Irabien, A. Photovoltaic solar electro-oxidation (PSEO) process for wastewater treatment. *Chem. Eng. J.* **2011**, *170*, 7–13. [CrossRef]
14. Rosa-Clot, M.; Tina, G.M.; Nizetic, S. Floating photovoltaic plants and wastewater basins: An Australian project. *Energy Procedia* **2017**, *134*, 664–674. [CrossRef]
15. Wu, W.; Christiana, V.I.; Chen, S.A.; Hwang, J.J. Design and techno-economic optimization of a stand-alone PV (photovoltaic)/FC (fuel cell)/battery hybrid power system connected to a wastewater-to-hydrogen processor. *Energy* **2015**, *84*, 462–472. [CrossRef]
16. Ganiyu, S.O.; Brito, L.R.D.; da Araújo Costa, E.C.T.; dos Santos, E.V.; Martínez-Huitle, C.A. Solar photovoltaic-battery system as a green energy for driven electrochemical wastewater treatment technologies: Application to elimination of brilliant blue FCF dye solution. *J. Environ. Chem. Eng.* **2019**, *7*, 102924. [CrossRef]
17. Valero, D.; Ortiz, J.M.; Exposito, E.; Montiel, V.; Aldaz, A. Electrochemical wastewater treatment directly powered by photovoltaic panels: Electrooxidation of a dye-containing wastewater. *Environ. Sci. Technol.* **2010**, *44*, 5182–5187. [CrossRef] [PubMed]
18. Strazzabosco, A.; Kenway, S.J.; Lant, P.A. Solar PV adoption in wastewater treatment plants: A review of practice in California. *J. Environ. Manag.* **2019**, *248*, 109337. [CrossRef]
19. Andrei, H.; Badea, C.A.; Andrei, P.; Spertino, F. Energic-environmental-economic feasibility and impact assessment of grid-connected photovoltaic system in wastewater treatment plant: Case study. *Energies* **2021**, *14*, 100. [CrossRef]
20. Mou, Y.; Xia, Y.; Zhang, S.; He, Y.; Shen, W.; Li, J. Aniline removed from simulated wastewater by electro-Fenton process using electric energy from photovoltaic modules. *Desalination Water Treat.* **2022**, *247*, 173–183. [CrossRef]
21. Marmanis, D.; Emmanouil, C.; Fantidis, J.G.; Thysiadou, A.; Marmani, K. Description of a Fe/Al electrocoagulation method powered by a photovoltaic system, for the (ore-)treatment of municipal wastewater of a small community in Northern Greece. *Sustainability* **2022**, *14*, 4323. [CrossRef]
22. Clerici, A. Efficienza energetica nel settore idrico. In Proceedings of the Efficienza Energetica—Tutela Dell'Ambiente, Opportunità di Crescita, Technical Workshop, Milan, Italy, 12 September 2011.
23. Vaccari, M. Il consumo energetico negli impianti di depurazione. In Proceedings of the Il Consumo di Energia Elettrica Negli Impianti di Depurazione: Opportunità di Risparmio, Meeting, Rimini, Italy, 8 November 2012.
24. Di Domenico, S. Analisi Delle Fognature e Relative Applicazioni Energetiche. Bachelor Dissertation, University of Bologna, Bologna, Italy, 2010; p. 176.
25. United Nations (UN). *Transforming Our World: The 2030 Agenda for Sustainable Development*; Technical Report A/RES/70/1; United Nations (UN): New York, NY, USA, 2015; p. 35.
26. Directive 2000/60/EC, European Parliament and of the Council, A Framework for Community Action in the Field of Water Policy, OJ L 327, 22.12.2000, p. 73. 2000. Available online: https://eur-lex.europa.eu/legal-content/EN/TXT/?uri=CELEX%3A3 2000L0060 (accessed on 1 August 2020).
27. Zhang, H.; Gong, W.; Bai, L.; Chen, R.; Zeng, W.; Yan, Z.; Li, G.; Liang, H. Aeration-induced CO_2 stripping, instead of high dissolved oxygen, have a negative impact on algae-bacteria symbiosis (ABS) system stability and wastewater treatment efficiency. *Chem. Eng. J.* **2020**, *382*, 122957. [CrossRef]
28. Liu, G.; Wang, J.; Campbell, K. Formation of filamentous microorganisms impedes oxygen transfer and decreases aeration efficiency for wastewater treatment. *J. Clean. Prod.* **2018**, *189*, 502–509. [CrossRef]
29. Pennsylvania Department of Environmental Protection. *The Activated Sludge Process, Part II, Module 16, Wastewater Treatment Plant, Operator, Certification Training*; Pennsylvania Department of Environmental Protection: Harrisburg, PA, USA, 2014; p. 114.
30. Capuano, M. Modello di Calcolo Diagnostico del Comparto di Aerazione in un Impianto di Depurazione Delle Acque Reflue Civili a Scala Reale. Master's Dissertation, Polytechnic of Torino, Torino, Italy, 2018; p. 164.
31. Gillot, S.; Héduit, A. Effect of air flow rate on oxygen transfer in an oxidation ditch equipped with fine bubble diffusers and slow speed mixers. *Water Res.* **2000**, *34*, 1756–1762. [CrossRef]

32. Lu, J.H.; Lei, H.Y.; Dai, C.S. Analysis of Henry's law and a unified lattice Boltzmann equation for conjugate mass transfer problem. *Chem. Eng. Sci.* **2019**, *199*, 319–331. [CrossRef]
33. Mizuta, K.; Shimada, M. Benchmarking energy consumption in municipal wastewater treatment plants in Japan. *Water Sci. Technol.* **2010**, *62*, 2256–2262. [CrossRef] [PubMed]
34. Campanelli, M.; Foladori, P.; Vaccari, M. *Consumi Elettrici ed Efficineza Energetica del Trattamento Delle Acque Reflue*; Maggioli Editore: Santarcangelo di Romagna, Italy, 2013; p. 391.
35. PVGIS. Photovoltaic Geographical Information System. Database. 2020. Available online: https://ec.europa.eu/jrc/en/pvgis (accessed on 1 January 2020).

Article

Transcalar Design: An Approach to Biodesign in the Built Environment

Ana Goidea [1,*], Dimitrios Floudas [2] and David Andréen [1]

[1] bioDigital Matter, Department of Architecture and the Built Environment, Lund University,
     221 00 Lund, Sweden; david.andreen@arkitektur.lth.se
[2] Microbial Ecology Group, Department of Biology, Lund University, 223 62 Lund, Sweden;
     dimitrios.floudas@biol.lu.se
*   Correspondence: ana.goidea@abm.lth.se; Tel.: +45-5018-2234

Abstract: Biodesign holds the potential for radically increasing the sustainability of the built environment and our material culture but comes with new challenges. One of these is the bridging of the vast differences of scale between microbiological processes and architecture. We propose that a transcalar design approach, which weaves together nonlinear dependencies using computational design tools and design methodologies through the biological generation of architectural components, is a way towards successful design implementations. Such design processes were explored in a laboratory-based fabrication and study of a column element. This column, named Protomycokion, serves to illustrate how design methodologies, particularly through the use of a demonstrator artefact, can serve to navigate the multiple scales, disciplines, and experiments that are necessary to engage the complexities of biodesign. Transcalar design processes embrace the adaptability, variability and interdependence of biological organisms and show possible gains with regard to material sustainability and increased performativity.

Keywords: biodesign; transcalar; transdisciplinary; architecture; 3D printing; biomaterials

1. Introduction

As the world is facing an urgent need to shift towards more sustainable practices, the construction industry, which accounts for massive resource use and carbon emissions, must develop its own path towards sustainability. One potential method is to build from materials that are renewable, circular, and do not require the use of raw and prime materials, e.g., through the use of waste streams or by-products. In this paper, we present a case study involving the use of forestry by-products which are transformed into building materials using live fungus and a 3D-printing process. Based on this case study, we suggest that a transcalar methodology that may be generally applicable within the emerging field of biodesign.

Biodesign is designing with, as or for living matter. In this paper, we employed the definition of biodesign provided by Myers and Antonelli [1] within the more specific context of biofabrication, which is "the incorporation of living organisms as essential components [...]. It goes beyond mimicry to integration, dissolving boundaries and synthesizing new hybrid typologies".

Biology is the most powerful manufacturing technology we know of. By harnessing properties that inherent in biology such as circularity, adaptability and self-organization, the field may hold significant potential for improving the sustainability of our material culture. Of particular interest to us is the construction industry, in which some of the biggest sources of pollution and resource consumption are found. Sustainability problems arise in linear consumption chains which rely on non-renewable resources. The negative ecological footprint of the built environment can be significantly reduced by employing biological growth in the manufacture of a new class of performative materials for architecture.

Selecting biological processes that take place at a molecular level and applying them to the scale of buildings and cities can be key to replacing mineral extraction and centralized, energy-intensive production with local circularity—but it comes with a host of new challenges. One of the most pressing is bridging the two fields' vastly different scales.

Although traditional architectural materials account for small scale behaviours such as moisture transport or thermal conductivity, they are traditionally employed as bulk materials with little spatial differentiation and homogenous behaviours. This is contrary to the biological world, wherein material differentiation and variability is continuous across scales [2]. The specificity, heterogeneity and dynamic nature of such systems is fundamental not only for the performative or functional output, but for the very formation and generation of structures [3] and therefore needs to be considered in biodesign.

This paper explores how these scales, i.e., the biomolecular to the architectural, can be bridged in a continuous and interrelated manner. What challenges does this present to the designer, and what methods and tools can be employed to overcome these challenges? Based on this question, we outline a methodology for the design and fabrication with living matter. The methodology was developed and implemented in the project Pulp Faction, which employs 3D printing with fungal lignocellulosic biocomposites in the making of an architectural-scale building component, named Protomycokion. The processes used in this project are studied in this paper and described from the perspective of transcalar design, and their general applicability and implications are discussed.

2. Background

The field of biodesign is gaining increasing momentum. The field is characterized by the use of nature-based solutions, including living agents in the making of new materials, and new classes of materials. Currently, there are projects employing several organisms in biofabrication for architectural elements, such as fungi, bacteria and plants; however, this paper will focus on the kingdom of fungi, as they are relevant to the case study presented here.

The 'Hy-Fi' tower at MOMA PS1 in New York constructed by The Living in collaboration with Arup and Ecovative from 2014 [4] is one of the early large-scale installations built from fungal materials in the form of stacked blocks and steel supporting arches. 'Mycotree', constructed by Block Research Group at ETH Zurich with the Karlsruhe Institute for Technology, was exhibited at the Seoul Biennale in 2017 [5] and is a compression-only structure made from fungal blocks and wood connectors. 'El Monolito Micelio' was produced in 2018 [6] as a monolithic cast in a plywood formwork. These projects all used casting, and while this method is useful for efficient mass-production, it also has some drawbacks, such as a lower level of possible customization and reduced growth (and therefore biotransformation) on the inside of the resulting components.

Through the introduction of digital fabrication in the production of such biomaterials, these limitations can potentially be removed. Elsacker et al. [7] used robotic wire-cutting for the processing of bulk fungal materials. The 'Tilted Arch' project [8] investigated the 3D printing of fungal biocomposites and the bio-welding of the fabricated components.

The research in this manuscript presents a novel methodology of integrating and orchestrating behaviour at multiple scales, through digital technologies for design and fabrication, for the production of biomaterials.

3. Materials and Methods
3.1. Terminology

In the biofabrication methodology of the Pulp Faction project, we employ several terms. *Substrate* is the mix of components before inoculation with fungus. This acts as a scaffolding onto which the living cells perform their biotransformation though some material remains in its original form at the end of the process, forming an in situ biocomposite. *Pulp* is the substrate that is inoculated with the living agent, and therefore becomes the living material that is 3D printed.

The term *transcalar* refers to processes and structures that range across multiple interconnected scales. This is a term that has been used more extensively in the field of global studies. Jan Aart Scholte distinguishes between *multilevel* and *transcalar*: Multilevel concerns each level separately whereas transcalar places the emphasis on the interrelation between the various scales or levels. "In contrast, a trans-scalar approach explains politics by treating spatial scales as overlapping, interrelated and mutually constitutive." [9].

By this definition, transcalar processes are nonlinear: it is not ideal to consider any singular scale in isolation without taking its interactions into account. Manuel de Landa describes nonlinear processes in a multitude of contexts, namely sociological, geological and not least biological. He states that such systems require new methodologies, particularly because nonlinear equations (and by extension, systems) are very difficult to solve analytically. They exhibit emergent properties: "...properties of the combination as a whole which are more than the sum of its individual parts. These emergent (or 'synergistic') properties belong to the interaction between parts, so it follows that a top-down analytical approach [...] is bound to miss precisely those properties" [10].

3.2. Methodology

In order to manage the transcalar and nonlinear aspects of biodesign, we relied on a research-by-design methodology with an emphasis on transdisciplinarity.

Architecture presents a wicked problem in that no solution can be derived from an exhaustive list of problem specifications. Such problems are not suitable for exclusively reductionist experimentation but require a reflection-in-action type of approach to the design task. The problem is further reinforced by the fact that living matter has its own agency. According to Sharma, experimental reductionism in combination with "the global perspective of systems-level experiments, [allows one to] link the fine and the coarse, the local and the global, and the bottom-up and top-down knowledge." [11].

Research-by-design methodology emphasises the importance of making, here suggested as a material practice with physical prototyping for the investigation of the problem and probing the solution space. This implies a series of material experimentations and prototyping growing in scope and resulting in a *demonstrator* [12], which in this research, is a Protomycokion. The prototypes explored sets of parameters that concern different aspects of the biofabrication (such as substrate composition, printing parameters, fungal species, methods of inoculation, growth time, etc.) through iterative testing in order to establish a workable design path.

The *demonstrator* speaks of what is in disciplinary terms called the architectural scale, i.e., a scale fitted to the needs and corporeal dimensions of human beings. The *demonstrator* is a synthesis of a temporally evolving spectrum of prototypes, bringing the divergent investigations into one concluding context: "Rather than presenting an array of possible solutions, the demonstrator necessitates the prioritisation of one solution space over another in decision-making." [13]. As in a wicked problem, the "information needed [to] understand the problem depends on one's idea for solving it" [14]. Following this, the solutions presented here are to be seen as the results of successive developments of a designed artefact, not as quantitively optimized solutions—solutions for this specific context that point out similar possible approaches in the future. The character of the problem and the chosen approach to produce and follow the building of a demonstrator, also means that this article is in a large part devoted to method descriptions combined with design reflections on varying scales.

As biodesign spans across a wide range of length-scales, we emphasized two important perspectives of scale in this context:

1. Addressing all scales with the specificities and transformations that take place at each level.
2. Linking the process of design across scales, i.e., in terms of how behaviours at one level effect and constrain across scalar boundaries.

The Pulp Faction project led to the development of a design and fabrication protocol that targets a number of variable and specific scales ranging from nanometres to meters. We developed a strategy of design that works at the level of each of these scales, connecting them in a reciprocal way. Although material scales are continuous and span several domains, we have for the sake of clarity chosen to present the scales in a linear manner starting from the smallest. In the following sections, we outline the transformations that take place at five different scales and present an interpretation of the architectural implications.

3.2.1. Nano

At the molecular level, transformations are of a chemical nature. The fungus grows on and inside the material, which results in the biotransformation of part of the original material into a living tissue. Elements of this transformation involve the partial consumption of cellulose and lignin and the gradual build-up of chitin, proteins, and other various carbohydrates in structured matrices. Through biofabrication, we employed the biochemical fungal factory to transform the existing material at the molecular level into compounds that can impart properties that did not originally exist in the substrate.

An additional transformation takes place through the metabolism of organic carbon found in the material, which is transformed into the leaving tissue of the fungal species consisting largely of protein, chitin, and extracellular polymeric substances (EPS). One component of this biotransformation process that is of particular interest is the production of EPS, which is common when microorganisms colonize surfaces (Figure 1). Their composition varies depending on nutrient condition, type of organism, growth stage, and other environmental factors [15]. EPS substances have different roles [16], but one of the most relevant in this project is that they anchor the hyphae to the substrate. Through adhesion and aggregation, they effectively act as a glue between these. The EPS is layered at nano and micro scales and grows to the millimetre scale when matured [15]. The conditions in which these are produced have design implications for several scales.

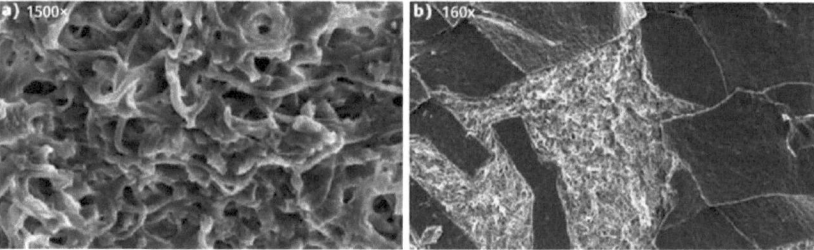

Figure 1. SEM microscopy of pre-formed biofilms of P. Ostreatus [17] Copyright 2017 Elsevier. (**a**) Compact 7 days old fungal biofilm showing hyphae cemented together with EPS matrix. (**b**) Fractured layer of EPS covering the surface of the fungal mat.

A further aspect of the molecular transformations is the production of hydrophobins, which are small proteins that increase the hydrophobicity of the mycelium [18]. We assume that the production of hydrophobins, which are a common element of fungal mycelium, along with chitin, which is itself hydrophobic, led to an overall hydrophobicity of the final biomaterial.

3.2.2. Micro

At the micro scale, we looked at the transformations through the biological lens. Filamentous fungi, such as the one used in Pulp Faction, produce cylindrical cells of a few micrometres' length, termed hyphae. The hyphae exhibit uniform growth and interconnect to form a complex, highly organized network of filaments that become the mycelium. The mycelium can cover large areas and volumes of substrate, to the extent that the total length of hyphae included in 1 g of soil can measure up to 600 km [19]. In this project, the nanoscale processes described above resulted in the partial biotransformation of the pulp into living mycelium. Here, the role of the mycelium is to surround and bind wood, cellulose, and clay particles into a matrix that consists of living cells and abiotic material. This is the next level of transformation whereby the more amorphous (lignin) and fibrous (cellulose) structures of wood are interconnected with the network of the fungal mycelium. At the same time, the mycelium acts as an extensive natural network of highways through which the fungus translocates nutrients across the construct to further colonize and biotransform the material (Figure 2). The microorganism freely determines the distribution of nutrients across the pulp; interestingly, this results in a relatively uniform type of growth across the material, at least at the milli and meso scales.

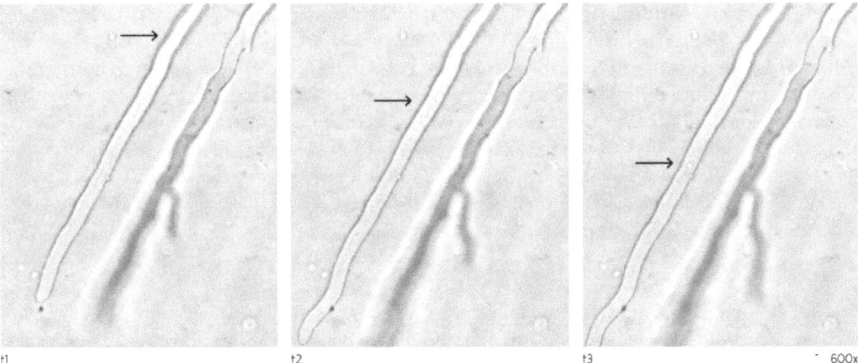

Figure 2. Microscopic imaging of growing hyphae with arrouw showing transport of particles. Photo by author.

A high ratio of fungal cells to the substrate is desired for a higher degree of biotransformation of the pulp. This occurs naturally over time, as the substrate becomes colonized. To accelerate the growth time, the strategy employed at this scale was to blend the inoculum. A fungus that was grown in a Petri dish for 5 days was blended with sterilized water, and this liquid inoculum was added to the substrate. The blending process cuts the mycelium into numerous fragments and their addition into the pulp results in the simultaneous development of many colonies, which eventually merge across the material. This results in a significant reduction in the time required for growth and a more homogeneous age of the mycelium.

3.2.3. Milli

This level is concerned with the larger material scale, wherein mechanical transformation can be observed. The main parts of the process at this scale were the composition of the substrate and the extrusion of the pulp.

Composition

The composition of the material is a crucial aspect of the research. There are several factors that influence the results in several ways, namely the water content, fibre size, and additives. Different scales have contradicting requirements regarding water content. For the stability of the component, a drier extruded material is desired. Additionally, the higher the water content, the higher the resulting volumetric shrinkage and distortion [20], providing another reason for lowering the water content in the pulp. However, a higher water content is necessary for a fast and homogenous colonization of the substrate by the fungus. A successful percentage that satisfies both conditions has been found at 59.4 percent of the total weight (wt%).

The fibre sources are wood fragments and paper pulp. Several sources have been tested and evaluated, with an emphasis on finding a working solution rather than the best possible composition. Besides water, the lignocellulosic fibres were at the highest percentage in the composition at 21.7 wt%. Out of these, cellulose fibres make up at 5.4 wt%. The size of the wood particles is of high importance, as larger particles improve the mechanical performance of the end result (under a threshold of 5 mm [21]) and increase fungal growth [22]. However, large wood particles impede the extrusion as they cause frequent clogging. Therefore, the largest fibres that successfully printed without clogging were employed. Filtering the wood particles with a sieve of mesh size 2 mm produced the most stable results.

Besides water and lignocellulosic fibres, additives were necessary due to the requirements of the 3D-printing process. Xanthan is a polysaccharide produced by the bacterial species Xanthomonas campestris. It was employed as a stabiliser to prevent water and fibres from separating in the process of extrusion, at 2.6 wt%. Clay powder as inorganic matter is a secondary additive to the substrate. Mixed with water, it results in a highly extrudable material, so when combined with the rest of the substrate it acts as a support material. Additionally, this reduced the amount of water necessary to achieve a continuous extrusion, which is desirable. However, it should ideally be kept minimal, as it does not contribute to conversion into fungal biomass. A percentage of 16.3 wt% (considerably less by volume) was found to be suitable for our process.

Extrusion

The inoculated substrate was extruded on a layer-by-layer basis, similar to FDM (fused deposition modelling) and LDM (liquid deposition modelling) 3D-printing methods. However, unlike FDM (which relies on the thermoplasticity of plastics for the binding of deposited layers) and LDM (which relies on the evaporation of water or chemical reactions to achieve rigidity [20]), there were no chemical or thermo-setting agents in the pulp. The binding took place post-extrusion in the growth stage, at which point the hyphae grow and fuse the layers together (Figure 3). This printing method is termed bioFDM (bio-fused deposition modelling).

Figure 3. Extrusion of pulp (**left**), and hyphae growing on printed surface (**right**). Photo by author.

The dimensioning of the printing nozzle is also at this scale, and it has repercussions for the lower and higher scales. A wider nozzle provides an increased stability of the printed component and because it deposits more material at once, it reduces the total printing time of the final column. However, it also reduces the surface to volume ratio—which as described below is not desirable as it lowers the total growth of the fungus. The dimensions that have been employed are similar to the project reference of the fungal combs (Termitomyces and termite symbiosis, [23]), where the expectation is that the fungal hyphae grow throughout the bulk of the pulp. The final nozzle size employed was 3.2 mm diameter.

Several properties that were defined at smaller scales could be observed here, namely hydrophobicity, dispersion in water, humidity absorption, tension, and compression strength.

3.2.4. Meso

This is the scale of the 3D-printed component (Figure 4), where the demands and constraints of the organism, the printing process, and structural integrity of the component itself as well as the larger macro scale all come into play. Each component was designed to connect to an adjacent one, following the overall computed structure.

Figure 4. Printed subcomponent. Photo by author.

The design was managed using computational models which are able to negotiate these disparate needs. The surface area to volume ratio (SA:V) was increased by a reaction-diffusion model. The SA:V in the 3D-printed component that was algorithmically generated was found to be 0.509, compared to 0.046 for the same size component if simplified for the casting process. This enhanced oxygen access, which maximized hyphae growth [23]. This led to higher EPS production, which induced the desired chemical and physical properties of the resulting biocomposite.

The bioFDM process relies on stabilizing the component during the growth stage and finalizing the rigidity at the desiccation stage—therefore in the printing stage it is weak. This limits the total height that the component could be printed at. A scaffolding system, either independent, robotic or 3D printed, could be used to overcome this limitation partially or fully.

However, geometry plays an important role at this scale. Curved and folded geometries are structurally more rigid compared to flat surfaces; therefore, by employing a complex algorithm, the stability was improved. A computation script was further employed to increase the connections between neighbouring channels in the extrusion toolpath. This introduced more lateral connections, which provided supports during printing and therefore reduced the weakness in the printing and growth stage. Moreover, these lateral supports strengthened the geometry in the desiccation stage, reducing global component distortions.

3.2.5. Macro

The macro scale is the demonstrator, where the output is experienced as architecture relating to the scale of the human body. To achieve the full extent of the macro scale, a two-step printing process was implemented. The building element was subdivided into smaller components (see above meso scale) that were individually printed, grown and dried. When the individual components had achieved their full strength, they were assembled and bonded together, facilitating the larger (macro) scale.

The bonding at this second stage utilised the same process as the first stage of printing, with living pulp being applied to each joint. When placed in a controlled high humidity environment, the mycelium in this joint grew into the dried components, effectively bonding them together as a result.

As the pulp dried, it contracted, resulting in a shrinkage of the final component. This was limited in the horizontal plane through the fabrication process, which resulted in a mostly vertical shrinkage. This was found to be approximately 20% and it was accounted for in the design process.

At this scale, the characteristics and behaviours of the smaller scales (nano, milli, meso) come into effect as carriers or enablers of architectural performance. The hyphae network covering the surface of the components not only binds and strengthens it but imparts hydrophobicity that reduces the risk of liquid water ingress. Because of the microscopic properties and arrangement of the fibres, water vapor can still be absorbed by or released from the material, allowing it to function as an effective humidity buffer.

The arrangement at the milli scale of the printed material, which was formed in response to the fungus' physiological requirements and fabrication process, also assists in these functions. Thus, a clear transcalar function becomes apparent. The high surface area and vertically connected voids facilitate the exchange of moisture, air and heat between the column and the surrounding (human inhabited) spaces or rooms. These voids also provide a pathway for liquid water runoff and permit the controlled and efficient drying of the structure. In their ultimate form, these interconnected and defined channels can perform important roles in managing the internal climate, effectively forming a building-scale vascular system.

The variable material appearance, influenced by a myriad of parameters and microscopic behaviours, transformed at the macro scale (Figure 5). Viewed together as a whole, the variation of texture and colour is perceived as unified. This effect was reinforced by the generative design, which never repeats itself yet follows a clearly distinguishable pattern, resulting from the reaction diffusion algorithm and the process of fabrication.

Figure 5. Protomycokion column. Photo by author.

4. Results

Central to the transcalar approach described and discussed in this paper is the interdependence of variable scales, systems and materials which results in nonlinear interactions and rapidly increasing complexity. These conditions, which are the norm in biological systems, place a hard limit on traditional engineering approaches due to exponential increase in formal and functional complexity [24]. Bentley suggests that nature and biological processes rely on a fundamentally different "design" logic which is better suited to complex and interrelated problems and that makes it possible to break through this "complexity ceiling".

The project and design processes outlined in this paper demonstrate that computational or algorithmic design enables a similar approach in architecture. Instead of drawing form, architects can define—through computer code—a series of processes that only have meaning when placed in a context. In responding to this context, the resulting form becomes locally adapted at multiple scales and can exhibit unlimited variability in principle while maintaining consistency in terms of the internal and external logics. Such locally operating algorithms can suggest and negotiate high levels of complexity and interdependence [25]. We also found that the use of digital fabrication serves an important role in linking the computational design to the complexities of the physical reality and the construction process. Without this technology, the making process becomes a bottleneck that forces top-down reductionism, eliminating or reducing the effectiveness of the computational design approach.

Data-driven design can span multiple scales and reach high resolutions without relying on the repetition and homogeneity of forms and material as is the norm in industrial mass-production. By encoding algorithmic behaviours into the making process and allowing these to interact with the biological processes themselves, a combination of specificity and large scale can be achieved. In this way, biological growth can be guided using digital tools. Emerging computational models enable new modes of creation that allow for a plurality of scales, languages and priorities to coexist, relate, and negotiate within a single model, including design intent, fungal needs, fabrication parameters, structural constraints and human requirements.

The design of Protomycokion relies on a series of algorithmic processes that make the transcalar relations possible. The critical aspect of digital fabrication is the ability to combine high specificity and articulation with large volumes, which is necessary when advancing the field of biodesign, increasing its capacity to make a profound change to resource-use and manufacturing in architecture. As Gorochowski states [26], "Being able to scale our ability to harness biology will be crucial for addressing the many grand challenges we face, such as shifts toward sustainable manufacturing, clean energy production, and new forms of advanced medicine. CAD applied to synthetic biology is likely to play a key role in realizing these ambitions".

5. Discussion

One of the most exciting aspects of using biofabrication in construction is the great potential for adaptation and variability. With regard to mycelium biocomposites, different fungal strains lead to different outcomes both in terms of fabrication process and the performance of the architectural object. From a biological point of view, growth speed under a broad range of conditions, branching patterns, genetic stability, competitiveness, and lack of spores and toxin production are important factors in the selection of a fungal strain. From an architectural point of view, factors such as tensile and compressive strength, fibre adhesiveness, heat conductivity, hydrophobicity, appearance and durability will all come into play and are influenced by the biological characteristics of different fungal strains, as well as biofabrication conditions. Depending on the intended application, these will be of varying importance and different strains or even combinations of strains may be relevant for different projects.

In different environments, various raw materials are likely to be available and sustainable. In Pulp Faction, forestry by-products were used, but in different contexts agricultural waste, recycled urban waste, or even on-site grown plant materials could be relevant. By adjusting the strain of fungus used, these could potentially all be suitable raw materials which means that the process is not per se reliant on centralised infrastructures or monocultures. This is a critical aspect for the overall sustainability of the biofabrication) paradigm. If biofabrication is scaled up and employed in the construction industry and follows previous industrial logics, problems will arise with regard to biodiversity, transportation and other issues. Local raw materials and local fungal and other microbial strains can shape how biomaterials blend and match with the local environment and can reduce the need for transportation. The potential of using locally sourced and highly varied raw material through the transformative power of microorganisms is a key component in battling these challenges.

Therefore, it is unsuitable to develop a single form, product, or process through which to implement biodesign and biofabrication. As has been described in the paper, the variables operating at all the different scales within the process are highly interdependent. The fungal strain used is not an independent factor, but influences and is influenced by the raw materials, the extrusion process and post treatment, and the architectural role and context the output has.

This is the core of the transcalar approach—the interdependence of the involved scales represents both the challenge and the potential of biodesign. Computer models based on algorithmic and self-organizing logics can regulate and negotiate such nonlinear processes and are critical for a successful and sustainable implementation of a biodesign construction paradigm.

6. Conclusions

The project output—the column *Protomycokion* and the processes through which it was designed and fabricated—serves as a proof-of-concept for the use of biofabrication in combination with 3D printing to create architectural-scale artefacts. It demonstrates that these can achieve properties that would otherwise be difficult if not impossible. Doing so introduces a vast range of scalar interdependencies that result in a nonlinear and complex design process. In the making of the Protomycokion, we demonstrated the first successful example of the 3D printing of an architectural-scale fungal lignocellulosic structure, demonstrating the potential of this approach. We outlined how this requires a new approach to generate and control the resulting complexity, which we defined as a transcalar design methodology. This is based on the integration of research by design, computational design and fabrication, as well as applied microbiology.

This transcalar process and its complex interdependence needs to be managed using computational design tools. These algorithmic approaches allow every scale to be individually addressed through its own internal logic, while the consequences for connected scales can be tracked and considered. In addition to the computational tools themselves, the research-by-design approach proved to be a powerful tool to address these interdependencies, and particularly, the use of a physical-design prototype facilitated the transdisciplinary workflows.

The design-centred methodology with a transcalar focus facilitates a rapid and agile exploration of complex and interdependent systems. This needs to be complemented with experiments undertaken in a more conventional reductionist manner. The design approach, and particularly the demonstrator, should be coupled in an iterative manner with these experiments, and serves multiple functions in that it allows for the rapid establishment of parameters and design species, links disciplines and facilitates interactions between them, communicates design and scientific intent and most of all it manifests the transcalar effects of decisions made at a reductionist level.

Through an explorative laboratory-based design approach, the study shows that there is the potential for more sustainable lines of production of architectural elements, where the use of locally fabricated biomaterials and the successively generated design of architectural elements can not only perform well technologically but also leaves room for advanced and adaptive architectural formation.

Author Contributions: Conceptualization, A.G. and D.A.; methodology, A.G., D.A. and D.F.; software, A.G.; validation, A.G. and D.F.; formal analysis, A.G., D.A. and D.F.; investigation, A.G.; resources, D.A. and D.F.; data curation, A.G.; writing—original draft preparation, A.G.; writing—review and editing, A.G., D.A. and D.F.; visualization, A.G.; supervision, D.A. and D.F.; project administration, D.A.; funding acquisition, D.A. All authors have read and agreed to the published version of the manuscript.

Funding: The making of the Protomycokion was funded by the Swedish National Board of Housing, Building and Planning (grant no. 6418/2018), and the article written with the support of Formas (grant no. 2020-00429).

Acknowledgments: The authors would like to thank Gunnar Sandin for the support and discussions.

Conflicts of Interest: The authors declare no conflict of interest. The funders had no role in the design of the study; in the collection, analyses, or interpretation of data; in the writing of the manuscript, or in the decision to publish the results.

References

1. Myers, W.; Antonelli, P. *Bio Design: Nature, Science, Creativity*; Museum of Modern Art: New York, NY, USA, 2012.
2. Weibel, E.R. Fractal geometry: A design principle for living organisms. *Am. J. Physiol. Lung Cell Mol. Physiol.* **1991**, *261*, L361–L369. [CrossRef] [PubMed]
3. Turner, J.S. Homeostasis, complexity, and the problem of biological design. *Emerg. Complex. Organ.* **2008**, *10*, 76–89.
4. Nagy, D.; Locke, J.; Benjamin, D. Computational brick stacking for constructing free-form structures. In *Proceedings of the Design Modelling Symposium: Modelling Behaviour*, 1st ed.; Springer: Cham, Switzerland, 2015; pp. 203–212. [CrossRef]
5. Heisel, F.; Lee, J.; Schlesier, K.; Rippmann, M.; Saeidi, N.; Javadian, A.; Nugroho, A.R.; Mele, T.V.; Block, P.; Hebel, D.E. Design, cultivation and application of load-bearing mycelium components: The MycoTree at the 2017 Seoul biennale of architecture and urbanism. *Int. J. Sustain. Energy Dev.* **2017**, *6*, 296–303. [CrossRef]
6. Dessi-Olive, J. Monolithic Mycelium: Growing Vault Structures. In Proceedings of the 18th International Conference Non-Conventional Materials and Technologies, Nairobi, Kenya, 24–26 July 2019. Available online: https://www.academia.edu/3990 9593/Monolithic_Mycelium_Growing_Vault_Structures (accessed on 13 February 2022).
7. Elsacker, E.; Søndergaard, A.; Van Wylick, A.; Peeters, E.; De Laet, L. Growing living and multifunctional mycelium composites for large-scale formwork applications using robotic abrasive wire-cutting. *Constr. Build. Mater.* **2021**, *283*, 122732. [CrossRef]
8. Modanloo, B.; Ghazvinian, A.; Matini, M.; Andaroodi, E. Tilted Arch; implementation of additive manufacturing and bio-welding of mycelium-based composites. *Biomimetics* **2021**, *6*, 68. [CrossRef] [PubMed]
9. Scholte, J.A. Civil society and global governance: Exploring transscalar connections. *Interest Groups Advocacy* **2019**, *8*, 490–498. [CrossRef]
10. De Landa, M. *A Thousand Years of Nonlinear History*; Zone Books: New York, NY, USA, 1997.
11. Sharma, S. Designing the Organism-Environment Relationship. Ph.D. Thesis, Massachusetts Institute of Technology, Cambridge, MA, USA, 2020.
12. Thomsen, M.R.; Tamke, M. Narratives of making: Thinking practice led research in architecture. In *Proceedings of the Communicating (by) Design 2009*; Elsevier: Brussels, Belgium, 2009; pp. 1–8.
13. Thomsen, M.R.; Tamke, M. Prototyping Practice: Merging Digital and Physical Enquiries. In *Rethink! Prototyping*; Springer: Cham, Switzerland, 2015; pp. 49–62.
14. Rittel, H.W.J.; Webber, M.M. Dilemmas in a General Theory of Planning. In *Policy Sciences*; Elsevier Scientific Publishing Company: Amsterdam, The Netherlands, 1973; Volume 4, pp. 155–169.
15. Gazzè, S.A.; Saccone, L.; Smits, M.M.; Duran, A.L.; Leake, J.R.; Banwart, S.A.; Ragnarsdottir, K.V.; McMaster, T.J. Nanoscale Observations of Extracellular Polymeric Substances Deposition on Phyllosilicates by an Ectomycorrhizal Fungus. *Geomicrobiol. J.* **2013**, *30*, 721–730. [CrossRef]
16. Costa, O.Y.; Raaijmakers, J.M.; Kuramae, E.E. Microbial extracellular polymeric substances: Ecological function and impact on soil aggregation. *Front. Microbiol.* **2018**, *9*, 1636. [CrossRef] [PubMed]
17. Válková, H.; Novotný, Č.; Malachová, K.; Šlosarčíková, P.; Fojtík, J. Effect of bacteria on the degradation ability of Pleurotus ostreatus. *Sci. Total Environ.* **2017**, *584–585*, 1114–1120. [CrossRef] [PubMed]
18. Berger, B.W.; Sallada, N.D. Hydrophobins: Multifunctional biosurfactants for interface engineering. *J. Biol. Eng.* **2019**, *13*, 1–8. [CrossRef] [PubMed]
19. Ekblad, A.; Wallander, H.; Godbold, D.L.; Cruz, C.; Johnson, D.; Baldrian, P.; Björk, R.G.; Epron, D.; Kieliszewska-Rokicka, B.; Kjøller, R.; et al. The production and turnover of extramatrical mycelium of ectomycorrhizal fungi in forest soils: Role in carbon cycling. *Plant Soil* **2013**, *366*, 1–27. [CrossRef]
20. Rosenthal, M.; Henneberger, C.; Gutkes, A.; Bues, C.-T. Liquid Deposition Modeling: A promising approach for 3D printing of wood. *Eur. J. Wood Wood Prod.* **2017**, *76*, 797–799. [CrossRef]
21. Elsacker, E.; Vandelook, S.; Brancart, J.; Peeters, E.; De Laet, L. Mechanical, physical and chemical characterisation of mycelium-based composites with different types of lignocellulosic substrates. *PLoS ONE* **2019**, *14*, e0213954. [CrossRef] [PubMed]
22. Schmidt, C.G.; Furlong, E.B. Effect of particle size and ammonium sulfate concentration on rice bran fermentation with the fungus rhizopus oryzae. *Bioresour. Technol.* **2012**, *123*, 36–41. [CrossRef] [PubMed]
23. Goidea, A.; Floudas, D.; Andréen, D. Pulp Faction: 3d Printed Material Assemblies Through Microbial Biotransformation. In *Fabricate 2020: Making Resilient Architecture*; Burry, J., Sabin, J., Sheil, B., Skavara, M., Eds.; UCL Press: London, UK, 2020; pp. 42–49. [CrossRef]
24. Bentley, P. Climbing Through Complexity Ceilings. In *Network Practices: New Strategies in Architecture and Design*; Burke, A., Tierney, T., Eds.; Princeton Architectural Press: New York, NY, USA, 2007; pp. 178–197.
25. Varenne, F. The Nature of Computational Things-Models and Simulations in Design and Architecture. In *Naturalizing Architecture: ArchiLab 2013*; Brayer, M.-A., Migayrou, F., Eds.; Hyx Editions: Orléans, France, 2013; pp. 96–105.
26. Gorochowski, T.E.; Karr, J.R.; Parmeggiani, F.; Yordanov, B. Editorial: Computer-Aided Biodesign Across Scales. *Front. Bioeng. Biotechnol.* **2021**, *9*, 700418. [CrossRef] [PubMed]

Article

Impact of the Height of Buildings on the Maintainability of Natural Stone Claddings

Cláudia Ferreira [1,*], Ana Silva [1] and Jorge de Brito [1,2]

[1] Civil Engineering Research and Innovation for Sustainability (CERIS), Instituto Superior Técnico, Universidade de Lisboa, Av. Rovisco Pais, 1049-001 Lisbon, Portugal; ana.ferreira.silva@tecnico.ulisboa.pt (A.S.); jb@civil.ist.utl.pt (J.d.B.)

[2] Department of Civil Engineering, Architecture and Georesources, Instituto Superior Técnico, Universidade de Lisboa, Av. Rovisco Pais, 1049-001 Lisbon, Portugal

*   Correspondence: claudiaarferreira@tecnico.ulisboa.pt

Abstract: The buildings' surroundings' environmental exposure conditions (e.g., orientation, location, altitude, distance from the sea, temperature, precipitation, presence of damp, exposure to prevailing winds, among others) have a considerable influence on the performance and durability of their envelope. Furthermore, the intensity of these conditions can vary significantly with the height of the building and, consequently, influence the degradation of different parts of the same building in different ways. In a tall building, the upper part is more prone to higher solar radiation levels, temperature variations, and exposure to wind–rain action. On the other hand, external elements at the bottom are more susceptible to high levels of pollution, especially in city centres. In this sense, the main purpose of this study was to analyse the degradation processes in buildings with different heights and understand whether the processes and maintenance requirements are statistically different. A sample of 203 natural stone claddings (NSC), located in Portugal, was used as case study. The sample was collected based on the diagnosis of the degradation condition of these claddings through in situ visual inspections. To predict the degradation process of NSC over time, a stochastic service life prediction model, based on Petri nets (PN), was implemented. This model allows evaluating the performance of NSC by encompassing the uncertainty of the future performance of the claddings. The results obtained through the degradation and maintenance models were compared with real case studies to highlight the real impact of buildings' height subjected to environmental exposure conditions on the maintainability of NSC.

Keywords: degradation; maintenance; environmental exposure conditions; tall buildings; natural stone claddings; Petri nets

1. Introduction

The cladding materials, applied in façades and roofs, are the buildings' first protection level and, therefore, they are exceptionally vulnerable to the environment degradation agents and mechanisms [1]. Consequently, the surrounding environmental exposure conditions have a strong impact on the rate and severity of degradation of these materials [2]. The service life and maintenance needs of the different cladding solutions are influenced by factors such as location, orientation, altitude, distance from the sea, precipitation, temperature, presence of damp, and exposure to prevailing winds [3,4]. The service life of façade claddings is very variable, depending on the material applied, the exposure conditions, even the geographical context, and the consequent users' performance requirements [5,6]. In fact, the service life of the cladding materials varies around the world. For example, the Aon Center, in Chicago was initially clad in Italian Carrara marble, but the severe thermal cycles and environmental loads of Chicago led to early cracking and bowing of the marble slabs, and the building had to be re-cladded with white granite 15 years later [7–9]. Similar constructive solution presented different service lives in other places, for example 21 years in Helsinki (Finland), 25 years in Malmö (Sweden) and Paris (France), and 31 years in Nyköping (Sweden) [10,11]. The variation of the environmental exposure conditions with height can also considerably affect the rate and severity of the claddings' degradation. A study performed by Westberg et al. [12] reveals that tall buildings are more susceptible to weather effects. In the Aon Center, most of the cracked slabs were located on the elevated part of the building, subjected to higher sunlight exposure [13].

The environmental exposure conditions at the top and bottom of a tall building are distinct. The upper part of the building is less protected from these conditions, namely solar radiation, temperature variations, and the combined action of precipitation and prevailing winds [14,15]. On the other hand, the façades at the bottom of buildings are subjected to a higher level of pollution in the air [16]. The main purpose of this study is to understand whether the degradation process in tall buildings is statistically different from that in low buildings and assess the impact of these differences on the maintenance requirements. To assess the impact of the building's height on the degradation and maintenance conditions of natural stone claddings in external façades over time, a stochastic service life prediction model, based on Petri nets (PN), is implemented. This model allows evaluating the performance of NSC by encompassing the uncertainty of the future performance of the claddings [17]. The case study selected is composed of 203 natural stone claddings (NSC), 110 in low buildings and 93 in high-rise buildings, located in Portugal. The sample was collected based on the diagnosis of the degradation condition of these claddings through in situ visual inspections. In the methodology developed, the degradation process and three maintenance strategies are assessed: (i) total replacement only; (ii) combination of minor interventions and total replacement; and (iii) combination of cleaning operations, minor interventions, and total replacement.

To the authors' best knowledge, there are no studies in the literature that address this issue. First, the maintenance planning of claddings is not yet fully implemented in our society (the maintenance of this element is still seen as non-essential) [18,19]. Furthermore, when degradation models are used to predict the evolution of anomalies and plan the maintenance activities, it is assumed that the environmental exposure conditions are equal in all building [20,21]. Nowadays, from the literature, it is known that environmental exposure conditions have a considerable influence on the degradation process [22], especially the microclimate. Therefore, the analysis of the degradation process for different buildings' heights is fundamental to define adequate degradation curves to correctly model the claddings' behaviour. By reducing the uncertainties in the degradation process, better maintenance plans can be developed and, consequently, higher savings in the maintenance plan can be reached.

The outline of this paper is as follows: Section 2 provides a background of the variation of environmental exposure conditions according to the buildings' height; in Section 3, the material analysed and the maintenance model implemented are described; Sections 4 and 5 present the results obtained and their discussion, respectively; and, finally, the conclusions are drawn in Section 6.

2. Background: Variation of the Environmental Exposure Conditions According to Buildings' Height

The façades' durability is strongly influenced by the microclimate [23]. Local climate concerns the overall climate of the region and is related with the topography, rural or urban context, altitude, and distance to the sea of the building [3]. On the other hand, microclimate depends on the specific location and characteristic of the building, such as [12] orientation, materials, height, and surface protection (by elements existing in the façade or by external surrounding elements). Therefore, the assumption that environmental exposure conditions are constant along the height of a building is an over-simplistic approach.

Several studies show that existing environmental conditions are directly related with the buildings' height. Elshaer et al. [24] used different configurations of buildings (standalone and different surrounding heights) to assess the impact of wind loads on tall buildings. The authors concluded that the mean pressure magnitudes of the wind are higher on the top of the building and increase with height. However, the surrounding buildings have a protective effect, mainly at the bottom of the building, since the mean pressure magnitudes of the wind decreases with the increase in height of the surrounding buildings. On the other hand, the increase in height of the surrounding buildings contributes to the turbulence induced by the incoming wind. The risk of turbulence is considerably high at the bottom of the building when the height of the surrounding buildings is, approximately, 75% of the height of the building under analysis.

The pollutant concentrations are also higher at street level [16]. Azimi et al. [25], in Chicago, and Makhelouf [26], in Paris, analysed the vertical distribution of pollution around high-rises. In both studies, the measurements carried out show considerable differences in the pollutant concentrations as a function of floor elevation. These concentrations are more significant at the bottom of the building mainly because of traffic density. Only the ozone concentration increases with the height of the building [25,27]. From previous studies, it is possible to understand that pollutants related to road traffic are severely harmful to outdoor surfaces due to the dry deposition process [28,29].

Wind-driven rain intensity is another important parameter in the degradation of the buildings' envelope elements. The wind-driven rain has an active role in the deposition of atmospheric pollutants on building façades [30]. Ge et al. [31], from field measurements of wind-driven rain on mid- and high-rise buildings, and Blocken et al. [30], from numerical models, observed that the wind-driven rain intensity increases as a function of floor elevation, reaching its maximum at the roof of the buildings. Furthermore, when the rain is acid, the impact in the degradation is higher, since the buildings' elements are exposed to acid environments for a long time [29,32].

Regarding temperature, although the results of Azimi et al. [25] show that temperature decreases with height, Charisi et al. [33] found that the more exposed parts of buildings present high surface temperatures due to the high radiative flux that the building façades are exposed to and, consequently, a higher temperature variation along the day. In the context of degradation of buildings' envelope elements, higher temperature variations are more harmful than a high stable temperature [34]. Since the top of the building is more exposed, the impact of temperature variations is more visible in these areas. Furthermore, the top of the building is also more prone to higher indices of UV radiation [35]. Solar exposure has a considerable importance in the aging of building materials [36,37].

3. Materials and Methods

To assess the impact of the building's height on the degradation and maintenance conditions of façades, 203 natural stone claddings were selected as case studies. For that purpose, a stochastic service life prediction model, based on PN [17], was implemented. A condition-based maintenance model means that inspections are an important activity in the maintenance planning. In other words, planning the maintenance activities to be carried out is possible only after the assessment of the NSC condition through an inspection.

A stochastic service life prediction model is used to the detriment of well-established models, such as the factorial method [38]. Although the factorial method is flexible and relatively easy to apply, this deterministic method is extremely sensitive to small changes in the sub-factors' quantification. As more durability sub-factors are adopted, the complexity of the method increases, and the reference service life becomes more difficult to establish in an objective way [39]. The implementation of PN overcomes these limitations. The graphical representation allows describing the problem in a more intuitive manner; it is more flexible, since it allows incorporating more rules in the model to accurately simulate more complex problems and, at the same time, keep the model size within manageable limits. Probabilistic distribution can also be used to describe the degradation phenomena, providing more relevant information regarding the risk of failure of the claddings.

The research methodology implemented is divided into three main steps (Figure 1). In the step 1, a statistical analysis of the database is carried out, where the differences of weighted area of the façade affected by visual, loss of integrity, and loss of adhesion anomalies, according to the building's height, are identified. In step 2, the optimal parameters of the degradation model for high and low buildings are estimated for different probabilistic distributions. The exponential distribution is used to validate the degradation model. After that, the best probabilistic distribution is chosen, and the degradation curves are estimated. Finally, in step 3, the impact of maintenance activities is analysed, and values of high and low buildings are compared with the values of the complete sample.

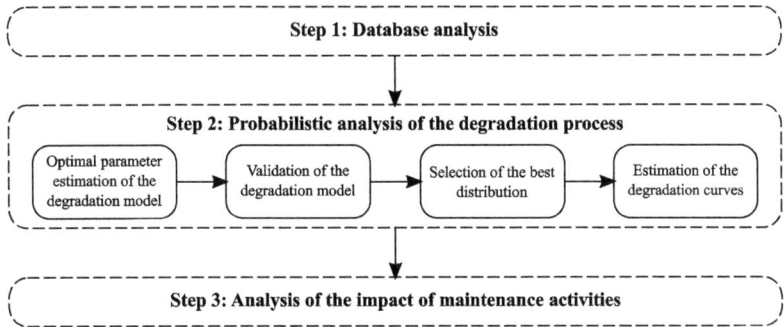

Figure 1. Diagram of the methodology implemented in this study.

3.1. Natural Stone Cladding

Over the years, several problems in natural stone claddings have been reported [11,40,41], derived mainly from inappropriate design, construction errors, and/or lack of maintenance [42,43]. The failure of NSC is extremely serious. The detachment of a stone element from the façade represents a high hazard to pedestrians and users [11,41,44]. Due to its unique appearance, natural stone provides an image of prestige and prosperity and is used as a cladding material in several buildings around the world, most of which are considered tall buildings. The knowledge of its behaviour and requirements is essential.

The database used in this study is composed of 203 NSC. A total of 54% of database elements correspond to low buildings (buildings up to five storeys) and 46% to high buildings (with more than five floors). The degradation condition of each NSC in the database was analysed based on in situ visual inspections.

The inspected buildings were randomly chosen. Buildings with different environmental exposures, locations, ages, heights, types of use, and types of stone were selected. The objective was to obtain a heterogeneous database. In terms of the type of stone, 35% of the database elements correspond to limestone, 27% to granite, and 38% to marble.

3.2. Classification System

The classification system to assess and characterise the degradation condition of buildings' claddings has been addressed by different authors [45–47]. In this study, a discrete classification system with five degradation conditions is used to assess the overall condition of NSC. This classification system was introduced by Silva et al. [39]. The overall degradation condition is determined through the severity of degradation index, S_w. Based on a visual assessment, the extent of the cladding affected by the different anomalies is recorded. The severity of degradation index is estimated by the ratio between the area affected by the anomalies observed in a NSC, weighted according to their severity, and a reference area equivalent to the total cladding area with the highest possible degradation condition (Equation (1)) :

$$S_w = \frac{\sum(A_n \times k_n \times k_{a,n})}{A \times \sum k_{max}}, \tag{1}$$

where k_n is the multiplying factor of anomaly n, as a function of its degradation condition (varying between 0 and 4); $k_{a,n}$ a weighting factor corresponding to the relative weight of the anomaly detected ($k_{a,n} \in R^+$); A_n the area of cladding affected by an anomaly n (in m^2); A the façade's area (in m^2); $\sum k_{max}$ the sum of the multiplying factors for the highest degradation condition of each anomaly type. The severity of degradation index, S_w, ranges between 0 and 100%. The anomalies, the weighting factors (k_n and $k_{a,n}$), and more details about the classification system can be consulted in Silva et al. [39].

Figure 2 illustrates the relationship between the severity of degradation, S_w, and the degradation condition, C, with some examples. Condition A ($S_w \leq 1\%$) represents a NSC with no visible degradation; in condition B ($1 < S_w \leq 8\%$), the NSC begins to present some visual anomalies (superficial dirt and stains) and some signs of loss of integrity (material degradation and cracking); condition C ($8 < S_w \leq 20\%$) corresponds to a NSC with slight degradation, with anomalies related to joints and substrate degradation and loss of integrity (open joint, scaling of the edges, and fracture); condition D ($20 < S_w \leq 45\%$) corresponds to a NSC with moderate degradation (there is an evolution on the condition C anomalies); and condition E ($S_w > 45\%$) represents a NSC with generalised degradation and severe defects.

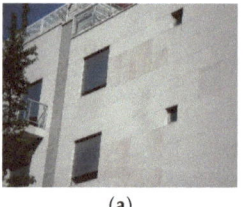 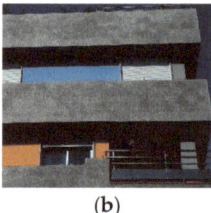  

(**a**) (**b**) (**c**) (**d**)

Figure 2. General appearance of NSC in the different degradation conditions: (**a**) condition A ($S_w \leq 1\%$); (**b**) condition B ($1 < S_w \leq 8\%$); (**c**) condition C ($8 < S_w \leq 20\%$); (**d**) condition D ($20 < S_w \leq 45\%$). No example is provided for condition E because there is no NSC in this condition in the database.

3.3. Maintenance Model

Beyond the degradation process, the maintenance model adopted also includes the inspection and maintenance processes. Since it is a stochastic model, the uncertainties that arise from the inspection records, from the natural variability of the degradation process, and from the efficiency/impact of the maintenance actions are considered. Therefore, to consider the propagation of uncertainties during a building's lifetime, in this model, a Monte Carlo simulation is used (the sample size considered is 50,000). More details about the maintenance model can be found in Ferreira et al. [17].

3.3.1. Degradation Process

To adjust the maintenance model to model NSC in low- and high-rise buildings, the estimation of the firing rates of the transitions of the degradation process from the database is a fundamental step. For that purpose, several probability distributions are analysed. The probability distribution that best describes the degradation process of the NSC is the one that minimises the differences between the predicted and observed data. The fit of the probability distribution parameters to the database is carried out through the maximum likelihood method [48]. The log likelihood, log L, measures the difference between the observed data and those estimated by the model (Equation (2)).

$$\log L = \sum \log p_{ij},\qquad(2)$$

The log likelihood is given by the summation of the logarithm of the probability of transition from degradation i to j, p_{ij}, of all observed transitions presented in the database.

3.3.2. Impact of the Maintenance Activities

The database is also used to estimate the impact that a maintenance activity has on the NSC. The impact of a maintenance activity is quantified by assessing the effect this activity has on the severity of degradation index, S_w [49]. The impact of maintenance activities on the removal or repair of the anomalies observed is defined based on the literature or expert judgement. These values are used to perform a theoretical correction of the anomalies in the different records presented in the database. After theoretical analysis, a new severity of degradation index is estimated and, consequently, a new degradation condition. By comparing these records with the original, the probability that a NSC improves its condition is estimated.

In this study, only three types of intervention are considered in the maintenance model: cleaning operations, minor interventions, and total replacement. Cleaning operations are applied to remove part of the aesthetical and visual defects (e.g., surface dirt, stains, and efflorescence) and reduce microbiological growth. Minor intervention is a more detailed action than cleaning operations. Besides covering cleaning operations, it also considers localised repair and/or partial replacement of the NSC due to cracks or local loss of adhesion. Finally, in the last level, the whole cladding is replaced. In terms of implementation, it is assumed that a cleaning operation is required when a cladding presents a condition B of degradation, a minor intervention when the degradation condition is C, and a total replacement when condition is D or E.

For NSC, the fixed costs (at year 0), the application zones, and the impacts of the various types of interventions are presented in Table 1. More specifically, these values mean, for example, that a cleaning operation in NSC has a cost of EUR 31.37/m², is applied in condition B, and improves the NSC's condition to A with a probability of 15%, leading to no significant improvement with a probability of 85%. The costs were adapted from the literature [50].

Table 1. Fixed costs, application zones, and impacts of the different maintenance activities.

Interventions	Cost (EUR/m²)	Application Zone	Impact of the Maintenance Activity (%)		
			P_A	P_B	P_C
Inspections	1.03	All	-	-	-
Cleaning operations	31.37	B	15.0	85.0	-
Minor interventions	68.80	C	0.0	80.4	19.6
Total replacement	149.51	D, E	100.0	-	-

3.3.3. Output of the Maintenance Model

The output of the maintenance model is given in terms of four parameters: service life, maintenance costs, efficiency index, and number of interventions over the time horizon.

Based on the literature, in this study, condition D defines the expected end of the service life (ESL) for NSC [39]. In the maintenance model, it is assumed that the ESL is reached when the probability of transition between conditions C and D is equal to 50% [23]. The maintenance costs correspond to the accumulated costs required, over the time horizon, t_h, to keep the NSC in operation (Equation (3)). These costs consider the costs related with inspections, $C_{inspection}$, and the other maintenance activities, $C_{maintenance}$. To consider future costs, a real discount rate, v, of 6% is considered [23].

$$C_{total} = \sum \frac{C_{inspection}}{(1+v)^t} + \sum \frac{C_{maintenance}}{(1+v)^t}, \tag{3}$$

The ability of maintenance strategy to maintain the NSC in a good condition is measured through the efficiency index (*EI*) (Equation (4)). The EI ranges between 0 and 1, and it is computed by the ratio between the area below the degradation curve with loss of performance, $\int S_w(t)\,dt$, and the area below the degradation curve when there is no degradation, $100 \cdot t_h$. The higher the *EI* value, the more efficient the maintenance strategy is over time [51].

$$EI = \frac{\int S_w(t)\, dt}{100 \times t_h},\qquad(4)$$

Finally, the number of total replacements corresponds to the average number of times that the cladding is totally replaced during the time horizon.

4. Results

In this study, the influence of the buildings' height on the degradation and maintenance of NSC is analysed. A time horizon of 150 years is considered in the several analyses performed. Furthermore, it is assumed that the NSC is in condition A at the beginning of the analysis (no visible degradation).

4.1. Degradation Condition of NSC According to the Façade's Height and the Environmental Exposure Conditions

As described in Equation (1), the severity of degradation index (and, consequently, the degradation condition) is estimated considering the area affected by the anomalies observed in a NSC.

Figure 3 shows the statistical analysis of the weighted area of the façade affected by visual anomalies according to the buildings' height. The main visual anomalies observed in the sample are colour change, damp stains, biological colonisation, and deposition of dirt or efflorescence (Figure 4). The results reveal that high buildings present higher areas affected by stains and by the deposition of biological agents. According to Neto and de Brito [52], these anomalies are mainly caused by wet–dry cycles and the action of water, by the presence of living organisms, and particles accumulation, higher buildings being more prone to this type of anomalies, as indicated by the sample.

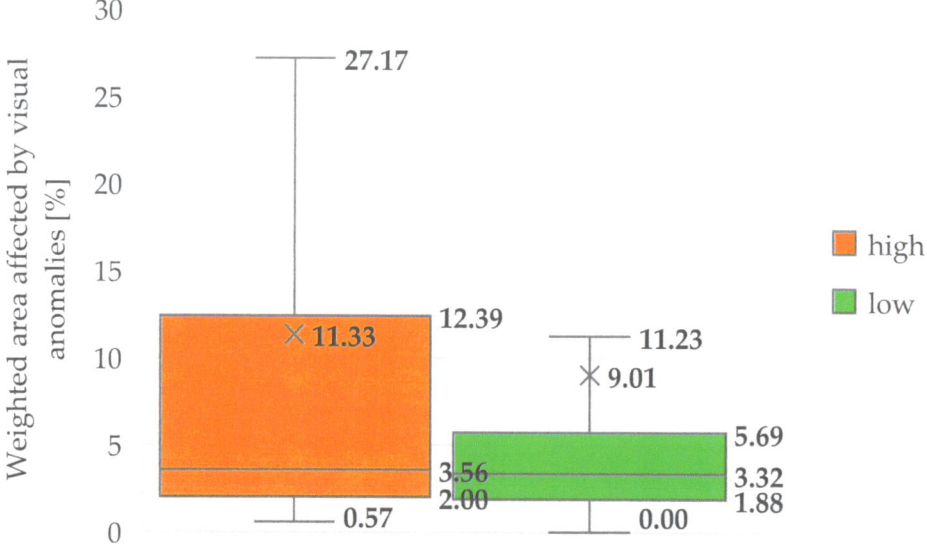

Figure 3. Boxplots of the weighted area of the façade affected by visual anomalies according to the buildings' height.

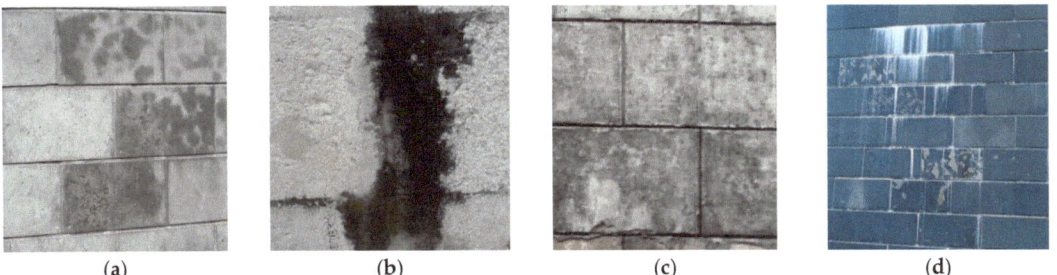

Figure 4. Illustrative examples of the visual anomalies observed in NSC: (**a**) damp stains; (**b**) biological colonisation; (**c**) dirt deposition; (**d**) efflorescence.

Concerning the anomalies related to the loss of integrity of NSC (loss, volume change, or degradation of the stone elements), the results reveal that these anomalies occur with a higher frequency in low buildings (Figures 5 and 6). These anomalies tend to be caused by chemical and biological actions, and the higher concentration of pollutants in the low buildings may justify these results [16]. On the other hand, physical actions, as impacts, and human actions can also promote these anomalies, and the lower parts of buildings are thus more susceptible to these actions.

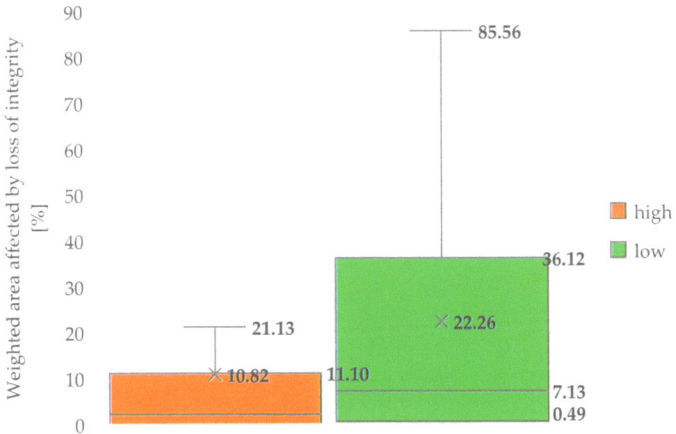

Figure 5. Boxplots of the weighted area of the façade affected by loss of integrity according to the buildings' height.

Figure 6. Illustrative examples of the loss of integrity anomalies observed in NSC located at the bottom wall of NSC façades.

Figure 7 presents a statistical analysis of the loss of adhesion anomalies according to the buildings' height and exposure to wind–rain action. For severe conditions of the combined action of wind and rain, high-rise buildings present higher areas affected by detachment, mainly due to the action of wet–dry cycles and thermal shocks. On the other hand, for a moderate exposure to wind–rain action, low buildings present higher areas affected by loss of adhesion anomalies. In this situation, these anomalies are mainly caused by other effects, such as excessive deformation of the substrate and structural-related movements of the walls, which are not directly related to the buildings' height.

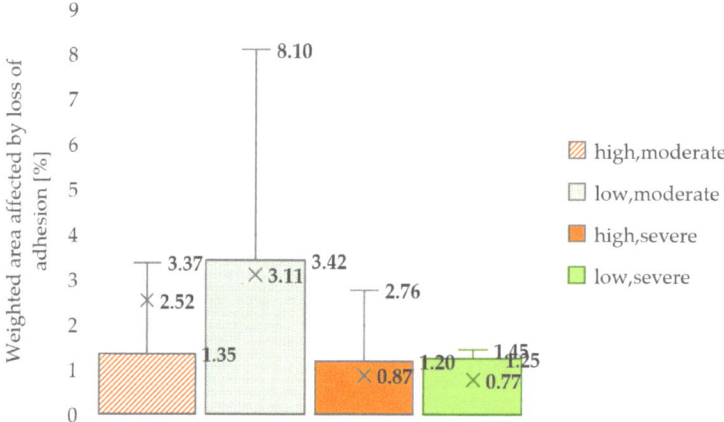

Figure 7. Boxplots of the weighted area of the façade affected by loss of adhesion anomalies according to the buildings' height and exposure to wind–rain action.

4.2. Probabilistic Analysis of the Degradation Process

To select the best probability distribution that describes the behaviour of the observed data, three probability distribution are analysed: exponential, Weibull, and lognormal. In addition, the parameters of the degradation process are also estimated through the Markov chains. Due to their wide application to model degradation processes [39,53–55], Markov chains are used to validate the degradation process in the Petri net maintenance model. In Table 2, the optimal parameters and the log likelihood value obtained for low and high buildings are compared, in terms of mean, T_i, and standard deviation, SD_i, of the permanence time in each degradation condition, with $i = \{A, B, C, D\}$.

Table 2. Comparison of the optimal parameters obtained for Markov chains and Petri net (exponential, Weibull, and lognormal) for low and high buildings.

Parameters		Low Buildings				High Buildings			
		Markov Chains	Exponential	Weibull	Lognormal	Markov Chains	Exponential	Weibull	Lognormal
Mean value (years)	T_A	5.4	5.6	4.6	4.9	6.0	5.0	4.2	6.5×10^3
	T_B	36.5	37.4	39.5	38.7	96.1	100.4	44.9	48.4
	T_C	81.7	77.1	26.2	29.0	111.1	129.8	16.8	18.6
	T_D	111.1	1.4×10^4	57.7	7.8×10^6	111.1	3.4×10^7	35.6	1.8×10^7
Standard deviation (years)	SD_A	5.4	5.6	4.4	5.8	6.0	5.0	19.5	9.3×10^{10}
	SD_B	36.5	37.4	12.4	14.5	96.1	100.4	7.5	11.6
	SD_C	81.7	77.1	2.1	14.5	111.1	129.8	0.6	0.4
	SD_D	111.1	1.4×10^4	3.2	4.9×10^7	111.1	3.36×10^7	1.8	1.4×10^8
$-\log L$			95.06	90.48	75.98	77.09	63.80	63.26	45.47	44.15

The validation of the degradation process in the Petri net maintenance model is carried out through the comparison exponential distribution and Markov chains results. For both heights, the values of the optimal parameters obtained through these two methodologies, for degradation conditions A, B, and C, are similar (Table 2). However, the differences observed in degradation condition D are already quite significant. The reason for this difference is related to a limitation of the database: it has no records in degradation condition E. The differences in the remaining degradation conditions occur due to sampling errors associated with the Monte Carlo simulation implemented in the Petri net degradation model. The above results can be confirmed in Figure 8. This figure presents the average degradation curves obtained for both methodologies and for heights. The curves are practically overlapped in degradation conditions A and B. In condition C ($8 < S_w \leq 20\%$), it is already possible to observe slight differences between the curves; but the differences from condition D ($20 < S_w \leq 45\%$) begin to be more pronounced. However, since it is assumed that the end of the service life is reached when the NSC reaches condition D, and there are no elements in condition E, it is considered that Petri Nets are adequate to describe the degradation process for both heights.

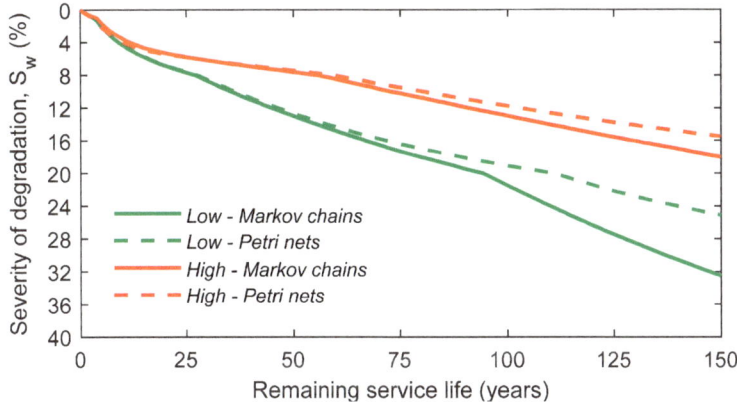

Figure 8. Comparison of the average degradation curves obtained for both models and heights.

After validation, the three probability distributions (exponential, Weibull, and lognormal) are compared to identify the distribution most suitable to describe the degradation process. By comparing the log likelihood values (Table 2), the results reveal that Weibull and lognormal distributions have a better fit to the historical data. These two probability distributions present the lowest log likelihood values for both heights. However, by analysing the optimal parameters, it is found that lognormal distribution has difficulties in modelling the permanence time in condition D for low buildings and in condition A and D for high buildings (Table 2). The values estimated are unrealistic. Therefore, based on these results, the Weibull distribution is selected as the more adequate distribution to describe the degradation process for both heights. In Figure 9, the average degradation curves obtained for the three probabilistic distributions and for both heights are compared. In this figure, the adequate fit of the Weibull distribution can be confirmed. According to the exponential and lognormal degradation curves, after 150 years, the severity of degradation index of the NSC is above 40% (i.e., condition E has not yet been reached). Since maintenance is not yet considered in the degradation curves, these two probability distributions reveal to be inadequate to describe the degradation process of NSC.

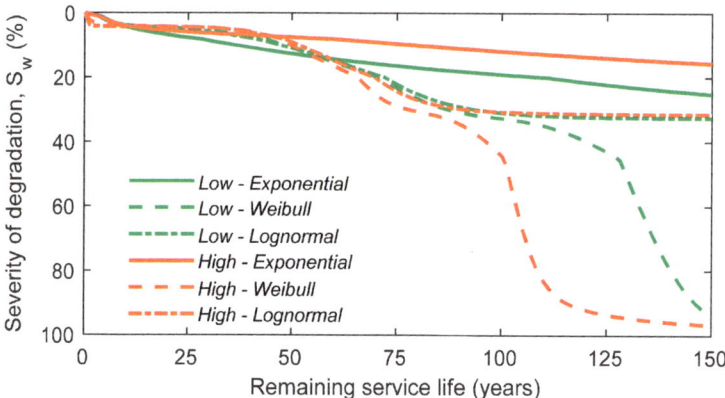

Figure 9. Comparison of the average degradation curves obtained for the three probabilistic distributions and for both heights.

Figure 10 presents the cumulative distribution functions (CDF) of the five degradation conditions for both heights computed with the Weibull distribution. The CDF allows evaluating the probability of the NSC moving from one condition to the next, the expected end of service life, and the permanence time of the NSC in each degradation condition. The ESL is identified in Figure 10 for both heights. For low buildings, an average service life of 71 years is obtained, and for high-rise buildings, that value is 65 years.

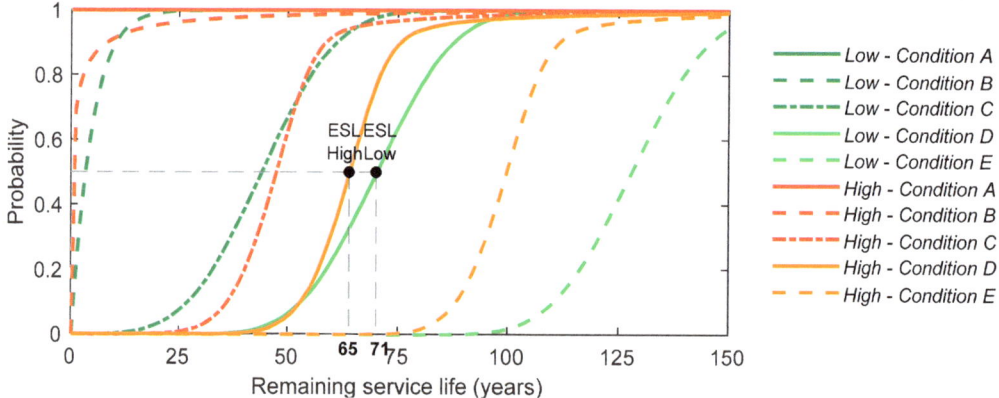

Figure 10. Cumulative distribution functions of the five degradation conditions over time horizon for both heights.

4.3. Comparison of the Different Maintenance Strategies

To introduce the impact of maintenance actions in low- and high-rise buildings, three maintenance strategies are analysed: (i) total replacement only; (ii) combination of minor interventions and total replacement; and (iii) combination of cleaning operations, minor interventions, and total replacement. These three maintenance strategies were defined based on previous works and on expert judgement [17,23,51]. For both heights, a periodicity between inspections of 5 years is considered.

In Figures 11 and 12, and Table 3, for both heights, the different parameters estimated for each maintenance strategy are compared. Furthermore, these results are compared with the values obtained for the complete sample of NSC. More details about the results of the complete sample can be found in Ferreira et al. [23,51].

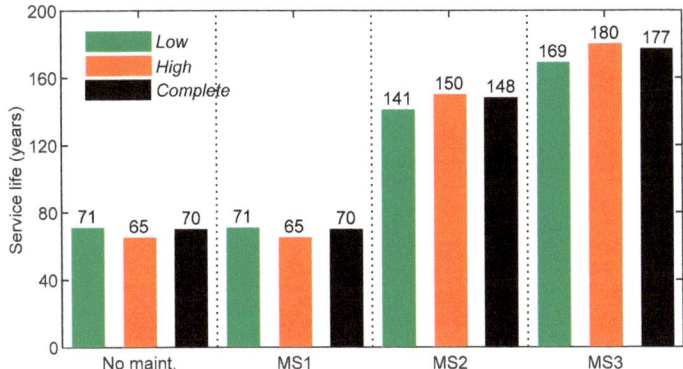

Figure 11. Comparison of the service life for both heights and for the complete sample.

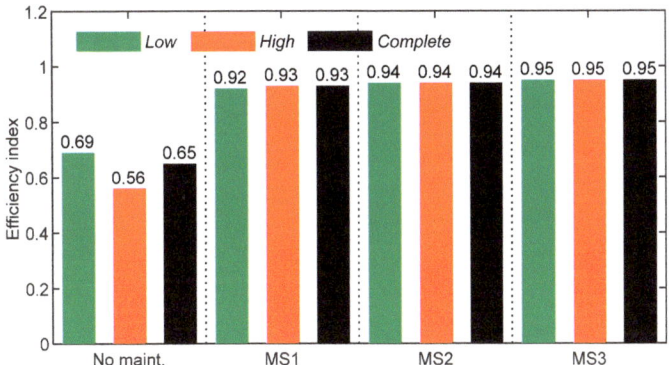

Figure 12. Comparison of the efficiency index for both heights and for the complete sample.

Table 3. Comparison of the total number of replacements and maintenance costs for both heights and for the complete sample.

Maintenance Strategy	Case Study	Maintenance Activity			Cost (EUR/m^2)
		Cleaning Operation	**Minor Intervention**	**Total Replacement**	
MS1	Low	-	-	1.7	6.01
	High	-	-	1.9	6.67
	Complete	-	-	1.7	5.98
MS2	Low	-	2.2	0.6	10.73
	High	-	2.1	0.5	8.40
	Complete	-	2.1	0.5	9.10
MS3	Low	5.7	2.0	0.3	45.85
	High	5.6	2.0	0.3	45.04
	Complete	5.6	2.0	0.3	44.65

Figure 11 compares the results of service life. In a simple way, they reveal that using preventive maintenance activities, such as cleaning operations and minor interventions, contributes to increasing the service life of NSC. These results are visible for both heights and in the complete sample. For the situations with maintenance (MS1, MS2, and MS3) and for the situation with no maintenance, the ESL ends when condition D is achieved. However, in MS1, MS2, and MS3, when condition D is achieved, the NSC is completely replaced, while in the situation with no maintenance, the NSC continues to degrade. This is the reason why the service lives obtained for MS1 and for the situation with no maintenance are the same. Since MS1 only includes total maintenance, the NSC degrades continuously until condition D without any maintenance being performed. The same behaviour can be observed for the situation with no maintenance. The difference between both situations is that in MS1, a total replacement is carried out when the degradation condition is D, while in situation with no maintenance, maintenance activities are not carried out.

Furthermore, as maintenance strategies become more complex (from MS1 to MS3), along with the increase in service life, the efficiency index also increases (Figure 12). This observation is valid for both heights and for the complete sample. This result means that using preventive maintenance activities increases the probability of the NSC remaining in the most favourable degradation conditions (such as conditions A and B) for longer. Consequently, the aesthetic appearance of the NSC is better during the time horizon.

On the other hand, the increase in complexity of the maintenance strategy translates into an increase in the global number of interventions and maintenance costs (Table 3), as expected. However, by closely analysing Table 3, it is found that, although the global number of interventions increased, the number of replacements was substantially reduced. This result is relevant because the replacement of all NSC is the most time-consuming maintenance activity, and reducing that number over the time horizon allows increasing the users' satisfaction. Regarding costs, there is a close relationship with the number of interventions, i.e., the increase in the number of interventions has a greater impact on the maintenance costs.

5. Discussion

Through a simple analysis of the results obtained with no maintenance, it is found that they are coherent with the studies in the literature [12,39]. By comparing the service life of NSC (Figure 10) for both heights, the results reveal that NSCs are more durable in short buildings than in tall buildings. These results show the environmental loads that tall buildings are subjected to (such as higher temperature [33], wind-driven rain intensity [30], and wind loads [24]) contribute to accelerating the degradation process of NSC.

From the results considering maintenance (Figures 11 and 12, and Table 3), it is understood that the characteristics of NSC's maintenance continue to depend on height. By starting the analysis with MS1 results, in general, the parameters estimated through the complete sample can be used to describe the behaviour in low buildings. However, the differences between the complete sample and the sample of the high-rise buildings are more significant but expected. High-rise buildings have a lower service life. Consequently, compared to low buildings, the maintenance activities of total replacement will occur sooner. Over time, this implies that the number of interventions and the maintenance cost will be higher. In terms of the efficiency index, since the values are very close, the only possible conclusion to draw is that the efficiency of MS1 is similar for both heights, although the impact of the maintenance activities is higher for higher buildings.

The results of MS2 may seem a little counter intuitive. They reveal that the service life for high-rise buildings is longer than for low buildings. This result is justified by the permanence time in condition B, T_B (Table 2). MS2 includes minor interventions and total replacement activities. Minor interventions have condition C as trigger, while for total replacement, it is condition D and E. Table 2 shows that the permanence time in the most favourable conditions (A and B) for high buildings is, approximately, 5 years longer. Consequently, minor interventions will occur earlier in low buildings, which implies a slightly higher number of interventions and maintenance costs. Another reason is the fact that the impact of minor interventions is the same for both heights (Table 1). Therefore, since they allow postponing the total replacement of the NSC for longer periods, minor interventions are more efficient in high-rise buildings. In terms of efficiency index, the values are again similar for both heights. For MS3, similar observations can be made. Finally, for MS2 and MS3, if the results of the complete sample are compared with those of low- and high-rise buildings, it can be observed that the parameters of the complete sample are more adequate to describe the behaviour in high-rise buildings.

6. Conclusions

In this study, the influence of the buildings' height on the degradation of natural stone claddings was assessed through a condition-based maintenance model. The literature review shows that claddings at the top of buildings are more prone to degradation. These elements are more exposed to wind loads, temperature variations, and wind-driven rain action. On the other hand, claddings at the bottom of the buildings are more subjected to pollutant concentrations. From a statistical analysis of the anomalies observed in the NSC database, these results are confirmed. The anomalies presented in high-rise buildings are mainly caused by wet–dry cycles and the action of water, while in low buildings, they are caused by chemical and biological actions. Based on that, and in order to understand whether the degradation curves of tall and short buildings are statistically different, the degradation process in these buildings was analysed. The results confirm that NSCs are more durable in low buildings than in high-rise buildings. The higher exposure to environmental loads of the tall buildings increases their degradation process. Later, the impact of these differences on the maintenance requirements was assessed. For that purpose, three maintenance strategies were analysed. This revealed a strong influence on service life. Although high-rise buildings present a lower service life when maintenance is not carried out, when associated with maintenance activities, their service lives are longer than those obtained for low buildings. This demonstrates that the degradation pattern of high- and low-rise buildings is different, and the use of the complete sample can introduce considerable uncertainties in modelling the degradation pattern of stone claddings. The use of the adequate degradation curve is essential for the correct modelling of the claddings' behaviour. Furthermore, no assumptions should be made regarding the behaviour of claddings based only on their degradation curve, especially when considering maintenance activities.

Since the different types of stone have different degradation patterns, strengths, and vulnerabilities, to increase the reliability of the results, degradation curves for the different types of stone should be used. However, this analysis is outside the scope of the present study, and as the sample is being complemented, more detailed analyses, such as this one, will be carried out.

Author Contributions: Conceptualisation, C.F., A.S. and J.d.B.; methodology, C.F. and A.S.; software, C.F.; validation, C.F. and A.S.; formal analysis, C.F. and A.S.; investigation, C.F. and A.S.; resources, C.F. and A.S.; data curation, A.S.; writing—original draft preparation, C.F. and A.S.; writing—review and editing, A.S. and J.d.B. All authors have read and agreed to the published version of the manuscript.

Funding: This research was funded by FCT (Portuguese Foundation for Science and Technology) through the project BestMaintenance-LowerRisks (PTDC/ECI-CON/29286/2017) and through research unit CERIS (UIDB/04625/2020).

Institutional Review Board Statement: Not applicable.

Informed Consent Statement: Not applicable.

Data Availability Statement: The data presented in this study are available on request from the corresponding author.

Acknowledgments: The authors gratefully acknowledge the support of CERIS from Instituto Superior Técnico, Universidade de Lisboa.

Conflicts of Interest: The authors declare no conflict of interest.

References

1. Sandak, A.; Sandak, J.; Brzezicki, M.; Kutnar, A. *Bio-Based Building Skin*; Springer International Publishing: Singapore, 2019.
2. Freitas, S.S.; de Freitas, V.P. Cracks on ETICS along thermal insulation joints: Case study and a pathology catalogue. *Struct. Surv.* **2016**, *34*, 57–72. [CrossRef]
3. Phillipson, M.C.; Emmanuel, R.; Baker, P.H. The durability of building materials under a changing climate. *Wiley Interdisc. Rev. Clim. Chang.* **2016**, *7*, 590–599. [CrossRef]

4. Silva, C.M.; Flores-Colen, I.; Coelho, A. Green roofs in Mediterranean areas—Survey and maintenance planning. *Build. Environ.* **2015**, *94*, 131–143. [CrossRef]
5. Silva, A.; de Brito, J.; Thomsen, A.; Straub, A.; Prieto, A.J.; Lacasse, M.A. Causal effects between criteria that establish the end of service life of buildings and components. *Buildings* **2022**, *12*, 88.
6. Silva, A.; de Brito, J. Service life of building envelopes: A critical literature review. *J. Build. Eng.* **2021**, *44*, 102646. [CrossRef]
7. Sun Moon, K. Dynamic interrelationship between the evolution of structural systems and façade design in tall buildings: From the home insurance building in Chicago to the present. *Int. J. High-Rise Build.* **2018**, *30*, 1–16.
8. Logan, J.M.; Hastedt, M.; Lehnert, D.; Denton, M. A case study of the properties of marble as building veneer. *Int. J. Rock Mech. Min. Sci. Geomech. Abstr.* **1993**, *7*, 1531–1537. [CrossRef]
9. Rudnicki, J.W. Geomechanics. *Int. J. Solids Struct.* **2000**, *37*, 349–358. [CrossRef]
10. Grelk, B.; Christiansen, C.; Schouenborg, B.; Malaga, K. Durability of marble cladding—A comprehensive literature review. *J. ASTM Int.* **2006**, *4*, 1–19.
11. Loughran, P. *Failed Stone: Problems and Solutions with Concrete and Masonry*; Birkhäuser: Basel, Switzerland, 2006.
12. Westberg, K.; Norén, J.; Kus, H. On using available environmental data in service life estimations. *Build. Res. Inf.* **2001**, *29*, 428–439. [CrossRef]
13. Newlin, J.; Jimenez, G.A.; Hester, D.; Blank, L.M. Thin marble facades: History, evaluation, and maintenance. In Proceedings of the 2010 Structure Congress, Orlando, FL, USA, 12–15 May 2010.
14. Straube, J.F.; Burnett, E.F.P. Simplified prediction of driving rain on buildings. In Proceedings of the International Building Physics Conference, Eindhoven, The Netherlands, 18–21 September 2000.
15. Moghtadernejad, S.; Mirza, M.S.; Chouinard, L.E. Facade design stages: Issues and considerations. *J. Archit. Eng.* **2019**, *25*, 04018033. [CrossRef]
16. Fu, X.; Liu, J.; Ban-Weiss, G.A.; Zhang, J.; Huang, X.; Ouyang, B.; Popoola, O.; Tao, S. Effects of canyon geometry on the distribution of traffic-related air pollution in a large urban area: Implications of a multi-canyon air pollution dispersion model. *Atmos. Environ.* **2017**, *165*, 111–121. [CrossRef]
17. Ferreira, C.; Neves, L.C.; Silva, A.; de Brito, J. Stochastic maintenance models for ceramic claddings. *Struct. Infrastruct. Eng.* **2020**, *16*, 247–265. [CrossRef]
18. Khalid, E.I.; Abdullah, S.; Hanafi, M.H.; Said, S.Y.; Hasim, M.S. The consideration of building maintenance at design stage in public buildings: The current scenario in Malaysia. *Facilities* **2019**, *37*, 942–960. [CrossRef]
19. British Standards Institution. *Code of Practice for the Design and Installation of Natural Stone Cladding and Lining—Part 1: General*; Technical Report No. 8298-1; British Standards Institution (BSI): London, UK, 2010.
20. Farahani, A.; Wallbaum, H.; Dalenbäck, J.O. Optimized maintenance and renovation scheduling in multifamily buildings—A systematic approach based on condition state and life cycle cost of building components. *Constr. Manag. Econ.* **2019**, *37*, 139–155. [CrossRef]
21. Ruparathna, R.; Hewage, K.; Sadiq, R. Multi-period maintenance planning for public buildings: A risk based approach for climate conscious operation. *J. Clean. Prod.* **2018**, *170*, 1338–1353. [CrossRef]
22. Barrelas, J.; Dias, I.S.; Silva, A.; de Brito, J.; Flores-Colen, I.; Tadeu, A. Impact of Environmental Exposure on the Service Life of Façade Claddings—A Statistical Analysis. *Buildings* **2021**, *11*, 615. [CrossRef]
23. Ferreira, C.; Barrelas, J.; Silva, A.; de Brito, J.; Dias, I.S.; Flores-Colen, I. Impact of Environmental Exposure Conditions on the Maintenance of Facades' Claddings. *Buildings* **2021**, *11*, 138. [CrossRef]
24. Elshaer, A.; Gairola, A.; Adamek, K.; Bitsuamlak, G. Variations in wind load on tall buildings due to urban development. *Sustain. Cities Soc.* **2017**, *34*, 264–277. [CrossRef]
25. Azimi, P.; Zhao, H.; Fazli, T.; Zhao, D.; Faramarzi, A.; Leung, L.; Stephens, B. Pilot study of the vertical variations in outdoor pollutant concentrations and environmental conditions along the height of a tall building. *Build. Environ.* **2018**, *138*, 124–134. [CrossRef]
26. Makhelouf, A. Impact assessment of the construction of tall buildings in a big town on the urban climate and the air pollution. *E3 J. Environ. Res. Manag.* **2012**, *3*, 64–74.
27. Villena, G.; Kleffmann, J.; Kurtenbach, R.; Wiesen, P.; Lissi, E.; Rubio, M.A.; Croxatto, G.; Rappenglück, B. Vertical gradients of HONO, NOx and O_3 in Santiago de Chile. *Atmos. Environ.* **2011**, *45*, 3867–3873. [CrossRef]
28. Baedecker, P.A.; Reddy, M.M.; Reimann, K.J.; Sciammarella, C.A. Effects of acidic deposition on the erosion of carbonate stone—Experimental results from the US National Acid Precipitation Assessment Program (NAPAP). *Atmos. Environ. B Urban Atmos.* **1992**, *26*, 147–158. [CrossRef]
29. Haneef, S.J.; Johnson, J.B.; Dickinson, C.; Thompson, G.E.; Wood, G.C. Effect of dry deposition of NOx and SO_2 gaseous pollutants on the degradation of calcareous building stones. *Atmos. Environ. A Gen. Top.* **1992**, *26*, 2963–2974. [CrossRef]
30. Blocken, B.; Dezsö, G.; van Beeck, J.P.A.J.; Carmeliet, J. Comparison of calculation models for wind-driven rain deposition on building facades. *Atmos. Environ.* **2010**, *44*, 1714–1725. [CrossRef]
31. Ge, H.; Nath, U.D.; Chiu, V. Field measurements of wind-driven rain on mid-and high-rise buildings in three Canadian regions. *Build. Environ.* **2017**, *116*, 228–245. [CrossRef]
32. Singh, A.; Agrawal, M. Acid rain and its ecological consequences. *J. Environ. Biol.* **2007**, *29*, 15.

33. Charisi, S.; Thiis, T.K.; Stefansson, P.; Burud, I. Prediction model of microclimatic surface conditions on building façades. *Build. Environ.* **2018**, *128*, 46–54. [CrossRef]
34. Ito, W.H.; Scussiato, T.; Vagnon, F.; Ferrero, A.M.; Migliazza, M.R.; Ramis, J.; de Queiroz, P.I.B. On the thermal stresses due to weathering in natural stones. *Appl. Sci.* **2021**, *11*, 1188. [CrossRef]
35. Blumthaler, M.; Ambach, W.; Ellinger, R. Increase in solar UV radiation with altitude. *J. Photochem. Photobiol. B Biol.* **1997**, *39*, 130–134. [CrossRef]
36. Careddu, N.; Marras, G. The effects of solar UV radiation on the gloss values of polished stone surfaces. *Constr. Build. Mater.* **2013**, *49*, 828–834. [CrossRef]
37. Määttä, J.; Piispanen, M.; Kymäläinen, H.R.; Uusi-Rauva, A.; Hurme, K.R.; Areva, S.; Sjöberg, A.-M.; Hupa, L. Effects of UV-radiation on the cleanability of titanium dioxide-coated glazed ceramic tiles. *J. Eur. Ceram. Soc.* **2007**, *27*, 4569–4574. [CrossRef]
38. International Organization for Standardization. *Buildings and Constructed Assets—Service Life Planning—Part 1: General Principles and Framework*; Technical Report No. 15686-1; International Organization for Standardization: Geneva, Switzerland, 2011.
39. Silva, A.; de Brito, J.; Gaspar, P.L. *Methodologies for Service Life Prediction of Buildings: With a Focus on Façade Claddings*; Springer International Publishing: Zurich, Switzerland, 2016.
40. Thai-Ker, L.; Chung-Wan, W. Challenges of external wall tiling in Singapore. In Proceedings of the Qualicer 2006: IX World Congress on Ceramic Tile Quality, Castellón, Spain, 12–15 February 2006.
41. Farmer, M.C.; Lyons, S.P. Stone cladding failure: The cause and consequences. In Proceedings of the Second Forensic Engineering Congress, San Juan, Puerto Rico, 21–23 May 2000.
42. Sousa, H.; Sousa, R. Durability of stone cladding in buildings: A case study of marble slabs affected by bowing. *Building* **2019**, *9*, 229. [CrossRef]
43. Huang, B.; Lu, W.; Günay, S. Shaking table tests of granite cladding with dowel pin connection. *Bull. Earthq. Eng.* **2020**, *18*, 1081–1105. [CrossRef]
44. Huang, B.; Lu, W.; Mosalam, K.M. Shaking table testing of granite cladding with undercut bolt anchorage. *Eng. Struct.* **2018**, *171*, 488–499. [CrossRef]
45. Shohet, I.M.; Puterman, M.; Gilboa, E. Deterioration patterns of building cladding components for maintenance management. *Constr. Manag. Econ.* **2002**, *20*, 305–314. [CrossRef]
46. Veritas, B. *Gestion Technique du Patrimoine—Réhabilitation et Maintenance, Guide Veritas du Bâtiment*; Bureau Veritas: Paris, France, 1993.
47. Gaspar, P.; De Brito, J. Service life estimation of cement-rendered facades. *Build. Res. Inf.* **2008**, *36*, 44–55. [CrossRef]
48. Kalbfleisch, J.D.; Lawless, J.F. The analysis of panel data under a Markov assumption. *J. Am. Stat. Assoc.* **1985**, *80*, 863–871. [CrossRef]
49. Ferreira, C.; Silva, A.; de Brito, J.; Dias, I.S.; Flores-Colen, I. The impact of imperfect maintenance actions on the degradation of buildings' envelope components. *J. Build. Eng.* **2021**, *33*, 101571. [CrossRef]
50. CYPE Price Generator. Available online: http://www.geradordeprecos.info/ (accessed on 14 March 2019).
51. Ferreira, C.; Silva, A.; de Brito, J.; Dias, I.S.; Flores-Colen, I. Definition of a condition-based model for natural stone claddings. *J. Build. Eng.* **2021**, *33*, 101643. [CrossRef]
52. Neto, N.; de Brito, J. Inspection and defect diagnosis system for natural stone cladding. *J. Mater. Civ. Eng.* **2011**, *23*, 1433–1443. [CrossRef]
53. Butt, A.A.; Shahin, M.Y.; Feighan, K.J.; Carpenter, S.H. Pavement performance prediction model using the Markov process. *Transp. Res. Rec.* **1987**, *1123*, 12–19.
54. Hawk, H.; Small, E.P. The BRIDGIT bridge management system. *Struct. Eng. Int.* **1998**, *8*, 309–314. [CrossRef]
55. Thompson, P.D.; Small, E.P.; Johnson, M.; Marshall, A.R. The Pontis bridge management system. *Struct. Eng. Int.* **1998**, *8*, 303–308. [CrossRef]

infrastructures

Article

Sustainability in the Civil Construction Sector Supported by Industry 4.0 Technologies: Challenges and Opportunities †

Jacqueline de Almeida Barbosa Franco [1,*], Ana Mariele Domingues [1], Nelson de Almeida Africano [2], Rafael Mattos Deus [1,2,3] and Rosane Aparecida Gomes Battistelle [2]

[1]   Department of Production Engineering, School of Engineering, São Paulo State University (UNESP), Av. Engenheiro Luiz Edmundo Carrijo Coube 14-01, Bauru 17033-360, SP, Brazil; ana.m.domingues@unesp.br (A.M.D.); rafaelmdeus@gmail.com (R.M.D.)
[2]   Department of Civil and Environmental Engineering, School of Engineering, São Paulo State University (UNESP), Av. Engenheiro Luiz Edmundo Carrijo Coube 14-01, Bauru 17033-360, SP, Brazil; nelson.africano@unesp.br (N.d.A.A.); rosane.battistelle@unesp.br (R.A.G.B.)
[3]   Faculdades Integradas de Jahu (FIJ), Street Tenente Navarro, 642, Jaú 17207-310, SP, Brazil
*   Correspondence: jacqueline.barbosa@unesp.br; Tel.: +55-149-9114-7804
†   This paper is an extended version of our paper published in Franco, J.; Domingues, A.M.; Africano, N.; Deus, R.; Battistelle, R. Opportunities for Civil Construction Growth Through Industry 4.0. In Proceedings of the First International Conference on Construction, Energy, Environment and Sustainability (CEES 2021) on the Topic of Sustainable Construction Materials and Technologies, Coimbra, Portugal, October 2021; pp. 1–15. It has been updated for publishing in the journal.

Abstract: The civil construction sector is under pressure to make construction processes more sustainable, that is, aligned with economic, social, and environmental sustainability. Thus, the research question considers: How do Industry 4.0 Technologies help civil construction face challenges and identify new opportunities to become sustainable? The general objective of this work is to offer a current overview of publications that associate the civil construction sector; Industry 4.0 Technologies and sustainability, and identify the challenges and opportunities of the Industry 4.0 Technologies set to contribute to sustainability achievement. The research method was a bibliographic review combined with bibliometric analysis in SCOPUS databases. The results show that civil construction faces the challenge of reducing the consumption of natural resources, ensuring safe work, and optimizing processes, especially handwork. However, the insertion of Industry 4.0 Technologies into civil construction has allowed sensors, robots, modelling and simulation systems, artificial intelligence, and drones to have their productivity, efficiency, safety, strategic and environmental management enhanced. Furthermore, Industry 4.0 Technologies can contribute to civil construction through innovative, sustainable, and technological solutions focused on the flow of work, which can provide growth through the balance of costs/benefits in the management of projects and works. Thus, it is expected that this article will contribute to discussions around the possibility of construction becoming sustainable with the support of Industry 4.0 Technologies.

Keywords: technologies 4.0; sustainable construction; construction industry challenges; construction industry opportunities; sustainability; construction 4.0; intelligent construction; sustainability; industry 4.0; sustainable construction processes

1. Introduction

According to Lezoche et al. [1], the historical evolution of industry is marked by four phases, the first of which is referred to as the First Industrial Revolution, with the advent of steam machines and the use of coal as fuel. The Second Industrial Revolution stood out for the emergence of electric power and serial production lines. The Third Industrial Revolution provided automation of machines, computers, and the Internet. Currently, the Fourth Industrial Revolution highlights the most abrupt change, where the concept

Infrastructures 2022, 7, 43. https://doi.org/10.3390/infrastructures7030043

https://www.mdpi.com/journal/infrastructures

of digitalization and the virtual world are responsible for technologically innovating the production processes. Figure 1 shows the evolutionary phases of the industry, from 1.0 to 4.0.

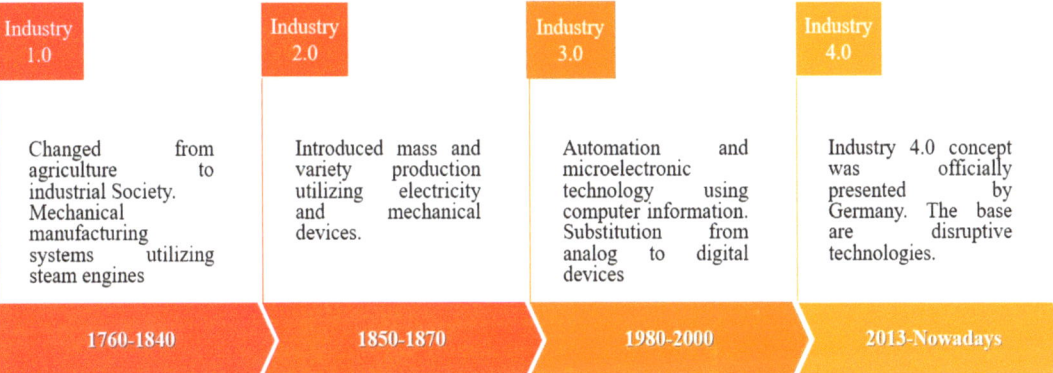

Figure 1. The Evolution from Industry 1.0 to 4.0. Source: Adapted from [2,3].

Industry 4.0 appeared for the first time in 2011 in Germany and is referred to as the fourth industrial revolution [4]. This concept aims to integrate technologies such as the Internet of Things (IoT), Industrial Internet of Things (IoT), Intelligent Objects, Big Data, Cloud Computing, Artificial Intelligence, 3D printing, Sensors, Actuators, Virtual and Augmented Reality [2,5] to create an environment of digital and intelligent manufacturing. Thus, the goal is to use these technologies to generate efficiency and optimize production processes continuously and upwardly by generating greater productivity, quality, and customization. The rapid advance in technological innovations in sensors, devices, information networks, and machine learning has helped robotics and automation progress rapidly, bringing improvements in several productive sectors [5]. In early 2020, during the COVID-19 pandemic [6] in Brazil, according to Zhou et al. [7] the use of technologies has shown its importance using Big Data in Geographic Information Systems (G.I.S.). Mainly regarding rapid visualization of information on epidemics, tracking of confirmed cases, transmission forecast, balance and management of supply and demand of material resources [8] and the use of artificial intelligence (A.I.) to identify the transmissibility of the virus, populations at risk, and thus the ability to establish the infection cycle and suggest effective and preventative control measures [9].

All productive sectors are under pressure to develop their activities sustainably, based on environmental, social, and economic pillars, to promote the future of current and new generations. The continuous growth of cities and society elicits various concerns for improved development and management of the multifaceted urban systems, including resilience and sustainability [10]. Thus, considering these new scenarios and paradigms, the civil construction sector stands out, which is still regarded as unsustainable when employing archaic processes and activities, collection procedures, data recording, less automated and incomplete monitoring that results in waste of materials and exacerbated use of natural resources, beyond the unavailability of qualified labor [11].

However, sustainability was defined in the World Commission on Environment and Development's 1987 Brundtland report 'Our Common Future' as 'development that meets the needs of the present without compromising the ability of future generations to meet their own needs' [12]. Since then, industries and business have also become part of the search for the sustainability of operations so that they can remain profitable and positively impact society and with concern about the environment's ability to regenerate, thus, the American businessman Elkington, defines the Triple Bottom Line (TBL) concept determining three pillars: economic, social and environmental with a focus on the business perspective [13]. The implementation of the Sustainable Development Goals (S.D.G.s) since 2016, is strengthened through the S.D.G. 9—Industry, Innovation and Infrastructure, civil construction to actively participate in this universal call, in search of sustainable development, which contributes to a change in business and construction models supported by people and technologies [14]. This new model supported by construction, society and environment contributes to the attainment of the seventeen goals proposed by the U.N., since it affects the entire supply chain and brings improvements in resource efficiency, error elimination, reduction in waste of materials, energy and transportation (S.D.G. 7; S.D.G. 14; S.D.G. 15), as well as help achieve poverty eradication (S.D.G. 1) and zero hunger (S.D.G. 2), good health and well-being (S.D.G. 3), gender equality (S.D.G. 5), clean water and sanitation (S.D.G. 6), decent work and economic growth (S.D.G. 8), reduction inequalities (S.D.G. 10), sustainable cities and communities (S.D.G. 11), responsible consumption and production (S.D.G. 12) and direct actions against global climate change (S.D.G. 13) [11].

Some review articles related to the Civil Construction and Industry 4.0 Technologies were published. However, the review scopes are concentrated in just one industry technology 4.0, such as patterns and trends IoT by Ghosh et al. [15], extrusion-based additive manufacturing with 3D printing analyzed by Valente et al. [16], Sepasgozar [17] studied the Digital Twin application to expedite a smart and sustainable built environment, Darko et al. [18] explored Building information modelling (BIM) and appointed the survey and future needs, and Zhang et al. [19] identified Virtual reality applications for the built environment. Furthermore, the implications for the sustainability pillars are not the main research focus, thus there is a gap regarding the Industry 4.0 Technologies main contributions to the Triple Bottom Line. Although these studies contributed to the state of the art in Civil Construction and Industry 4.0 Technologies, this paper adds to these previous reviews the systematization of the Industry 4.0 Technologies set that can help us to face current civil construction challenges and contribute to the identification of opportunities through practical examples in order to permit the sector to achieve sustainability.

Along these lines, discussions aimed at improving production patterns and using resources through new approaches, practices and innovative technologies that enable the construction sector to develop in a structured and sustainable way become essential. Construction 4.0 presents a promising initiative that helps other industrial sectors improve productivity indicators by optimizing operational processes using innovative technologies. Thus, the general objective of this work is to offer a current overview of publications that associate the civil construction sector; Industry 4.0 Technologies and sustainability and identify the challenges and opportunities of Industry 4.0 Technologies set to contribute to sustainability achievement. After this introduction, the paper is structured into five additional sections. Section 2 presents the literature review. Section 3 presents the research methodology. Section 4 presents the bibliometric results. Section 5 presents the discussion and systematizes the challenges and opportunities through a table and, finally, Section 6 presents the final considerations.

2. Literature Review

Construction 4.0 is the application of the concepts of Industry 4.0 in the construction sector, that is, the application of digital technologies and processes adapted to the construction environment [20]. Construction represents one of the largest industries in the world, which contributes to around 13 percent of the global gross domestic product (GDP) [16]. In Brazil, the forecast of the civil construction sector's gross domestic product (GDP) is expected to increase by over 22 percent until 2025 [21]. However, this sector is responsible for the use of scarce natural resources [15], exacerbation of fossil energy source use even considering its limitation and delivery capacity [22]; increasing greenhouse gas emissions and global warming at large [23], energy consumption [17] generation of big quantities of solid wastes which are difficult to apply to waste management [24], and low use of technologies [25].

An abundance of research activity has been conducted to optimize civil construction utilizing Industry 4.0 Technologies, but review studies available on the topics are limited in terms of examples of using technologies and their final applications, and, mainly, in terms of the implications for the sustainability of the construction industry. Relevant studies review the use of only one technology in construction, such as IoT [15], 3D printing [26–28] and Virtual and Augmented Reality [19,27]. Others have reviewed a joint application of technologies such as BIM and IoT [17], Blockchain and BIM together in disaster recovery of buildings [29], or application of BIM to applications under construction in forum sites [30]. None of these studies present detailed discussions on the environmental, social and economic impacts of adopting new technologies in operations.

Nevertheless, some studies have comprehensively revealed the application of Industry 4.0 Technologies in construction [31–33]. However, these studies also have a limited scope in terms of Triple Bottom Line contemplate [33] which reviews the implications of adopting smart technologies for sustainable construction and the positive consequences for health, safety, and the environment. These analyses are restricted to operations carried out on site, that is, while the construction project is being carried out.

Thus, it is noted that the implications for sustainability are not the main target of the reviews conducted so far. Despite the growing interest in the application of Industry 4.0 Technologies in construction, there is a knowledge gap regarding contributions to the sustainability dimensions of the adoption of such technologies in the construction production chain [34]. The researchers are more focused on the technical aspects of [31]. Environmental, social, socio-cultural and ethical issues are yet under explored in research relating to the adoption of Industry 4.0 Technologies in civil construction [32].

3. Research Methodology

To understand state of the art, identify knowledge and possible research gaps, the research method employed was an exploratory bibliographic review combined with bibliometric analysis [35]. To ensure transparency and traceability of the results reported here, the Preferred Reporting Items for Systematic Reviews and Meta-Analysis (PRISMA) protocol [36,37] was implemented to conduct the research. Figure 2 presents the diagram with the literature review flow; the diagram model was adapted from [38]. The research was carried out on the SCOPUS database in February 2022, using the title, abstract and keyword options, applying the following query and boolean operators:

(1) "CONSTRUCTION" OR "CIVIL CONSTRUCTION" OR "CONSTRUCTION TECHNOLOGY" OR "CONSTRUCTION 4.0" OR "INTELLIGENT CONSTRUCTION" AND;

(2) "TECHNOLOGIES 4.0" OR "INDUSTRIES 4.0" OR "INDUSTRY 4. 0" OR "THE 4th INDUSTRIAL REVOLUTION" OR "THE FOURTH INDUSTRIAL REVOLUTION" AND;

(3) "SUSTAINABLE" OR "SUSTAINABILITY" OR "TRIPLE BOTTOM LINE" OR "SUSTAINABLE DEVELOPMENT".

The approach has a qualitative character since it aims to deepen the knowledge on how the fourth industrial revolution can contribute to advances in civil construction. Table 1 show the inclusion and exclusion criteria applied on SCOPUS database.

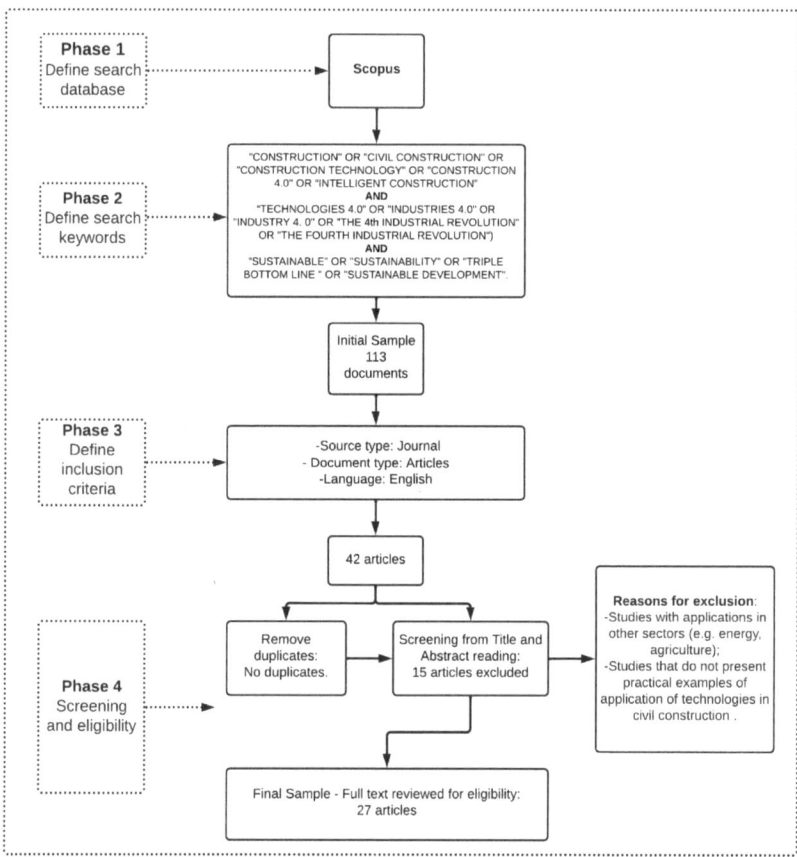

Figure 2. Literature review process flow diagram. Source: Adapted from [38].

Table 1. Inclusion and Exclusion Criteria.

Search Criteria	Inclusion Criteria	Exclusion Criteria
Database	SCOPUS	Other databases
Topic	Title, abstract and keywords	Words that were not present in the title, abstract and keywords
Publication Period	Without restriction	Without restriction
Document Type	Articles	Other documents
Publication Stage	Without restriction	Without restriction
Source	Journals	Books and Conferences
Language	English	Other languages

4. Results

The search returned 113 publications, and after applying the filter, applications resulted in 42 articles and after reading and reviewing, 27 articles fell within the research, which were submitted to a systematic and bibliometric analysis through the VOSviewer software. There has been an evolution of the subject over the last few years, but few publications on the SCOPUS platform have addressed the specific keywords. The search covers articles published in journals peer reviewed between the years 2017 and 2022, before that, there were only two papers published in 2016 at conferences proceedings. There is an increasing trend in the number of publications over the last years, especially from 2021, increasing exponentially, with 69.2% of articles being published only in the previous year. The analysis of the publications' distribution per year on the Table 2 reveals that the interest in adopting Industry 4.0 Technologies in construction has emerged within the last five years, being still a developing topic, with few theoretical and empirical investigations.

Table 2. Bibliographic Analysis Review.

Number of Articles	Authorship	Year	Country	Title	Technologies 4.0 Applied in Civil Construction
1	[39]	2022	Poland	Digitization in the Design and Construction Industry-Remote Work in the Context of Sustainability: A Study from Poland	Digitalization of services (remote work)
2	[40]	2021	Australia	Adoption of blockchain technology through digital twins in the construction industry 4.0: A PESTELS approach	Blockchain/Digital Twins
3	[41]	2021	Australia	Project data categorization, adoption factors, and non-functional requirements for blockchain based digital twins in the construction industry 4.0	Blockchain/Digital Twins
4	[42]	2021	Slovakia	Simulation modeling of aerial work completed by helicopters in the construction industry focused on weather conditions	Digital Simulation Model
5	[43]	2021	Spain	Circular economy in the building and construction sector: A scientific evolution analysis	Building Information Modeling (BIM)
6	[44]	2021	Hungary	Construction 4.0 organizational level challenges and solutions	Augmented and Virtual Reality
7	[35]	2021	China	Understanding digital transformation in advanced manufacturing and engineering: A bibliometric analysis, topic modeling and research trend discovery	BIM/Digital Twins/Additive Manufacturing (3D)

Table 2. *Cont.*

Number of Articles	Authorship	Year	Country	Title	Technologies 4.0 Applied in Civil Construction
8	[45]	2021	South Korea	The engineering machine-learning automation platform (Emap): A big-data-driven AI tool for contractors' sustainable management solutions for plant projects	Artificial Intelligence (Machine Learning)/Big Data
9	[46]	2021	Czech Republic	Safety of construction from the point of view of population protection in the context of industry 4.0 in the Czech Republic	BIM
10	[28]	2021	Italy	Building envelope prefabricated with 3D printing technology	3D printing for prefabricated components to building
11	[47]	2021	Poland	Global water crisis: Concept of a new interactive shower panel based on IoT and cloud computing for rational water consumption	IoT and cloud computing
12	[48]	2021	Italy	Smart green prefabrication: Sustainability performances of industrialized building technologies	Premanufactured Building Technologies
13	[49]	2021	Nigeria	The disruptive adaptations of construction 4.0 and industry 4.0 as a pathway to a sustainable innovation and inclusive industrial technological development	All 4.0 Technologies
14	[50]	2021	United Kingdom	Distributed manufacturing: A new digital framework for sustainable modular construction	Modular building construction (Premanufactured); IoT; BIM; Advances in Materials
15	[51]	2021	Malaysia	Assessing predicting factors: Good management practices towards the successful implementation of green supply chain management (gscm) in IBS construction project	Industrialized Building System (IBS) and Digitalization

Table 2. *Cont.*

Number of Articles	Authorship	Year	Country	Title	Technologies 4.0 Applied in Civil Construction
16	[52]	2021	United Arab Emirates	Construction Industry 4.0 and Sustainability: An Enabling Framework	Building information modeling and automation vis-à-vis others such as cyber–physical systems and smart materials, with significant growth expected in the future for blockchain- and three-dimensional-printing-related technologies.
17	[53]	2021	Nigeria/South Africa	Effect of the Fourth Industrial Revolution on Road Transport Asset Management Practice in Nigeria	robotics, mobility, virtual and augmented reality, Internet of things and cloud computing, machine learning, artificial intelligence, blockchain, three-dimensional (3D) printing drones and digital engineering.
18	[54]	2021	South Africa	3D printing for sustainable low-income housing in South Africa: A case for the urban poor	three-dimensional (3D) printing), factor analysis aided by 3D printing technology, accessibility of technology
19	[55]	2021	India	Actionable strategy framework for digital transformation in AECO industry	Three-dimensional (3D) scanning, BIM, Drones/Augmented Reality/IOT/Machine Learning/Cloud Computing/Big Data/Sensors
20	[56]	2020	Spain	Skill needs of the civil engineering sector in the European Union countries: Current situation and future trends	(BIM), the Internet of Things (IoT), 3D laser scanning and component printing, big data analytics, augmented reality (AR), robotic construction, artificial intelligence (AI), sensor systems, intelligent materials, drones
21	[57]	2020	Cyprus (First author)	Building information modeling applications in smart buildings: From design to commissioning and beyond A critical review	BIM/ IOT (and digital design techniques, research in building design and optimization, BIM and LCA monitoring and tools)
22	[58]	2020	Australia	Criteria development for sustainable construction manufacturing in Construction Industry 4.0: Theoretical and laboratory investigations	Three-dimensional (3D) printing construction, software Strand7 Finite Element Analysis, Physical and mechanical properties of samples

Table 2. *Cont.*

Number of Articles	Authorship	Year	Country	Title	Technologies 4.0 Applied in Civil Construction
23	[59]	2020	Malaysia	Integrating building information modeling (BIM) and sustainability to greening existing building: Potentials in Malaysian construction industry	Building Information Modeling (BIM), building lifecycles and technology and digitization in the construction industry.
24	[60]	2020	Nigeria	Disruptive technological innovations in construction field and fourth industrial revolution intervention in the achievement of the sustainable development goal 9	BIM/Drones/Robots/ Artificial Intelligence
25	[61]	2019	Malaysia	Developing a framework for life cycle assessment of construction materials through building information modeling (BIM)]	BIM
26	[62]	2018	Croatia	Architectural programs as corporate communications platforms	IoT
27	[63]	2017	Italy	Emergency: innovative prefabricated construction components for an eco-solidarity architecture	Printing machine to produce panels prefabricated

Note that most publications are in European and Asian countries, but there are very few articles that relate to construction, sustainability, and technologies 4.0. Thus far, there are no American publications. Among developing countries, including the BRICS members (Brazil, Russia, India, China, and South Africa), only Brazil and Russia have not contributed to the advancement of research in these areas. The lack of financial resources and a proper management system for construction, informal construction, and demolition waste represent the main challenges that developing countries need to face [64,65]. Although there is no Brazilian article that stands out in the analysis, Brazil is still a country that suffers from challenges in sustainable construction, such as lack of more efficient government policies, lack of specialized labor, productivity losses and time with routine construction, problems in the disposal of construction waste and few uses and applicability of technologies 4.0 in favor of sustainable construction [66]. The publication's distribution is presented in Figure 3.

The most relevant publications on the subject are concentrated in articles, representing more than 40.6% of the total published in five years. The main areas of indexation of journals are Engineering with 25.3% of publications; followed by Social Sciences with 18.9%; Environmental Sciences with 13.7%; Energy with 12.6% and 29.5% distributed in small percentages among the other areas. This distribution reveals that the technical and academic areas are the most engaged in the growth process of Industry 4.0 Technologies, aligned with the concepts of sustainability and civil construction.

By using VOSviewer software, based on the network of 27 articles extracted from the SCOPUS database, the keywords density visualization presents the co-occurrence of keywords. The more keywords around the node and the higher their frequency, the deeper the color appears (shown in yellow in Figure 4. It can be seen from the map that the top five keywords with high frequency in the research are: Industry 4.0 (18 times);

Sustainable Development (12 times); Sustainability (13 times); Construction 4.0 (8 times), and Innovation (6 times). At the same time, the others are a subset of it. The analysis of the nodes, which presents the strongest links on the map, reveals that current research aims to use technologies to help construction to achieve higher sustainability standards, thus contributing to sustainable development goals.

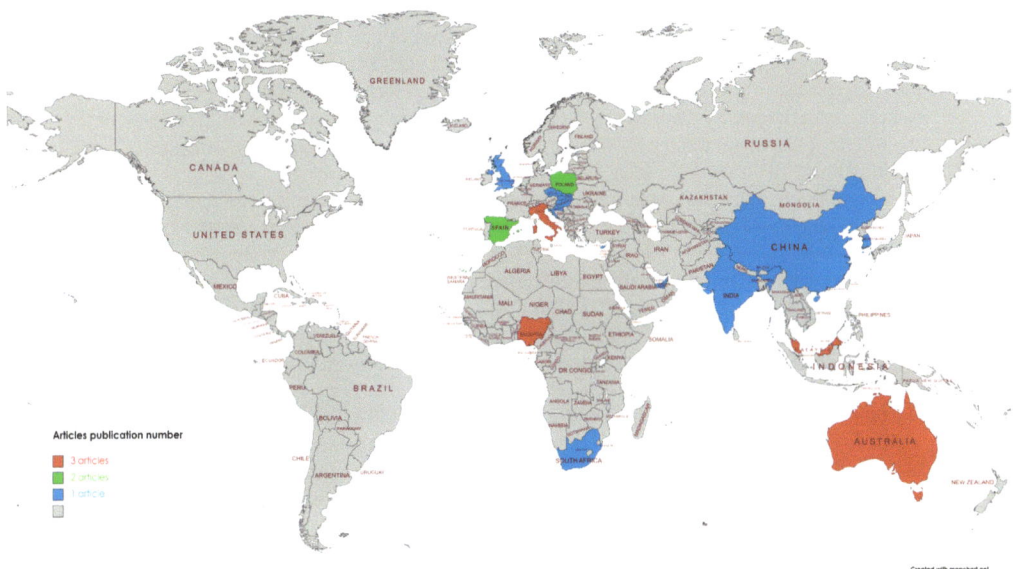

Figure 3. Countries with the highest number of publications in the last five years. Source: Own elaboration supported by MapChart tool, 2021.

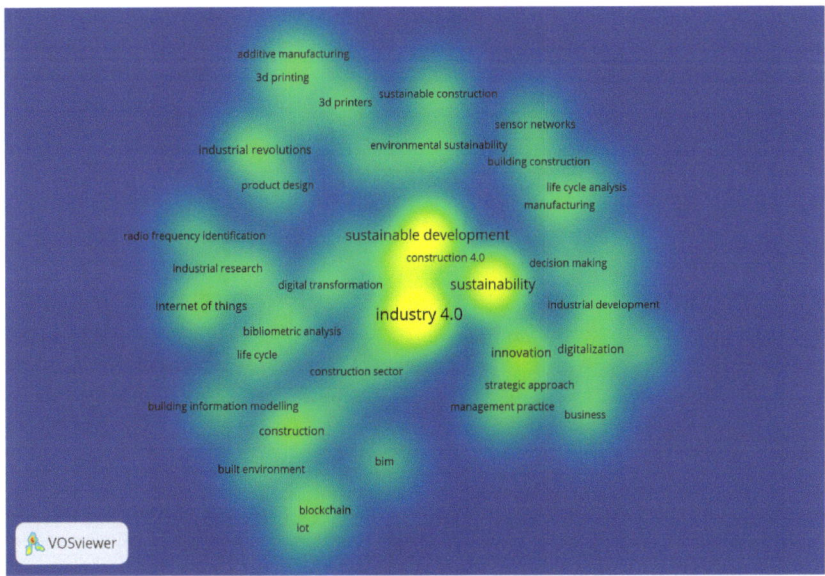

Figure 4. Keywords Co-occurrence Density map. Source: Own elaboration supported by VOSviewer, 2021.

The secondary cluster with the higher density is composed of the keywords (innovation and strategic approach and management practice), signaling that the implementation of technologies in construction depends on a new innovative approach in relation to the strategic and operational activities of the construction. This is also reinforced by the proximity to the term (digitalization), the core of the industry 4.0 concept.

There are also weaker links and intensity, these being mainly constituted by keywords related to individual technologies (3D printing; building information modeling; sensor networks) and managerial practices that can operationalize the themes of the central cluster. Technologies that are used together appear close to each other, for example, the terms (Blockchain and IoT) share a strong link since Blockchain technology is being implemented in IoT-enabled digital systems to avoid data and information vulnerability that travels over the Internet. Likewise, the terms (additive manufacturing and 3D printing) are due to 3D printing being the most used technology for additive manufacturing.

In addition, there is a concern with the sustainability of constructions gaining strength through the terms (life cycle analysis and manufacturing and building construction and sensor networks), which also indicates a change in the standard of assessment of environmental impacts in the construction industry, where the use of emissions data and resource consumption are collected with the help of sensors to feed environmental impact assessment systems.

The main result of the bibliometric review presents a description of the applicability of Industry 4.0 Technologies associated with civil construction. As shown in Figure 5, the revolution seen in the construction industry is marked by the adoption of disruptive technologies. In the content analysis of the articles, we identified 15 Industry 4.0 Technologies applied in the Construction. The most investigated technologies in the literature are Building Information Modeling (BIM) and 3D printing and scanning, being analyzed in 12 articles each. Then, IoT and Artificial Intelligence, represent the next most investigated with 7 and 6 articles, respectively. This analysis shows that there are many gaps regarding the implementation and impact of many technologies in the context of construction.

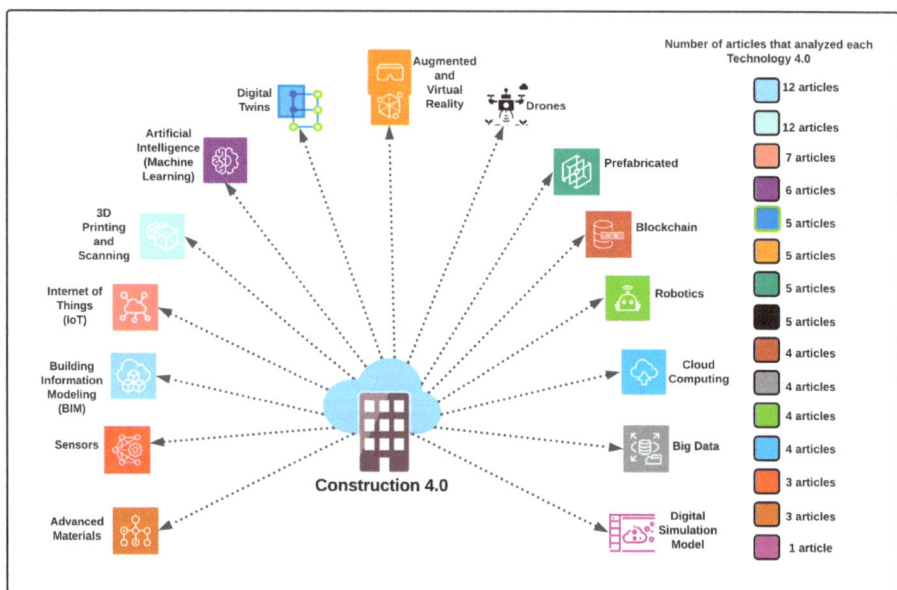

Figure 5. Technological contributions to civil construction. Source: Own elaboration supported by Lucidchart Educational Software, 2021.

5. Discussion

The construction industry plays an essential role in a country's economic growth, mainly in developing countries such as Brazil, where the construction sector represents one of the largest sectors of the global economy, employing about 7% of the population every year [48]. However, civil construction has been criticized for activities and processes that generate a loss of materials, overuse of natural resources, high volumes of waste whilst obstructing achievement of the sustainable development goals (S.D.G.s) goals [67].

In highlighting the civil construction sector, it is necessary to understand that it is an area facing many challenges in maintaining its activities and consequently in achieving sustainable development goals, given that the construction production chain significantly impacts the three pillars of sustainability. Furthermore, construction remains one of the least digitalized and innovative sectors in using Industry 4.0 Technologies. It is only ahead of agriculture, which occupies last place in the McKinsey Global Institute Industry Digitization Index [68]. Although construction is moving towards automation, it still has no links to promising topics such as sustainability [69].

The construction sector bears the highest rates of work accidents worldwide, improving the implementation of technologies can be seen as a social solution to the health and safety of workers [33]. Technologies for information management and visualization are instrumental in enhancing human perceptions and interpretations of complicated project information [70]. Furthermore, an essential contribution of the industry 4.0 technologies use in construction lies in the possibility of automated data collection for environmental impact assessments in a life cycle approach, called Life Cycle Assessment (LCA). In LCA studies, the availability of specific data, inputs and outputs associated with the production of materials, products and processes is a challenge for the execution of reliable studies. The lack of data compromises the quality of the study and the validity of the results found. Thus, [61] propose a framework in which BIM can automate data collection and LCA studies in the context of construction, allowing recognition of the environmental load of materials, processes and operations and direct design improvements to reduce such impacts. Data collection for the LCA is operationalized through the integration of sensors and IoT enabled devices to BIM [57]. Green BIM for environmental sustainability can be used for monitoring and management over a building's full life cycle, and should then be considered in future research [71].

The adoption of Industry 4.0 Technologies can support the construction industry to implement Circular Economy standards and consequently achievement of the S.D.G.s, promoting resource efficiency from project inception to end-of-life. By incorporating circular design requirements into the technologies, such as design for disassembly, deconstruction, and recycling, it is possible to reduce the use of non-renewable natural resources, properly manage the waste stream, and close the materials loop [43,72]. Table 3 systematizes and compares the evolution of methods employed in construction separated by current challenges and opportunities for the main Industry 4.0 Technologies identified in construction.

Table 3. Challenges and Opportunities in the construction sector. Source: elaborated by the authors.

Technology	Challenges	Opportunities Construction Industry 4.0
1. Pre-manufacture Items produced outside the construction site	The use of conventional construction methods is associated with increased costs, incompatibility of skills, loss of productivity, quality, safety and sustainability and an aging workforce that has reached its limits [73]	Prefabricated items generate savings of financial resources and time as they are installed with more agility [74]. Example: Prefabricated houses, where the structures of the houses are built industrially and only assembled on the construction site [75]. In the context of pre-molded materials, the use of Drywall stands out, which are light and versatile plaster partitions with the function of prevention of superstructures in constructions, used in larger scale in Europe and the U.S.A. [74]

Table 3. *Cont.*

Technology	Challenges	Opportunities Construction Industry 4.0
2. Advances in Materials Green materials, nanomaterials, self-cure materials and reuse and recycled materials	Emphasis of the production function in civil construction, mainly concentrated in the use of such products as metallurgical, ferrous, and non-ferrous [76]. Construction and demolition wastes (C.D.W.) are generated at a large scale in the construction sector [77,78]	The changes in materials seek greater strength, greater durability, better appearance, better workability, and molding. Example: Live concrete or self-repairing, a mixture of ingredients that grows and regenerates itself, used to assemble structures in remote areas to fill cracks [79]. Another example is the use of moringa oleifera in wastewater treatment, which allows the kneading of concrete [80]. The replacement of natural aggregates with C.D.W. recycled aggregates in construction materials, such as mortars, has environmental benefits [77,78]
3. 3D Printing Additive manufacturing technique, where the printer adds layer by layer to print walls and other components	Partially digitalized business and company models [81]	Faster construction and assembly with less waste, where the printing is performed on the construction site itself and pre-made parts made of concrete or metals [82]. Examples: The construction of a 1100 m^2 two-story house with one day of printing, two days of assembly and requirement of only three workers [82]. Another example is the manufacture of masks and protective equipment by students from Universidade Estadual Paulista de Guaratinguetá, Ilha Solteira and Tupã during the COVID-19 pandemic [83–85]
4. Exoskeletons Wearable robotic device, which amplifies human strength up to 20 times	The execution of repetitive operations or actions that require excessive effort have always been the main causes of musculoskeletal injuries in people working on production or construction lines [86]	Used to help workers carry heavy materials on the construction site, avoiding physical stress and injuries [87]. Example: The Industry 4.0 Technologies program leads companies to rethink processes and consider human factors, ergonomics, and sustainability. This leads to a new trend, which places workers in a modern intelligent factory, allowing them to take advantage of interconnected tools [88]
5. Drones/UAVs Unmanned, remotely controlled aircraft	Work performed manually and the need to enter confined spaces and high works, two of the most dangerous practices in civil construction [89]	Used for structure construction, mapping, and monitoring. Example: On the construction site, it performs the mapping and topography of areas and soil, together with 3D scanning and photogrammetry, monitors the progress and quality of structures [90]
6. Augmented Reality Virtualization and interaction with the environment	Creating the model of a building has always been a complex task, especially for existing structures, as it has always included the adoption of traditional methods and physical tools for collecting information [91]	Devices allow interaction with the project in an immersive digital structure. Example: Visualization and interaction with the architectural projects before the realization, which allows the correction of errors. Use of augmented reality glasses to detect defects in constructions [73]
7. Big Data Collection and storage of large amount of construction data	The use of Big Data, marked the dematerialization of information and separates it from its physical carriers, storage, transmission, and processing equipment [92]	Collection of data from works to retain knowledge and assist in future works. Example: Access to Google and NASA Earth Exchange Climate Data Centers, Satellite Images and Weather Information, Ground, Water and Geospatial Data from the Resource Conservation Service for planning and control during the project creation phase [1]

Table 3. *Cont.*

Technology	Challenges	Opportunities Construction Industry 4.0
8. Internet of Things (IoT) Connects all objects present in the environment and transmits data in real time through wireless sensors	Previous global technologies are marked by the widespread adoption of mobile devices connected to the "common Internet" without interconnectivity between devices [93]	It allows the connection and collection of information of the machines, materials, vehicles, and people present on the construction site, in real time. Example: Monitoring of delivery trucks in real time, so that the site is properly and promptly prepared to receive the resources, without harming the flow [94]. IoT can also guarantee the quality of the concrete, where sensors connected to smartphones are linked to the reinforcement and warn when the material has reached a reliable resistance level [95]
9. Sensors Installed in numerous objects to allow the capture of information and the implementation of corrective actions	The analysis was based on the tactile–visual contact, that is, the method of execution through simple probing [96]	Traceability of materials since each tool present in the work has an identity. Together with the Internet of things, they can collect information and make corrective actions in real time. Example: Using digital maps to obtain general information about the terrain through high-definition cameras with sensors mounted on drones to explore specific areas [68]. The Edge, one of the most sustainable buildings in the world, uses sensors to manage the lighting system, which allows it to manage the energy generated and adapt the lighting and air ventilation according to the internal use [97]
10. Artificial Intelligence (AI) Computers learn and recognize events, capture, and share information in real time	It is difficult to control the processes on the construction site efficiently because there was no integrated way to verify information about people, materials and equipment in real time to perform corrective actions [82]	A.I. can monitor hundreds of activities simultaneously on the construction site by monitoring and detecting irregularities. Example: Monitoring schedules, costs, safety risks, warning about deviations in schedules, or failure to meet safety standards, which allows quick action to correct the problem [82]
11. Building Information Modeling (BIM) Digital platform that integrates all construction information throughout the life cycle, using various virtualization and simulation technologies	The construction work, besides taking more time, involved complicated processes, such as management, process control and quality control to completion, which generated numerous problems [98]. Besides that, the unforeseen ground conditions are some of the main contributors to construction cost overruns and late completion [99]	It integrates all the projects and all those involved in construction. Example: BIM contains information on geometry, materials, structure, thermal efficiency and energy performance, installations, production costs [100]. Augmented reality can give digital instructions that virtually overlap the workspace, directing the masons, step by step, during the construction process [101]
12. Blockchain A digital ledger system that creates a distributed, immutable storage of data and information on a network	Data and information shared by value chain members across the project lifecycle are fragmented and vulnerable to manipulation, causing inefficiencies and unreliability [41]	Blockchain is a reliable system for information security of shared data with BIM and IoT. Example: Blockchain implementation reduces data fragmentation and increases trust and transparency of contracts and project processes, allowing secure and assertive management of information, which results in increased collaboration and efficiency [41]
13. Digital Twin An exact virtual replica of the environment or a physical object that provides real-time performance data	The lack of structure and poor digitalization in the construction industry makes it difficult to implement technologies that have the power to improve processes throughout the project lifecycle, such as the Digital Twin [41]	Digital Twin benefits the entire project lifecycle by providing real-time monitoring of data. Example: Automated and simultaneous monitoring of progress and compliance with safety and quality specifications, logistics, resource planning and predictive maintenance [41,102]

Practical Implications and Future Directions

The contributions from the abovementioned reinforce the present article on the challenges and opportunities regarding the usage of Industry 4.0 Technologies, which can help the construction sector and bring improvements in sustainability concerning social, economic, and environmental pillars. Moreover, this highlights that the subject needs further attention by the academy, as there remains an extensive effort required in research related to the topic.

After carrying out the bibliographic research, identifying the selected works and developing the bibliometric and content analysis, several issues can be highlighted in relation to the concept of Construction, Industry 4.0 technologies, and Sustainability. The results revealed a growing field of research and trending topics that will gain more relevance. However, they also indicate that individual technologies are not well connected to sustainability initiatives, with a limited number of experts operating somewhat in isolation and who offer single-point solutions, mainly technical solutions, instead of taking an integrated management "holistic" approach necessary to plan new industrial and residential projects around the world.

Despite the contributions, it is understood that there are limitations in our study, since it qualitatively reviews, that is, only subjectively. Our review analysis is limited by search terms applied only in the Scopus database. The use of certain keywords and selection criteria defined in journal articles and in English bears some restrictions, therefore, all literature that includes publications in other languages and other forms of publication are not reflected in this study. While these limitations present useful avenues for future research to explore and expand on the results of this study, future studies may also focus on expanding the keyword set and use other types of publications, databases, and books, even news with ideas and practices that remain out of the analyses. Another important point is the development of empirical research covering different professionals in the civil construction stakeholder chain and at the strategic, tactical, and operational levels. Therefore, we wish to emphasize the lack of studies focusing on or integrating different Industry 4.0 Technologies highlights gaps such as:

1. The publication's analysis distribution per year reveals that the interest in adopting Industry 4.0 Technologies in construction has emerged within the last five years, being still a "hot topic", with few theoretical and empirical investigations;
2. Thus far, there are no American publications. Among developing countries, including the BRICS members (Brazil, Russia, India, China and South Africa), only Brazil and Russia have not contributed to the advancement of research in these areas;
3. Lack the implementation and impact of many technologies in the context of construction;
4. How two or more technologies can be diffused, that is, worked together; or
5. There are still technical challenges related to the integration of different technologies. Future research should investigate the challenges encountered in the joint application of different technologies, both in theory and in practice;
6. Empirical studies with qualitative and quantitative approaches showing the real advances in the applicability of technological tools in construction;
7. The impacts of industry technology 4.0 affect which and how the pillars of sustainability operate;
8. Proposals for models that allow replicability within the topic's construction, technology and sustainability;
9. Most articles explore the relationship between industry 4.0 technologies in construction from an economic and some environmental point of view, however, few also address the social pillar.

The practical implications of the results of the review allow future research efforts/activities in Industry 4.0 Technologies and sustainability in construction to be developed as discussed through this manuscript. The study benefits researchers and professionals in the construction industry. For researchers, the identified gaps reveal areas of high priority for future research, mainly highlighting the need to relate Industry 4.0 Technologies and sustainability of civil construction activities. Moreover, this study can help managers understand the integrations between Construction and Industry 4.0 Technologies to achieve better operational and environmental organizational results. For the construction industry, the study expands knowledge about available technologies and raises awareness of the latest applicability within construction and expands the potential to become a sustainable sector, which ensures good construction practices, is concerned with workers' health and productivity, and additionally preserves the environment and continues growth economically. The study exposes missing gaps from current research: a broader consideration of the construction adjustments needed to accommodate the use of Industry 4.0 Technologies to make the sector more sustainable. Therefore, these gaps in the literature should direct future research to strengthen the use of Industry 4.0 Technologies in construction to contribute to the sustainability and circularity dimensions of the processes. To continue and stimulate discussions, Table 4 displays some positive and negative impacts of the use of Industry 4.0 Technologies in civil construction from the perspective of the Triple Bottom Line, which can serve as inspiration for increasingly comprehensive and in-depth research.

Table 4. Industry 4.0 Technologies Impacts to the Triple Bottom Line. Source: elaborated by the authors.

Industry 4.0 Technologies	Triple Bottom Line		
	Social	Economic	Environmental
1. Pre-manufacture	Improve health and safety of workers and local community; Access to habitation with low cost [48]	Improve quality, time, and cost, because construction activities are led within controlled environment [48,63]	Prefabricated reduce natural resources use and increase the effectiveness of waste management at the end-of-life, as the disassembly and recovery materials is facilitated; Reducing of local CO_2 emissions, particulate matter and noise [48]
2. Advances in Materials	Income generation for civil construction waste recycling plants and employees so that the material becomes a problem and a sustainable output [102]	The positive uses of solid waste technological treatment are considered beneficial from the economic and environmental point of view and saving the natural resources [24]	
3. 3D Printing	Low-income housing [54]	3D printing allows for mass customization and fast implementation, which can reduce costs [28,58] 3D printing reduces the cost of construction due to zero waste; it uses recycled materials and it decreases the use of transport [56]	Optimization of resources (energy and materials) use and waste management due to the high precision in the use of materials, which does not generate waste, and the incorporation of recycled materials for the deposition in 3D [58]
4. Exoskeletons	Reduction in work accidents and preservation of health and safety [102]	Costs with trained workers and investment in training [102]	Exoskeleton system it is possible to innovate the architectural image, to support an equitable and sustainable development based on the prevention and risk management and extend the useful life cycle of the built environment [103]
5. Drones/UAVs	Lack of regulatory and administrative interventions to guide the UAVs' safe operation on construction sites [104]	Low-cost unmanned aerial system [70]	To obtain data and images from underneath floating buildings, drones can be equipped with cameras and sensors to collect characteristic construction information [105]

Table 4. *Cont.*

Industry 4.0 Technologies	Triple Bottom Line		
	Social	Economic	Environmental
6. Augmented Reality	Training of workers and prevention of occupational risks [56]	Planning of works in the virtual environment, with a preview of the necessary operations and processes, making it possible to correctly dimension and optimize financial resources [106]	Optimizes the use of resources in all phases of the project, from design to use, identifying potential areas for improvement in energy and water consumption, preventing errors and defects through early visualization of events in the virtual environment [107,108]
	Augmented reality or virtual reality can increase customers' understanding the final product early in the design phase, avoiding changes during the project execution and consequently avoiding redesign costs [55]		
7. Big Data	Using big data, information on work progress and suppliers and employees payments are distributed through blockchain-based smart contracts for appropriate project managerial [34] Big Data-generated data in the stages of a project is collected and formalized into a repository to be used as a knowledge base [45]		The use of cloud-based big data enables building sustainability management as a means of predicting, managing, and monitoring the impacts of a building project on the environment [71]
8. Internet of Things (IoT)	IoT maintain safety and health of workers through real-time alerting of potential falls and collisions [109] IoT can monitoring urban places exposed to extreme environmental conditions, as areas subject to flooding and landslides, minimizing or preventing deaths in natural disasters [62]	Automated real-time data collection saves resources as it streamlines the planning, communication, control and optimization of processes, inventories, preventive maintenance, time and budgets [15,110]	Real-time monitoring of parameters on emissions and consumption of resources, such as water and energy, to reducing resource scarcity [47]
9. Sensors	Sensors monitoring health parameters of workers and the environment avoiding ergonomic injuries and release of harmful substances [33].	Due to the wide variety of pollutants in the civil construction, pollutant monitoring technologies should play a significant role in the very near future as the technologies of low cost sensors evolve fast [22]	
10. Artificial Intelligence (AI)	A challenge for the current management model, such as the replacement of manual activities with digital activities, also continuous workers and knowledge transfer from other sectors [44]	Artificial Intelligence can predict and respond to potential risks in a construction project cycle, reducing design changes and rework predicts, design cost estimating, design error check, change in order forecast, and predictive maintenance, bringing potential environmental benefits by optimizing the use of resources [45]	
11. Building Information Modeling (BIM)	Monitoring health and safety issues—reduction of work accidents. The BIM are able automatically detect safety hazards and suggest preventive actions to workers [57] Population protection requirements can be incorporated in the information modeling system, helping to choose places safe and sustainable to build [46]	BIM increasing productivity and efficiency of operations and process; Decrease of time execution and improve quality of the projects [60] BIM can provide accurate statistics, facilitating cost estimation, construction schedule control and provide spatial and time information [15].	The use of BIM models contributes to assess and improve: energy performance; CO_2 emissions; resource efficiency and waste management; air quality [57] Use BIM to improve design from the projects conception, for example, design for disassembly and deconstruction, contributes to reduce the use of resources and improve waste management in construction [43]

Table 4. *Cont.*

Industry 4.0 Technologies	Triple Bottom Line		
	Social	Economic	Environmental
12. Blockchain	Increased collaboration and transparency among stakeholders. Data security [41]	Cost reduction by eliminating indirect costs and inefficiencies [41]	Improves waste management through the traceability material in the entire project lifecycle [41]
13. Digital Twin	Facilities management, by employing state of the art technologies such as digital twins and digital asset management to improve the environmental issues resulting from the careless consumption of energy related to the greenhouse effect and that can interfere in the societal quality of life [22].	A DT can be used to learn and suggest new scenarios before building a product, manufacturing tools and equipment, because developing a construction process, and planning for developing, avoiding loose time, natural resources and money [17,40].	

6. Final Considerations

The general objective of this work is to offer a current overview of publications that associate the civil construction sector; Industry 4.0 Technologies and sustainability, and identify the challenges and opportunities of the Industry 4.0 Technologies set to contribute to sustainability achievement. This study helps researchers and practitioners, with tables of reference that serve as a guide to advance the study of technologies and to address the current shortcomings of such technologies, while enhancing their sustainability contributions to processes in future building construction. To the best of the authors' knowledge, this study is the first of its kind using Civil Construction, Industry 4.0 Technologies, and Sustainability to propose a unified table to help managers and academics understand these relationships.

In the current scenario, where the civil construction industry continues to generate a large waste of resources such as water, energy and materials, the use of technologies can help improve the performance and competitiveness of the sector, in addition to contributing to achieving sustainable development goals. The central premise behind the use of technologies associated with Industry 4.0 is to generate efficiency and optimize production processes in a continuous and upward manner, that is, the use of resources in a reduced, precise, intelligent, and autonomous way, which generates greater productivity, quality and customization. Thus, from the bibliographic and bibliometric review, it is possible to verify that disruptive technologies support the new industrial paradigm, that can be applied in building, to improve the performance of the construction sector and render it more sustainable and intelligent using modeling systems and virtual simulation of projects, 3D printing, robots, drones, sensors, and the Internet of things (IoT).

The bibliometric review identified state of the art methods relating to Civil Construction; Industry 4.0 Technologies and Sustainability and pointed out that there are still few papers in this field and there remain gaps to be explored, not only by civil engineering, but by professionals and multidisciplinary researchers. Furthermore, it was noted that technologies are still secondary on the research topics, showing that there is space for them to be empirically explored and to become protagonists in the coming years. Another point is the developing countries, including Brazil, which are still adept at manual civil construction and poorly trained and digitalized, allows for growth in performance of the industry 4.0 technologies and Sustainability and solidification of the tools and practices that transform the current context. These findings also reflect in academic contributions, directing new lines of research in possible research gaps addressed in this article.

Infrastructures **2022**, *7*, 43

Through a bibliographic review of the literature, the research was able to point out what Industry 4.0 Technologies, challenges, and opportunities Civil Construction has experienced. From the review, it was possible to identify and present in a structured way the applicability of the industry 4.0 technologies within the scope of civil construction, by elaborating a comparison between the adoption of technological tools and the previous scenario of the sector.

That is why investing in technological intelligence means directing the strategy towards flexibility, which can significantly favor the civil construction sector, especially in issues of cost reduction, improvements, and alternatives to the productive process in search of transformation in the way of acting, thinking and doing. Therefore, it is concluded that Industry 4.0 Technologies can contribute to civil construction through innovative, sustainable, and technological solutions focused on the flow of work, which are able to provide growth to civil construction through the balance of costs/benefits in the management of projects and works. For future studies, the development of a systematic review of the literature is recommended, which can identify other opportunities and challenges, besides the practical and applicability of the use of new technologies aligned with the environmental, social, and economic pillars in the scope of civil construction.

Author Contributions: Conceptualization, J.d.A.B.F., A.M.D., N.d.A.A. and R.A.G.B.; Methodology, J.d.A.B.F., A.M.D., N.d.A.A. and R.A.G.B.; Validation, J.d.A.B.F., A.M.D., N.d.A.A. and R.A.G.B.; Formal analysis, J.d.A.B.F., A.M.D. and N.d.A.A.; Investigation, J.d.A.B.F., A.M.D. and N.d.A.A.; Data curation, J.d.A.B.F., A.M.D. and N.d.A.A.; Writing—Original Draft, J.d.A.B.F., A.M.D. and N.d.A.A.; Writing—Review and Editing, R.A.G.B.; Supervision, R.M.D. and R.A.G.B. All authors have read and agreed to the published version of the manuscript.

Funding: The APC was funded by PROAP/CAPES via PROPG/UNESP.

Data Availability Statement: Not applicable.

Acknowledgments: The authors would like to thank the post-Graduation program in Production Engineering of School of Engineering (UNESP Bauru) for administrative and technical support.

Conflicts of Interest: The authors declare no conflict of interest. The funders had no role in the design of the study; in the collection, analyses, or interpretation of data; in the writing of the manuscript, or in the decision to publish the results.

References

1. Lezoche, M.; Hernandez, J.E.; Díaz, M.M.E.A.; Panetto, H.; Kacprzyk, J. Agri-food 4.0: A survey of the supply chains and technologies for the future agriculture. In *Computers in Industry*; Elsevier B.V.: Amsterdam, The Netherlands, 2020; Volume 117, p. 103187. [CrossRef]
2. Xu, L.D.; Xu, E.L.; Li, L. Industry 4.0: State of the art and future trends. *Int. J. Prod. Res.* **2018**, *56*, 2941–2962. [CrossRef]
3. Yin, Y.; Stecke, K.E.; Li, D. The evolution of production systems from Industry 2.0 through Industry 4.0. *Int. J. Prod. Res.* **2017**, *56*, 848–861. [CrossRef]
4. Zhou, K.; Liu, T.; Zhou, L. Industry 4.0: Towards future industrial opportunities and challenges. In Proceedings of the 2015 12th International Conference on Fuzzy Systems and Knowledge Discovery (FSKD), Zhangjiajie, China, 15–17 August 2015; pp. 2147–2152.
5. Oztemel, E.; Gursev, S. Literature review of Industry 4.0 and related technologies. *J. Intell. Manuf.* **2018**, *31*, 127–182. [CrossRef]
6. Candido, D.D.S.; Watts, A.; Abade, L.; Kraemer, M.U.G.; Pybus, O.G.; Croda, J.; de Oliveira, W.; Khan, K.; Sabino, E.C.; Faria, N.R. Routes for COVID-19 importation in Brazil. *J. Travel Med.* **2020**, *27*, taaa042. [CrossRef] [PubMed]
7. Zhou, C.; Su, F.; Pei, T.; Zhang, A.; Du, Y.; Luo, B.; Cao, Z.; Wang, J.; Yuan, W.; Zhu, Y.; et al. COVID-19: Challenges to GIS with Big Data. *Geogr. Sustain.* **2020**, *1*, 77–87. [CrossRef]
8. Livingston, E.H.; Desai, A.; Berkwits, M. Sourcing Personal Protective Equipment During the COVID-19 Pandemic. *JAMA* **2020**, *323*, 1912–1914. [CrossRef]
9. McCall, B. COVID-19 and artificial intelligence: Protecting health-care workers and curbing the spread. *Lancet Digit. Health* **2020**, *2*, e166–e167. [CrossRef]
10. Tzioutziou, A.; Xenidis, Y. A Study on the Integration of Resilience and Smart City Concepts in Urban Systems. *Infrastructures* **2021**, *6*, 24. [CrossRef]
11. Keogh, M.; Smallwood, J.J. The role of the 4th Industrial Revolution (4IR) in enhancing performance within the construction industry. In *IOP Conference Series: Earth and Environmental Science*; IOP Publishing: Bristol, UK, 2021; Volume 654, p. 012021. [CrossRef]

12. The World Commission on Environment and Development (WCED). Our Common Future. 1987. Available online: https://sustainabledevelopment.un.org/content/documents/5987our-common-future.pdf (accessed on 14 January 2022).
13. Elkington, J. *Cannibals with Forks: The Triple Bottom Line of Business of 21st Century*, 1st ed.; Capstone Publishing Limited Oxford Centre for Innovation: Oxford, UK, 1994.
14. UN. Sustainable Development Goals. United Nations. 2015. Available online: https://sustainabledevelopment.un.org/sdgs (accessed on 14 April 2020).
15. Ghosh, A.; Edwards, D.J.; Hosseini, M.R. Patterns and trends in Internet of Things (IoT) research: Future applications in the construction industry. *Eng. Constr. Arch. Manag.* **2020**, *28*, 457–481. [CrossRef]
16. Valente, M.; Sibai, A.; Sambucci, M.; Valente, M.; Sibai, A.; Sambucci, M.; Valente, M.; Sibai, A.; Sambucci, M.; Valente, M.; et al. Extrusion-Based Additive Manufacturing of Concrete Products: Revolutionizing and Remodeling the Construction Industry. *J. Compos. Sci.* **2019**, *3*, 88. [CrossRef]
17. Sepasgozar, S.M.E. Differentiating Digital Twin from Digital Shadow: Elucidating a Paradigm Shift to Expedite a Smart, Sustainable Built Environment. *Buildings* **2021**, *11*, 151. [CrossRef]
18. Darko, A.; Chan, A.P.; Yang, Y.; Tetteh, M.O. Building information modeling (BIM)-based modular integrated construction risk management—Critical survey and future needs. *Comput. Ind.* **2020**, *123*, 103327. [CrossRef]
19. Zhang, Y.; Liu, H.; Kang, S.-C.; Al-Hussein, M. Virtual reality applications for the built environment: Research trends and opportunities. *Autom. Constr.* **2020**, *118*, 103311. [CrossRef]
20. Dallasega, P.; Rauch, E.; Linder, C. Industry 4.0 as an enabler of proximity for construction supply chains: A systematic literature review. *Comput. Ind.* **2018**, *99*, 205–225. [CrossRef]
21. STATISTA. Forecast of the Infrastructure Construction Sector's Gross Domestic Product (GDP) in Brazil from 2021 to 2025. Statista Research Department. 2022. Available online: https://www.statista.com/statistics/1140201/brazil-infrastructure-construction-gdp/ (accessed on 10 February 2022).
22. Fokaides, P.; Apanaviciene, R.; Černeckiene, J.; Jurelionis, A.; Klumbyte, E.; Kriauciunaite-Neklejonoviene, V.; Pupeikis, D.; Rekus, D.; Sadauskiene, J.; Seduikyte, L.; et al. Research Challenges and Advancements in the field of Sustainable Energy Technologies in the Built Environment. *Sustainability* **2020**, *12*, 8417. [CrossRef]
23. Mesa, J.A.; Fúquene-Retamoso, C.; Maury-Ramírez, A. Life Cycle Assessment on Construction and Demolition Waste: A Systematic Literature Review. *Sustainability* **2021**, *13*, 7676. [CrossRef]
24. Ahmed, H.M.; Abdelhaffez, G.S.; Ahmed, A.A. Potential use of marble and granite solid wastes as environmentally friendly coarse particulate in civil constructions. *Int. J. Environ. Sci. Technol.* **2020**, *19*, 889–896. [CrossRef]
25. Bogue, R. What are the prospects for robots in the construction industry? *Ind. Robot.* **2018**, *45*, 1–6. [CrossRef]
26. Bedarf, P.; Dutto, A.; Zanini, M.; Dillenburger, B. Foam 3D printing for construction: A review of applications, materials, and processes. *Autom. Constr.* **2021**, *130*, 103861. [CrossRef]
27. Jamali, K.; Kaushal, V.; Najafi, M. Evolution of Additive Manufacturing in Civil Infrastructure Systems: A Ten-Year Review. *Infrastructures* **2021**, *6*, 108. [CrossRef]
28. Volpe, S.; Sangiorgio, V.; Petrella, A.; Coppola, A.; Notarnicola, M.; Fiorito, F. Building Envelope Prefabricated with 3D Printing Technology. *Sustainability* **2021**, *13*, 8923. [CrossRef]
29. Nawari, N.O.; Ravindran, S. Blockchain and Building Information Modeling (BIM): Review and Applications in Post-Disaster Recovery. *Buildings* **2019**, *9*, 149. [CrossRef]
30. Yin, X.; Liu, H.; Chen, Y.; Al-Hussein, M. Building information modelling for off-site construction: Review and future directions. *Autom. Constr.* **2019**, *101*, 72–91. [CrossRef]
31. Newman, C.; Edwards, D.; Martek, I.; Lai, J.; Thwala, W.D.; Rillie, I. Industry 4.0 deployment in the construction industry: A bibliometric literature review and UK-based case study. *Smart Sustain. Built Environ.* **2020**, *10*, 557–580. [CrossRef]
32. Oesterreich, T.D.; Teuteberg, F. Understanding the implications of digitisation and automation in the context of Industry 4.0: A triangulation approach and elements of a research agenda for the construction industry. *Comput. Ind.* **2016**, *83*, 121–139. [CrossRef]
33. Xu, M.; Nie, X.; Li, H.; Cheng, J.C.; Mei, Z. Smart construction sites: A promising approach to improving on-site HSE management performance. *J. Build. Eng.* **2022**, *49*, 104007. [CrossRef]
34. Yevu, S.K.; Yu, A.T.; Darko, A. Digitalization of construction supply chain and procurement in the built environment: Emerging technologies and opportunities for sustainable processes. *J. Clean. Prod.* **2021**, *322*, 129093. [CrossRef]
35. Lee, C.-H.; Liu, C.-L.; Trappey, A.J.; Mo, J.P.; Desouza, K.C. Understanding digital transformation in advanced manufacturing and engineering: A bibliometric analysis, topic modeling and research trend discovery. *Adv. Eng. Inform.* **2021**, *50*, 101428. [CrossRef]
36. Liberati, A.; Altman, D.G.; Tetzlaff, J.; Mulrow, C.; Gøtzsche, P.C.; Ioannidis, J.P.A.; Clarke, M.; Devereaux, P.J.; Kleijnen, J.; Moher, D. The PRISMA Statement for Reporting Systematic Reviews and Meta-Analyses of Studies That Evaluate Health Care Interventions: Explanation and Elaboration. *PLoS Med.* **2009**, *6*, e1000100. [CrossRef]
37. Page, M.J.; McKenzie, J.E.; Bossuyt, P.M.; Boutron, I.; Hoffmann, T.C.; Mulrow, C.D.; Shamseer, L.; Tetzlaff, J.M.; Akl, E.A.; Brennan, S.E.; et al. The PRISMA 2020 statement: An updated guideline for reporting systematic reviews. *Int. J. Surg.* **2021**, *88*, 105906. [CrossRef]
38. Zamani, S.H.; Rahman, R.A.; Fauzi, M.A.; Yusof, L.M. Government pandemic response strategies for AEC enterprises: Lessons from COVID-19. *J. Eng. Des. Technol.* 2022; *in press*. [CrossRef]

39. Orzeł, B.; Wolniak, R. Digitization in the Design and Construction Industry—Remote Work in the Context of Sustainability: A Study from Poland. *Sustainability* **2022**, *14*, 1332. [CrossRef]
40. Teisserenc, B.; Sepasgozar, S. Project Data Categorization, Adoption Factors, and Non-Functional Requirements for Blockchain Based Digital Twins in the Construction Industry 4.0. *Buildings* **2021**, *11*, 626. [CrossRef]
41. Teisserenc, B.; Sepasgozar, S. Adoption of Blockchain Technology through Digital Twins in the Construction Industry 4.0: A PESTELS Approach. *Buildings* **2021**, *11*, 670. [CrossRef]
42. Bisták, A.; Hulínová, Z.; Neštiak, M.; Chamulová, B. Simulation Modeling of Aerial Work Completed by Helicopters in the Construction Industry Focused on Weather Conditions. *Sustainability* **2021**, *13*, 13671. [CrossRef]
43. Norouzi, M.; Chàfer, M.; Cabeza, L.F.; Jiménez, L.; Boer, D. Circular economy in the building and construction sector: A scientific evolution analysis. *J. Build. Eng.* **2021**, *44*, 102704. [CrossRef]
44. Nagy, O.; Papp, I.; Szabó, R.Z. Construction 4.0 Organisational Level Challenges and Solutions. *Sustainability* **2021**, *13*, 12321. [CrossRef]
45. Choi, S.-W.; Lee, E.-B.; Kim, J.-H. The Engineering Machine-Learning Automation Platform (*EMAP*): A Big-Data-Driven AI Tool for Contractors' Sustainable Management Solutions for Plant Projects. *Sustainability* **2021**, *13*, 10384. [CrossRef]
46. Slivkova, S.; Brumarova, L.; Kluckova, B.; Pokorny, J.; Tomanova, K. Safety of Constructions from the Point of View of Population Protection in the Context of Industry 4.0 in the Czech Republic. *Sustainability* **2021**, *13*, 9927. [CrossRef]
47. Czajkowski, A.; Remiorz, L.; Pawlak, S.; Remiorz, E.; Szyguła, J.; Marek, D.; Paszkuta, M.; Drabik, G.; Baron, G.; Paduch, J.; et al. Global Water Crisis: Concept of a New Interactive Shower Panel Based on IoT and Cloud Computing for Rational Water Consumption. *Appl. Sci.* **2021**, *11*, 4081. [CrossRef]
48. Gallo, P.; Romano, R.; Belardi, E. Smart Green Prefabrication: Sustainability Performances of Industrialized Building Technologies. *Sustainability* **2021**, *13*, 4701. [CrossRef]
49. Lekan, A.; Clinton, A.; Owolabi, J. The Disruptive Adaptations of Construction 4.0 and Industry 4.0 as a Pathway to a Sustainable Innovation and Inclusive Industrial Technological Development. *Buildings* **2021**, *11*, 79. [CrossRef]
50. Turner, C.; Oyekan, J.; Stergioulas, L. Distributed Manufacturing: A New Digital Framework for Sustainable Modular Construction. *Sustainability* **2021**, *13*, 1515. [CrossRef]
51. Sharifah-NurFarhana, S.S.; Rohana, M.; Afzan, A.Z.; Nadia, Z.; Yon Syafni, S. *Assessing Predicting Factors: Good Management Practices Towards the Successful Implementation of Green Supply Chain Management (GSCM) in IBS Construction Project*; CIDB: Kuala Lumpur, Malaysia, 2021.
52. Balasubramanian, S.; Shukla, V.; Islam, N.; Manghat, S. Construction Industry 4.0 and Sustainability: An Enabling Framework. *IEEE Trans. Eng. Manag.* **2021**, *33*, 1–19. [CrossRef]
53. Gambo, N.; Musonda, I. Effect of the Fourth Industrial Revolution on Road Transport Asset Management Practice in Nigeria. *J. Constr. Dev. Ctries* **2021**, *26*, 19–43. [CrossRef]
54. Aghimien, D.; Aigbavboa, C.; Aghimien, L.; Thwala, W.; Ndlovu, L. 3D Printing for sustainable low-income housing in South Africa: A case for the urban poor. *J. Green Build.* **2021**, *16*, 129–141. [CrossRef]
55. Bhattacharya, S.; Momaya, K. Actionable strategy framework for digital transformation in AECO industry. *Eng. Constr. Arch. Manag.* **2021**, *28*, 1397–1422. [CrossRef]
56. Akyazi, T.; Alvarez, I.; Alberdi, E.; Oyarbide-Zubillaga, A.; Goti, A.; Bayon, F. Skills Needs of the Civil Engineering Sector in the European Union Countries: Current Situation and Future Trends. *Appl. Sci.* **2020**, *10*, 7226. [CrossRef]
57. Panteli, C.; Kylili, A.; Fokaides, P.A. Building information modelling applications in smart buildings: From design to commissioning and beyond A critical review. *J. Clean. Prod.* **2020**, *265*, 121766. [CrossRef]
58. Tahmasebinia, F.; Sepasgozar, S.M.E.; Shirowzhan, S.; Niemela, M.; Tripp, A.; Nagabhyrava, S.; Mansuri, Z.; Alonso-Marroquin, F. Criteria development for sustainable construction manufacturing in Construction Industry 4.0: Theoretical and laboratory investigations. *Constr. Innov.* **2020**, *20*, 379–400. [CrossRef]
59. Zulkefli, N.S.; Mohd-Rahim, F.A.; Zainon, N. Integrating Building Information Modelling (BIM) and Sustainability to Greening Existing Building: Potentials in Malaysian Construction Industry. *Int. J. Sustain. Constr. Eng. Technol.* **2020**, *11*, 76–83. [CrossRef]
60. Lekan, A.; Aigbavboa, C.; Babatunde, O.; Olabosipo, F.; Christiana, A. Disruptive technological innovations in construction field and fourth industrial revolution intervention in the achievement of the sustainable development goal 9. *Int. J. Constr. Manag.* **2020**, 1–12. [CrossRef]
61. Zainon, N.; Lun, G.W.; Zaid, N.S.M.; Myeda, N.E.; Aziz, N.M. Developing a Framework for Life Cycle Assessment of Construction Materials through Building Information Modelling (BIM). *Int. J. Innov. Creat. Chang.* **2019**, *10*, 253–276.
62. Homadovski, A. Arhitektonski programi kao komunikacijske platforme korporacija. *Prost. Znan. Časopis Arhit. Urban.* **2018**, *26*, 82–93. [CrossRef]
63. Sperimentazione, R.E.; Sferra, A.S. Emergency: Innovative prefabricated construction components for an eco-solidarity architecture. *TECHNE-J. Technol. Archit. Environ.* **2017**, *14*, 328–334. [CrossRef]
64. Doussoulin, J.P.; Bittencourt, M. How effective is the construction sector in promoting the circular economy in Brazil and France? A waste input-output analysis. *Struct. Chang. Econ. Dyn.* **2021**, *60*, 47–58. [CrossRef]
65. Manjia, M.B.; Abanda, H.F.; Pettang, C. A Contribution to the Sustainable Construction Indicators Evaluation in Developing Countries: The Case of Cameroon. *Lect. Notes Netw. Syst.* **2017**, *72*, 137–148. [CrossRef]

66. Nunes, K.; Mahler, C.F. Comparison of construction and demolition waste management between Brazil, European Union and USA. *Waste Manag. Res.* **2020**, *38*, 415–422. [CrossRef]
67. Ogunmakinde, O.E.; Egbelakin, T.; Sher, W. Contributions of the circular economy to the UN sustainable development goals through sustainable construction. *Resour. Conserv. Recycl.* **2021**, *178*, 106023. [CrossRef]
68. Agarwal, R.; Chandrasekaran, S.; Mukund, S. *Imagining Construction's Digital Future*; McKinsey & Company: Hong Kong, China, 2016. Available online: https://www.mckinsey.com/business-functions/operations/our-insights/imagining-constructions-digital-future (accessed on 28 April 2020).
69. Lu, K.; Jiang, X.; Tam, V.W.Y.; Li, M.; Wang, H.; Xia, B.; Chen, Q. Development of a Carbon Emissions Analysis Framework Using Building Information Modeling and Life Cycle Assessment for the Construction of Hospital Projects. *Sustainability* **2019**, *11*, 6274. [CrossRef]
70. Li, D.; Lu, M. Integrating geometric models, site images and GIS based on Google Earth and Keyhole Markup Language. *Autom. Constr.* **2018**, *89*, 317–331. [CrossRef]
71. Wong, J.K.W.; Zhou, J. Enhancing environmental sustainability over building life cycles through green BIM: A review. *Autom. Constr.* **2015**, *57*, 156–165. [CrossRef]
72. Oreto, C.; Massotti, L.; Biancardo, S.A.; Veropalumbo, R.; Viscione, N.; Russo, F. BIM-Based Pavement Management Tool for Scheduling Urban Road Maintenance. *Infrastructures* **2021**, *6*, 148. [CrossRef]
73. Bock, T. The future of construction automation: Technological disruption and the upcoming ubiquity of robotics. *Autom. Constr.* **2015**, *59*, 113–121. [CrossRef]
74. FIA. Tecnologia na Construção Civil: O que é, Importância e Exemplos. Fundação Instituto de Administração (FIA). 2020. Available online: https://fia.com.br/blog/tecnologia-na-construcao-civil/ (accessed on 3 April 2020).
75. Alves, N. Casas Pré-Fabricadas: Tipos, Vantagens e Como Funciona. CONSTRUCT. 2017. Available online: https://constructapp.io/pt/casas-pre-fabricadas/ (accessed on 3 April 2020).
76. Bahia, L.D.; Pinheiro, B.R. Evolução dos Indices de Tecnologia dos Complexos Têxtil e Construção Civil no Brasil (1985–2009). 2017. Available online: https://www.econstor.eu/handle/10419/177508 (accessed on 15 May 2020).
77. Garcia-Troncoso, N.; Xu, B.; Probst-Pesantez, W. Development of Concrete Incorporating Recycled Aggregates, Hydrated Lime and Natural Volcanic Pozzolan. *Infrastructures* **2021**, *6*, 155. [CrossRef]
78. Gomes, R.I.; Bastos, D.; Farinha, C.B.; Pederneiras, C.M.; Veiga, R.; de Brito, J.; Faria, P.; Silva, A.S. Mortars with CDW Recycled Aggregates Submitted to High Levels of CO_2. *Infrastructures* **2021**, *6*, 159. [CrossRef]
79. Zeeberg, A. Bricks Alive! Scientists Create Living Concrete. *The New York Times*. 2020. Available online: https://www.nytimes.com/2020/01/15/science/construction-concrete-bacteria-photosynthesis.html (accessed on 15 April 2021).
80. de Almeida Corrêa e Silva, T.; De Paula, H.M. Gestão da água em usina de concreto: Análise do emprego de Moringa oleifera no tratamento de água residuária e proposta de reuso após tratamento. *Matéria* **2019**, *24*. [CrossRef]
81. Riedl, R.; Benlian, A.; Hess, T.; Stelzer, D.; Sikora, H. On the Relationship Between Information Management and Digitalization. *Bus. Inf. Syst. Eng.* **2017**, *59*, 475–482. [CrossRef]
82. WEF. Winsun: Demonstrating the Viability of 3D Printing at Construction Scale. World Economic Forum. 2016. Available online: https://www.futureofconstruction.org/case/winsun/ (accessed on 24 December 2021).
83. UNESP. Unesp/Tupã Iniciará Fabricação de Máscaras de Proteção. Universidade Estadual Paulista Júlio de Mesquita Filho (UNESP). 2020. Available online: https://www.tupa.unesp.br/#!/noticia/614/unesp-tupa-iniciara-fabricacao-de-mascaras-de-protecao (accessed on 22 April 2021).
84. UNESP. Unesp Produz Equipamentos para Apoiar Saúde do Vale do Paraíba. Universidade Estadual Paulista Júlio de Mesquita Filho (UNESP). 2020. Available online: https://www2.unesp.br/portal#!/noticia/35698/unesp-produz-equipamentos-para-apoiar-saude-do-vale-do-paraiba/ (accessed on 22 April 2021).
85. UNESP. Universidade Pública Unida pelo SUS-Soluções Contra o COVID-19. Universidade Estadual Paulista Júlio de Mesquita Filho (UNESP). 2020. Available online: https://www.feis.unesp.br/index.php/estagios/#!/departamentos/engenharia-mecanica/grupos/gpea/ (accessed on 22 April 2021).
86. Salvadore, G.; Rota, E.; Corsi, E.; Colombina, G. Industrial Wearable Robots: A HUMANufacturing Approach. *IFMBE Proc.* **2019**, *76*, 1729–1733. [CrossRef]
87. Baldwin, E. Esqueletos Robóticos Podem Ajudar os Trabalhadores da Construção Civil a Partir de 2020. ArchDaily. 2020. Available online: https://www.archdaily.com.br/br/908668/esqueletos-roboticos-podem-ajudar-os-trabalhadores-da-construcao-civil-a-partir-de (accessed on 22 April 2021).
88. Farinaccio, R. Testamos um Exoesqueleto Simples usado na Indústria Automobilística. Techmundo. 2018. Available online: https://www.tecmundo.com.br/produto/128710-testamos-exoesqueleto-simples-usado-industria-automobilistica.htm (accessed on 22 April 2021).
89. Kas, K.A.; Johnson, G.K. Using unmanned aerial vehicles and robotics in hazardous locations safely. *Process Saf. Prog.* **2019**, *39*, e12066. [CrossRef]
90. Antunes, J. Should You Choose LiDAR or Photogrammetry for Aerial Drone Surveys? UAV Expo. 2018. Available online: https://www.commercialuavnews.com/construction/choose-lidar-photogrammetry-aerial-drone-surveys (accessed on 22 April 2021).
91. Castronovo, F.; Awad, B.; Akhavian, R. Implementation of Virtual Design Reviews in the Generation of As-Built Information. In *Construction Research Congress (CRC)*; American Society of Civil Engineers (ASCE): Reston, VA, USA, 2018.

92. Legner, C.; Eymann, T.; Hess, T.; Matt, C.; Böhmann, T.; Drews, P.; Mädche, A.; Urbach, N.; Ahlemann, F. Digitalization: Opportunity and Challenge for the Business and Information Systems Engineering Community. *Bus. Inf. Syst. Eng.* **2017**, *59*, 301–308. [CrossRef]
93. Covington, M.J.; Carskadden, R. Threat implications of the Internet of Things. In Proceedings of the 2013 5th International Conference on Cyber Conflict (CYCON 2013), Tallinn, Estonia, 4–7 June 2013. Available online: https://ieeexplore.ieee.org/abstract/document/6568380 (accessed on 22 April 2021).
94. Woodhead, R.; Stephenson, P.; Morrey, D. Digital construction: From point solutions to IoT ecosystem. *Autom. Constr.* **2018**, *93*, 35–46. [CrossRef]
95. Nakamura, J. 5 Inovações na Construção Civil que Estão Agitando o Mercado. BUILDIN Construção e Informação. 2019. Available online: https://www.sienge.com.br/blog/inovacoes-na-construcao-civil/ (accessed on 10 April 2021).
96. de Matos Nogueira, R.; Santos, J.S.; dos Santos, R.P.; Galvão, B.B.; Swartele, J.C.; Santos, R.C.; De, R.D.; Nogueira, M.; De Andrade, W.V.; Júlio, S.; et al. Importância Da Sondagem Spt Na Construção Civil. *Rev. Pesqui. Ação* **2019**, *5*, 171–178. Available online: https://revistas.brazcubas.br/index.php/pesquisa/article/view/683 (accessed on 10 April 2021).
97. CELERE. Um dos Prédios Mais Sustentáveis do Mundo e o Impacto da Internet das Coisas na Construção. Equipe CELERE. 2018. Available online: https://celere-ce.com.br/construcao-civil/predios-mais-sustentaveis-do-mundo-internet-das-coisas/ (accessed on 6 January 2022).
98. Cho, Y.S.; Lim, N.Y.; Joung, W.S.; Jung, S.H.; Choi, S.K. Management of Construction Fields Information Using Low Altitude Close-range Aerial Images. *Korean J. Geomat.* **2014**, *32*, 551–560. [CrossRef]
99. Lee, M.L.; Lee, Y.L.; Goh, S.L.; Koo, C.H.; Lau, S.H.; Chong, S.Y. Case Studies and Challenges of Implementing Geotechnical Building Information Modelling in Malaysia. *Infrastructures* **2021**, *6*, 145. [CrossRef]
100. Craveiro, F.; Duarte, J.P.; Bartolo, H.; Bartolo, P.J. Additive manufacturing as an enabling technology for digital construction: A perspective on Construction 4.0. *Autom. Constr.* **2019**, *103*, 251–267. [CrossRef]
101. Franco, J.T. Assim é Construída uma Parede de Tijolos Utilizando Realidade Aumentada. ArchDaily. 2019. Available online: https://www.archdaily.com.br/br/908796/assim-e-construida-uma-parede-de-tijolos-utilizando-realidade-aumentada (accessed on 6 January 2022).
102. Brum, E.M.; Pandolfo, A.; Berticelli, R.; Kalil, R.M.L.; Pasquali, P.B. Economic, social and environmental aspects of the sustainability of a construction waste recycling plant. *Gestão Produção* **2021**, *28*, e5120. [CrossRef]
103. Bellini, O.E. Adaptive Exoskeleton Systems: Remodelage for Social Housing on Piazzale Visconti (BG). In *Regeneration of the Built Environment from a Circular Economy Perspective*; Springer: Cham, Switzerland, 2019; pp. 363–374. [CrossRef]
104. Jeelani, I.; Gheisari, M. Safety challenges of UAV integration in construction: Conceptual analysis and future research roadmap. *Saf. Sci.* **2021**, *144*, 105473. [CrossRef]
105. de Lima, R.L.P.; Boogaard, F.C.; Sazonov, V. Assessing the Influence of Floating Constructions on Water Quality and Ecology. In *WCFS2020*; Springer: Singapore, 2022; pp. 397–406. [CrossRef]
106. Rodrigues, M. Civil Construction Planning Using Augmented Reality. In *Sustainability and Automation in Smart Constructions*; Springer: Cham, Switzerland, 2021; pp. 211–217. [CrossRef]
107. Ahmed, S. A Review on Using Opportunities of Augmented Reality and Virtual Reality in Construction Project Management. *Organ. Technol. Manag. Constr. Int. J.* **2019**, *11*, 1839–1852. [CrossRef]
108. Delgado, J.M.D.; Oyedele, L.; Demian, P.; Beach, T. A research agenda for augmented and virtual reality in architecture, engineering and construction. *Adv. Eng. Inform.* **2020**, *45*, 101122. [CrossRef]
109. Kanan, R.; Elhassan, O.; Bensalem, R. An IoT-based autonomous system for workers' safety in construction sites with real-time alarming, monitoring, and positioning strategies. *Autom. Constr.* **2018**, *88*, 73–86. [CrossRef]
110. Gamil, Y.; Abdullah, M.A.; Abd Rahman, I.; Asad, M.M. Internet of things in construction industry revolution 4.0: Recent trends and challenges in the Malaysian context. *J. Eng. Des. Technol.* **2020**, *18*, 1091–1102. [CrossRef]

Article

A Discussion on Winter Indoor Hygrothermal Conditions and Hygroscopic Behaviour of Plasters in Southern Europe

Alessandra Ranesi [1,2,*], Magda Posani [2,3,4], Rosário Veiga [2] and Paulina Faria [1]

1   CERIS—Civil Engineering Research and Innovation for Sustainability, NOVA School of Science and Technology, NOVA University of Lisbon, Quinta da Torre, 2829-516 Caparica, Portugal; mpr@fct.unl.pt
2   National Laboratory for Civil Engineering, Avenida do Brasil 101, 1700-066 Lisbon, Portugal; posani@ibi.baug.ethz.ch (M.P.); rveiga@lnec.pt (R.V.)
3   CONSTRUCT (LFC—Building Physics Laboratory), Faculty of Engineering of the University of Porto—FEUP, R. Dr. Roberto Frias, 4200-465 Porto, Portugal
4   Chair of Sustainable Construction, Institute of Construction and Infrastructure Management (IBI), ETH Zürich, Stefano-Franscini-Platz 5, 8093 Zürich, Switzerland
*   Correspondence: a.ranesi@campus.fct.unl.pt; Tel.: +39-389-9975619

Abstract: In Southern European countries, due to the specific climate, economy and culture, a permanent heating practice during winter is not widely adopted. This may have a significant effect on the performance of indoor coating materials, typically tested considering hygrothermal conditions in the range of 33–75% relative humidity (RH) and 20–25 °C, which are common in continuously heated buildings. In this study, the indoor climate of four bedrooms located in Lisbon, Portugal, was monitored under operational conditions. Based on the data monitored in the case studies, characteristic ranges of indoor hygrothermal conditions were defined and compared to those considered in standard test procedures. In addition, numerical simulations were adopted to compare the hygroscopic performance of four plasters under operational conditions observed on-site. Results show that the four rooms, intermittently heated or unheated, do not provide comfort conditions over 50% of the wintertime, with temperatures lower and RH higher than the ones recommended by the standards. The MBVs resulting from simulations (under operational conditions) are qualitatively in agreement with the MBVs obtained under standard testing conditions. Nonetheless, future studies are recommended to evaluate if standard tests are quantitatively representative of the hygroscopic performance of coating materials in the Southern European scenario.

Keywords: hygrothermal comfort; indoor climate; moisture buffering; hygroscopic behaviour; southern Mediterranean countries; hygrometric regulation

1. Introduction

The importance of indoor environmental quality (IEQ) is currently largely acknowledged, due to the extended amount of time people spend indoors [1]. Consequently, the study of parameters such as indoor thermal comfort [2–4], indoor air quality [5], perceived quality [6] and the correlation with human health [7] gained importance in research. In this context, increasing attention has been paid to the use of building materials [8] and hygroscopic coating systems [9,10] that can help to passively regulate indoor relative humidity (RH). The idea is to exploit the moisture buffering ability of the materials to regulate indoor hygrometric conditions. Indeed, hygroscopic materials tend to adsorb moisture when RH rises and then release it when the air becomes drier [11], thus moderating the peaks in indoor RH and reducing operational energy demands [12,13] while passively improving indoor comfort [14].

To evaluate and compare the moisture buffering ability of materials, the NORDTEST protocol [15,16] is often adopted. This test procedure was defined by a research group working on the specific scenario of North European countries [17] and it is based on the hypothesis of continuously heated buildings (e.g., indoor set-point temperature of 23 °C [18]). The methodology was defined considering an occupancy of 8 h per day, which is typical of offices and bedrooms [19]. Three possible ranges of RH were proposed, and the one normally adopted spans from 33% to 75%. Even though some other procedures exist, for instance ISO 24353 [20], the NORDTEST method is the most largely adopted one, because it provides a quantitative evaluation of the moisture buffering capacity [17] through a single parameter: the practical Moisture Buffering Value (MBV). Hence, this test procedure allows to compare the potential effectiveness of different hygroscopic materials and coating systems through their MBVs.

Despite the great contribution provided by the introduction of the NORDTEST procedure, some doubts may arise when it is adopted in the context of Southern European countries. In fact, in Southern Europe, a permanent heating practice is not commonly adopted, especially in residential buildings [21]. On one hand, this is a consequence of the milder winter conditions. On the other, the combination of low incomes and high energy costs leads to a general "Lack of Motivation to Heat", which is extremely high in Portugal, Romania and Greece, and lower but still relevant in other Southern European countries such as Spain, Croatia and Italy [21]. In this context, a relevant share of the population is found to be unable to keep the house adequately warm [22,23]. Due to the low indoor temperatures (T), high RH levels can be expected. The scenario of Southern Europe may thus require a complementary approach that differs from the standard test conditions defined for the case of Northern Europe by the NORDTEST protocol.

This study aims to evaluate the indoor hygrothermal conditions in four case studies located in Lisbon (Portugal) and intends to open a discussion on the applicability of standard tests on the moisture buffering ability of building materials, in the context of Southern Europe. The detailed methodology is schematized in Figure 1.

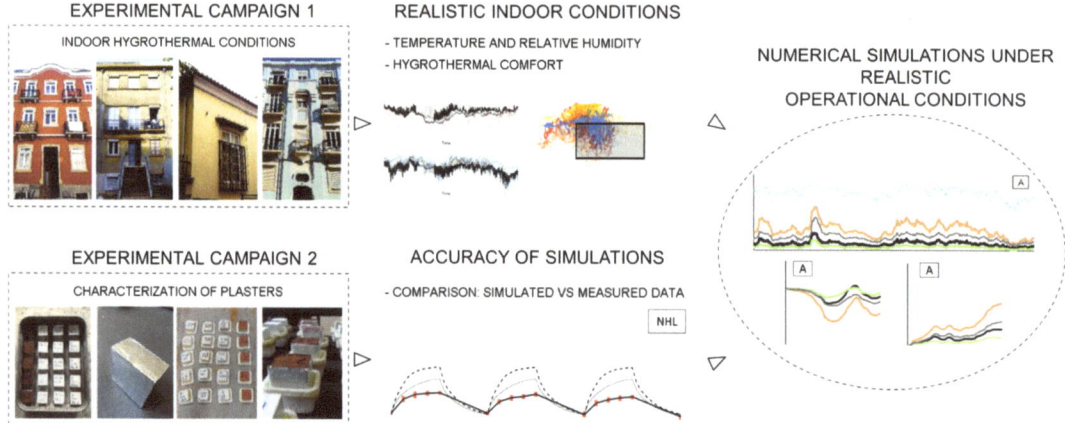

Figure 1. Schematic representation of the methodology followed in the study.

The monitoring was performed during winter, when the passive relative humidity regulation can be significant since windows are kept closed for most of the time. Moreover, it was possible to verify the complaints of the bedrooms' users, who reported the spaces to be cold and moist during winter. The dataset, thus obtained, was examined to evaluate the fluctuation of indoor RH to be compared to the scenario adopted in the NORDTEST. To facilitate the comparison between real conditions and testing ones, the data were recorded in bedrooms, which better represents (for residential) the type of space (occupation for 1/3 of the day) considered in the NORDTEST. The indoor climate data obtained on-site were then used as input in numerical simulations, to evaluate the hygroscopic behaviour of different plasters under realistic operational conditions. Results were compared to the

MBVs of the plasters obtained under standard conditions (via laboratory tests), to assess if they were representative of their potential hygroscopic behaviour under the observed real conditions.

2. Materials and Methods

2.1. Case Studies Selected and Indoor Monitoring Campaign

Four case studies were selected for the experimental indoor monitoring campaign. In each one, the air temperature (T) and relative humidity (RH) were continuously recorded during winter 2021. The four buildings are located in the core of the city of Lisbon, and their location is displayed in Figure 2. All the buildings were built before the first Portuguese regulation on thermal requirements for buildings was published [24]. This is a very common condition in the Portuguese building stock, where 85% of the building stock, reported in 2011, dated back to before the 1990s [25]. The bedrooms under study are subjected to one-person occupancy and they are intermittently heated by the users with electric-heating devices, or not heated at all.

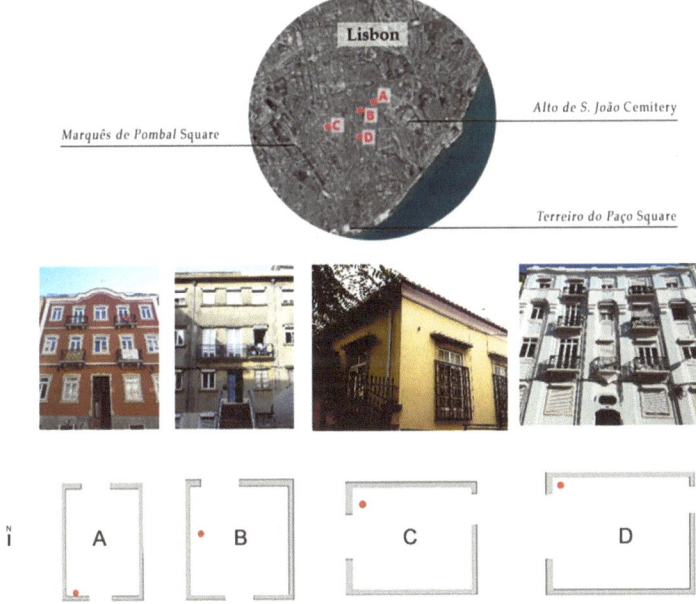

Figure 2. Selected case studies: location in the map of Lisbon, building facades, and plans of the monitored bedrooms (openings: interior door and outdoor-facing window). In each room, a red dot indicates the position of the data-logger used to monitor the indoor hygrothermal conditions.

Case study A, Figure 2A, is located in a three-floor building whose envelope was recently refurbished. The bedroom considered is on the 1st floor, and it has an area of about 7.5 m^2. It has one external wall, which is north-oriented, and a balcony. Case study B, Figure 2B, is located in a building that looks like the result of a social housing project of the second half of the 20th century. The bedroom selected is on the upper ground floor and has an area of about 8.4 m^2. It has one external wall, north-oriented, with one window. Case study C, Figure 2C, is a room of a detached house with an individual owner. The bedroom analysed is on the upper ground floor and it has an area of about 7.5 m^2. The bedroom has one external wall, west-oriented, with a window. Case study D, Figure 2D, is located on the 3rd and last floor of an apartment building. It has a floor area of about 11 m^2 and one external wall with a balcony, west-oriented.

The indoor monitoring campaign was performed by means of two data-loggers HOBO UX100-003 (accuracy: ±0.21 °C, ±3.5% for 25–85% RH and 5% out of this range) and two HOBO U12-013 (accuracy: ±0.35 °C, ±2.5% for 10–90% RH and 5% out of this range). The sampling interval adopted was 10 min and the final hygrothermal data were defined as the hourly average values of T and RH obtained from the recordings, as in previous studies [26,27]. The data-loggers were positioned inside paper boxes (open on the top) to avoid the interference of drafts and solar radiation in the measurements. Furthermore, the equipment was located on the top of different pieces of furniture, at 70–180 cm from the floor, to minimize direct interactions between the bedrooms' users and the sensors. Finally, a minimum distance of 10 cm was kept between the walls and the data-loggers. The hourly data of outdoor T and RH were provided by the Portuguese Institute of Sea and Atmosphere (IPMA) [28], from a local meteorological station.

The monitoring campaign was performed during winter because it is the period when a passive regulation of RH can be very beneficial for improving hygrothermal comfort. Indeed, during winter the air change rates are low because windows are kept closed for most of the time, and the lower the air change rates the higher the potential impact of the materials on indoor RH [10]. In addition, due to the typically moderate use of heating in Southern Europe, high RH levels can occur. Wintertime was approximated considering the period 15 November–31 March, based on the degree days' calculation. Since the Portuguese legislation [29] that defines the degree days does not include a specific identification for the starting and ending date of the heating period (which is hereby considered to define wintertime), an Italian standard was taken as a reference [30]. This choice was considered suitable for the scope since both Portugal and Italy are Southern European countries, and the selected period appeared representative of wintertime in Lisbon.

2.2. Statistical Analysis of Indoor Hygrothermal Conditions and Indoor Comfort

Once the set of hygrothermal data from the case studies was acquired, it was statistically evaluated through cumulative frequency plots. The 25th and 75th percentiles, also known as the upper and lower quartiles [31], were considered to identify a typical range of indoor conditions. Similarly, a wider range was defined by using the 10th and 90th percentiles.

To evaluate whether the indoor environments were cold and moist, as reported by the bedroom users, the data obtained in the monitoring were compared to the comfort requirements found in the literature. Indoor comfort depends on a variety of factors that can be difficult to forecast for residential buildings, due to the uncertainty on the activities performed, the variability of clothing, the uncontrolled use of the windows, and so forth. Thus, calculations concerning the predicted mean vote (PMV) and predicted percentage of dissatisfied (PPD), as indicated in standards ISO 7730 [32] and ASHRAE 55 [33], are disregarded in favour of a more simplified evaluation. A zone of acceptable hygrothermal comfort was defined according to the following observations. During winter the temperature should be higher than 16 °C to guarantee neutral or comfort sensation for the occupants, as referred by Peeters et al. [34] for bedrooms. Standard EN 16798-1 [35] indicates a maximum temperature of 25 °C for bedrooms belonging to category III (acceptable, moderate level of expectation on indoor comfort). In addition, standard EN 15,251 [36] suggests an RH level within the range 20–70%, for buildings in category III. Therefore, in order to account for an additional indication of the literature, the minimum acceptable RH level was increased to 30% [7], to avoid excessive drying out of the skin and of the mucous membranes.

2.3. Plaster Characterization

Four plastering mortars were selected to be used in the simulations. The mortars were prepared by mechanical mixing and water was added to achieve suitable workability (assessed through flow table test [37]). The mortars and their consistence were the following:

E—commercial plaster based on clayish earth produced by EMBARRO [38] with a consistence by flow table of 170 ± 10 mm;

CL—1:3 volumetric ratio of hydrate air lime CL 90-S and siliceous sand (0–4 mm) with a consistence by flow table of 151 ± 5 mm;

NHL—1:3 volumetric ratio of natural hydraulic lime NHL3.5 and siliceous sand (0–4 mm) with a consistence by flow table of 150 ± 5 mm;

Cem—1:4 volumetric ratio of CEM II/B-L 32.5N and siliceous sand (0–2 mm) with a consistence by flow table of 140 ± 3 mm.

A detailed description and characterization of the plastering mortars can be found in a previous study [39]. The Moisture Buffering Values (MBVs) were calculated considering the experimental results obtained following the NORDTEST protocol [17] and the ISO 24353 standard [20]. MBVs were calculated on the average of five specimens for each plaster (40 × 40 × 20 mm^3). According to the NORDTEST protocol [17], the specimens were cyclically exposed to steps of RH 33% (16 h)–75% (8 h) until quasi-steady-state equilibrium was reached. When tested according to the ISO 24353 [20], the cyclic condition of *middle humidity level* (12 h at 75% RH followed by 12 h at 50% RH) was chosen. Temperature was fixed at 23 ± 0.5 °C during the entire test in both cases. The difference between the two methods lies in the range of RH considered (minimum of 33% or 50%) and in the period of exposure to different hygrometric conditions (12–12 h; 16–8 h). The MBV results are reported in Table 1.

Table 1. Plaster MBVs (g/m^2·%RH) according to the NORDTEST and ISO 24353 testing protocols.

Plaster	NORDTEST	ISO 24353
E	1.493 ± 0.09	1.327 ± 0.08
CL	0.416 ± 0.04	0.267 ± 0.03
NHL	0.799 ± 0.03	0.537 ± 0.02
Cem	0.843 ± 0.07	0.660 ± 0.05

The physical and hygric characterization of the plasters was performed in previous studies [39–42]. The material properties needed for the simulations were defined following the indication of Posani, Veiga and Freitas [43], based on the results of the experimental campaigns. Thermal properties were considered of minor importance in this study, and they were thus approximated using the values provided in the WUFI database [44] for similar materials. The main data adopted for the simulations are summarized in Table 2.

Table 2. Plaster properties adopted in numerical simulations.

Plaster	P_o (%)	ρ_{Dry} (kg/m^3)	μ (-)	A_w (kg/m^{2}s$^{0.5}$)	* λ_{Dry} (W/(mK))
E	29.9	1743	9.07	0.50	0.5
CL	25.8	1720	7.43	1.71	0.7
NHL	26.2	1779	9.32	2.40	0.7
Cem	20.2	1919	20.42	0.43	1.2

Notation: Po—open porosity, ρ_{Dry}—dry bulk density, μ—water resistance factor, A_w—capillary water absorption, λ_{Dry}—thermal conductivity, * not measured but approximated considering values from WUFI database.

The sorption isotherm is recognized to be one of the most important material properties when simulating the impact of hygroscopic materials on indoor RH [45]. They were defined for both the adsorption and desorption phases, according to standard ISO 12571 [46]. Five specimens (40 × 40 × 20 mm^3) for each plaster were tested. They were first dried at 60 °C, then they were kept under constant hygrothermal conditions until equilibrium was reached, using a climatic chamber FITOCLIMA 700EDTU. The steps of RH considered were the following: 30%, 50%, 70%, 80%, and 95% RH, while the temperature was constantly kept at 23 ± 0.5 °C.

2.4. Numerical Simulations

The software adopted for mono-dimensional hygrothermal simulations is WUFI Pro 5 [44], which allows performing mono-dimensional hygrothermal simulations of multi-layered wall cross-sections under realistic climatic conditions. This software was chosen for several reasons. First, it offers a detailed calculation model of combined heat and moisture transport, which includes liquid transport, vapour diffusion, and hygroscopic behaviour of porous materials [44]. Furthermore, WUFI Pro has been validated through several years of field and laboratory testing [47–51], and it is widely adopted to investigate passive regulation of humidity due to hygroscopic building materials [52–55]. In addition, the software allows introducing material properties as input data, thus plasters can be modelled according to the information obtained in laboratory tests. Additionally, the software accounts for hourly data of boundary conditions, thus the indoor climate can be introduced in the model based on the microclimate monitoring performed in the case studies.

In this study, numerical simulations are first adopted to reproduce the standard test on moisture adsorption/desorption defined by ISO 24353 [20]. The results numerically obtained are compared to the experimental results observed in the laboratory. The accuracy of the model for representing the hygroscopic behaviour of the plasters is consequently discussed. The plasters are then simulated considering the indoor climatic conditions measured on-site and the results are discussed in comparison with MBV experimentally obtained. The comparison aims to evaluate if standard test conditions are representative of materials adopted in the context of Southern Europe, where indoor climatic conditions can become colder and moister than in northern countries, due to the different heating habits.

2.4.1. Simulations under Standard Conditions

Dynamic numerical simulations have been largely applied to study the hygroscopic behaviour of building materials. Nonetheless, modelling hygroscopic materials requires some simplifications, in particular concerning their sorption isotherm. Building materials can show a residual moisture content at the end of desorption, due to the effect of capillary forces which make the uptake of water molecules in the porous network easier than their removal [56]. This behaviour is also known as moisture hysteresis [57]. Thus, the curves obtained during the adsorption and desorption phases can be quite different from each other.

In WUFI software, the sorption isotherm is assumed as a bijective function, thus two separate curves cannot be introduced for adsorption and desorption, and a simplification must be adopted. In the literature, two approaches emerge for operating this simplification: some studies consider the adsorption isotherm only [58], and others use the average values obtained combining adsorption and desorption curves [59]. Both simplifications are applied in this research and evaluated. The materials modelled according to the two approaches are simulated under the standard conditions adopted in the laboratory test as in ISO 24353 [20]. Then, the results obtained with the two simplifications are compared to those measured in the laboratory. Based on the outcomes of this comparison, the simplification offering more accurate results is chosen for the forthcoming simulations. The NORDTEST procedure was not replicated via numerical simulation due to the very little data available, namely only one measurement after each phase of adsorption or desorption. Consequently, it was of minor interest for the sake of comparing measured and simulated values.

More in detail, this first set of simulations is performed as follows. First, the materials were modelled as horizontal components, having a thickness of 2 cm, and a sealing material was applied on the bottom (a vapour barrier with a S_d = 1500 m). The lateral sealing is not modelled since the simulations run under the hypothesis of an infinite plane component, thus the conditions at the border do not influence the results. The upper and lower boundary conditions adopted are those of the experimental test, namely a constant temperature of 23 °C and cycles of 12 h of constant RH, which is alternatively kept at 75% or 50%. To replicate the test performed in the laboratory, the initial condition of the material is 23 °C and moisture content stabilized at 63% RH. The results of the first 4 cycles, i.e., a total of 48 h, are not represented, while the following ones are reported in comparison to those measured in the laboratory, in terms of moisture content per unit of surface in the samples.

2.4.2. Simulations under Realistic Operational Conditions

The plasters are then simulated under realistic operational conditions, considering the indoor data recorded on-site and a typical Portuguese wall assembly.

Since all case studies have different walls, a typical configuration is adopted to have comparable results, while being representative of the Portuguese building stock. The geometry consists of a whole-brick structure, 34 cm thick, as characteristic of traditional Portuguese brick-masonry walls with medium thickness [60]. On the exterior side, 2 cm of lime-cement render is considered, finished with acrylic paint, to account for a typically refurbished façade. At the indoor-facing side of the wall, a 2 cm thick layer of plaster is adopted (E, CL, NHL, and Cem, alternatively). The initial conditions in the plasters are assumed as in equilibrium with air at 20 °C and 60% RH, which is considered to be a realistic assumption, based on the indoor hygrothermal data observed on-site. Outdoor boundary conditions are defined using typical weather data of Lisbon, namely those provided in the Test Reference Year from the WUFI database. At the interior side of the walls, the microclimate adopted is the one recorded on-site during winter, in the four case studies, alternatively.

Results are evaluated in terms of moisture content in the plaster, per unit of surface. Then, the variation of moisture content in the plasters is observed in detail during a 2-day period. Based on the results, the hygroscopic behaviour observed under realistic operational conditions is discussed and compared to the results obtained in terms of MBV in standard tests.

3. Results and Discussion

3.1. Indoor Climate

Figure 3 shows the hourly data of T and RH obtained in the indoor environmental monitoring, versus the ones recorded by IPMA for the outdoor climate, from November 2020 to March 2021. According to the collected data, during winter the outdoor temperature and relative humidity were in the ranges 1–26 °C and 40–100% RH, respectively, with T being lower than 16 °C for most of the time and RH being generally above 75%. Regarding indoor climates, hygrothermal conditions were in the ranges of 10–28 °C and 21–90% RH in the period considered.

3.2. Statistical Evaluation

To analyse the typical range of variation of indoor T and RH, a statistical evaluation was performed, and the results are shown in Figure 4.

The curve of accumulated frequency shows that the lower threshold value considered in the NORDTEST is not very representative of the indoor hygrometric conditions analysed. Indeed, this condition was never reached in case studies C and D, while such low levels of RH, namely below 35%, are obtained for less than 5% of the time in the other two case studies. This result indicates that an RH level around 33% is not representative of a typical daily low point of RH, but it is more of an exceptional condition, in the case studies considered. This outcome is coherent with the heating strategy adopted in the case studies. While continuous heating may lead to low levels of RH, intermittent or absent heating leads to lower indoor temperatures, with consequently higher RH levels.

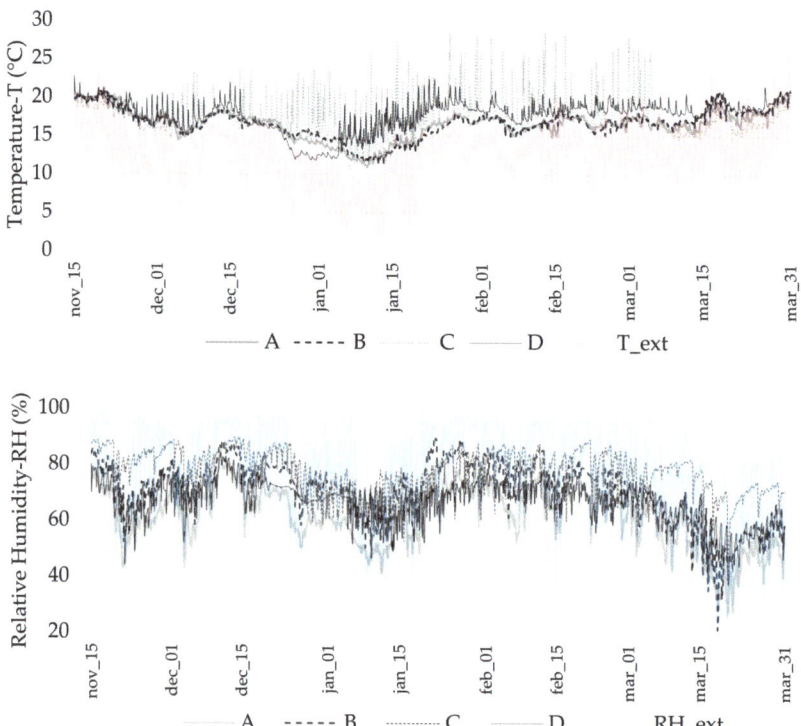

Figure 3. Hourly average air temperature (°C) and relative humidity (%) data recorded by IPMA in the city of Lisbon and the same parameters recorded in the four bedrooms (A, B, C and D), for the period 15 November 2020–31 March 2021.

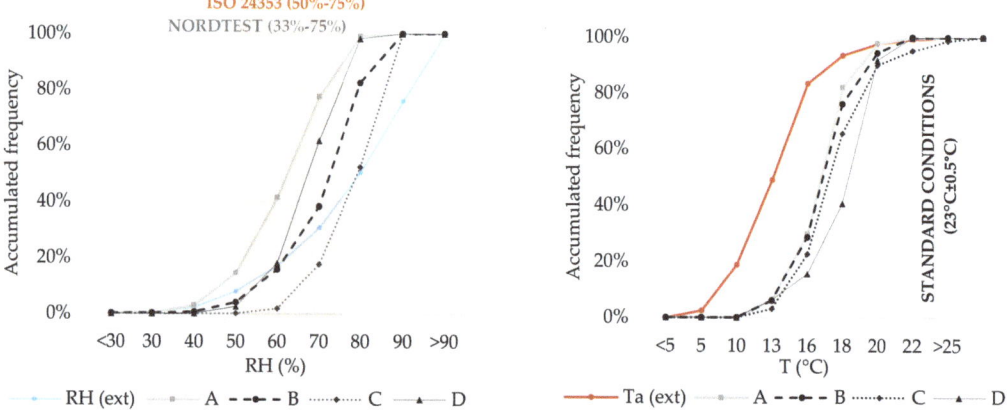

Figure 4. Frequency distribution of hourly RH and T data recorded in the four bedrooms under study in Lisbon and in the outdoor climate, from November 2020 to March 2022.

As far as the upper limit value of the NORDTEST is concerned, i.e., 75% RH, it seems quite representative of a typical condition of high RH in case studies A and D. In these two rooms, indoor hygrometric conditions are below this value at least 80% of wintertime.

On the contrary, much higher RH levels can be found in case studies B and C, where an RH above 75% is detected during 60% and 40% of the winter period, respectively. Even for temperature, the standard range considered in laboratory testing (23 °C ± 0.5 °C) does not seem to represent typical indoor conditions in the analysed bedrooms. Indeed, temperatures below 22.5 °C are found for more than 90% of the time in all the rooms taken into analysis.

The outcomes of the monitoring seem consistent with previous indoor monitoring campaigns performed in buildings located in Portugal. Indeed, in a study on a prototype of an un-refurbished classroom [3], on social housing [61], and on residential apartments [62], RH levels were frequently falling in the range 50–80% RH during winter. In addition, in the three studies, indoor temperature was found to be below 22.5 °C for almost the whole winter period considered in the monitoring (entire winter in [3,62], and only February in [61]).

In order to have a representation of a typical range for indoor RH and T fluctuations, two intervals are hereby considered: the 90th–10th percentile (P90–P10%) and the more restrictive interval 75th–25th percentile (P75%, P25%). Considering all case studies, the average values of P25% and P75% are 63%—16 °C and 76%—18.5 °C, whereas the average values obtained for P10% and P90% are 56%—14.5 °C and 82%—19.5 °C, as reported in Figure 5.

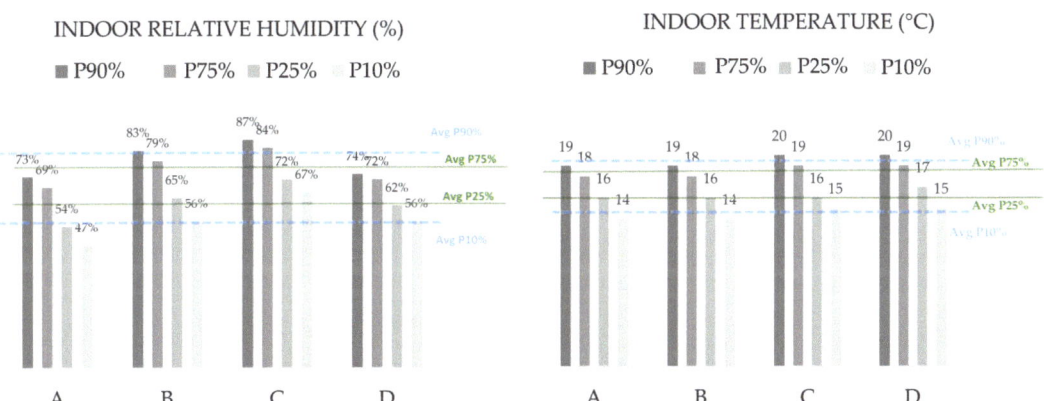

Figure 5. Values of the 90th, 75th, 25th, and 10th percentiles in the dataset of indoor relative humidity and temperature recorded in each case study, during winter. The blue and green lines indicate the average values obtained from the percentiles of the 4 case studies.

According to this analysis, a typical range of fluctuation would be 63–76% RH and 16–18.5 °C (considering 25th–75th percentiles), or 56–82% for RH and 14.5–19.5 °C (accounting for 10th–90th percentiles). The proposed ranges are hereby assumed as representative of the indoor climates considered, and they are compared to the indication of ISO 24353 [20] and NORDTEST [17] for the RH range to consider during the tests.

From the qualitative comparison provided in Figure 6, the step 50–75% RH suggested by ISO 24353 [20] for a "middle humidity level" appears to better estimate the indoor datasets than the NORDTEST. In the latter, the minimum RH appears extremely lower than the values of indoor RH registered, and it is significantly below the limits estimated with P10% and P25%. This difference between typical testing conditions and real climates might result in an overestimation of the potential benefits of hygroscopic materials applied in the Southern European context. In fact, the conditions of the NORDTEST have a greater range of RH and a much lower minimum value, which would probably result in higher MBV of the materials than at "more realistic conditions". For this reason, it could be valuable to have further studies aimed to evaluate the scenario of Southern European countries and a possible complementary approach to adopt for applications of hygroscopic materials within this context. Regarding the temperature, both the methods (ISO and NORDTEST) account for a T of 23 ± 0.5 °C, which is quite far from the ranges hereby observed (16–18.5 °C and 14.5–19.5 °C). Even though the effect of T on the moisture buffering capacity of building materials is hardly ever investigated, according to Mazhoud et al. [63] a linear correlation between T and MBV exists, probably for the effect of T on saturation vapour pressure [64]. The possibility of considering a specific temperature for Southern European countries might be an option to consider in future investigations.

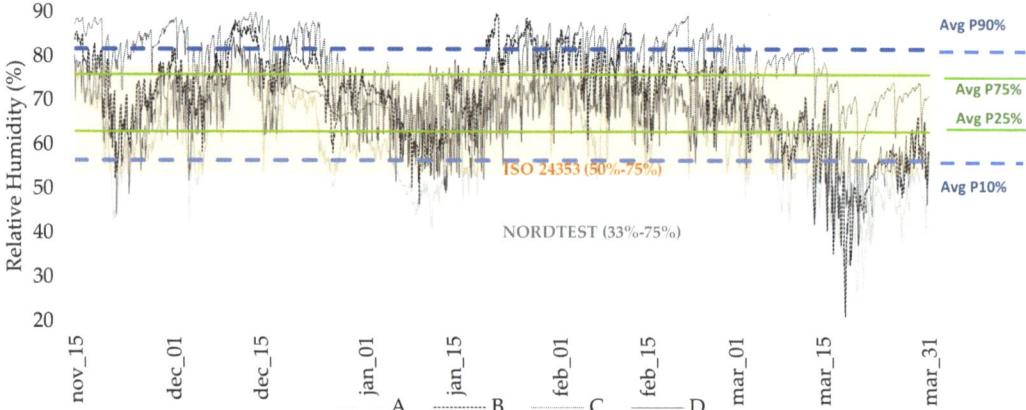

Figure 6. Indoor RH in each of the four bedrooms. The blue and green lines indicate the average values found in the case studies, in terms of 10th, 25th, 75th and 90th percentile of RH. For comparison, the ranges of RH considered in the NORDTEST [17] and the ISO 24353 [20] are also reported, in grey and orange hatches, respectively.

3.3. Indoor Comfort

Comparing the datasets obtained via indoor monitoring with the comfort zone roughly defined through four points in Figure 7, it emerges that all case studies are out of the hygrothermal comfort area for a large share of wintertime. In case studies A and D indoor RH and T are out of the comfort zone for at least 50% of wintertime, a percentage that increases to 75% and about 90% in case studies B and C, respectively.

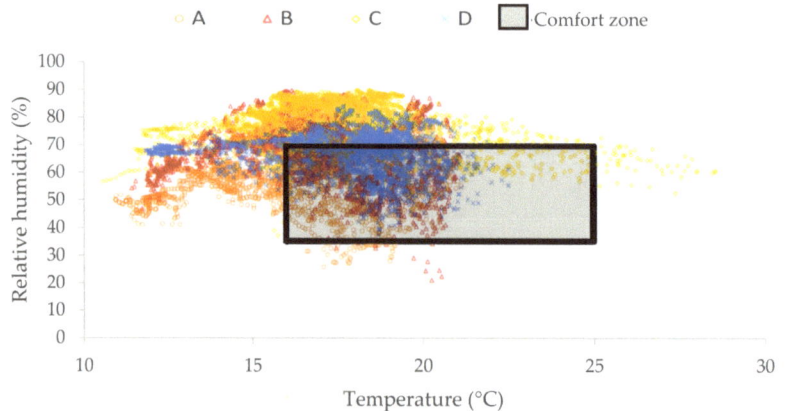

Figure 7. Graphic comparison between the hygrothermal datasets registered on-site in case studies A to D, and the comfort zone defined through 4 points (16;30); (16;70); (25;30); (25;70).

The comparison reported in Figure 7 shows that discomfort conditions are mainly due to high RH and/or low T. This result is in agreement with the feedback given by the users and with the observation raised in the literature concerning the typical lack of comfort in Southern European residential spaces.

3.4. Sorption Isotherms of the Plasters

The sorption isotherms of the plasters are shown in Figure 8. For each plaster, the adsorption and the desorption phases are represented by a continuous and a dotted line, respectively. All the plasters present some hysteresis, showing a residual moisture content at the end of the desorption phase. For E and NHL plasters, the hysteresis is very low, and the adsorption and desorption curves almost overlap. The other two plasters, CL and CEM, have higher hysteresis.

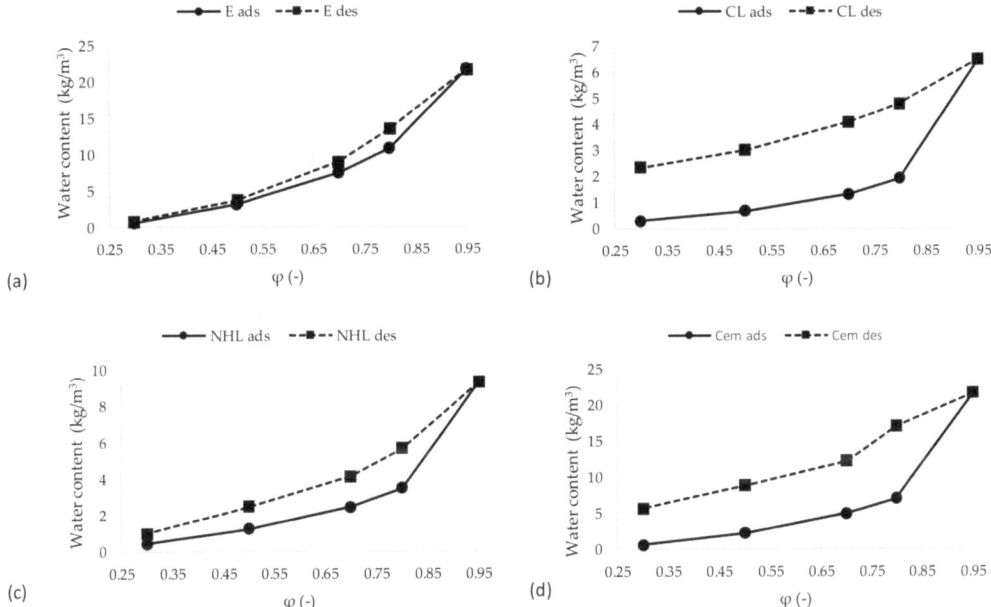

Figure 8. Sorption isotherms of the mortars based on: (**a**) earth; (**b**) air lime CL90-S; (**c**) natural hydraulic lime NHL 3.5 and (**d**) cement II/B-L 32.5N.

3.5. Simulations

3.5.1. Simulations under Standard Conditions

Figure 9 shows the results of numerical simulations compared to those obtained in the experimental characterization of the plasters. Numerical simulations were run both considering the average of adsorption and desorption curves—simulated (AVG)—and only accounting for the adsorption curve—simulated (ADS). For E and Cem, the two curves (AVG and ADS) are almost overlapped. On the contrary, CL and especially NHL show more relevant differences when different assumptions are made to simplify their sorption isotherms. Namely, more accurate results were obtained considering only the adsorption curve. Thus, for the simulations presented in the following section, this simplification (ADS) is adopted to model the sorption isotherm of the four plasters considered.

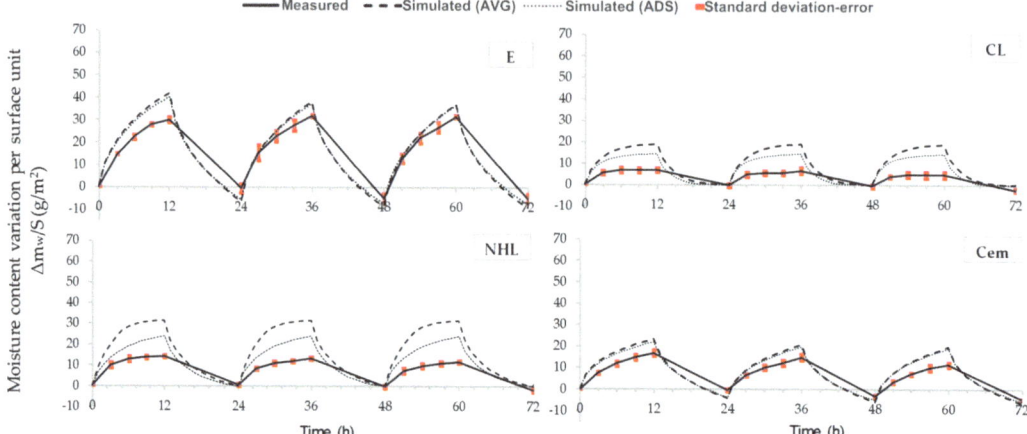

Figure 9. Three cycles of moisture content variation per unit of surface, displayed among time for each plaster: E—earth, CL—air lime, NHL—natural hydraulic lime and Cem—cement-based; *Continuous*—plaster laboratory results tested according to ISO 24353 [20] and relative standard deviation; *dashed*—hourly measures on simulation based on sorption/desorption average curve; *dotted*—hourly measures on simulation based on adsorption.

Moreover, all simulations appear to overestimate the moisture content in the materials during the adsorption process. This outcome seems less relevant for E and Cem, and more significant for CL and NHL. Nonetheless, simulations still appear representative of the different behaviour of materials, meaning that materials showing higher moisture content variation in the laboratory do also have higher changes of moisture content in the simulations. For this reason, the model adopted is considered suitable for a qualitative comparison of the hygroscopic behaviour of the plasters under realistic operational conditions.

Finally, similar differences between measured and simulated water content in building materials, during alternated cycles of high and low humidity, were also observed in previous studies [65–67].

3.5.2. Simulations under Realistic Operational Conditions

The results obtained via dynamic hygrothermal simulations under realistic operational conditions are presented in Figure 10. In the first four graphics, Figure 10a, the moisture content per unit area is represented with different colours for each plaster, for the indoor conditions of case studies A, B, C and D. The initial moisture content of plasters is assumed as the one at 60% RH, which corresponds to a different value depending on the sorption isotherm of each material. Although this difference in initial water content is noticeable, it is not relevant for the discussion on RH regulation. In this regard, what matters is the variation in the moisture content of the plaster, not its absolute value. Results shown in Figure 10a suggest that the variation of moisture content is stronger in plasters E and Cem, rather than in CL and NHL.

The fluctuation of moisture content is shown more in detail for two periods of 2 days, and the results are displayed in Figure 10b. The eight graphics reported in the figure confirm the previous observations. In all the scenarios considered, the largest fluctuations of moisture content are observed in the earthen plaster (E), followed by plasters based on cement (Cem), natural hydraulic lime (NHL) and hydrated air lime (CL), in this order. An exception is observable in the graphic on the right referring to case C, where the difference between E and Cem, and between NHL and CL, does not seem relevant. The ranking observed is in agreement with the MBVs experimentally obtained following the standard ISO 24353 [20] and the NORDTEST procedure [17]. The simulation results obtained under operational conditions show that in Southern European countries with low heating habits, the analysed standard tests used to quantify moisture buffering are qualitatively representative of the hygroscopic performance of materials under real operational conditions.

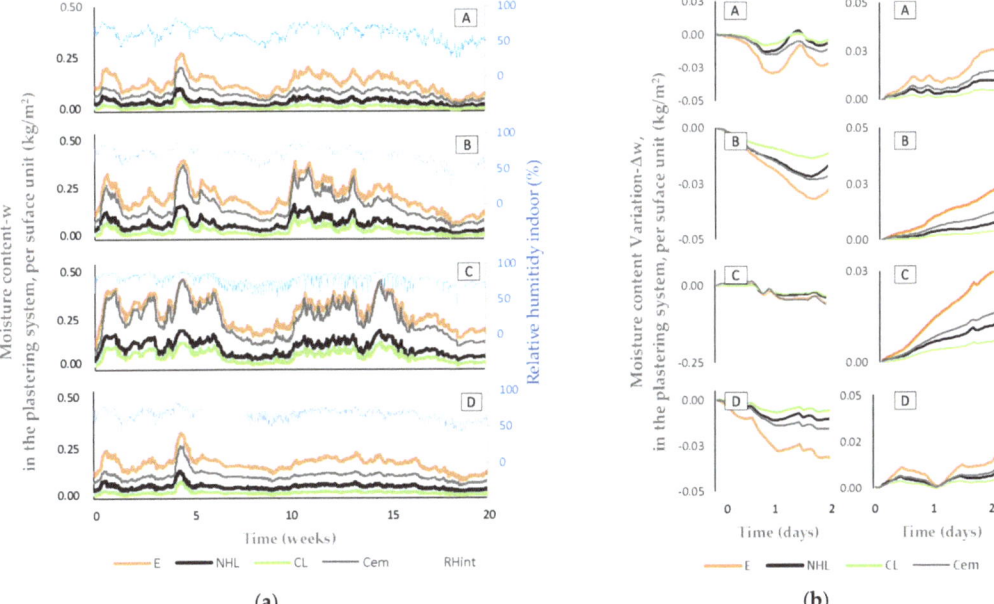

(a)   (b)

Figure 10. Simulation results of the moisture behaviour of the four plasters for each study case: (a) moisture content per unit of surface (m_w/S) during the entire winter period; (b) moisture content variation per unit of surface (Δm_w/S) during two periods of 2 days each, respectively, starting on 20 February and 21 March. From top to bottom, the graphics correspond to the results obtained considering the indoor climate recorded in case studies A, B, C and D.

Finally, the earth-based plaster, E, seems to be the most promising for further studies on indoor air quality improvement. This outcome is consistent with the observations in Cascione et al. [15], where an experimental campaign conducted at the room level showed that a clayey earth plaster was more effective than a lime-based one, for stabilizing indoor RH. Thus, earth-based plasters appear extremely appealing thanks to the additional benefits given by the low environmental impact and infinite recycling possibilities of earth [68].

4. Conclusions

This study presents the results obtained in an indoor hygrothermal monitoring campaign performed in four bedrooms of different buildings in Lisbon, during wintertime. The datasets obtained were analysed, and characteristic ranges of temperature and relative humidity were defined. Mono-dimensional dynamic hygrothermal simulation tools were adopted to simulate the hygroscopic performance of four plasters, under the operational conditions measured on-site.

The outcomes of the indoor monitoring campaign allowed to define the following conclusions:

- The microclimates of the four case studies are found to be well represented by the hygrothermal ranges of 63–76% RH and 17.5 ± 1.5 °C, which were defined considering the 25th and 75th percentiles of the dataset distributions.
- In terms of RH, the ISO 24353 sets the closest values to the characteristic ranges defined for the four case studies according to the monitoring. The standard adopts

the condition 50% to 75% RH, differently from the NORDTEST procedure, which is typically used considering the range 33–75% RH. Overall, the humidity range adopted in the ISO standard appears more representative of the microclimates observed on-site. Indeed, the lower RH value adopted in the NORDTEST (33%) is rarely reached in the datasets presented in this study. RH below this value is observed for less than 5% of the time and only in two case studies.

- Considering the temperature, the values prescribed in both the ISO 24353 standard and the NORDTEST protocol (22.5–23.5 °C) are higher than those observed in the case studies during almost the entire wintertime.
- In terms of indoor comfort, it was observed that the case studies are often out of the comfort area—over 50% of wintertime—mainly due to high relative humidity and low temperature. This outcome is consistent with the complaints of the bedrooms' users. Furthermore, it is aligned with the literature concerning the inability of keeping residential spaces sufficiently warm in Southern Europe.

Dynamic hygrothermal simulations allowed to give a rough evaluation of the moisture buffering ability of the plasters, under realistic operational conditions. The main remarks defined from the simulation results are the following:

- The fluctuation in the moisture content of the plasters was qualitatively in agreement with the ranking based on the MBV determined by both the NORDTEST procedure and ISO 24353 standard. Thus, the standard test procedures for evaluating the moisture buffering capacity of building materials might be representative also for the context of Southern European housing, despite its colder and moister indoor conditions. Further studies are needed to evaluate this point more in depth, accounting for the more accurate results obtainable through whole-building simulation models.
- The earth-based plaster, above all, showed the widest fluctuations in water content under realistic operational conditions. This result suggests that this material could be promising for passive regulation of indoor relative humidity.

Forthcoming studies will be focused on quantitatively evaluating the effect of the plasters on indoor RH regulation, by means of whole-building simulation tools. These evaluations will be used to further assess the suitability of standard tests to represent the hygroscopic behaviour of plasters in intermittently heated/unheated spaces, typical of Southern European countries.

Author Contributions: Conceptualization, investigation, writing—original draft preparation, A.R.; conceptualization, software, writing—original draft preparation, M.P.; supervision, writing—review and editing, R.V. and P.F. All authors have read and agreed to the published version of the manuscript.

Funding: This research is funded by the Portuguese Foundation for Science and Technology: PD/BD/150399/2019, PD/BD/135192/2017 (first and second authors are part of the Doctoral Training Programme EcoCoRe) and UIDB/04625/2020 (Civil Engineering Research and Innovation for Sustainability Unit—CERIS).

Institutional Review Board Statement: Not applicable.

Acknowledgments: The authors would like to acknowledge the support provided by CONSTRUCT-LFC (Institute of R&D in Structures and Construction at FEUP) and also by the National Laboratory for Civil Engineering, through projects PRESERVe and REuSE, as well as the help offered by IPMA, who provided for the outdoor climate dataset considered in the study.

Conflicts of Interest: The authors declare no conflict of interest.

References

1. Diffey, B.L. An overview analysis of the time people spend outdoors. *Br. J. Dermatol.* **2011**, *164*, 848–854. [CrossRef] [PubMed]
2. Curado, A.; Freitas, V.P.; Ramos, N.M. Variability assessment of thermal comfort in a retrofitted social housing neighborhood based on "in situ" measurements. *Energy Procedia* **2015**, *78*, 2790–2795. [CrossRef]
3. Barbosa, F.C.; Freitas, V.P.; Almeida, M. School building experimental characterization in Mediterranean climate regarding comfort, indoor air quality and energy consumption. *Energy Build.* **2020**, *212*, 109782. [CrossRef]

4. Caro, R.; Sendra, J.J. Are the dwellings of historic Mediterranean cities cold in winter? A field assessment on their indoor environment and energy performance. *Energy Build.* **2021**, *230*, 110567. [CrossRef]
5. Almeida, R.M.; Freitas, V.P. IEQ assessment of classrooms with an optimized demand controlled ventilation system. *Energy Procedia* **2015**, *78*, 3132–3137. [CrossRef]
6. Darling, E.K.; Cros, C.J.; Wargocki, P.; Kolarik, J.; Morrison, G.C.; Corsi, R.L. Impacts of a clay plaster on indoor air quality assessed using chemical and sensory measurements. *Build. Environ.* **2012**, *57*, 370–376. [CrossRef]
7. Wolkoff, P. Indoor air humidity, air quality, and health—An overview. *Int. J. Hyg. Environ. Health* **2018**, *221*, 376–390. [CrossRef]
8. McGregor, F.; Heath, A.; Maskell, D.; Fabbri, A.; Morel, J.C. A review on the buffering capacity of earth building materials. *Proc. Inst. Civ. Eng. Constr. Mater.* **2016**, *169*, 241–251. [CrossRef]
9. Liuzzi, S.; Stefanizzi, P. Experimental study on hygrothermal performances of indoor covering materials. *Int. J. Heat Technol.* **2016**, *34*, S365–S370. [CrossRef]
10. Ferreira, C.; de Freitas, V.P.; Delgado, J.M.P.Q. The influence of hygroscopic materials on the fluctuation of relative humidity in museums located in historical buildings. *Stud. Conserv.* **2020**, *65*, 127–141. [CrossRef]
11. Posani, M.; Veiga, M.R.; de Freitas, V.P. Towards resilience and sustainability for historic buildings: A review of envelope retrofit possibilities and a discussion on hygric compatibility of thermal insulations. *Int. J. Archit. Herit.* **2021**, *15*, 807–823. [CrossRef]
12. Ramos, N.M.; de Freitas, V.P. The evaluation of hygroscopic inertia and its importance to the hygrothermal performance of buildings. In *Heat and Mass Transfer in Porous Media*; Springer: Berlin, Germany, 2012; pp. 25–45.
13. Wargocki, P.; Wyon, D.P. Providing better thermal and air quality conditions in school classrooms would be cost-effective. *Build. Environ.* **2013**, *59*, 581–589. [CrossRef]
14. Cintura, E.; Nunes, L.; Esteves, B.; Faria, P. Agro-industrial wastes as building insulation materials: A review and challenges for Euro-Mediterranean countries. *Ind. Crops Prod.* **2021**, *171*, 113833. [CrossRef]
15. Cascione, V.; Maskell, D.; Shea, A.; Walker, P.; Mani, M. Comparison of moisture buffering properties of plasters in full scale simulations and laboratory testing. *Constr. Build. Mater.* **2020**, *252*, 119033. [CrossRef]
16. Gonçalves, H.; Gonçalves, B.; Silva, L.; Vieira, N.; Raupp-Pereira, F.; Senff, L.; Labrincha, J.A. The influence of porogene additives on the properties of mortars used to control the ambient moisture. *Energy Build.* **2014**, *74*, 61–68. [CrossRef]
17. Rode, C.; Peuhkuri, R.H.; Mortensen, L.H.; Hansen, K.K.; Time, B.; Gustavsen, A.; Ojanen, T.; Ahonen, J.; Svennberg, K.; Harderup, L.E.; et al. *Moisture Buffering of Building Materials*; Technical University of Denmark, Department of Civil Engineering: Lyngby, Danmark, 2005.
18. Rode, C.; Peuhkuri, R. The Concept of Moisture Buffer Value of Building Materials and Its Application in Building Design. In Proceedings of the 8th International Conference and Exhibition on Healthy Buildings, Lisbon, Portugal, 4–8 June 2006.
19. Rode, C.; Peuhkuri, R.H.; Time, B.; Svennberg, K.; Ojanen, T. Moisture buffer value of building materials. In *Heat-Air-Moisture Transport: Measurements on Building Materials*; ASTM International: West Conshohocken, PA, USA, 2007; pp. 111–122.
20. ISO 24353; Hygrothermal Performance of Building Materials and Products—Determination of Moisture Adsorption/Desorption Properties in Response to Humidity Variation. International Organization for Standardization: Geneva, Switzerland, 2008.
21. Magalhães, S.A.; de Freitas, V.P. A Complementary Approach for Energy Efficiency and Comfort Evaluation of Renovated Dwellings in Southern Europe. In Proceedings of the 11th Nordic Symposium on Building Physics, Trondheim, Norway, 11–14 June 2017.
22. Magalhães, S.A.; de Freitas, V.P.; Alexandre, J.L. Energy Certification Label vs. Passive Discomfort Index for Existing Dwellings. In Proceedings of the XIII International Research-Technical Conference on the Problems of Designing, Construction and Use of Low Energy Housing, Krakow, Poland, 11–13 September 2018. [CrossRef]
23. Atanasiu, B.; Kontonasiou, E.; Mariottini, F. *Alleviating Fuel Poverty in the EU—Investing in Home Renovation, a Sustainable and Inclusive Solution*; Buildings Performance Institute Europe (BPIE): Brussels, Belgium, 2014.
24. *Portuguese Regulation of Thermal Behaviour Characteristics of Buildings*; Decreto-Lei n° 40/90, de 6 de Fevereiro; Portuguese Legislation: Lisbon, Portugal, 1990. (In Portuguese)
25. INE; LNEC. *The Housing Stock and Its Rehabilitation—Analysis and Evolution*, 2013th ed.; Statistics Portugal—INE; National Laboratory for Civil Engineering—LNEC: Lisbon, Portugal, 2011; ISBN 978-989-25-0246-5. (In Portuguese)
26. Posani, M.; Veiga, M.R.; de Freitas, V.P.; Kompatscher, K.; Schellen, H. Dynamic Hygrothermal Models for Monumental, Historic Buildings with HVAC Systems: Complexity Shown through a Case Study. In Proceedings of the 12th Nordic Symposium on Building Physics—NSB2020, Tallinn, Estonia, 6–9 September 2020. [CrossRef]
27. Posani, M.; Veiga, M.R.; de Freitas, V.P. Thermal retrofit for historic massive walls in temperate climates: Risks and opportunities. In Proceedings of the 4° Encontro de Conservação e Reabilitação de Edifícios—ENCORE 2020, Lisbon, Portugal, 3–6 November 2020.
28. Portuguese Institute for Sea and Atmosphere (Instituto Português do Mar e da Atmosfera)—IPMA. 2021. Available online: http://www.ipma.pt/pt/ (accessed on 14 June 2021).
29. *Portuguese Energy Regulation of Buildings*; Despacho n° 15793-K/2013; Portuguese Legislation: Lisbon, Portugal, 2013. (In Portuguese)
30. Italian Energy Regulation of Buildings; Decreto del Presidente della Repubblica n° 74 del 16 aprile 2013. 2013. Available online: https://www.gazzettaufficiale.it/eli/id/2013/06/27/13G00114/sg (accessed on 13 February 2022). (In Italian)

31. Chambers, J.M.; Cleveland, W.S.; Kleiner, B.; Tukey, P.A. *Graphical Methods for Data Analysis*, 1st ed.; Chapman and Hall/CRC: Boca Raton, FL, USA, 2017.
32. *ISO 7730*; Ergonomics of the Thermal Environment—Analytical Determination and Interpretation of Thermal Comfort Using Calculation of the PMV and PPD Indices and Local Thermal Comfort Criteri. International Organization for Standardization: Geneva, Switzerland, 2005.
33. *ASHRAE 55*; Thermal Environmental Conditions for Human Occupancy. American Society of Heating, Refrigerating and Air-Conditioning Engineers: Atlanta, GA, USA, 2020.
34. Peeters, L.; de Dear, R.; Hensen, J.; D'haeseleer, W. Thermal comfort in residential buildings: Comfort values and scales for building energy simulation. *Appl. Energy* **2009**, *86*, 772–780. [CrossRef]
35. *EN 16798-1*; Energy Performance of Buildings—Ventilation for Buildings—Part 1: Indoor Environmental Input Parameters for Design and Assessment of Energy Performance of Buildings Addressing Indoor Air Quality, Thermal Environment, Lighting and Acoustics. European Committee for Standardization: Brussels, Belgium, 2019.
36. *EN 15251*; Indoor Environmental Input Parameters for Design and Assessment of Energy Performance of Buildings Addressing Indoor Air Quality, Thermal Environment, Lighting and Acoustics. European Committee for Standardization: Brussels, Belgium, 2007.
37. *EN 1015-3*; Methods of Test for Mortar for Masonry—Part 3: Determination of Consistence of Fresh Mortar (by Flow Table). European Committee for Standardization: Brussels, Belgium, 1999.
38. Embarro Universal. Available online: https://www.embarro.com/en/ (accessed on 4 February 2022).
39. Ranesi, A.; Faria, P.; Veiga, M.R. Traditional and modern plasters for built heritage: Contribution 2 for relative humidity passive regulation. *Heritage* **2021**, *4*, 2337–2355. [CrossRef]
40. Santos, A.R. The Influence of Natural Aggregates on the Performance of Replacement Mortars for Ancient Buildings: The Effects of Mineralogy, Grading and Shape. Ph.D. Thesis, Instituto Superior Técnico, Lisbon, Portugal, 2019.
41. Santos, A.R.; Veiga, R.; Santos Silva, A.; de Brito, J.; Álvarez, J.I. Evolution of the microstructure of lime based mortars and influence on the mechanical behaviour: The role of the aggregates. *Contruction Build. Mater.* **2018**, *187*, 907–922. [CrossRef]
42. Pederneiras, C.; Veiga, R.; de Brito, J. Physical and mechanical performance of coir fiber-reinforced rendering mortars. *Materials* **2021**, *14*, 823. [CrossRef]
43. Posani, M.; Veiga, R.; de Freitas, V.P. Thermal mortar-based insulation solutions for historic walls: An extensive hygrothermal characterization of materials and systems. *Constr. Build. Mater.* **2022**, *315*, 125640. [CrossRef]
44. Fraunhofer Institute for Building Physics IBP. Available online: https://wufi.de/en/software/product-overview/ (accessed on 29 March 2021).
45. Ferreira, C.; de Freitas, V.P.; Ramos, N.M. Quantifying the influence of hygroscopic materials in the fluctuation of relative humidity in museums housed in old buildings. In Proceedings of the 10th Nordic Symposium on Building Physics, Lund, Sweden, 15–19 June 2014.
46. *ISO 12571*; Hygrothermal Performance of Building Materials and Products—Determination of Hygroscopic Sorption Properties. International Organization for Standardization: Geneva, Switzerland, 2013.
47. Mundt Petersen, S.; Arfvidsson, J. Comparison of field measurements and calculations of relative humidity and temperature in wood framed walls. In Proceedings of the 15th International Meeting of Thermophysical Society, Valtice, Czech Republic, 3–5 November 2010.
48. Mundt Petersen, S.; Harderup, L.H. Validation of a one-dimensional transient heat and moisture calculation tool under real conditions. In Proceedings of the Thermal Performance of the Exterior Envelopes of Whole Buildings XII International Conference, Clearwater, FL, USA, 1–5 December 2013.
49. Alev, Ü.; Targo, K.; Marko, T.; Martti-Jaan, M. Air leakage and hygrothermal performance of an internally insulated log house. In Proceedings of the 10th Nordic Symposium on Building Physics—NSB 2014, Lund, Sweden, 15–19 June 2014.
50. Stöckl, B.; Daniel, Z.; Hartwig, M.K. Hygrothermal simulation of green roofs-new models and practical application. In Proceedings of the 10th Nordic Symposium on Building Physics—NSB 2014, Lund, Sweden, 15–19 June 2014.
51. Villmann, B.; Slowik, V.; Wittmann, F.H.; Vontobel, P.; Hovind, J. Time-dependent moisture distribution in drying cement mortars—Results of neutron radiography and inverse analysis of drying tests. *Restor. Build. Monum.* **2014**, *20*, 49–62. [CrossRef]
52. Ferreira, C.; Freitas, V.P.; Delgado, J.M.P.Q. The influence of mass tourism and hygroscopic inertia in relative humidity fluctuations of museums located in historical buildings. In *Building Pathology, Durability and Service Life*; Delgado, J.M.P.Q., Ed.; Springer: Cham, Switzerland, 2020; Volume 12, pp. 121–144.
53. Cascione, V.; Maskell, D.; Shea, A.; Walker, P. A review of moisture buffering capacity: From laboratory testing to full-scale measurement. *Constr. Build. Mater.* **2019**, *200*, 333–343. [CrossRef]
54. Liuzzi, S.; Rubino, C.; Martellotta, F.; Stefanizzi, P.; Casavola, C.; Pappalettera, G. Characterization of biomass-based materials for building applications: The case of straw and olive tree waste. *Ind. Crops Prod.* **2020**, *147*, 112229. [CrossRef]
55. Evrard, A.; De Herde, A. Hygrothermal performance of lime-hemp wall assemblies. *J. Build. Phys.* **2010**, *34*, 5–25. [CrossRef]
56. Claude, S.; Ginestet, S.; Bonhomme, M.; Escadeillas, G.; Taylor, J.; Marincioni, V.; Korolija, I.; Altamirano, H. Evaluating retrofit options in a historical city center: Relevance of bio-based insulation and the need to consider complex urban form in decision-making. *Energy Build.* **2019**, *182*, 196–204. [CrossRef]

57. Libralato, M.; De Angelis, A.; D'Agaro, P.; Cortella, G.; Qin, M.; Rode, C. Damage risk assessment of building materials with moisture hysteresis. In Proceedings of the 8th International Building Physics Conference, Copenhagen, Denmark, 25–27 August 2021. [CrossRef]
58. Kunzel, H.M. *Simultaneous Heat and Moisture Transport in Building Components*; Fraunhofer Institute of Building Physics: Stuttgart, Germany, 1995; ISBN 3-8167-4103-7.
59. Rode, C. Combined Heat and Moisture Transfer in Building Constructions. Ph.D. Thesis, Technical University of Denmark, Lyngby, Denmark, 1990.
60. Pina dos Santos, C.A.; Rodrigues, R. *ITE54—Thermal Transmission Coefficients of Opaque Elements of Building Envelope*; National Laboratory of Civil Engineering: Lisboa, Portugal, 2009. (In Portuguese)
61. Ramos, N.M.; Almeida, R.M.; Simões, M.L.; Delgado, J.M.; Pereira, P.F.; Curado, A.; Soares, S.; Fraga, S. Indoor hygrothermal conditions and quality of life in social housing: A comparison between two neighbourhoods. *Sustain. Cities Soc.* **2018**, *38*, 80–90. [CrossRef]
62. Magalhães, S.A. Comparison between the Passive Discomfort Index and the Energy Class of Rehabilitated Residential Buildings in Southern Europe (Original title, in Portuguese: Comparação do Índice de Desconforto Passivo com a Classe Energéticade Edifícios de Habitação Reabilitados do Sul da Europa). Ph.D. Thesis, Faculty of Engineering of the University of Porto, Porto, Portugal, 2020; p. 85.
63. Mazhoud, B.; Collet, F.; Pretot, S.; Chamoin, J. Hygric and thermal properties of hemp-lime plasters. *Build. Environ.* **2016**, *96*, 206–216. [CrossRef]
64. Ramos, N.M.M.; Delgado, J.M.P.Q.; de Freitas, V.P. Influence of finishing coatings on hygroscopic moisture buffering in building elements. *Constr. Build. Mater.* **2010**, *24*, 2590–2597. [CrossRef]
65. Kaczorek, D. Moisture buffering of multilayer internal wall assemblies at the micro scale: Experimental study and numerical modelling. *Appl. Sci.* **2019**, *9*, 3438. [CrossRef]
66. Colinart, T.; Lelièvre, D.; Glouannec, P. Experimental and numerical analysis of the transient hygrothermal behavior of multilayered hemp concrete wall. *Energy Build.* **2016**, *112*, 1–11. [CrossRef]
67. Goto, Y.; Wakili, K.G.; Frank, T.; Stahl, T.; Ostermeyer, Y.; Ando, N.; Wallbaum, H. Heat and moisture balance simulation of a building with vapor-open envelope system for subtropical regions. *Build. Simul.* **2012**, *5*, 301–314. [CrossRef]
68. Du, Y.; Habert, G.; Brumaud, C. Influence of tannin and iron ions on the water resistance of clay materials. *Constr. Build. Mater.* **2022**, *323*, 126571. [CrossRef]

infrastructures

Article

Bio-Wastes as Aggregates for Eco-Efficient Boards and Panels: Screening Tests of Physical Properties and Bio-Susceptibility †

Eleonora Cintura [1,2,3,*], **Paulina Faria** [1,3], **Marta Duarte** [2] and **Lina Nunes** [2,4]

1   Department of Civil Engineering, NOVA, School of Science and Technology, NOVA University of Lisbon,
    2829-516 Caparica, Portugal; paulina.faria@fct.unl.pt
2   National Laboratory for Civil Engineering, Avenida do Brasil 101, 1700-066 Lisbon, Portugal;
    mduarte@lnec.pt (M.D.); linanunes@lnec.pt (L.N.)
3   CERIS, Civil Engineering Research and Innovation for Sustainability, IST, 1049-001 Lisbon, Portugal
4   Azorean Biodiversity Group (cE3c), University of the Azores, 9700-042 Angra do Heroísmo, Portugal
*   Correspondence: e.cintura@fct.unl.pt
†   This paper is an extended version of our paper published in Cintura E., Nunes L. and Faria P.,
    Characterization of agro-wastes to be used as aggregates for eco-efficient insulation boards. In Proceedings of
    the 2021 International Conference on Construction, Energy Environment & Sustainability (CEES), Coimbra,
    Portugal, 12–15 October 2021; ISBN: 978-989-54499-1-0.

Abstract: Screening tests were developed or adapted from RILEM recommendations, standards and past studies, and carried out to characterize some agro-industrial wastes and to assess their feasibility as aggregates for eco-efficient building composites. Spent coffee grounds, grape and olive press waste and hazelnut shells were used, as well as maritime pine chips as control material. Particle size distribution, loose bulk density, thermal conductivity and hygroscopicity properties were analysed. The selected bio-wastes did not show good thermal insulation properties if compared with some bio-wastes already studied and used for thermal insulation composites. Values of loose bulk density and thermal conductivity were between 325.6–550.5 kg/m^3 and 0.078–0.107 W/(m·K); moisture buffering values higher than 2.0 g/(m^2·%RH). Biological susceptibility to mould and termites were also tested, using not yet standardized methods. The low resistance to biological attack confirms one of the greatest drawbacks of using bio-wastes for building products. However, final products properties may be changed by adding other materials, pre-treatments of the wastes and the production process.

Keywords: agro-industrial waste; bio susceptibility; board; coffee ground; grape press waste; hazelnut shell; insulation; olive pomace; panel; thermal properties

1. Introduction

The global climate is changing as a consequence of human activity and the problem has become so serious that the European Commission is calling for a climate-neutral Europe by 2050 [1]. To reach such an ambitious goal, the strategic importance of the construction sector is clear. Indeed, the building industry is recognized to have a strong environmental impact for several reasons. Among them are energy consumption, production of solid waste and harmful gases, and the lack of insulation of the existing building stock, responsible for high energy losses [2–4]. The urgent need for more sustainable building practices is leading to increased research focused on the production, transport and use of building materials that can be shown to have a lower impact on the environment [5,6]. In this context, eco-friendly insulation materials and composites emerge as an interesting solution. They can reduce energy consumption, mitigate the production of harmful wastes, reduce the waste volumes to manage and passively control hygrothermal conditions, improving indoor air quality and comfort [7,8].

Nowadays, a significant amount of research focuses on the feasibility of using bio-wastes to produce several building materials, such as binders, mortars and concrete, plasters, masonry blocks, insulation boards, and coating panels. That is due to the large production of bio-wastes and their good potential in construction practices [9,10]. The use of bio-wastes can both lower production costs and encourage circular economy practices, as well as being an innovative method for waste disposal [5,11–13].

Several recent studies attempted to evaluate the feasibility of producing composite boards using bio-wastes. For example, Eschenhagen et al. [14] analysed boards made up of Miscanthus (*Miscanthus* spp.) fibres, sunflower (*Helianthus annuus* L.) stalks and natural binders (starch-based binder, wood glue made of casein and bone glue made of gelatine). Composites were obtained with a density of 190 kg/m^3 (average value) and thermal conductivity between 0.057 W/(m·K) and 0.068 W/(m·K) for Miscanthus fibres, 280 kg/m^3 and 0.065–0.077 W/(m·K) for sunflower stalks. Considering the reference value of 0.065 W/(m·K) as the maximum thermal conductivity of a good thermal insulator material [15], these bio-wastes showed potential for insulation boards production. Ali et al. [16] evaluated the possibility of making boards using wheat and agave straw bonded with corn starch. The resulting composites also showed good potential as insulating boards with thermal conductivity values of about 0.052 W/(m·K). Nunes et al. [17] produced cement-bonded particleboards replacing maritime pine (*Pinus pinaster* Ait.) chips with banana tree (*Musa* sp.) pseudostem waste. The researchers demonstrated that the increase in banana fibre content from 0% to 75% (by weight) reduced thickness swelling from 0.38% to 0.11%, improving dimensional stability.

Among the large number of past studies that considered bio-wastes for boards' production, only a few detailed the properties of the bio-aggregates individually. Table 1 presents a summary of the particle size of bio-aggregates already used for boards' production.

Table 1. Particle size of bio-aggregates already studied for boards' production.

References	Description	Particle Size (mm)
Wong et al. [18]	Particleboard of grapevine and pine chips (0.25–1.00 mm particles used for the surface layer; 1.00–6.00 mm for the core) and mixed with melamine modified urea-formaldehyde (MUF). Three layers were formed, and hot-pressed (T = 170 °C, pressure = 3.6 MPa, time = 5 min).	0.25–6.00
Binici et al. [19]	Insulation composite of sunflower stalk fibre, sunflower stalk sponge and wheat stalks shredded to reach dimensions of 5–10 mm, vermiculite and gypsum as a binder. Materials were dry mixed, the water was added, and the fresh mortars were placed in moulds in three layers and compacted.	5–10
Liuzzi et al. [20]	Insulation composite of straw fibres (size = 30 mm) and olive fibres (size = 20 mm) mixed with a sodium silicate solution Na$_2$ O$_n$ (SiO$_2$) without pressing. The materials were cured at environmental conditions for 28 days and finally dried at 50 °C until constant mass.	20–30
Eschenhagen et al. [14]	Insulation composite of Miscanthus and sunflower stalk fibre grounded with a 1.5 cm screen and sieved to obtain fibres equal or bigger than 10 mm, starch-based binder, wood glue made of casein and bone glue made of gelatine.	≥10
Pavelek and Adamová [21]	Insulation boards consisted of a premanufactured panel filled with shredded rapeseed (*Brassica napus*) and woodchips from coniferous trees (sandwich panel).	<0.25–8
Mati-Baouche et al. [22]	Insulation composite of sunflower stalks (shredded and sieved to obtain particle size between 1 and 6.3 mm) and chitosan from shrimp shell. The materials were mixed, pressed (pressure between 1 × 10^{-3} − 32 × 10^{-3} MPa) and then dried in an oven (T 50 °C, time = 50 h).	1–6.3
Pásztory et al. [23]	Insulation composite of chipped black locust (*Robinia pseudoacacia*) tree bark and urea-formaldehyde (UF) based resin, by pressing at T = 120 °C for 6 s per final mm thickness.	<1–45
Binici et al. [24]	Insulation composite of corn stalks (particle size between 0.5–4 mm), epoxy resin, gypsum and Portland cement (CEM I 42.5). Materials were mixed for 5 min, compacted (T = 20 °C, time = 1 min, pressure = 0.07–0.27 MPa) and dried at 50 °C for 50 h.	0.5–4
Wang et al. [25]	Cement-bonded particleboard made up shredded grapevine stalk, cement and 3% calcium chloride (CaCl$_2$) by weight of cement. The boards were cold pressed (pressure = 1.25 MPa, time = 8 h) and then conditioned at T = (20 ± 2) °C, RH = (65 ± 5)% for 28 days.	9–80
Kusumah et al. [26]	Particleboard of sweet sorghum (*Sorghum bicolor* L. Monech) bagasse and citric acid dissolved in water as adhesive. Citric acid was sprayed onto the dried particles and the boards are hot-pressed (T = 200 °C, time = 10 min, maximum pressure = 6.5 MPa).	0.9–5.9
Buratti et al. [27]	Panels of rice husk (length 9 mm, width of 1 mm) and cold-water-based polyurethane glue (density = 1000 kg/m^3). For comparison samples of cork (size 0.8 mm–1 mm) and glue were fabricated (they were cured at T = 100 °C, time between 90–120 min).	9 0.8–1

Particle size is one of the most studied properties of aggregates but remains unknown for many bio-wastes. The reported methods and experimental tests tend to focus on the composites [10]. The analysis of the bio-wastes should be further investigated since their characteristics will be certainly linked to the performance of the final products [28]. Knowing bio-wastes properties allows more conscious choices to be made to achieve the final requirements for the produced composites [29]. Along with the European Standards for aggregates in general, the Recommendations of RILEM Technical Committee 236-BBM "Bio-aggregate-based building materials" [30] have been widely used to study properties of bio-aggregates. For example, Page et al. [31] used them to characterize hemp shiv and flax fibres; Laborel-Préneron et al. [32] to analyse barley straw, hemp shiv and corn cob; Antunes et al. [33] to evaluate rice husk properties; Barbieri et al. [34] to study wheat husk. Using the same methods allows conforming the procedures and guarantees an easier comparison between different materials. However, complementary characterization may be important and further test procedures may be needed. As bio-based products are frequently vulnerable to biological deterioration, bio-susceptibility tests are a good example of this need.

Due to their organic composition, and factors like the presence of nutrients and microorganisms in the raw materials, as well as typical high hygroscopicity, bio-based wastes are often prone to biological deterioration [35,36]. Bio susceptibility is indeed recognised as one of the main drawbacks of bio-based building materials [37,38]. It can lead to modified properties and eventually to reduced durability. In particular, besides the obvious aesthetic impact, mould growth on interior applications can also lead to health risks for building users, namely respiratory diseases, such as asthma and allergic rhinitis [39]. Insect attack can also be a major cause of deterioration of building materials, thus worsening their performance. In the case of bio-based components and structures, subterranean termites represent the highest hazard in Mediterranean countries [40,41] and can be used as model organisms to evaluate susceptibility. The biological resistance of raw materials provides useful information and can help to forecast their impact on the final performance of composite materials. Thus, it is an important property that has to be considered to optimize the design of bio-based products.

Taking into consideration the previous information, this article reports the characterization of four bio-wastes analysed individually to determine their properties as raw materials: spent coffee grounds, grape press waste, olive press waste and hazelnut shells. Typically, spent coffee grounds are usually disposed of in landfills, used as composting and fermentation or as animal feed, such as olive and grape pomace [42,43]. Hazelnut shells are used for combustion and heating [44].

Maritime pine (*Pinus pinaster* Ait.) chips were considered as control material, as its characteristics are better known and recycling is frequent, namely from construction and demolition waste. These bio-wastes were chosen considering the referenced feasibility of using them as building materials and their world production, focusing on Euro-Mediterranean [10]. The use of local materials decreases the environmental impact derived from the transport and consumption phases and secures high availability. The results were compared with other bio-based materials already studied and used as aggregates (cork waste particles, corn cob particles, hemp shiv, and rice husk), namely for producing boards and panels. The potential of the analysed bio-wastes as aggregates for this type of composite production and, how to optimize their use, was discussed. This work also aims at both describing and discussing the methods to evaluate properties of bio-aggregates, some not so common, as the cases of bio-susceptibility tests, and reporting the obtained properties, comparing with literature whenever possible. The study reduces the gaps of knowledge found in literature and evaluates the feasibility of using complementary bio-wastes to produce composite boards and panels.

2. Materials and Methods

2.1. Materials

Spent coffee grounds were provided by the central bar of the National Laboratory of Civil Engineering (LNEC), Lisbon, Portugal. They are usually thrown away for waste disposal. They were air-dried at room temperature for 6 weeks over an absorbent paper, regularly stirred to improve the dry rate. Grapes and olive press wastes were provided by Esporão company located in Reguengos de Monsaraz, Portugal. They were spread over a plastic tarp for 7 and 10 weeks, respectively, to air dry and also regularly mixed to allow better ventilation. Olive press waste needed a longer drying period due to the initial high amount of liquid content that, according to the producer, depends on the olives' quality of each season. Hazelnut shells were provided by Borges Agricultural & Industrial Nuts SA company, located in Reus, Spain. This bio-waste was used as received. Details on the cellulose, hemicellulose and lignin content of these bio-wastes have been described previously by Cintura et al. [10], such as their disposal and use.

To simulate recycled pine wood a maritime pine board, obtained from a local wood shop (Lisbon, Portugal), was cross cut and then shredded in a laminar mill five times to reach a chip dimension of less than 10 mm. Figure 1 shows the analysed materials and their colour scale according to the PANTONE Uncoated RGB scale [45].

(a) (b) (c) (d) (e)

Figure 1. Bio-wastes size and colour scale after air drying: (**a**) grape press waste; (**b**) hazelnut shells; (**c**) olive press waste; (**d**) spent coffee grounds; (**e**) maritime pine chips.

After air drying, the materials were sampled as described by Amziane et al. [30], they were placed on a flat surface into a pile that was divided into quarters. Two parts were selected and further divided into quarters. This procedure was repeated until having enough material to carry out the laboratory tests. Sampling guarantees a better mixture of particles, avoiding the segregation between the coarser and finer ones.

2.2. Methods

Experimental tests were performed after drying the bio-wastes at 60 °C until a constant mass was reached (change in mass of less than 0.1% over 24 h), except for bio-susceptibility tests for which the bio-wastes were dried also at 103 °C for 24 h. Then, they were stabilised in a conditioning room (T = (20 ± 2) °C, (60 ± 5)% relative humidity (RH)), adapting the method proposed by Amziane et al. [30] to equilibrate at known laboratory conditions. All the laboratory tests were performed without pressing the bio-aggregates. Table 2 summarizes the tests performed, the samples and relevant references. Further details are presented in the following sections.

Table 2. Summary of laboratory tested properties, samples, considered/adapted references and standards.

Properties		Samples	References and Contribution	Description	Strengths	Limitations
Physical properties	Particle size distribution	3 samples of 100 g of the materials	Amziane et al. [30] described the method and reported EN 933-2 [46]	Sieving methods by using 200 mm diameter sieves	Widely used method: easier comparison between different aggregates considering the same laboratory test	Sieving time is not specified; for the considered agro-industrial wastes, a sample of 45 ± 10 g in case of 200 mm diameter sieves is too small
	Loose bulk density	Cylindrical glass (diameter = 6 cm height = 11 cm) filled with 3 samples of the material	Amziane et al. [30] introduced the method; Laborel-Préneron et al. [32] provided a detailed description too	By considering aggregates' weight and the corresponding volume of water	Applicability to different bio-aggregates	It could be less rapid and immediate than EN 1097-3 [47] (replacement of the volume of aggregate with a volume of water)
		Cylindrical plastic container (100 mL) filled with 3 samples of the material	EN 1097-3 [47] described the laboratory test	The ratio between mass and volume	Fast laboratory test	Not specific for bio-aggregates
	Thermal conductivity	5 different points of the surface of an open container (diameter = 18.50 cm, high = 5.80 cm) filled with the material	Antunes et al. [33] evaluated the thermal conductivity of bio-aggregates by using the transient method; Liuzzi et al. [20] described its advantages and reasons to use it	Transient method	Possibility of analysing small samples (faster stabilization at different RH) and loose aggregates	Fast evaluation; the results could be as not precise as other methods (e.g., heat flow)
	Water absorption	3 samples of 25 g of the materials	Amziane et al. [30] introduced the method; use and details are described by Laborel-Préneron et al. [32]	Difference between dry and wet mass	Possibility of testing loose aggregates	No specification of opening mesh (permeable bag could be better described) and of water's temperature; possible compaction of the aggregates; rotation speed should be automatically controlled
	Sorption/desorption properties	3 plastic box (11.0 cm × 14.8 cm, high = 2 cm) with an open-top surface filled with the materials	ISO 24353 [48] described the laboratory test; Rode et al. [49] provided the MBV classification	Samples at different RH	Same sorption/desorption time (12 h); not developed considering indoor conditions in a specific area (differently from Rode et al. [49])	The lack of a numeric classification in ISO 24353 [48] makes difficult the comparison between different aggregates and the discussion of the results
Bio susceptibility	Mould	5 + 5 Petri dishes (diameter = 9 cm) filled with similar volumes of materials. Two exposure methods	ASTM D5590-17 [50] provided information about the test and the evaluation; Parracha et al. [51] detailed the adaptations to the material	Evaluation of contaminated surface	Different exposure methods could be considered; the control secures the validation of the tests	Subjective/visual evaluation
	Termites	3 Petri dishes (diameter = 9 cm), moistened calibrated sand on one side and similar volumes of materials on the other	Nunes and Duarte [52] provided information to develop the test	Termites' survival	Innovative laboratory test to analyse loose aggregates	Control of moulds development for high sugar content materials

2.2.1. Particle Size Analysis, Loose Bulk Density and Thermal Conductivity

Grain size analysis was carried out using the mechanical sieves method, considering Amziane et al. [30], as mentioned in Table 2. Due to the different grain sizes of the studied materials, the apertures of the successive openings of the sieves covered a wide range (from 10 mm to 0.125 mm) in accordance with EN 933-2 [46]. The sieving time, not specified in the considered references, was 3.5 min. The particle size distribution curve was determined by considering the average values of the three samples.

Bio-wastes loose bulk density was calculated considering two different methods. The first one considered the method presented by Amziane et al. [30] and Laborel-Préneron et al. [32]. An empty cylindrical glass was weighed and then filled with the material until half the volume. The container was sealed and upend ten times and shaken to obtain a horizontal surface. The level of the material was marked. The material was removed, and the container was filled with water and weighed. The loose bulk density was determined by Equation (1). The average value of the three tested samples was considered significant when the coefficient of variation was less than 5%.

$$\rho_{Aggregate}\left(\frac{kg}{m^3}\right) = \frac{m_{Aggregate}}{m_{H_2O}}\rho_{H_2O} \tag{1}$$

The second method, based on EN 1097-3 [47], consisted of calculating the ratio between the mass and the volume of the materials. A cylindrical container with a known volume (V) was weighted (m_1), filled by dropping the material from a height of 40 cm, shaken to obtain a horizontal surface without compacting the material, and weighted again (m_2). The loose bulk density was calculated by Equation (2).

$$\rho_{Aggregate}\left(\frac{kg}{m^3}\right) = \frac{m_2 - m_1}{V} \tag{2}$$

Measurements of thermal conductivity in building materials may be performed through steady-state methods or transient methods. In this work, a transient method was adopted, considering the method reported by Antunes et al. [33] and Liuzzi et al. [20], as reported in Table 2. The transient method offers several benefits [53,54], in particular the smaller dimension of the testing area. This allowed performing the measurement in different parts of the surface of each sample, indicated in Figure 2a. Bio-wastes' thermal conductivity was measured by using an ISOMET 2104 Heat Transfer Analyser with a 60 mm diameter contact probe API 210412, ranging values between 0.04 and 0.30 W/(m·K). To evaluate the correlation between the thermal conductivity and RH, the samples were stabilised in a climatic chamber (Fitoclima 300 EDTU) at T = 23 °C, RH = 50%, then T = 23 °C, RH = 75%. When constant mass was reached (change in mass of less than 0.1% over 24 h), thermal conductivity was calculated, protecting the samples from the airflow during the measurement by a cover box (Figure 2b). To validate this method, mass was controlled before and after the test to guarantee a variation of less than 0.1%. The average value of the five measurements was considered significant if the coefficient of variation was less than 5%.

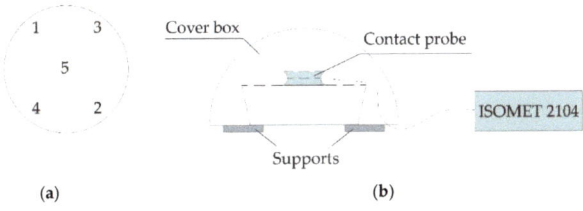

Figure 2. (a) Points where thermal conductivity was calculated; (b) Method to calculate thermal conductivity (adapted from Cintura et al. [29]).

2.2.2. Water Absorption and Sorption/Desorption Properties

For the water absorption test, based on Amziane et al. [30] and Laborel-Préneron et al. [32], an empty permeable bag was put in water until reached complete wetting. Then it was put in a salad spinner, turned 100 times (approximatively two rotations/second) and tared. It was filled with 25 g of each of the bio-wastes (m_0) and immersed in water. After one minute, the permeable bag with the waste was removed from the water, put in the salad spinner, turned 100 times again, and weighed. The permeable bag was put in the water again and this procedure was repeated after 1 min, 15 min, 4 h and then every 24 h until a constant mass was reached (change in mass less than 0.1% over 24 h). Water absorption was determined considering Equation (3), where m_A is the wet mass.

$$W(\%) = \frac{m_A - m_0}{m_0} \times 100 \tag{3}$$

The average value of three tested samples of each material was considered significant when the coefficient of variation was less than 5%. By knowing the bulk density of the bio-wastes, it was possible to determine the ratio between the volume of the absorbed water and the volume of the considered bio-wastes. The water absorption of the bio-wastes allows making considerations about the influence they may have on the workability of future composites.

The hygroscopicity of the bio-wastes was determined by considering the moisture adsorption/desorption capacity in response to humidity variation through cyclic tests, as indicated in ISO 24353 [48]. The plastic boxes filled with the materials (open-top surface = A), were preconditioned at T = (23 ± 2) °C and RH = (63 ± 2)% in a climatic chamber (Fitoclima 1000) until constant mass was reached (change in mass of less than 0.1% over 24 h) and weighed ($m_0 = m_{d(n-1)}$). Then they were conditioned at T = (23 ± 2) °C, RH = (75 ± 2)% for 12 h and weighed every 3 h (moisture sorption process, m_{an}), and at T = (23 ± 2) °C, RH = (50 ± 2)% for 12 h (moisture desorption process, m_{dn}). The cyclic value of the moisture adsorption content, $\rho_{A,ac}$, and the moisture desorption content, $\rho_{A,dc}$, were calculated according to Equations (4) and (5) to determine the variation of moisture adsorbed/desorbed content over time.

$$\rho_{A,ac}\left(\frac{kg}{m^2}\right) = \frac{m_{an} - m_{d(n-1)}}{A} \tag{4}$$

$$\rho_{A,dc}\left(\frac{kg}{m^2}\right) = \frac{m_{an} - m_{dn}}{A} \tag{5}$$

The moisture content difference between adsorption and desorption is calculated considering Equation (6).

$$\rho_{A,sc}\left(\frac{kg}{m^2}\right) = \rho_{A,ac} - \rho_{A,dc} \tag{6}$$

For easier comparison of the results with literature values, the moisture buffering value (MBV) was also calculated, adapting the method defined by Rode et al. [49]. MBV is the average value between MBV for the sorption phase (MBV$_a$) calculated as reported in Equation (7), and MBV for the desorption phase (MBV$_d$) calculated as reported in Equation (8). The last three cycles and the average values of each bio-waste was considered.

$$MBV_a\left(g/\left(m^2 \cdot \% \, RH\right)\right) = \frac{m_{an} - m_{d(n-1)}}{A \times \left(RH_{high} - RH_{low}\right)} \tag{7}$$

$$MBV_d\left(g/\left(m^2 \cdot \% \, RH\right)\right) = \frac{m_{an} - m_{dn}}{A \times \left(RH_{high} - RH_{low}\right)} \tag{8}$$

In these equations, m_{an} (g) is the value of the mass at the end of the sorption phase, $m_{d(n-1)}$ is the value of the mass at the end of the desorption phase of the previous cycle, m_{dn} is the value of the mass at the end of the desorption phase, A (m^2) is the exposed surface, RH_{high} is the highest value of RH (75%) and RH_{low} is the lowest one (50%, based on ISO 24353 [48], differently from Rode et al. [49]). The MBV of the analysed materials, calculated as described, can be compared with MBVs of literature even when calculated under different conditions. Indeed, the reference to RH variation included in the value makes the comparison easier [55].

2.2.3. Bio Susceptibility to Mould and Termites

To evaluate the bio-susceptibility to moulds, two different exposure methods were applied. Ten Petri dishes (diameter = 9 cm) were used for each bio-waste under test with five dishes containing 20 mL of culture media (4% malt, 2% agar). A similar amount of previously steam sterilized bio-wastes (approx. 13 mL) was added to each Petri dish and all plates were inoculated with 1 mL of a mixed spore suspension of *Aspergillus niger* and *Penicillium funicullosum*. The fungal strains used came from LNEC' fungal collection.

The Petri dishes with culture media were left for four weeks at (22 ± 1) °C and (70 ± 5)% RH. Five Whatman n° 1 filter papers (diameter = 45 mm) were used as controls for this exposure method. The inoculated dishes without culture media were conditioned for the same time and at the same temperature but at 100% RH. For these, maritime pine chips were considered as reference material.

The samples were visually graded each week and mould growth was estimated considering the classification provided in Table 3. At the end of the four weeks, the samples were also visualized under a stereo microscope (Olympus SZX12) to confirm the grading results. Carrying out the bio susceptibility test with and without culture media allowed evaluating the materials both in favourable conditions for mould growth and as they are (raw materials).

Table 3. Rate of mould growth adapted from ASTM D5590-17 [50].

Rating	Description	Contaminated Surface (%)
0	None	0
1	Traces of growth	<10
2	Light growth	10 to 30
3	Moderate growth	30 to 60
4	Heavy growth	>60

For testing against subterranean termites, a protocol was developed following previous work [52]. Three Petri dishes (diameter = 9 cm) for each bio-waste were half filled with approx. 7 mL of the materials and on the other half similar amounts of moistened (25% w/w) Fontainebleau™ sand were placed. Groups of 50 termites (*R. grassei*) were then introduced on each Petri dish. The termites were field collected (Sesimbra, Portugal) and maintained at optimal conditions until required for testing but never more than two months.

All tested samples were left for four weeks at (24 ± 1) °C and (80 ± 5)% RH, constantly monitored to control both termites' survival and mould growth. At the end of this period, the percentage of survival of the termites was evaluated and mould growth was qualitatively estimated. Because of the well-known durability of maritime pine, its chips were considered as controls to validate the test. A survival level lower than 50% would not be accepted [41]. Mould growth can have a limiting impact on termite survival and therefore was also closely followed.

3. Results and Discussion

3.1. Particle Size Analysis

Figure 3 shows the particle size distribution of the considered bio-wastes.

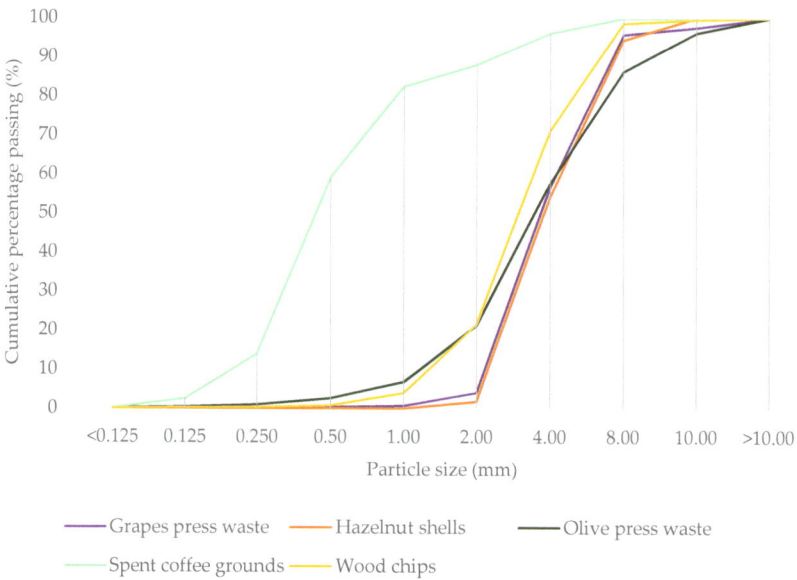

Figure 3. Particle size distribution of the tested bio-wastes and the wood chips.

Spent coffee grounds have grain sizes much lower than the other selected bio-wastes and the control; thus, for insulation boards, they might play a better role as fine aggregates. The other bio-wastes present more similar characteristics (particle size of about 1–8 mm).

The comparison between the results and literature values reported in Table 1 allows evaluating if shredding the bio-wastes will be required in case of using them for boards' production. The grain size of the analysed bio-wastes is in the range of the considered past studies, in which it varies between 0.25 mm and 80 mm. Therefore, shredding the bio-wastes to produce boards does not seem to be necessary. This guarantees a more sustainable practice since the bio-wastes can be used directly as they are as by-products. The shredding may be necessary in case of compressed panels' production for which a finer grain size might be more adequate [17].

Collet [56] reported some past studies about the influence of aggregates' grain size on the thermal properties of the composites. The results demonstrate that the finer are the particles, the higher is the thermal conductivity. Laborel-Préneron et al. [32] demonstrated that, in earth-straw composites, the shorter are the pieces of straw, the higher is the compressive strength. Future studies could deepen the influence of grain size on the properties of boards since it can affect physical and mechanical properties [17,18]. The influence of sieving time on the results of the grain size analysis of bio-aggregates could be further investigated, too. The test could be carried out considering several sieving times, evaluating the differences in the results and defining which guarantees the smallest deviation in the grains size distribution, as Martínez-García et al. [57] reported.

3.2. Loose Bulk Density and Thermal Conductivity

Table 4 reports the results of loose bulk density of the bio-wastes analysed by the two methods, comparing them with literature values.

Values of the considered bio-wastes have the same order of magnitude of literature ones. The main differences derive from different types and particle sizes that widely affects the values of loose bulk density [58]. Wood chips show the lowest values of loose bulk density, as expected. Grape press waste could be the best aggregate to produce thermal insulation boards since it has the lowest loose bulk density value between the bio-wastes.

Table 4. Measured loose bulk density of the analysed bio-wastes and comparison with literature values.

Material	Loose Bulk Density (kg/m³)		Literature Values (kg/m³)	Reference
	According to Amziane et al. [30]	According to EN 1097-3 [47]		
Grapes press waste	343.88 ± 12.00	325.60 ± 5.82	105 ± 5 [a] 1449 ± 2 [b] 1420 ± 3 [c]	Wong et al. [18] David et al. [59] David et al. [59]
Hazelnut shells	550.50 ± 19.53	549.66 ± 11.92	230	Çöpür et al. [60]
Olive press waste	449.43 ± 8.60	427.32 ± 9.62	1251 [d] 616 [e]	Liuzzi et al. [61] del Río Merino et al. [62]
Spent coffee grounds	478.81 ± 5.40	447.73 ± 5.13	380 ± 20 [f]	Massaro Sousa and Ferreira [63]
Wood chips	256.98 ± 8.10	250.20 ± 4.59	130 ± 2 [g]	Wong et al. [18]

[a] Particles of grapevine milled to a thickness of <1 mm particles; [b] Wine pomace; [c] Vine shoots; [d] Olive pruning waste; [e] Olive stone; [f] Grain sizes between 600 and 500 μm; [g] Commercial pine.

Considering the materials chosen for comparison, granular cork waste derived from cork panels, bottles cap manufacturing, cork industry (not expanded cork) showed values of about 150–160 kg/m³ [64]. For expanded cork granulate, Brás et al. [65] reported values of 112 kg/m³ and Nóvoa et al. [66] values of 220 kg/m³. For corn cob, Ansell et al. [58] obtained values of about 344–406 kg/m³. Laborel-Préneron et al. [32] evaluated corn cob and hemp shiv, achieving results of 497 kg/m³ and 153 kg/m³, respectively. For hemp shiv, Page et al. [31] reported values of 110 kg/m³. Antunes et al. [33] studied rice husk, reporting a loose bulk density of 85 kg/m³. The selected bio-wastes have a higher loose bulk density, except for corn cob evaluated by Laborel-Préneron et al. [32]. In this case, only hazelnut shells show higher values. Grape press waste has a loose bulk density closer to the one of corn cob evaluated by Ansell et al. [58].

Table 5 shows the values of thermal conductivity of the analysed bio-wastes. The thermal conductivity values are higher than the required to consider a material as thermal insulation, namely not lower than 0.065 W/(m·K) [15]. None of the tested bio-wastes can be classified as such. To produce boards with good thermal resistance using these bio-aggregates, it will be necessary to combine them with other materials with good thermal insulation properties or produce them in a way that air is entrapped within the composite in small volumes. Grape press waste has the lowest thermal conductivity, similar to one of the wood chips: it seems the most promising bio-aggregates to produce composites with good thermal insulation performance. Taking into account the correlation with loose bulk density, thermal conductivity values are in line with the expected since there is a direct proportionality [67]. Hazelnut shells have the worst thermal insulation behaviour (the highest thermal conductivity), having the highest loose bulk density; grape press wastes and maritime pine chips show the lowest values of thermal conductivity, having the lowest values of loose bulk density.

Table 5. Thermal conductivity of the analysed bio-wastes and comparison with literature values.

Material	Thermal Conductivity (W/(m·K))		Literature Values (W/(m·K))	References
	T = 23 °C, RH = 50%	T = 23 °C, RH = 70%		
Grape press waste	0.078 ± 0.002	0.081 ± 0.002	-	
Hazelnut shells	0.107 ± 0.003	0.115 ± 0.003	0.1	Çuhadaroğlu [68]
Olive press waste	0.089 ± 0.004	0.097 ± 0.003	-	
Spent coffee grounds	0.092 ± 0.002	0.099 ± 0.005	0.2	Lachheb et al. [69]
Wood chips	0.077 ± 0.001	0.082 ± 0.002	0.0568–0.0629 [a]	Cetiner and Shea [7]

[a] Materials particle size between 1 mm–4 mm, conditioned at RH = 50%.

Considering the materials chosen for comparison, all the bio-wastes have higher values of thermal conductivity, except for the one of corn cob. However, the test conditions of temperature and RH are frequently not defined.

Figures 4 and 5 show the correlations between thermal conductivity and RH, and between thermal conductivity and loose bulk density. As expected, the thermal conductivity increases proportionally to RH and the loose bulk density, for all tested bio-wastes. Figure 5 also reports the values of the materials chosen for comparison, being the lower thermal conductivity justified by lower loose bulk density.

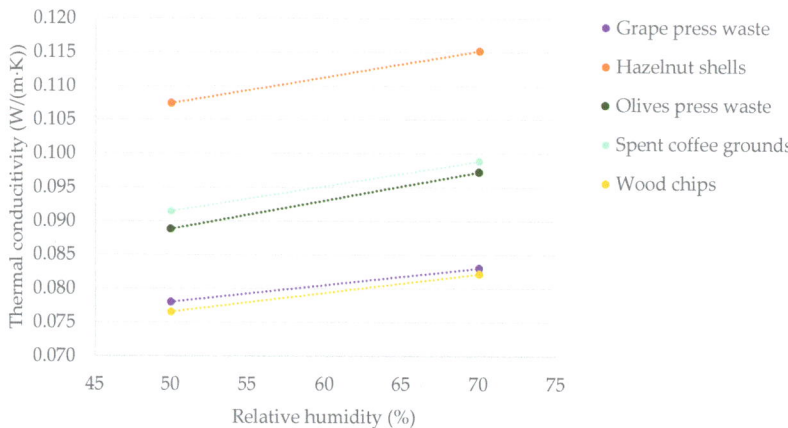

Figure 4. Correlation between thermal conductivity and RH of the tested bio-wastes.

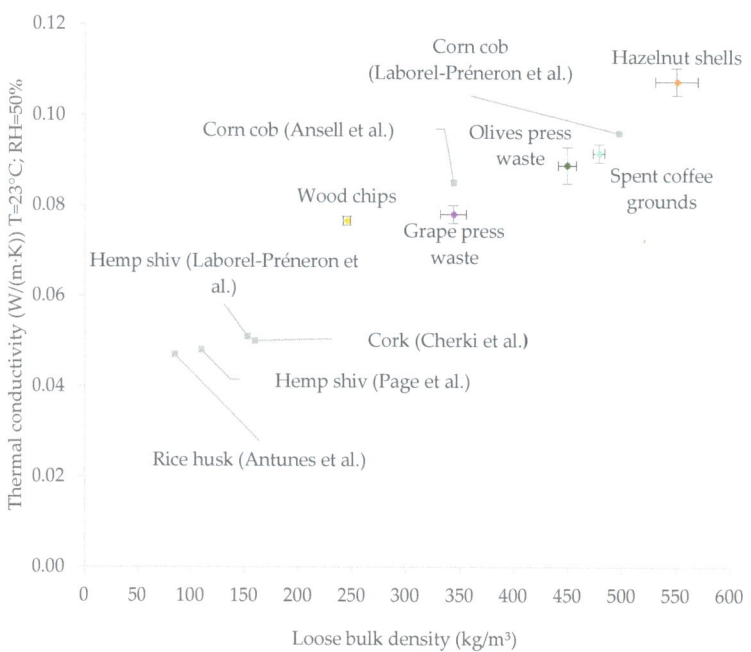

Figure 5. Correlation between thermal conductivity and loose bulk density of bio-wastes, compared with some literature values: Page et al. [31]. Laborel-Préneron et al. [32], Antunes et al. [33], Ansell et al. [58] and Cherki et al. [64].

Gomes et al. [70] and Cherki et al. [64] reported values of thermal conductivity of expanded granular cork of about 0.035–0.070 W/(m·K) and 0.049–0.050 W/(m·K), respectively. For hemp shiv, Laborel-Préneron et al. [32] reported values of 0.051 W/(m·K) while Page et al. [31] of 0.048 W/(m·K). Antunes et al. [33] evaluating rice husk achieved results of about 0.047 W/(m·K). Comparing with the results of Laborel-Préneron et al. [32], among the tested bio-wastes only hazelnut shells have a higher thermal conductivity than corn cob's one (0.096 W/(m·K)). Considering the results of Ansell et al. [58], the thermal conductivity of corn cob (0.085 W/(m·K)) is higher than grape press waste and wood chips. Despite these results, the analysed bio-wastes may be used as bio-aggregates for insulation composite boards and panels' production, if the composition and methods are able to improve the insulation performance.

3.3. Water Absorption and Sorption/Desorption Properties

Figure 6 reports the results of water absorption of the five studied bio-wastes considering the method proposed by Amziane et al. [30], and Table 6 presents the water absorption after 48 h.

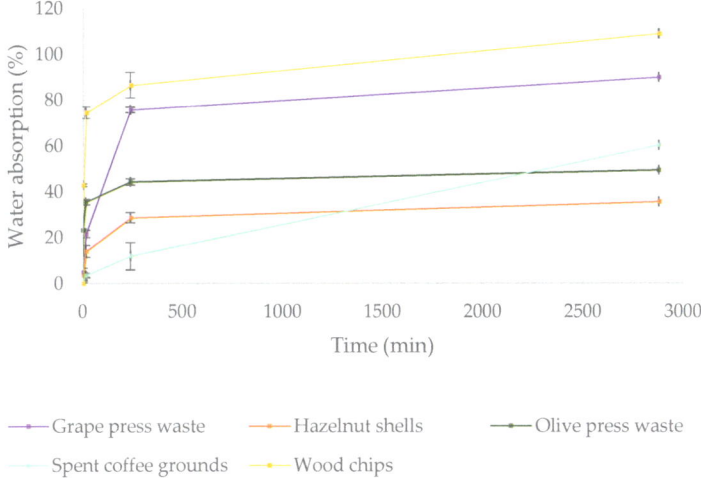

Figure 6. Water absorption as a function of time, tested according to Amziane et al. [30].

Table 6. Water absorption of the bio-wastes after 48 h of immersion.

Bio-Waste	Absorption after 48 h (%)
Grape press waste	89.7 ± 1.2
Hazelnut shells	35.5 ± 2.2
Olive press waste	49.3 ± 2.1
Spent coffee grounds	60.1 ± 6.0
Wood chips	108.7 ± 5.6

Except for the spent coffee grounds, the analysed bio-wastes show a similar behaviour along time (Figure 6), starting to saturate after approx. 4 h of immersion, although with different levels of water absorption. Comparing with past studies [32,33], the correlation between water absorption and time is similar.

Regarding the absorption after 48 h (2880 min, Table 6), the different percentages can be observed. The results were compared with some literature ones determined by the same method [30]. Laborel-Préneron et al. [32] reported that water absorption after 48 h for corn cob is 123% and 380% for hemp shiv. Page et al. [31] obtained values of about 450% for hemp shiv. Antunes et al. [33] of about 300% for rice husk.

Values of water absorption of the analysed bio-waste are lower than in the literature. The discrepancy is probably caused by the considered method that could lead to differences in the results: the used permeable bags could be different, an eventual compaction of the materials during the permeable bag's closing or inside the bags, as well as the compaction of the material during the absorbing phase and the manual rotation speed. To ensure a direct comparison between different materials, the method should be complemented. For example, the opening mesh of the permeable bag should be defined according to the grain size of the bio-aggregates, or the rotation time could be controlled automatically to avoid manual operation mistakes. Another important factor that could influence the water absorption capacity is the temperature of the water, as demonstrated by Bouasker et al. [71].

Most materials absorb a greater quantity of water during the first 24 h. Hazelnut shells show the lowest water saturation content. They achieved the lowest value of water absorption after 24 h (32.9 ± 2.6)%, followed by olive press waste (48.9 ± 1.6)%. Wood chips and grape press waste show the highest values of water absorption after the first 24 h ((101.9 ± 1.6)% and (88.0 ± 0.7)%, respectively).

Information about water absorption is extremely useful for future boards' production in case of using a hydraulic matrix, as Laborel-Préneron et al. [32] reported. To better investigate this property, the ratio between the volume of absorbed water and the volume of the materials was calculated and its evolution with time is reported in Figure 7.

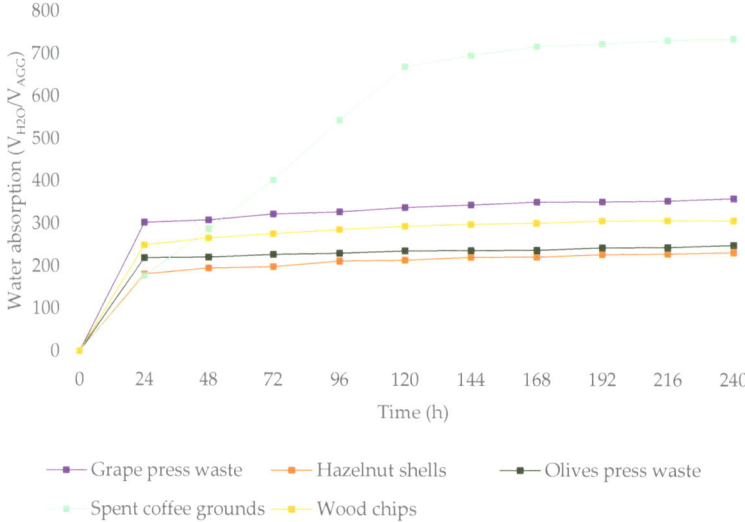

Figure 7. Variation of water absorption during time considering the ratio of the volume of absorbed water and the volume of the material.

Supposing to produce boards or panels by wet methods and by defining the percentages of the components in volumes, with the same quantities of bio-wastes, composites with hazelnut shells should absorb less water. Composites with grape press waste will probably need more water for production than the others to obtain the same workability because more water will be absorbed by the bio-wastes. Figure 7 also shows that, differently from the evaluation of water absorption in terms of mass, wood chips show lower water absorption than grapes press waste. Again, the performance of spent coffee grounds differs greatly from the other bio-wastes. This one shows a slower water absorption: after 120 h it is still absorbing water and the constant mass is reached only after 10 days. The difference between spent coffee grounds and the other bio-wastes may depend on the different grain sizes but other characteristics of the coffee grounds may also have influence.

Figure 8 shows the variation in moisture adsorbed/desorbed content over time for the considered bio-wastes.

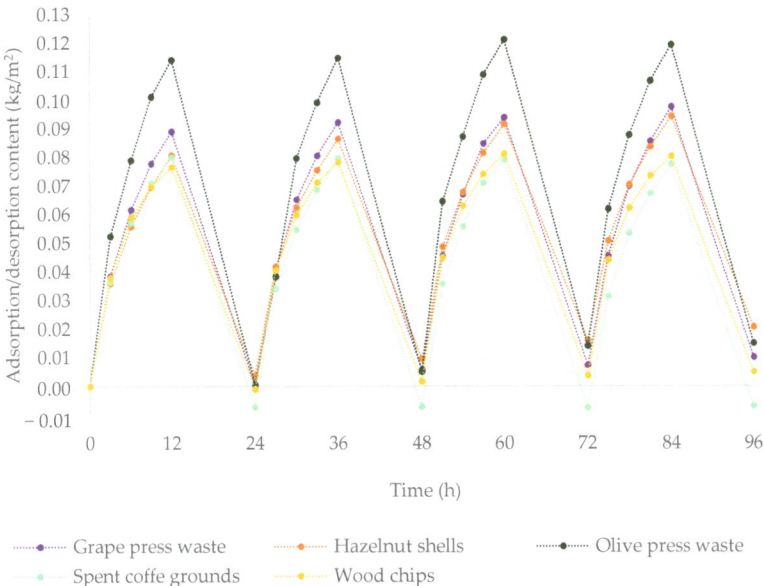

Figure 8. Moisture adsorption/desorption content for four cycles between 50% and 75% RH.

As Collet [56] and Romano et al. [72] reported, hygroscopicity properties widely affect the thermal behaviour of the composites and the control of the dynamic moisture changes. MBV values show the potential of bio-aggregates as hygric regulators [58]. For these reasons, the obtained results could anticipate some of the future properties of the boards.

Olive press waste achieved the highest values of moisture adsorption ($\rho_{A,ac}$ between 0.114 kg/m^2 and 0.116 kg/m^2) and desorption content ($\rho_{A,ad}$ between 0.104 kg/m^2 and 0.113 kg/m^2) during the four cycles. Wood chips and hazelnut shells reached the lowest values both in the sorption and desorption phases. Values of moisture sorption are between 0.076 kg/m^2 and 0.080 kg/m^2 for wood chips, between 0.078 kg/m^2 and 0.083 kg/m^2 for hazelnut shells. As for desorption, the values are between 0.074 kg/m^2 and 0.078 kg/m^2 and between 0.074 kg/m^2 and 0.077 kg/m^2, respectively.

Considering the moisture content difference between sorption and desorption, $\rho_{A,sc}$, values of grape press waste, olives press waste and wood chips are close to zero during the first cycle (between −0.001 kg/m^2 and 0.001 kg/m^2). Hence, these aggregates have similar sorption and desorption capacity. The first cycle shows not already stabilized bio-wastes moisture capacity. Except for wood chips and spent coffee grounds, sorption capacity is greater than desorption. During the second cycle, the bio-wastes sorption capacity improved. For all the bio-wastes, moisture adsorption content, $\rho_{A,ac}$, is greater than moisture desorption content, $\rho_{A,ad}$. After the first cycle, also for spent coffee grounds the moisture content difference is near to zero (maximum value of 0.001 kg/m^2). Hazelnut shells showed the greatest moisture content difference for all the cycles (values between 0.004 kg/m^2 and 0.006 kg/m^2), with higher moisture sorption capacity than desorption.

However, the moisture content differences are very small for all the bio-wastes and during all cycles, less than 0.01 kg/m^2. Furthermore, the measurement method (opening and closing of the climatic chamber) might have determined an error that has to be taken into consideration. As Romano et al. [72] reported, the difference between the bio-wastes might depend on a micro-capillary network formation that is created during water molecules sorption/desorption.

Table 7 reported MBV values [g/(m^2·% RH)] and the classification provided by Rode et al. [49]: Negligible: MBV = 0.0–0.2; Limited: MBV = 0.2–0.5; Moderate:

MBV = 0.5–1.0; Good: MBV = 1.0–2.0; Excellent: MBV $\geq$ 2.0. MBV. Values were calculated to allow a comparison between the bio-wastes and other already studied materials. Indeed, a gap in literature did not allow a comparison to be made between the variation in sorption/desorption content during time of the analysed materials and the ones considered for comparison evaluated by the same test.

Table 7. MBV of analysed bio-wastes classified according to Rode et al. [49].

Materials	MBV (g/(m^2·% RH))	Classification according to Rode et al. [49]
Grape press waste	3.54 ± 0.09	Excellent
Hazelnut shells	3.13 ± 0.16	Excellent
Olives press waste	4.38 ± 0.13	Excellent
Spent coffee grounds	3.44 ± 0.01	Excellent
Wood chips	3.10 ± 0.06	Excellent

Olive press waste showed the highest MBV, the wood chips and the hazelnut shells had the lowest ones. In composites' production, olives press waste might guarantee a greater sorption/desorption capacity. They could therefore be the worst aggregates to produce thermal insulation boards, but the best ones in the case of indoor coating panels. Indeed, a high moisture buffering capacity can contribute to the passive control of the internal conditions and indoor air quality. However, these considerations should be verified: the performance of the composites widely varies depending on the complementary components (binders, additives) and the production method. Future studies should be devoted to determining the properties of these bio-wastes when combined with other materials to produce building composites. Overall, even in case of performances worse than the ones of typical composites, the use of bio-wastes replacing raw materials may offer a competitive and more sustainable solution than other common ones. Furthermore, it would be interesting to investigate the relationship between the bio-aggregates and composites' properties.

According to Ansell et al. [58], a correlation of linear proportionality was expected between loose bulk density and MBV values for natural fibres. They showed that MBV increased with bulk density for hemp shiv, flax shiv, wheat straw and rape shiv. Holcroft and Shea [73] obtained different results considering hemp-lime: the lower the density, the higher the MBV. In the present study, the comparison between the materials does not allow defining a correlation between loose bulk density and MBV. MBV varies depending on other parameters too (e.g., grain size, chemical composition). Cintura et al. [10] reported chemical compositions of the analysed bio-wastes by considering past studies. The researchers accounted it as an important parameter that influences materials' physical and mechanical features. They supposed that the selected bio-wastes may have good moisture buffering capacity, confirmed by the results of the present study.

Considering literature values of some of the materials chosen for comparison, corn cob showed values of 3.24 g/(m^2·% RH) [58], higher only than hazelnut shells' ones. Hemp shiv had values of about 2.09–2.53 g/(m^2·% RH) [58], lower than the ones of all analysed bio-wastes. This demonstrates that the selected bio-wastes have good hygroscopicity behaviour. It might be a drawback for insulation boards production, even if, as anticipated, the performances will depend on the final compositions.

3.4. Bio Susceptibility to Mould and Termites

Figure 9 gives an idea of the mould growth over the five materials and the control when inoculated with culture media and after four weeks.

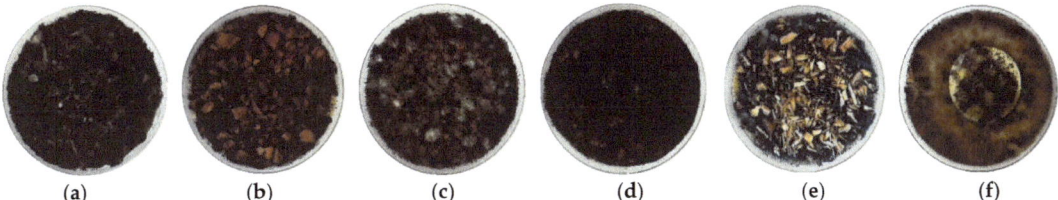

Figure 9. Mould growth (test with culture media) after four weeks: (**a**) grape press waste; (**b**) hazelnut shells; (**c**) olive press waste; (**d**) spent coffee grounds (**e**) wood chips; (**f**) filter paper control.

All the analysed bio-wastes with culture media are highly susceptible to mould attack, as expected. They reached the maximum value (4-contaminated surface more than 60%) during the second week of testing. The culture media contributes to the biological attack by increasing the sugar content available to the fungi. The controls (Figure 9f) demonstrated the validity of the test; all replicates reached grade 4 also on the second week of exposure.

Table 8 reports the results of weekly mould growth for the samples without culture media and Figure 10 shows the materials after four weeks of exposure.

Table 8. Average rate (±standard deviation) of mould growth for the samples without culture media.

Material	Mould Development			
	Week 1	Week 2	Week 3	Week 4
Spent coffee grounds	2.20 (±0.45)	3.00	4.00	4.00
Grape press waste	3.00	4.00	4.00	4.00
Olive press waste	3.00	4.00	4.00	4.00
Hazelnut shells	0.40 (±0.55)	2.30 (±0.45)	3.00	4.00
Wood chips	0.40 (±0.55)	1.40 (±0.55)	1.80 (±0.45)	2.70 (±0.67)

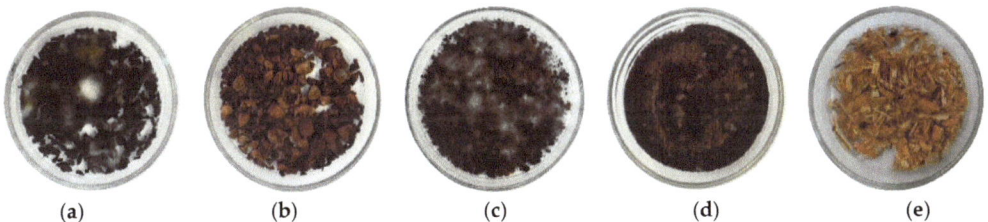

Figure 10. Mould growth (test without culture media) after four weeks of exposure: (**a**) grape press waste; (**b**) hazelnut shells; (**c**) olive press waste; (**d**) spent coffee grounds; (**e**) wood chips.

Even without surrounding the culture media, all the analysed bio-wastes have a high susceptibility to mould. Differently from the previous results, the samples reached the maximum value during the third week of testing, confirming the higher susceptibility caused by culture media (Figure 9). The biological attack of the controls (Figure 10e) demonstrated the validity of the test: being wood chips, mould growth was expected. They were rated as 2.70 (contaminated surface between 30% and 60%) after four weeks, hence all the bio-wastes showed a lower biological resistance.

Hazelnut shells showed similar behaviour to control during the first week, being both rated as 0.4. Nonetheless, this bio-waste reached the maximum values at the end of testing as the others. Grape and olive press waste showed the lowest resistance to mould, being rated at 4 during the second week. Spent coffee grounds reached the maximum value during the third week. As previously anticipated, high hygroscopicity improves mould growth. Considering the results of water adsorption, they could be considered consistent with the bio susceptibility ones: olives and grapes press waste showed the highest moisture buffering capacity, hazelnut shells and wood chips the lowest one. However, considering only the correlation between hygroscopicity and biological attack is an oversimplification. Bio susceptibility depends also on many other factors such as materials' composition, pH, surface properties, roughness, chemical and physical capabilities of mould species [51,74]. Mould growth could be further investigated since these laboratory tests aim at showing an initial assessment. The results confirm that, as bio-based materials, all the tested bio-wastes have a high susceptibility to mould.

Past research reported that caffeine improves the biological resistance of wood, lowering fungal growth. Kwaśniewska-Sip et al. [75] diluted caffeine into a water solution to treat Scots pine (*Pinus sylvestris* L.) samples; Šimůnková et al. [76] considered Norway spruce (*Picea abies* L. Karst.) samples. In both cases, caffeine solution improved wood's biological resistance. Nevertheless, even if spent coffee grounds could be a source of chemicals that can moderate mould growth, they cannot be used to avoid the biological attack, as Barbero-López et al. [77] reported. Indeed, the raw material is known as a good material to allow mould growth [78,79], as confirmed also in the present study.

Table 9 reports the results related to the susceptibility to subterranean termites, considering the average value for each bio-waste. The survival rate of the maritime pine (higher than 50%) confirms the validity of the test. Figure 11 shows the samples after the four weeks.

Table 9. Average rate (±standard deviation) of survival of *R. grassei* colonies for the bio-wastes.

Material	Survival Rate (%)	Mould Development *
Spent coffee grounds	0.00	Extensive
Grape press waste	63.33 (±27.30)	Limited
Olives press waste	0.00	Extensive
Hazelnut shells	10.67 (±9.45)	Limited
Wood chips	81.33 (±4.62)	Limited

* Visually and qualitatively evaluated after four weeks.

(a)   (b)   (c)   (d)   (e)

Figure 11. Termites' survival and mould growth after four weeks exposure: (**a**) grape press waste; (**b**) hazelnut shells; (**c**) olive press waste; (**d**) spent coffee grounds; (**e**) wood chips.

The termites were able to consume all bio-wastes, though their ability to survive was highly influenced by both the available cellulose they could use and the fast development of moulds that they were not able to limit. The bio-waste with the highest amount of cellulose (grape press waste with small parts of grapevine) [10] was not surprisingly the most consumed by termites and the one that kept the highest survival rate of the termites during the test period. Hazelnut shells have better resistance to termites than wood chips, but they are not completely unaffected: 10.67% of the termites survived deteriorating a part of the material. Cintura et al. [10] reported that hazelnut shells have a cellulose content of about 22.90−34.60%. According to past studies, wood chips have a cellulose content of about 32.09−50.00% [80–82]. The results are in line with this information: termites probably fed on hazelnut shells, but the cellulose content, i.e., the necessary nutrients to survive, was not enough, hence they slowly died.

Termites' survival for spent coffee grounds and olives press waste was rated at 0%, but these results cannot be considered as a demonstration of their best resistance to termites. Indeed, these materials also showed a high mould growth (Table 9 and Figure 11a,d) that could be the cause of termites' mortality. Šimůnková et al. [76] investigated caffeine's resistance from termites, applying a caffeine and water solution on wood and exposing the samples to *Reticulitermes flavipes* (Kollar). The results of their study demonstrated that caffeine improves the biological resistance of wood. Nevertheless, as previously anticipated, this cannot demonstrate good resistance to termites of spent coffee grounds. As Cintura et al. [10] reported, collecting information from several past studies, cellulose content in this bio-waste is between 8.60–52.42%. The range of variation is high, but spent coffee grounds have the lowest values when compared with the other considered bio-wastes. This information and the results of the present work cannot confirm a high termite resistance with spent coffee grounds, also due to the mould formation during the four weeks. Maybe this bio-waste could be used as a source of caffeine to apply on future eco-efficient boards/panels.

3.5. Comparison between Bio-Wastes and Wood Chips

As previously anticipated, maritime pine chips were considered as control material. Table 10 reports a comparison between the properties of the bio-wastes and wood chips, considering their use as thermal insulation materials. It shows which properties could be considered better (in green) or worse (in orange) than maritime pine ones for thermal insulation boards. The maximum/minimum values are highlighted with stronger shades of green/orange. When they are not highlighted, there is no difference between the considered bio-waste and wood chips. When they are highlighted in grey, more considerations have to be made. It is important to remind that this work presents some screening tests and properties of bio-aggregates. The performance of the final composites will widely depend on their composition and production method.

Table 10. Comparison between values of considered bio-wastes and maritime pine chips for thermal insulation boards.

Properties	Materials				
	Wood Chips	Grape Press Waste	Hazelnut Shells	Olives Press Waste	Spent Coffee Grounds
Loose bulk density (kg/m^3)	245.14	343.88	550.5	449.43	478.81
Thermal conductivity T = 23 °C, RH = 50% (W/(m·K))	0.077	0.078	0.107	0.089	0.092
Thermal conductivity T = 23 °C, RH = 75% (W/(m·K))	0.082	0.081	0.115	0.097	0.099
Absorption capacity after 48 h (%)	108.7	89.7	35.5	49.3	60.1
MBV (g/(m^2·% RH)) *	3.02	3.5	2.94	4.18	3.38
Bio-susceptibility to mould with culture media	4	4	4	4	4
Bio-susceptibility to mould without culture media	2.7	4	4	4	4
Bio-susceptibility to termites—Survival rate (%)	81.33	63.33	10.67	n.a. *	n.a. *

* Note: MBV—see detailed evaluation below; n.a. not available—the results need confirmation.

The analysed bio-wastes have higher values of loose bulk density and thermal conductivity than maritime pine chips. This may result in composites with worse thermal insulating performances than wood-based ones. A higher loose bulk density of the aggregates could be a drawback for thermal insulation boards' production, a benefit in case of coating panels'. The values of absorption capacity after 48 h are lower for the selected bio-wastes; hence, they may secure a higher water resistance when used in composites. For MBV, the values are higher than wood chips' ones, except for hazelnut shells. It seems that composites produced with the bio-wastes could have a higher contribution as moisture regulators than wood-based ones, guaranteeing better passive equilibrium of indoor humidity levels. This could be a benefit in case of internal coating panels' production, and a drawback in case of external panels or thermal insulation boards. A high MBV could affect the durability of the building composites. In terms of bio-susceptibility, the analysed bio-wastes show low resistance to mould, as well as wood chips. For termites, the outcomes of spent coffee grounds and olive press waste cannot be considered as a demonstration of high resistance: they could result from mould growth. Hazelnut shells show better resistance to termites' attacks than wood chips, but they are not completely unaffected. For eco-efficient building products, this drawback should be further investigated and solved.

The comparison between bio-wastes allows concluding that grape press waste is the most similar to maritime pine chips. It may be a good replacement of wood particles in future boards' production, even if many other factors play an important role (e.g., binders, production phase, treatments).

The final performance of panels and boards produced with the studied bio-wastes will strongly depend on their composition. The selected binders could both moderate or increase the benefits or the drawbacks of using these bio-wastes as aggregates. For example, for a hydraulic matrix, the use of water could cause the degradation of the bio-wastes and increase mould growth. Differently, a binder with a pH higher than 10 could guarantee less vulnerability to biological attack [51]. The thermal insulation properties could be improved by using a binder that secures the bonding of the aggregates by leaving a porous network between them.

Furthermore, the use of additives and the mixture with other material may widely affect the properties of the final product. For example, citric acid can moderate biological susceptibility and water absorption [83–85]. Past studies reported that boric acid, lime and potassium benzoate moderate mould growth [37,86,87]. On the other hand, they might increase the values of bulk density and thermal conductivity.

Pre-treatments of the bio-wastes may influence their properties, as Antunes et al. [33] demonstrated. As for the production methods, the curing phases [88] may be important, depending on the binder matrix. A fast and ventilated drying environment for the curing of the final product could avoid mould growth. Finally, the production process may widely affect the final properties. For example, pressing the composites increases bulk density and mechanical resistance, while just moulding could guarantee boards with lower bulk density and better thermal insulation properties.

Future studies could further investigate how all these parameters can influence eco-efficient boards and panels' performance.

4. Conclusions

This study investigated the properties of some bio-wastes (grape and olive press waste, hazelnut shells and spent coffee grounds), available in Euro-Mediterranean countries, to evaluate the feasibility of using them as aggregates for composite boards and panels. Maritime pine chips were considered as control, simulating recycled timber. Particle size distribution, loose bulk density, thermal conductivity, water absorption and hygroscopic properties were assessed, but particularly bio susceptibility to mould and termites was also analysed. From the results obtained, the following conclusions can be drawn:

- Grain size analysis demonstrated that shredding these bio-wastes to produce insulation boards does not seem necessary. Spent coffee grounds differ from the other bio-wastes and, for composites' production, they might be used as fine aggregates.
- The selected bio-wastes do not show by themselves good thermal insulation characteristics. Combining them with other materials, pre-treatments or production processes could improve the thermal insulation performance of the final products.
- The analysed bio-wastes have good hygroscopic behaviour, with high MBV, an advantage in case of the production of indoor coating boards to secure a passive control of indoor relative humidity and comfort.
- For all bio-wastes, the results confirmed the high biological susceptibility to the tested organisms. This drawback must be further investigated and mitigated for composites' production, namely by combining the bio-wastes with materials resistant to biological attack or by specific pre-treatments.

- Using the recommendations of RILEM TC 236-BBM "Bio-aggregate-based building materials" to evaluate properties of bio-wastes, considered as raw materials, allows them to be analysed and guarantees a simple comparison between different ones. However, some additional details for testing should be included, as well as complementary insect and fungi bio-susceptibility tests.

The present study both describes laboratory tests to analyse bio-wastes properties and provides a preliminary assessment of the considered ones, filling gaps in the literature. Using the selected bio-wastes as aggregates may be a competitive and more sustainable solution than the use of the traditional aggregates. Future studies will deepen the feasibility of producing eco-efficient composites and evaluate the properties of boards or panels.

Author Contributions: Conceptualization, Methodology, Validation, Investigation, Formal analysis, Data Curation, Writing—Original Draft, Visualization, E.C.; Conceptualization, Methodology, Writing—Review & Editing, Supervision, Project administration, L.N.; Investigation, Methodology, M.D.; Conceptualization, Writing—Review & Editing, Supervision, Funding acquisition, P.F. All authors have read and agreed to the published version of the manuscript.

Funding: This research was funded by the Portuguese Foundation for Science and Technology (FCT- Fundação para a Ciência e a Tecnologia), with PhD grant PD/BD/150579/2020, as part of the Eco-Construction and Rehabilitation Program (EcoCoRe).

Data Availability Statement: Data are available from the corresponding author upon request.

Acknowledgments: The authors are grateful to the CERIS research unit (project UIDB/04625/2020). The authors also acknowledge the help provided by Bruno Esteves, Polytechnic Institute of Viseu, and Susana Filipe Barreiros, NOVA School of Science and Technology, NOVA University of Lisbon, for helping in providing some of the materials analysed in this work.

Conflicts of Interest: The authors declare no conflict of interest.

References

1. Posani, M.; Veiga, M.D.R.; Peixoto de Freitas, V.; Kompatscher, K.; Schellen, H. Dynamic Hygrothermal Models for Monumental, Historic Buildings with HVAC Systems: Complexity shown through a case study. *E3S Web Conf.* **2020**, *172*, 15007. [CrossRef]
2. Viel, M.; Collet, F.; Lanos, C. Development and characterization of thermal insulation materials from renewable resources. *Constr. Build. Mater.* **2019**, *214*, 685–697. [CrossRef]
3. Nguyen, D.M.; Grillet, A.; Diep, T.M.H.; Bui, Q.; Woloszyn, M. Characterization of hygrothermal insulating biomaterials modified by inorganic adsorbents. *Heat Mass Transf.* **2020**, *56*, 2473–2485. [CrossRef]
4. Hung Anh, L.D.; Pásztory, Z. An overview of factors influencing thermal conductivity of building insulation materials. *J. Build. Eng.* **2021**, *44*, 102604. [CrossRef]
5. Binici, H.; Aksogan, O. Eco-friendly insulation material production with waste olive seeds, ground PVC and wood chips. *J. Build. Eng.* **2016**, *5*, 260–266. [CrossRef]
6. Ntimugura, F.; Vinai, R.; Harper, A.; Walker, P. Mechanical, thermal, hygroscopic and acoustic properties of bio-aggregates—Lime and alkali—Activated insulating composite materials: A review of current status and prospects for miscanthus as an innovative resource in the South West of England. *Sustain. Mater. Technol.* **2020**, *26*, e00211. [CrossRef]
7. Cetiner, I.; Shea, A.D. Wood waste as an alternative thermal insulation for buildings. *Energy Build.* **2018**, *168*, 374–384. [CrossRef]
8. Cintura, E.; Gomes, M.I. Influence of Humidity on Environmental Sustainability, Air Quality and Occupant Health. *World Acad. Sci. Eng. Technol. Int. J. Environ. Ecol. Eng.* **2020**, *14*, 8–13. [CrossRef]
9. De Azevedo, A.R.; Amin, M.; Hadzima-Nyarko, M.; Saad Agwa, I.; Zeyad, A.M.; Tayeh, B.A.; Adesina, A. Possibilities for the application of agro-industrial wastes in cementitious materials: A brief review of the Brazilian perspective. *Clean. Mater.* **2022**, *3*, 100040. [CrossRef]
10. Cintura, E.; Nunes, L.; Esteves, B.; Faria, P. Agro-industrial wastes as building insulation materials: A review and challenges for Euro-Mediterranean countries. *Ind. Crops Prod.* **2021**, *171*, 113833. [CrossRef]
11. Heniegal, A.M.; Ramadan, M.A.; Naguib, A.; Agwa, I.S. Study on properties of clay brick incorporating sludge of water treatment plant and agriculture waste. *Case Stud. Constr. Mater.* **2020**, *13*, e00397. [CrossRef]
12. Priyadarshini, M.; Giri, J.P.; Patnaik, M. Variability in the compressive strength of non-conventional bricks containing agro and industrial waste. *Case Stud. Constr. Mater.* **2021**, *14*, e00506. [CrossRef]
13. Mahieu, A.; Alix, S.; Leblanc, N. Properties of particleboards made of agricultural by-products with a classical binder or self-bound. *Ind. Crops Prod.* **2019**, *130*, 371–379. [CrossRef]
14. Eschenhagen, A.; Raj, M.; Rodrigo, N.; Zamora, A.; Labonne, L.; Evon, P.; Welemane, H. Investigation of Miscanthus and Sunflower Stalk Fiber-Reinforced Composites for Insulation Applications. *Adv. Civ. Eng.* **2019**, *2019*, 1–7. [CrossRef]

15. *AFNOR NF P75-101:1983*; Isolants Thermiques Destinés au Bâtiment—Définition. AFNOR: Paris, France, 1983.
16. Ali, M.; Alabdulkarem, A.; Nuhait, A.; Al-Salem, K.; Almuzaiqer, R.; Bayaquob, O.; Salah, H.; Alsaggaf, A.; Algafri, Z. Thermal analyses of loose agave, wheat straw fibers and agave/wheat straw as new hybrid thermal insulating materials for buildings. *J. Nat. Fibers* **2020**, *18*, 2173–2188. [CrossRef]
17. Nunes, L.; Cintura, E.; Parracha, J.L.; Fernandes, B.; Silva, V.; Faria, P. Cement-Bonded Particleboards with Banana Pseudostem Waste: Physical Performance and Bio-Susceptibility. *Infrastructures* **2021**, *6*, 86. [CrossRef]
18. Wong, M.C.; Hendrikse, S.I.S.; Sherrell, P.C.; Ellis, A.V. Grapevine waste in sustainable hybrid particleboard production. *Waste Manag.* **2020**, *118*, 501–509. [CrossRef]
19. Binici, H.; Aksogan, O.; Dıncer, A.; Luga, E.; Eken, M.; Isikaltun, O. The possibility of vermiculite, sunflower stalk and wheat stalk using for thermal insulation material production. *Therm. Sci. Eng. Prog.* **2020**, *18*, 100567. [CrossRef]
20. Liuzzi, S.; Rubino, C.; Martellotta, F.; Stefanizzi, P.; Casavola, C.; Pappalettera, G. Characterization of biomass-based materials for building applications: The case of straw and olive tree waste. *Ind. Crops Prod.* **2020**, *147*, 112229. [CrossRef]
21. Pavelek, M.; Adamová, T. Bio-waste thermal insulation panel for sustainable building construction in steady and unsteady-state conditions. *Materials* **2019**, *12*, 2004. [CrossRef]
22. Mati-Baouche, N.; De Baynast, H.; Lebert, A.; Sun, S.; Lopez-Mingo, C.J.S.; Leclaire, P.; Michaud, P. Mechanical, thermal and acoustical characterizations of an insulating bio-based composite made from sunflower stalks particles and chitosan. *Ind. Crops Prod.* **2014**, *58*, 244–250. [CrossRef]
23. Pásztory, Z.; Ronyecz Mohácsiné, I.; Börcsök, Z. Investigation of thermal insulation panels made of black locust tree bark. *Constr. Build. Mater.* **2017**, *147*, 733–735. [CrossRef]
24. Binici, H.; Aksogan, O.; Demirhan, C. Mechanical, thermal and acoustical characterizations of an insulation composite made of bio-based materials. *Sustain. Cities Soc.* **2016**, *20*, 17–26. [CrossRef]
25. Wang, C.G.; Zhang, S.G.; Wu, H. Performance of Cement Bonded Particleboards Made from Grapevine. *Adv. Mater. Res.* **2013**, *631–632*, 765–770. [CrossRef]
26. Kusumah, S.S.; Umemura, K.; Yoshioka, K.; Miyafuji, H.; Kanayama, K. Utilization of sweet sorghum bagasse and citric acid for manufacturing of particleboard I: Effects of pre-drying treatment and citric acid content on the board properties. *Ind. Crops Prod.* **2016**, *84*, 34–42. [CrossRef]
27. Buratti, C.; Belloni, E.; Lascaro, E.; Merli, F.; Ricciardi, P. Rice husk panels for building applications: Thermal, acoustic and environmental characterization and comparison with other innovative recycled waste materials. *Constr. Build. Mater.* **2018**, *171*, 338–349. [CrossRef]
28. Viel, M.; Collet, F.; Lanos, C. Chemical and multi-physical characterization of agro-resources' by-product as a possible raw building material. *Ind. Crops Prod.* **2018**, *120*, 214–237. [CrossRef]
29. Cintura, E.; Nunes, L.; Faria, P. Characterization of agro-wastes to be used as aggregates for eco-efficient insulation boards. In Proceedings of the CEES 2021—International Conference on Construction, Energy, Environment and Sustainability, Coimbra, Portugal, 12–15 October 2021; ISBN 978-989-54499-1-0.
30. Amziane, S.; Collet, F.; Lawrence, M.; Magniont, C.; Picandet, V.; Sonebi, M. Recommendation of the RILEM TC 236-BBM: Characterisation testing of hemp shiv to determine the initial water content, water absorption, dry density, particle size distribution and thermal conductivity. *Mater. Struct.* **2017**, *50*, 167. [CrossRef]
31. Page, J.; Sonebi, M.; Amziane, S. Design and multi-physical properties of a new hybrid hemp-flax composite material. *Constr. Build. Mater.* **2017**, *139*, 502–512. [CrossRef]
32. Laborel-Préneron, A.; Magniont, C.; Aubert, J.-E. Characterization of barley straw, hemp shiv and corn cob as resources for bioaggregate based building materials. *Waste Biomass Valorization* **2017**, *9*, 1095–1112. [CrossRef]
33. Antunes, A.; Faria, P.; Silva, V.; Brás, A. Rice husk-earth based composites: A novel bio-based panel for buildings refurbishment. *Constr. Build. Mater.* **2019**, *221*, 99–108. [CrossRef]
34. Barbieri, V.; Lassinantti Gualtieri, M.; Siligardi, C. Wheat husk: A renewable resource for bio-based building materials. *Constr. Build. Mater.* **2020**, *251*, 118909. [CrossRef]
35. Gradeci, K.; Labonnote, N.; Time, B.; Köhler, J. Mould growth criteria and design avoidance approaches in wood-based materials—A systematic review. *Constr. Build. Mater.* **2017**, *150*, 77–88. [CrossRef]
36. Tobon, A.M.; Andres, Y.; Locoge, N. Impacts of test methods on the assessment of insulation materials' resistance against moulds. *Build. Environ.* **2020**, *179*, 106963. [CrossRef]
37. Palumbo, M.; Lacasta, A.M.; Navarro, A.; Giraldo, M.P.; Lesar, B. Improvement of fire reaction and mould growth resistance of a new bio-based thermal insulation material. *Constr. Build. Mater.* **2017**, *139*, 531–539. [CrossRef]
38. Viel, M.; Collet, F.; Lecieux, Y.; François, M.L.M.; Colson, V.; Lanos, C.; Hussain, A.; Lawrence, M. Resistance to mold development assessment of bio-based building materials. *Compos. Part B Eng.* **2019**, *158*, 406–418. [CrossRef]
39. Ginestet, S.; Aschan-Leygonie, C.; Bayeux, T.; Keirsbulck, M. Mould in indoor environments: The role of heating, ventilation and fuel poverty. A French perspective. *Build. Environ.* **2020**, *169*, 106577. [CrossRef]
40. Ewart, D.; Nunes, L.; De Troya, T.; Kutnik, M.; Dhang, P. Termites and a changing climate. In *Climate Change Impacts on Urban Pests*; Dhang, P., Ed.; CAB International: Wallingford, UK, 2016; pp. 80–94.
41. Duarte, S.; Nunes, L.; Kržišnik, D.; Humar, M.; Jones, D. Influence of zwitterionic buffer effects with thermal modification treatments of wood on symbiotic protists in reticulitermes grassei clément. *Insects* **2021**, *12*, 139. [CrossRef]

42. Echeverria, M.C.; Nuti, M. Valorisation of the Residues of Coffee Agro-industry: Perspectives and Limitations. *Open Waste Manag. J.* **2017**, *10*, 13–22. [CrossRef]
43. Pedras, B.M.; Regalin, G.; Sá-Nogueira, I.; Simões, P.; Paiva, A.; Barreiros, S. Fractionation of red wine grape pomace by subcritical water extraction/hydrolysis. *J. Supercrit. Fluids* **2020**, *160*, 104793. [CrossRef]
44. Demirer, H.; Kartal, İ.; Yıldırım, A.; Büyükkaya, K. The Utilisability of Ground Hazelnut Shell as Filler in Polypropylene Composites. *Acta Phys. Pol. A* **2018**, *134*, 254–256. [CrossRef]
45. PANTONE Uncoated RGB Scale. Available online: https://www.ab-pulverlacke.de/pdf/sonderfarbton/pantone.pdf (accessed on 23 June 2021).
46. *EN 933-2*; Tests for Geometrical Properties of Aggregates. Determination of Particle Size Distribution. Test Sieves, Nominal Size of Apertures. CEN: Brussels, Belgium, 2020.
47. *EN 1097-3*; Tests for Mechanical and Physical Properties of Aggregates Part 3: Determination of Loose Bulk Density and Voids. CEN: Brussels, Belgium, 1998.
48. *ISO 24353*; Hygrothermal Performance of Building Materials and Products—Determination of Moisture Adsorption/Desorption Properties in Response to Humidity Variation. International Organization for Standardization: Geneva, Switzerland, 2008.
49. Rode, C.; Peuhkuri, R.H.; Mortensen, L.H.; Hansen, K.K.; Time, B.; Gustavsen, A.; Ojanen, T.; Ahonen, J.; Svennberg, K.; Arfvidsson, J.; et al. *Moisture Buffering of Building Materials*; (BYG Report No. R-127); Technical University of Denmark, Department of Civil Engineering: Lyngby, Denmark, 2005; ISBN 8778771951.
50. *ASTM D5590-17*; Determining the Resistance of Paint Films and Related Coatings to Fungal Defacement by Accelerated Four-Week Agar Plate Assay. ASTM International: Pennsylvania, PA, USA, 2017.
51. Parracha, J.L.; Borsoi, G.; Flores-Colen, I.; Veiga, R.; Nunes, L.; Dionísio, A.; Gomes, M.G.; Faria, P. Performance parameters of ETICS: Correlating water resistance, bio-susceptibility and surface properties. *Constr. Build. Mater.* **2021**, *272*, 121956. [CrossRef]
52. Nunes, L.; Duarte, S. *Termiticide Transmission Test. CEN/TC38/WG24 Round Robin Test*; Test Report 007UPB2017; LNEC: Lisbon, Portugal, 2017; 6p.
53. Posani, M.; Veiga, R.; de Freitas, V.P. Thermal mortar-based insulation solutions for historic walls: An extensive hygrothermal characterization of materials and systems. *Constr. Build. Mater.* **2022**, *315*, 125640. [CrossRef]
54. Czajkowski, Ł.; Kocewicz, R.; Weres, J.; Olek, W. Estimation of Thermal Properties of Straw-Based Insulating Panels. *Materials* **2022**, *15*, 1073. [CrossRef]
55. Ranesi, A.; Veiga, M.R.V.; Faria, P. Laboratory characterization of relative humidity dependent properties for plasters: A systematic review. *Constr. Build. Mater.* **2021**, *304*, 124595. [CrossRef]
56. Collet, F. Hygric and thermal properties of bio-aggregate based building materials. In *RILEM State-of-the-Art Reports*; Springer: Dordrecht, The Netherlands, 2017; Volume 23, pp. 125–147. ISBN 9789402410310.
57. Martínez-García, C.; González-Fonteboa, B.; Carro-López, D.; Pérez-Ordóñez, J.L. Mussel shells: A canning industry by-product converted into a bio-based insulation material. *J. Clean. Prod.* **2020**, *269*, 122343. [CrossRef]
58. Ansell, M.P.; Lawrence, M.; Jiang, Y.; Shea, A.; Hussain, A.; Calabria-Holley, J.; Walker, P. Natural plant-based aggregates and bio-composite panels with low thermal conductivity and high hygrothermal efficiency for applications in construction. In *Nonconventional and Vernacular Construction Materials*; Elsevier: Sawston, UK, 2020; pp. 217–245. ISBN 9780081027042.
59. David, G.; Vannini, M.; Sisti, L.; Marchese, P.; Celli, A.; Gontard, N.; Angellier-Coussy, H. Eco-Conversion of Two Winery Lignocellulosic Wastes into Fillers for Biocomposites: Vine Shoots and Wine Pomaces. *Polymers* **2020**, *12*, 1530. [CrossRef]
60. Çöpür, Y.; Güler, C.; Akgül, M.; Taşçıoğlu, C. Some chemical properties of hazelnut husk and its suitability for particleboard production. *Build. Environ.* **2007**, *42*, 2568–2572. [CrossRef]
61. Liuzzi, S.; Rubino, C.; Stefanizzi, P.; Petrella, A.; Boghetich, A.; Casavola, C.; Pappalettera, G. Hygrothermal properties of clayey plasters with olive fibers. *Constr. Build. Mater.* **2018**, *158*, 24–32. [CrossRef]
62. Del Río Merino, M.; Guijarro Rodríguez, J.; Fernández Martínez, F.; Santa Cruz Astorqui, J. Viability of using olive stones as lightweight aggregate in construction mortars. *Rev. Constr.* **2017**, *16*, 431–438. [CrossRef]
63. Massaro Sousa, L.; Ferreira, M.C. Spent coffee grounds as a renewable source of energy: An analysis of bulk powder flowability. *Particuology* **2019**, *43*, 92–100. [CrossRef]
64. Cherki, A.; Remy, B.; Khabbazi, A.; Jannot, Y.; Baillis, D. Experimental thermal properties characterization of insulating cork—gypsum composite. *Constr. Build. Mater.* **2014**, *54*, 202–209. [CrossRef]
65. Brás, A.; Leal, M.; Faria, P. Cement-cork mortars for thermal bridges correction. Comparison with cement-EPS mortars performance. *Constr. Build. Mater.* **2013**, *49*, 315–327. [CrossRef]
66. Nóvoa, P.J.R.; Ribeiro, M.C.; Ferreira, A.J.; Marques, A. Mechanical characterization of lightweight polymer mortar modified with cork granulates. *Compos. Sci. Technol.* **2004**, *64*, 2197–2205. [CrossRef]
67. Brouard, Y.; Belayachi, N.; Hoxha, D.; Ranganathan, N.; Méo, S. Mechanical and hygrothermal behavior of clay—Sunflower (*Helianthus annuus*) and rape straw (*Brassica napus*) plaster bio-composites for building insulation. *Constr. Build. Mater.* **2018**, *161*, 196–207. [CrossRef]
68. Çuhadaroğlu, B. Thermal conductivity analysis of a briquette with additive hazelnut shells. *Build. Environ.* **2005**, *40*, 942–948. [CrossRef]

69. Lachheb, A.; Allouhi, A.; El Marhoune, M.; Saadani, R.; Kousksou, T.; Jamil, A.; Rahmoune, M.; Oussouaddi, O. Thermal insulation improvement in construction materials by adding spent coffee grounds: An experimental and simulation study. *J. Clean. Prod.* **2019**, *209*, 1411–1419. [CrossRef]
70. Gomes, M.G.; Flores-Colen, I.; Melo, H.; Soares, A. Physical performance of industrial and EPS and cork experimental thermal insulation renders. *Constr. Build. Mater.* **2019**, *198*, 786–795. [CrossRef]
71. Bouasker, M.; Belayachi, N.; Hoxha, D.; Al-Mukhtar, M. Physical characterization of natural straw fibers as aggregates for construction materials applications. *Materials* **2014**, *7*, 3034–3048. [CrossRef]
72. Romano, A.; Bras, A.; Grammatikos, S.; Shaw, A.; Riley, M. Dynamic behaviour of bio-based and recycled materials for indoor environmental comfort. *Constr. Build. Mater.* **2019**, *211*, 730–743. [CrossRef]
73. Holcroft, N.; Shea, A. Effect of compaction on moisture buffering of hemp-lime insulation. *First Int. Conf. Bio-Based Build. Mater.* **2015**, *33*, 542–546.
74. Stefanowski, B.K.; Curling, S.F.; Ormondroyd, G.A. A rapid screening method to determine the susceptibility of bio-based construction and insulation products to mould growth. *Int. Biodeterior. Biodegrad.* **2017**, *116*, 124–132. [CrossRef]
75. Kwaśniewska-Sip, P.; Cofta, G.; Nowak, P.B. Resistance of fungal growth on Scots pine treated with caffeine. *Int. Biodeterior. Biodegrad.* **2018**, *132*, 178–184. [CrossRef]
76. Šimůnková, K.; Reinprecht, L.; Nábělková, J.; Hýsek, Š.; Kindl, J.; Borůvka, V.; Lišková, T.; Šobotník, J.; Pánek, M. Caffeine—perspective natural biocide for wood protection against decaying fungi and termites. *J. Clean. Prod.* **2021**, *304*, 127110. [CrossRef]
77. Barbero-López, A.; Ochoa-Retamero, A.; López-Gómez, Y.; Vilppo, T.; Venäläinen, M.; Lavola, A.; Julkunen-Tiitto, R.; Haapala, A. Activity of spent coffee ground cinnamates against wood-decaying fungi in vitro. *BioResources* **2018**, *13*, 6555–6564. [CrossRef]
78. Andreola, F.; Borghi, A.; Pedrazzi, S.; Allesina, G.; Tartarini, P.; Lancellotti, I.; Barbieri, L. Spent coffee grounds in the production of lightweight clay ceramic aggregates in view of urban and agricultural sustainable development. *Materials* **2019**, *12*, 3581. [CrossRef]
79. Murthy, P.S.; Madhava Naidu, M. Sustainable management of coffee industry by-products and value addition—A review. *Resour. Conserv. Recycl.* **2012**, *66*, 45–58. [CrossRef]
80. Wang, X.; Li, H.; Cao, Y.; Tang, Q. Cellulose extraction from wood chip in an ionic liquid 1-allyl-3-methylimidazolium chloride (AmimCl). *Bioresour. Technol.* **2011**, *102*, 7959–7965. [CrossRef]
81. Cotana, F.; Cavalaglio, G.; Gelosia, M.; Nicolini, A.; Coccia, V.; Petrozzi, A. Production of Bioethanol in a Second Generation Prototype from Pine Wood Chips. *Energy Procedia* **2014**, *45*, 42–51. [CrossRef]
82. Karunanithy, C.; Muthukumarappan, K.; Gibbons, W.R. Extrusion Pretreatment of Pine Wood Chips. *Appl. Biochem. Biotechnol.* **2012**, *167*, 81–99. [CrossRef]
83. Indrayani, Y.; Setyawati, D.; Munawar, S.S.; Umemura, K.; Yoshimura, T. Evaluation of Termite Resistance of Medium Density Fiberboard (MDF) Manufacture from Agricultural Fiber Bonded with Citric Acid. *Procedia Environ. Sci.* **2015**, *28*, 778–782. [CrossRef]
84. Widyorini, R.; Umemura, K.; Isnan, R.; Putra, D.R.; Awaludin, A.; Prayitno, T.A. Manufacture and properties of citric acid-bonded particleboard made from bamboo materials. *Eur. J. Wood Wood Prod.* **2016**, *74*, 57–65. [CrossRef]
85. Nataraj, D.; Sakkara, S.; Meenakshi, H.N.; Reddy, N. Properties and applications of citric acid crosslinked banana fibre-wheat gluten films. *Ind. Crops Prod.* **2018**, *124*, 265–272. [CrossRef]
86. Santos, T.; Nunes, L.; Faria, P. Production of eco-efficient earth-based plasters: Influence of composition on physical performance and bio-susceptibility. *J. Clean. Prod.* **2017**, *167*, 55–67. [CrossRef]
87. De Carvalho, P.S.; Nora, M.D.; da Rosa, L.C. Development of an acoustic absorbing material based on sunflower residue following the cleaner production techniques. *J. Clean. Prod.* **2020**, *270*, 122478. [CrossRef]
88. Cabral, M.R.; Nakanishi, E.Y.; Mármol, G.; Palacios, J.; Godbout, S.; Lagacé, R.; Savastano, H.; Fiorelli, J. Potential of Jerusalem Artichoke (*Helianthus tuberosus* L.) stalks to produce cement-bonded particleboards. *Ind. Crops Prod.* **2018**, *122*, 214–222. [CrossRef]

Article

Design and Thermal Characterization of Two Construction Solutions with and without Incorporation of Macroencapsulated PCM

António Figueiredo [1,*], Filipe Rebelo [1], António Samagaio [2], Romeu Vicente [1] and Jorge Lira [3]

1   RISCO-Research Centre for Risks and Sustainability in Construction, Civil Engineering Department, University of Aveiro, 3810-193 Aveiro, Portugal; filiperebelo@ua.pt (F.R.); romvic@ua.pt (R.V.)
2   Department of Environment and Planning, University of Aveiro, 3810-193 Aveiro, Portugal; samagaio@ua.pt
3   SteelMe, Maia, 4475-830 Oporto, Portugal; jorge.lira@5dhome.pt
*   Correspondence: ajfigueiredo@ua.pt

Abstract: Improving the energy efficiency of new and existing building stock while fostering the use of renewable energy is one of the major goals of the Renovation Wave initiative promoted by the European Union. In this framework, the present research focuses on the design of an innovative and efficient construction solution for an external envelope and internal partitions that can improve energy efficiency and thermal comfort in lightweight construction technology for buildings. The use of phase change materials (PCMs), particularly in the macroencapsulated form, in building construction solutions or components enhances the buildings' thermal mass without significantly increasing the solutions' weight. Therefore, the solution herein developed is essentially targeted at lightweight building technology since the incorporation of a macroencapsulated PCM core will allow to store and release large amounts of energy per volume unit, in order to attenuate high indoor temperature fluctuations. In the scope of this study, the use of a thermally active core in a lightweight construction solution was designed and thermally characterized. Thus, an experimental campaign on the thermal properties of the solution containing macroencapsulated PCMs was performed, intended for applications in two twin full-scale cold-formed steel lightweight tiny houses. Regarding the hot box heat flux meter approach, the results revealed the following: good correlation between thermal conductivity and mean specimen temperatures for both construction assemblies tested, and significant thermal amplitude reduction with the use solution containing the macroencapsulated PCM core.

Keywords: thermal conductivity; phase change materials; energy efficiency; thermal energy storage; lightweight buildings

1. Introduction

The European Union policy framework for energy and environmental strategy focuses on the ambitious goal of reducing energy consumption and greenhouse gas emissions by improving buildings' energy efficiency, from new to existing building stock, assuring comfortable and healthier indoor environment conditions for the users [1,2]. Almeida et al. [3], achieved potential energy savings of 48% in terms of electricity consumption in the EU, revealing a potential improvement in the residential sector behavior, highlighting the importance of the rapid implementation of European regulations. Additionally, during the last decade, a noticeable trend to implement prefabricated and lightweight building components combined with a modular approach to construction has been observed. Despite lightweight construction typology representing an economic and ecological alternative to common building heavyweight solutions, it is also an excellent solution for retrofitting and refurbishment; however, it still presents challenging issues in terms of thermal performance, due to the lack of thermal mass and consequent reduced thermal inertia, a known

Infrastructures **2022**, *7*, 27. https://doi.org/10.3390/infrastructures7030027   https://www.mdpi.com/journal/infrastructures

drawback of this particular construction system. Thus, the present research is motivated by the pursuit of coupling the development of enhanced lightweight building assemblies: for future resilient and sustainable buildings to be energy efficient; to compensate for the reduced thermal inertia by using phase change materials (PCMs); and to mitigate the use of lightweight building technology in different climate contexts.

Innovative building solutions and components containing PCM have been the subject of numerous studies over the last years, highlighting the following: development of solutions for lightweight buildings [4–6]; PCM incorporation into mortars [7–9], bricks [10–12], and thermally activated concrete slabs [13,14]; gypsum plaster wallboards [15–17]; in panels for cooling purposes [18]; screed mortars [19,20]; microencapsulation and positioning into attic spaces [21]; and buildings' features optimization [4,5,22].

Despite the well-known advantages on the use of building components containing PCMs, several authors have reported important issues that must be considered regarding their use in buildings. Kuznik et al. [23] investigated the use of PCMs in a renovation project by comparing two rooms: one with wallboards containing PCMs, and the other with standard wallboards without PCM. The authors concluded that the use of PCMs increased the indoor thermal comfort in the room containing PCM wallboards; however, they also concluded that for several days, the latent heat storage capacity of the PCMs was not fully exploited due to its incomplete discharge overnight. Thus, a correct system design is mandatory, including the PCM operating temperature range as well as the positioning conditions where the PCM will be applied. Sun et al. [24] investigated the thermal performance of a room by simulating four different inorganic composite PCMs, which were simultaneously located into the wall air cavities and also combined with a double-layer of PCM into a radiant floor system. These combined PCM-containing solutions, leading to a reduction of 21.2% in the annual energy consumption. The authors also highlighted three parameters with extreme influence on the PCM efficiency and, consequently, on the building energy consumption: the thickness of the PCM layer; the thermal conductivity; and the relative position between the heat source and the PCM layers in the radiant floor systems. Thus, excessive layer thickness of PCM (and amount) as well as high values of thermal conductivity could lead to the worst results in terms of indoor thermal conditions, also leading to increased materials' costs during installation. Aligned with these issues, Xu et al. [25] highlighted that the PCM performance is affected by numerous factors, such as PCM layer thickness, melting range temperature, thermal conductivity, latent heat fusion, and the existence or absence of an air gap between the PCM and the covering layer. The authors concluded that the thickness of the PCM layer should not exceed 20 mm and the latent heat of fusion should be larger than 120 kJ kg^{-1} to be fully exploited.

Regarding the research concerning buildings with low thermal inertia, Kośny et al. [26] studied several possibilities to improve buildings' thermal behavior by applying solutions containing PCM. A total of five different solutions were investigated, including different types of insulation, position and thickness of the PCM layer, as well as type of PCM arrangement (condensed and dispersed). A time shift in peak temperatures was observed, shifting and reducing the number of operating hours of the air conditioning system, from daytime peak to night time. An inversion in the direction of the heat flow was also observed, allowing the use of passive cooling to the building. Thus, it is possible to acknowledge that the addition of PCM to the insulation layer translates to a substantial improvement in the thermal performance for this type of building. In this context, Rebelo et al. [8] presented a full thermophysical characterization of an innovative cementitious mortar incorporating microencapsulated PCMs, also targeted for low thermal mass buildings located in warm climates. The developed mortars are intended to be applied in contact with the insulation layer by the inner surface of the building envelope walls, aiming indoor passive thermal regulation toward mitigating the overheating phenomena in lightweight construction systems. Soares et al. [27] proposed the use of drywalls with phase change materials to overcome the low thermal inertia of LSF systems. This research work has the objective of optimizing 10 different factors with direct influence in the efficiency of the PCM–

drywalls use. The authors concluded that the use of PCM–drywalls in LSF constructive systems allows to achieve a better building performance for all studied climates, with an optimum solution for each climate. In a review regarding the energy efficiency and thermal performance of LSF construction, Soares et al. [27] presented numerous commercial PCM-based solutions for LSF construction. In this study, five different examples of commercial PCM boards for dry construction, containing microencapsulated PCMs, can be consulted. Regarding macroencapsulated PCM, Santos et al. [28] presented three different solutions: ceiling tiles with a honeycomb core filled with PCM; aluminum-laminated panel containing a PCM that can be used after the plasterboard layer; and suspended ceiling tiles with PCM bags placed above.

Figueiredo et al. [4] performed an optimization study toward overheating reduction for buildings with low thermal inertia subjected to a Mediterranean climate. The authors attained a reduction of overheating risk by up to 24% in the cooling season, due to the optimization of the following parameters: ventilation rate; PCM melting temperate range; PCM position into construction solutions; and combining different melting temperatures in the same construction solution. The authors highlighted that the complete charge–discharge cycle of the PCM on a daily basis is only possible considering an effective compromise with the PCM melting temperature and ventilation rate selection.

These studies have paved the way to confirm that the use of PCMs as a second skin of the insulation layer substantially improves the building's thermal performance. However, we identified a literature gap regarding the type of PCM, such as salt hydrates due to their lower cost and form of macroencapsulation in building components, despite its huge potential for reduction in buildings' energy demand. Hence, the development and the thermal characterization of a thermally enhanced construction solution containing a salt hydrate PCM is proposed, suitable for incorporating into lightweight construction assemblies. Additionally, the developed PCM enhanced solution is also adequate for use at the inner surface of existing buildings in retrofit scenarios, targeting the reduction in internal overheating whilst promoting indoor passive thermal regulation, especially in warm climate conditions.

2. Materials and Methods

Previously, a numerical parametric simulation was carried out to support the PCM melting range for experimental development of the building solution with a thermally activated core. An experimental campaign to determine the thermal properties of a thermally enhanced solution based on a lightweight cold-formed steel solution containing macroencapsulated PCMs was performed, used in the scope of a comparison between two twin full-scale tiny houses located at the University of Aveiro campus (Portugal). The thermal characterization of the solution was performed in three phases:

(i)   Characterize the acquired PCM (RUBITHERM SP21E–manufacturer product reference) enthalpy–temperature curves by means of differential scanning calorimetry (DSC) analysis;

(ii) Determine the equivalent thermal conductivity of the thermally active core solution (with PCM layer) and its comparison to a reference solution (without PCM), through the hot box heat flux meter method in steady state conditions;

(iii) Analyze indoor temperature behavior in free floating conditions (passive chamber) as consequence of a controlled induced temperature (active chamber), using the hot box apparatus.

The methodology of the present work begins with the case study definition regarding the two tiny houses that will be used for a future real-scale evaluation of the indoor thermal comfort conditions comprising the lightweight external envelope solutions. The second step of this work was developed, resourcing a dynamic simulation, using the EnergyPlus^{TM} software. This step aims to define the adequate PCM melting temperature range to be applied in the construction solution, by changing the PCM operational temperature range according to the manufacturer options (commercial based solutions with different melting temperatures and enthalpy). From the parametric study resulted the selection over a commercially available PCM from RUBITHERM with reference SP21E. This PCM consists of a product based on salt–water mixtures and additives and it was macroencapsulated into aluminum cases with dimensions of 450 m × 300 m × 15 m, thus containing approximately 2 kg of pure PCM per macrocapsule. Macrocapsules consist of two shaped aluminum plates attached to each other, forming a final thickness of 15 mm (aluminum plates containing PCM). They are joined at two centerd points and joined together at their frames (see Figure 1). This macrocapsule, due to its composition based on aluminum, allow high heat transfer between the PCM and the materials in contact with the aluminum macrocapsule. This specific PCM solution was selected instead of a conventional paraffinic PCM-based solution, due to the fact that the paraffinic PCMs reveal relatively low ignition resistance. Thus, and compared to the generic paraffinic solutions, salt hydrate based PCMs are not flammable and therefore highly recommended for construction solution incorporation.

Figure 1. PCM encapsulated in aluminum container.

The main manufacturers' characteristics of the selected PCM are listed in Table 1.

Table 1. PCM properties used in this research (technical data from the manufacturer).

Designation from Manufacturer	Product Material	Melting Temperature/°C Range	Crystallization Temperature/°C Range	Latent Heat Capacity/kJ kg^{-1}	Thermal Conductivity/W m^{-1} °C^{-1}
SP21E	Salt–water mixtures and additives	22–23	21–19	170	0.50

Finally, as a third step, two building solutions of the representative external envelope walls (reference solution without PCM and thermally enhanced solution with PCM) were thermally characterized in laboratory conditions and compared.

3. Case Study Definition

3.1. Tiny Houses—Real Scale Case Study

The present case study is depicted in Figure 2, consisting of two lightweight buildings with a cold-formed steel assembly, commonly designated as a light steel frame (LSF) structure, with a treated floor area of 35 m², which corresponds to a volume of 125 m³. A building with this area, geometry and construction system is considered representative of a typical tiny house that is easily erected in densely constructed urban areas. This construction technology was chosen for the two tiny houses due to the growing tendency for prefabricated construction systems, the faster building technology and the current trend of residential downsizing and changing ownership/use. The LSF construction technology offers a significant cost reduction potential, allowing, at the same time, improved quality control due to the nature of the structure assembly. However, as previously stated, this building technology presents low thermal inertia and a significant risk of overheating as its major weaknesses. Therefore, there is a need to improve the building construction technology with the use of functionalized materials to define advanced building solutions to overcome its inherent reduced thermal inertia.

(**a**) (**b**)

Figure 2. Tiny houses case study: (**a**) 3D design view of the tiny houses; (**b**) tiny houses under construction.

As observed in Figure 2, the largest glazed surfaces are southwest-oriented to potentiate the solar heat gains. However, for the sake of comparison and attaining reliable results, no shading solutions and/or systems were used in this phase to prevent overheating in the warm season, thereby expecting a higher risk of overheating during the summer season.

For this study, one of the external envelopes (walls and roof) of the tiny houses was constructed with the standard solutions to act as the reference cell, while the other tiny house was executed comprising the thermally enhanced core solution in order to be compared to the reference cell in terms of indoor thermal behavior.

3.2. Construction Solutions of the Reference Tiny House

The building's envelope walls, floor and roof are composed of LSF structural elements, with the thermal insulation layer installed on the exterior surface. In Table 2 are listed the characteristics of the insulation thickness and the thermal transmission coefficient (*U*-values) of the adopted construction solutions for the ground floor level, facade walls, and roofing system, namely, the insulation thickness and *U*-value of the envelope construction solutions.

Table 2. Insulation thickness and *U*-value of the envelope construction solutions.

Opaque Construction Element	Mineral Wool * Insulation Thickness (mm)	U-Value (W m^{-2} °C^{-1})
Ground floor slab	60	0.54
Façade walls	60	0.47
Flat roof	40	0.63

* Thermal conductivity of 0.037 W m^{-1} °C^{-1}.

Focusing on the external envelope walls, Figure 3 presents the standard construction solution, applied in the reference tiny house. The ground floor and the roof assembly solutions are equivalent in terms of material layers (although with different thicknesses). The wall construction solution test specimen presented in Figure 3 have dimensions of $800 \times 650 \times 190$ mm^3.

With respect to the glazed envelope, the windows are composed of aluminum frames (U_{Frame} = 2.40 W m^{-2} °C^{-1}) with double glazing (U_{Glass} = 1.00 W m^{-2} °C^{-1}) and a solar heat gain coefficient of 0.21. This solution consists of a 6 mm thick exterior glazing pane, a 16 mm wide argon gas filled space, and a second laminated glazing pane of 8.76 mm.

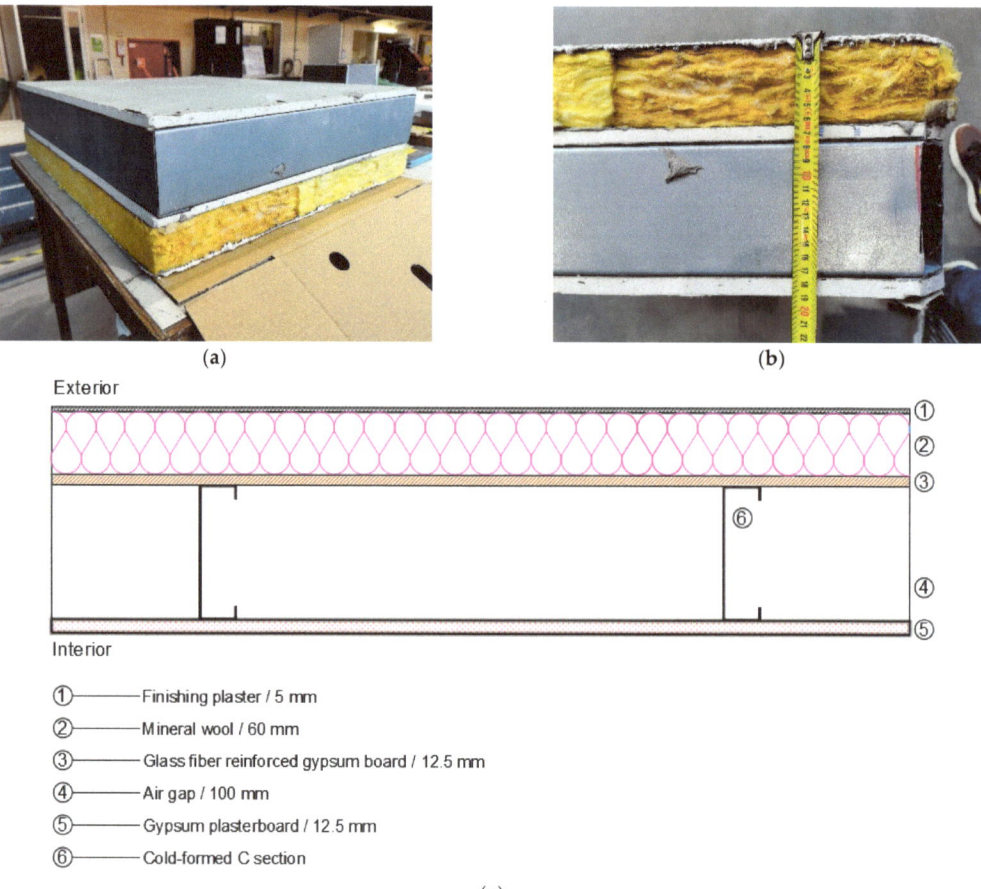

(a)   (b)

Exterior

Interior

①————Finishing plaster / 5 mm
②————Mineral wool / 60 mm
③————Glass fiber reinforced gypsum board / 12.5 mm
④————Air gap / 100 mm
⑤————Gypsum plasterboard / 12.5 mm
⑥————Cold-formed C section

(c)

Figure 3. Construction solution of the envelope walls: (**a**) 3D view of wall component; (**b**) cross section view of the wall component; (**c**) layered composition of the reference solution.

3.3. Construction Solutions with Active Core-PCM Macrocapsule

Based on the reference envelope wall, an enhanced construction solution is presented in this section. This solution as well as the PCM macrocapsule core position within it, are defined based on experience from studies developed by the authors [4]. In these, an optimization process was performed, incorporating different PCM solutions (the PCM operating temperature range was defined based on dynamic simulation analysis (See Section 3.4)) as well as their position in the exterior envelope construction solution, targeting two objective functions: the reduction in the overheating rate and heating demand. In [4], it was concluded that the PCM charging and discharging process (phase change) is more effective when the PCM is positioned closest to the innermost layer of the construction solution. In this sense, as depicted in Figure 4, the same location was selected for the position of the PCM core, immediately behind the finishing layer of the gypsum plasterboard.

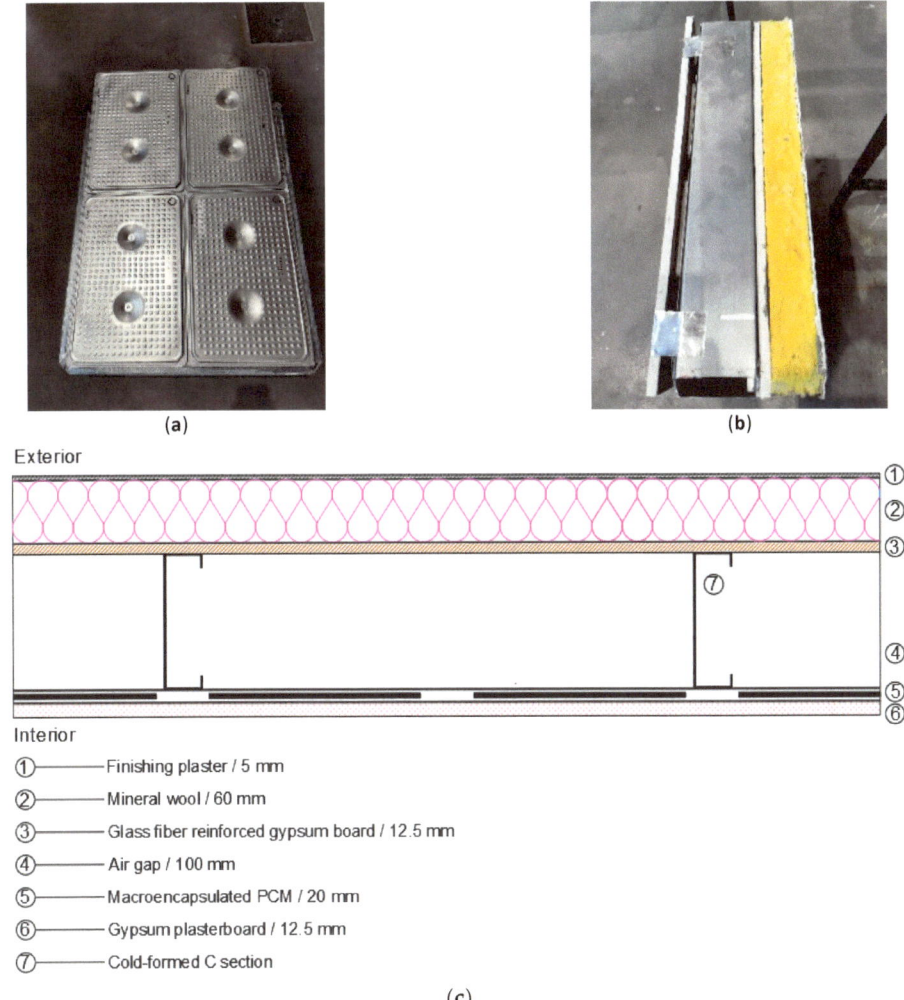

Exterior

Interior

① ——————— Finishing plaster / 5 mm
② ——————— Mineral wool / 60 mm
③ ——————— Glass fiber reinforced gypsum board / 12.5 mm
④ ——————— Air gap / 100 mm
⑤ ——————— Macroencapsulated PCM / 20 mm
⑥ ——————— Gypsum plasterboard / 12.5 mm
⑦ ——————— Cold-formed C section

(c)

Figure 4. Construction solution of the envelope walls for the thermally enhanced tiny house (test cell): (**a**) macroencapsulated PCM with aluminum case; (**b**) cross section of the enhanced solution; (**c**) layered composition of the enhanced solution.

3.4. Whole Building Dynamic Simulation

This section presents the whole building dynamic simulation carried out to perform a parametric study to define the most adequate and effective trade-off between the PCM selection and the operating temperature range, to fully exploit the potential of the PCM charging and discharging process on a daily cycle. The use of enhanced solutions containing PCM requires a careful design of the construction solutions, starting from the selection of the PCMs' operating temperature range; otherwise, the full potential of the material latent heat may be underexplored, including the external boundary conditions and internal use profile (internal gains). Thus, to fulfil this purpose, the whole building dynamic simulation software EnergyPlus[TM] was used to numerically analyze the dynamic thermal behavior of the tiny house, comprising the enhanced solution with PCMs applied in the external envelope walls. Due to the use of PCMs in the present work, the conduction transfer function (CTF) model for the algorithm of surface heat balance calculation methodology was used. Regarding the thermal zones, the model has two thermal zones dividing the ground and the elevated floor areas (Figure 5).

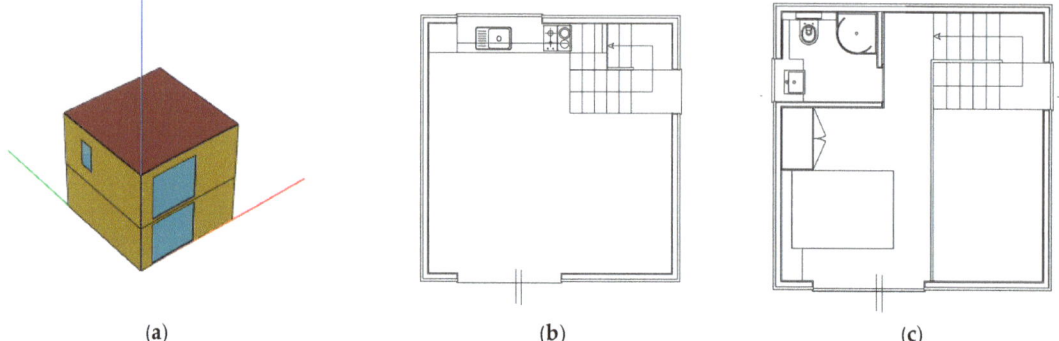

(a)   (b)   (c)

Figure 5. Numerical model design in EnergyPlus^{TM}: (**a**) 3D model; (**b**,**c**) tiny house architectural blueprints (no scale).

Regarding the weather conditions, the case study is located in the Aveiro region, in the north central coastal region of Portugal, approximately 10 km from the Atlantic Ocean. Considering the Köppen-Geiger climate World Map classification for a simplified weather characterization, Aveiro is classified as a "Csb" subtype climate region with rainy winters, dry summers and an average air temperature in the warmest month of 22 °C.

4. Results and Discussion

4.1. PCM Selection Using Dynamic Simulation

As previously mentioned, the PCM operating temperature range was selected through numerical simulation of the building thermal behavior in free-running conditions. The expected thermal regulation effect of the PCM is to buffer the temperature fluctuation in the cooling season during the day to prevent overheating risk (indoor temperature above 25 °C). During the heating season, the effect of the PCM is expected to store heat during the day and release the absorbed thermal energy during the night period to avoid an excessive temperature drop of the indoor air temperature, thus balancing diurnal and nocturnal indoor temperatures in a passive manner.

Since overheating can be defined as the number of hours for which the indoor temperature is above 25 °C on an annual analysis, according to Figure 6, it is possible to conclude that all analyzed possible PCM solutions are subjected to high overheating risk, highlighting longer periods for the reference scenario and for the scenario containing PCM with a peak melting temperature closest to the upper temperature limit for indoor thermal comfort, establishing overheating (indoor temperature above 25 °C). Furthermore, it is possible to conclude that the use of PCMs with high peak melting temperature can increase the risk of overheating, hindering indoor spaces to manage to decrease the indoor air temperature during the night period. Thus, the best result was attained for the construction solution with PCM SP21E, revealing a total of 4% of the year in thermal discomfort by overheating.

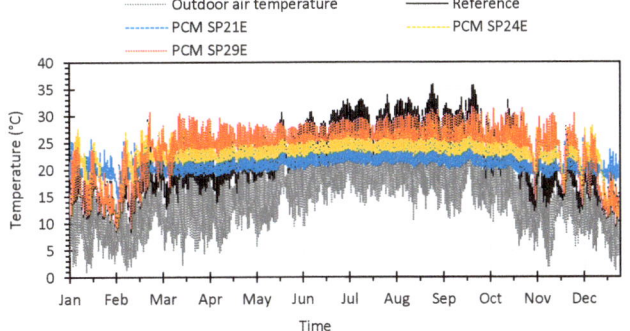

Overheating → Indoor temperature > 25 °C

Reference – 3147 hours

PCM SP21E – 357 hours

PCM SP24E – 2271 hours

PCM SP29E – 5398 hours

Figure 6. Annual indoor air temperature results: reference model vs. model with thermally enhanced solutions comprising different PCM operating temperature ranges.

4.2. PCM Thermal Characterization: Differential Scanning Calorimetry and T-History

The relationship of enthalpy as a function of temperature is one of the most important thermal properties of PCMs, as it reveals the material thermal behavior in terms of phase change and latent heat capacity. Differential scanning calorimetry (DSC) analysis is a laboratory test in which the PCM samples are submitted to controlled temperatures for heating and cooling cycles at specific heating and cooling rates, and the corresponding heat fluxes are recorded, thus providing the relevant information about the temperatures and the associated specific enthalpies, according to the PCM's crystallization and melting processes. For obtaining the phase change temperature range as well as the enthalpy (or specific heat capacity) as a function of temperature, DSC tests were performed on the pure sample of Rubitherm PCM SP21E. Before testing, due to the hygroscopic properties of this PCM solution, the samples were frozen at 0 °C, according to the manufacturer recommendation. Then, the test was executed for heating and cooling cycles within a temperature range comprehended between 10 and 50 °C at the heating and cooling rates of 1 °C min^{-1}, and the weight of the PCM samples was approximately 32.15 mg. The experimental results obtained are presented in Figure 7 for the heating and cooling cycles, respectively.

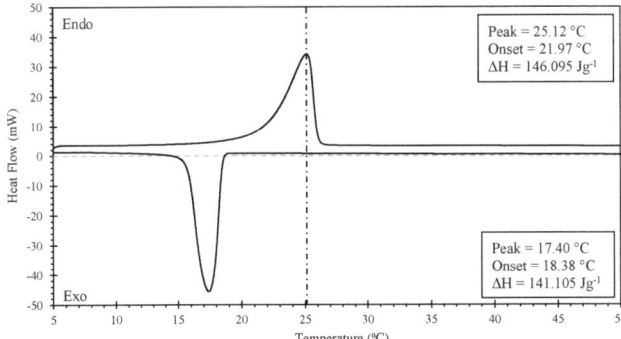

Figure 7. DSC curves for the pure samples of the Rubitherm PCM SP21E.

Regarding Figure 7, a difference between the peak melting and peak crystallization temperatures was observed, thus revealing the existence of a supercooling phenomenon (around 7.72 °C of supercooling). Regarding the manufacturer technical data, the expected peak melting temperature should occur at 21 °C; however, during the melting phase of the PCM, a peak melting temperature of 25.12 °C was attained. During the crystallization phase, the peak crystallization was attained for a temperature value of 17.40 °C.

Given the attained differences in terms of expected (technical datasheet) and experimentally obtained (DSC) peak melting temperatures, a new test was executed using the T-history approach, as presented in Figure 8.

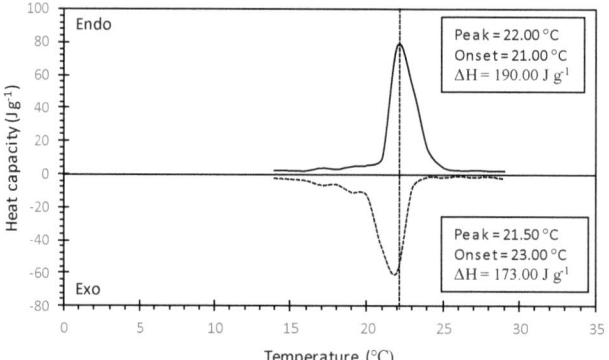

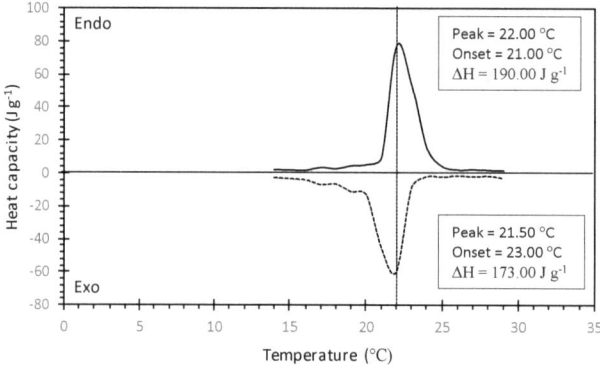

Figure 8. T-history analysis to measure enthalpy for the pure PCM SP21E.

In this test methodology, pure PCM samples with approximately 15 gr of weight were heated up to 60 °C in a water bath until completely melted and then cooled down to 10 °C to find the supercooling degree.

Comparing the DSC curves with the T-history test, changes in thermal behavior were registered regarding the peak melting temperatures, onset temperature values and enthalpy, despite the fact that the PCM tested was exactly the same product, collected from the same batch.

The differences observed for the results may be related to the total amount of the sample tested (and how it was collected) for the two approaches. Despite DSC analysis being a standard tool for the measurement of latent heat of PCMs, this specific method requires a very reduced material sample. This characteristic may not be problematic with homogeneous materials. Nevertheless, salt hydrate PCMs present local heterogeneities, which may induce sampling errors to the DSC tests, thus not allowing to be obtained the representative properties of the compound [29–31]. The T-history method proved to be more suitable for salt hydrate based PCMs.

4.3. Hot Box Heat Flux Meter

To evaluate the impact of incorporating the PCMs into the construction solution of the external envelope walls in terms of equivalent thermal conductivity, the hot box heat flux meter approach was used. The hot box apparatus consists of two chambers with controlled conditions of temperature and relative humidity, separated by a mounting ring where the test specimen is installed. This test was developed to evaluate the equivalent thermal conductivity of the representative wall specimens, from the base wall solution (reference wall) to the developed solution containing the PCM macrocapsules (enhanced solution). As previously referred, the enhanced wall solution comprises an inner layer (located behind the gypsum plaster wallboard) containing the aluminum macrocapsules of PCM. Both specimens were instrumented with heat flux meters on both sides (HTflux), with PT100 sensors inside the chambers (Figure 9).

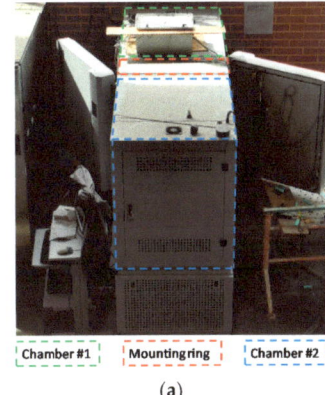

(a)

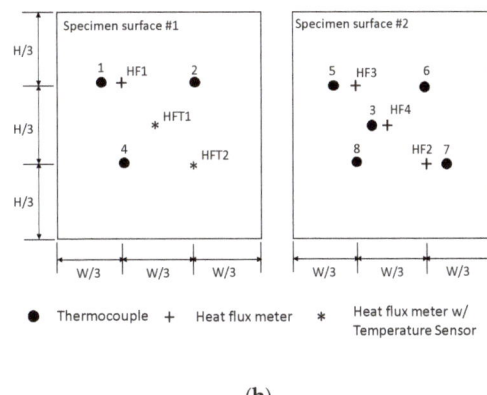

(b)

Figure 9. Hot box heat flux meter approach: (**a**) hot box apparatus (**b**) schematic layout of heat flux meter and temperature sensors positioning on the specimens' surfaces.

The first test was conducted with the goal of characterizing the equivalent thermal conductivity of the reference wall, followed by the enhanced wall containing PCM macro-capsules. Thus, in Figure 9, it is presented the experimental results of the heat fluxes as a function of the temperature increase in steps of steady state conditions. For both wall specimens, 17 steady state steps were defined.

Analyzing the results from Figure 10, a value of 0.13 W m^{-1} °C^{-1} was obtained for the thermal conductivity (at a temperature step of 22 °C) as a function of the mean specimen temperature for the reference wall, and a value of 0.12 W m^{-1} °C^{-1} for the enhanced wall was also obtained for the equal temperature step.

Due to the observed variance in the heat flow as a function of the temperature evolu-tion, specially highlighted in the case of the construction solution containing PCM, a full characterization regarding the thermal conductivity as a function of the mean specimen temperature for both wall solutions is presented in Figure 11.

The obtained results for thermal conductivity exhibited an increasing trend with an excellent correlation between the thermal conductivity values and the mean specimen temperatures, as corroborated by the square correlation coefficient (R^2) attained of 0.98, for the reference wall solution. Thus, the performed test on the reference solution to attain the thermal conductivity evolution along the temperature increase resulted in a thermal conductivity comprehended between 0.08 and 0.33 W m^{-1} °C^{-1} for a temperature range between 14.87 and 42.55 °C.

For the enhanced wall solution with PCM macrocapsules, it was observed that during the phase change transition zone (assigned in the plot with a gray box), thermal conductivity values tend to maintain stability, followed by a slight decrease, thus revealing significant discrepancies in this parameter. This behavior occurs due to the simultaneous influence of temperature rise and phase change fraction of the PCM, in addition to the coexistence of two physical states with different thermophysical properties, evidencing the PCM's inherently non-linear nature [32]. The evaluated thermal conductivity values are comprehended between 0.08 and 0.11 W m^{-1} °C^{-1} for temperature intervals from 15.04 to 19.00 °C below the phase change transition range, and thermal conductivity values above the phase change transition range are comprehended between 0.12 and 0.28 W m^{-1} °C^{-1} for mean specimen temperatures of 26.79 to 42.58 °C, respectively. The obtained results for both stages (before and after the phase change range) reveals an excellent R^2, demonstrating an excellent fit to the experimental data.

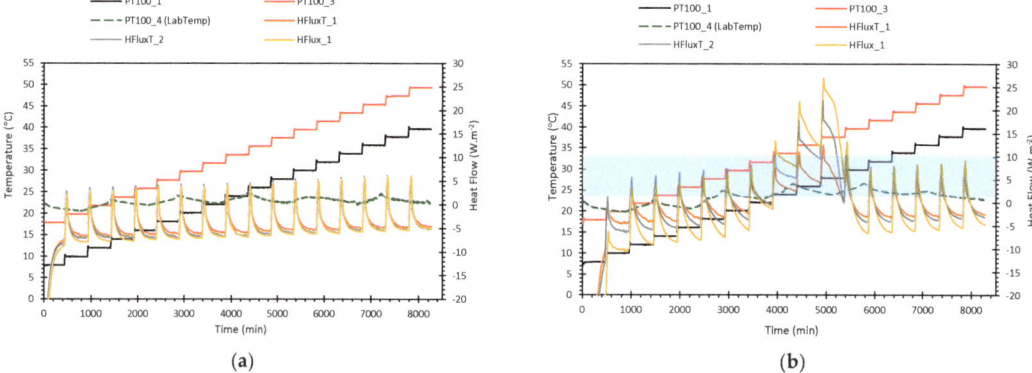

Figure 10. Hot box results: heat flux evolution when wall specimens are subjected to different temperature steps. (**a**) Reference construction solution; (**b**) enhanced construction solution with PCM macrocapsules.

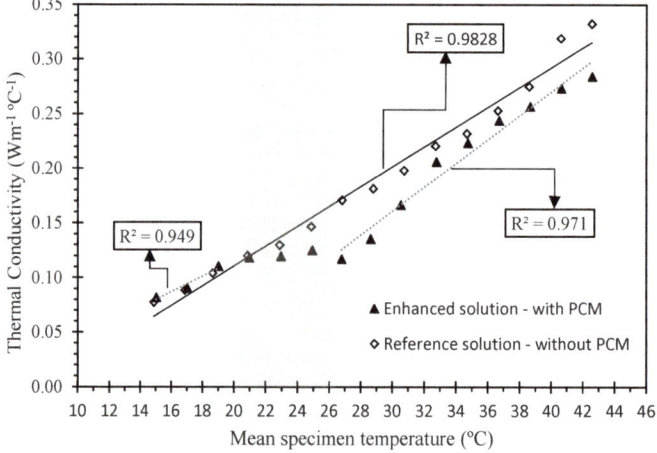

Figure 11. Equivalent thermal conductivity as function of the mean specimen temperature for both construction solutions.

Additionally, with the objective of comparing the thermal behavior of both wall solutions (the reference and the enhanced solution) when subjected to a temperature differential, simulating the indoor and outdoor temperature evolution of a daily cycle, the hot box apparatus was again used. Thus, the indoor temperature behavior was characterized in free-running conditions (using one chamber in passive conditions) as a consequence of a controlled temperature (using the other chamber in active metering mode).

Comparing the air temperature values inside the passive chamber (simulating indoor conditions) of both solutions, in Figure 12, a very expressive reduction in the temperature fluctuation was observed for the enhanced wall with PCM macrocapsules. A difference of 4 °C between curves was obtained for the period of the day in which we attained the maximum daily temperature inside the passive chamber. However, the fluctuation reduction presented in the temperature evolution curve of the construction solution containing PCM (red curve), observed after completing a cycle of 24 h, is an indicator that the latent heat of the PCM will not be fully discharged considering a daily cycle. This behavior is observed by the reduction in the temperature difference between curves during the third cycle of the test (hours: 60 to 75).

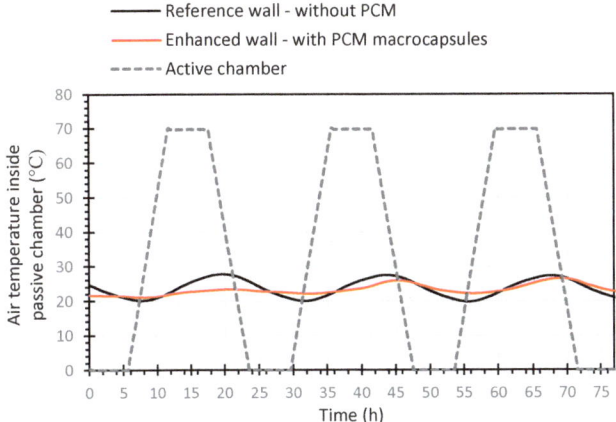

Figure 12. Hot box results: indoor air temperature profiles.

Analyzing the differences obtained between temperature curves, experimentally assessed, it is concluded that the use of PCM as a thermal regulator in the tiny houses certainly will contribute to the indoor thermal comfort in both seasons along the year with promising results.

5. Conclusions

The present study provides a meaningful contribution for passive thermal regulation strategies for indoor spaces, using a lightweight construction solution containing macroencapsulated salt hydrate based PCM. DSC and t-history analysis were used to characterize the thermal behavior of the PCM, and the hot box tests were used for thermal conductivity characterization of the construction solutions.

DSC analysis allowed the observation of several differences in the PCM thermophysical properties when compared with the manufacturer's datasheet. The T-history analysis revealed an increased accuracy of the latent heat behavior when compared with the manufacturer's datasheet rather than DSC. The T-history method proved to be more suitable for non-pure substances as well as for salt hydrate based PCMs. Thermophysical characterization revealed by the experimentally obtained heat storage capacity of 190 J g^{-1} allows to classify the use of salt hydrate PCMs as a possible alternative solution to the usual paraffinic-based PCMs.

Using the hot box approach, a good correlation between the equivalent thermal conductivity values and mean specimen temperatures was attained for the reference construction solution (without PCM) and for the enhanced construction solution containing PCM, when the mean specimen temperature is located outside the phase change transition zone (PCM completely solid and completely liquid). Thermal conductivity values tend to maintain stability during the phase change temperatures range, followed by a considerable decrease, thus revealing a non-linear behavior. Comparing the obtained values for thermal conductivity of both solutions, a reduction of 12.6% (average value) was observed in this thermal property, due to the addition of the PCM macrocapsules in the reference constructive solution.

Concerning the hot box approach test, with only one active chamber and the other chamber in free-running conditions, to evaluate the thermal regulation effect of the PCM, good results in terms of mitigating overheating rate reduction were attained. This proves that the use of salt hydrate based (macroencapsulated) PCMs incorporated into the envelope walls in such a construction system is suitable to compensate for the lack of thermal inertia of lightweight construction typologies, such as LSF buildings. Nevertheless, the hot box test revealed the importance of adequately select the operating temperature range of the PCMs, as a function of the desired indoor temperature range. On the other hand, the weight of the PCM incorporated into the construction solution plays a significant role in the overall efficiency since the excessive weight of PCM may not be fully charged/discharged for a daily cycle, as observed with the hot box test.

This study highlights the high potential for the development of innovative construction solutions incorporating salt hydrate based PCM macrocapsules, suitable to be incorporated into lightweight constructions toward new and existing buildings.

Author Contributions: All the authors have contributed to multiple tasks throughout this research. Conceptualization, A.F., A.S. and R.V.; methodology, A.F., A.S., J.L., F.R. and R.V.; validation, A.F. and F.R.; formal analysis, A.F., A.S., J.L., F.R. and R.V.; investigation, A.F., A.S., F.R. and R.V.; resources, A.F., J.L.; data curation, A.F., F.R. and R.V.; writing—original draft preparation, A.F. and F.R.; writing—review and editing, A.F., A.S., J.L., F.R. and R.V.; visualization, A.S. and R.V.; supervision, A.S. and R.V.; project administration, A.S.; funding acquisition, A.S. All authors have read and agreed to the published version of the manuscript.

Funding: This research was funded by the project THERMACORE—Performance of a wall or slab with a thermally active core in buildings in Portugal, POCI-01-0145-FEDER-030364, with the financial support of FCT—Fundação para a Ciência e Tecnologia/MCTES and was also supported by the Foundation for Science and Technology (FCT)-Aveiro Research Centre for Risks and Sustainability in Construction (RISCO), Universidade de Aveiro, Portugal [FCT/UIDB/ECI/04450/2020].

Institutional Review Board Statement: Not applicable.

Informed Consent Statement: Not applicable (study not involving humans).

Data Availability Statement: Not applicable.

Conflicts of Interest: The authors declare no conflict of interest.

References

1. Soares, N.; Bastos, J.; Pereira, L.D.; Soares, A.; Amaral, A.R.; Asadi, E.; Rodrigues, E.; Lamas, F.B.; Monteiro, H.; Lopes, M.A.R.; et al. A review on current advances in the energy and environmental performance of buildings towards a more sustainable built environment. *Renew. Sustain. Energy Rev.* **2017**, *77*, 845–860. [CrossRef]
2. EPBD Directive 2018/844/EU. Directive 2018/844/EU of the European Parliament and of the Council of 30 May 2018. *Off. J. Eur. Communities Union* **2018**, *19*, 75–91.
3. De Almeida, A.; Fonseca, P.; Schlomann, B.; Feilberg, N. Characterization of the household electricity consumption in the EU, potential energy savings and specific policy recommendations. *Energy Build.* **2011**, *43*, 1884–1894. [CrossRef]
4. Figueiredo, A.; Vicente, R.; Oliveira, R.; Rodrigues, F.; Samagaio, A. Multiscale modelling approach targeting optimisation of pcm into constructive solutions for overheating mitigation in buildings. *Appl. Sci.* **2020**, *10*, 8009. [CrossRef]
5. Kishore, R.A.; Bianchi, M.V.A.; Booten, C.; Vidal, J.; Jackson, R. Parametric and sensitivity analysis of a PCM-integrated wall for optimal thermal load modulation in lightweight buildings. *Appl. Therm. Eng.* **2021**, *187*, 116568. [CrossRef]
6. Adilkhanova, I.; Memon, S.A.; Kim, J.; Sheriyev, A. A novel approach to investigate the thermal comfort of the lightweight relocatable building integrated with PCM in different climates of Kazakhstan during summertime. *Energy* **2021**, *217*, 119390. [CrossRef]
7. Salgueiro, T.; Samagaio, A.; Gonçalves, M.; Figueiredo, A.; Labrincha, J.; Silva, L. Incorporation of phase change materials in an expanded clay containing mortar for indoor thermal regulation of buildings. *J. Energy Storage* **2021**, *36*, 102385. [CrossRef]
8. Rebelo, F.; Figueiredo, A.; Vicente, R.; Ferreira, V.M. Study of a thermally enhanced mortar incorporating phase change materials for overheating reduction in buildings. *J. Energy Storage* **2022**, *46*, 103876. [CrossRef]

9. Gencel, O.; Hekimoğlu, G.; Sarı, A.; Sutcu, M.; Er, Y.; Ustaoglu, A. A novel energy-effective and carbon-emission reducing mortars with bottom ash and phase change material: Physico-mechanical and thermal energy storage characteristics. *J. Energy Storage* **2021**, *44*, 103325. [CrossRef]

10. Saxena, R.; Ali, S.F.; Rakshit, D. PCM incorporated bricks: A passive alternative for thermal regulation and energy conservation in buildings for Indian conditions. In *Eco-Efficient Materials for Reducing Cooling Needs in Buildings and Construction*; Elsevier: Amsterdam, The Netherlands, 2021; pp. 303–328.

11. Al-Yasiri, Q.; Szabó, M. Thermal performance of concrete bricks based phase change material encapsulated by various aluminium containers: An experimental study under Iraqi hot climate conditions. *J. Energy Storage* **2021**, *40*, 102710. [CrossRef]

12. Bondareva, N.S.; Sheremet, M.A. Influence of phase change material melting point and its location on heat and mass transfer in a brick. *J. Energy Storage* **2021**, *42*, 103122. [CrossRef]

13. Millers, R.; Korjakins, A.; Lesinskis, A. Thermally activated concrete slabs with integrated PCM materials. *E3S Web Conf.* **2019**, *111*, 01080. [CrossRef]

14. Figueiredo, A.; Lapa, J.; Vicente, R.; Cardoso, C. Mechanical and thermal characterization of concrete with incorporation of microencapsulated PCM for applications in thermally activated slabs. *Constr. Build. Mater.* **2016**, *112*, 639–647. [CrossRef]

15. Maleki, B.; Khadang, A.; Maddah, H.; Alizadeh, M.; Kazemian, A.; Ali, H.M. Development and thermal performance of nanoencapsulated PCM/ plaster wallboard for thermal energy storage in buildings. *J. Build. Eng.* **2020**, *32*, 101727. [CrossRef]

16. Song, Y.; Li, C.; Yu, H.; Tang, Y.; Xia, Z. Optimization of the phase-change wallboard test method: Experimental and numerical investigation. *J. Energy Storage* **2020**, *30*, 101559. [CrossRef]

17. Li, C.; Yu, H.; Song, Y. Experimental investigation of thermal performance of microencapsulated PCM-contained wallboard by two measurement modes. *Energy Build.* **2019**, *184*, 34–43. [CrossRef]

18. Millers, R.; Korjakins, A.; Lešinskis, A.; Borodinecs, A. Cooling panel with integrated PCM layer: A verified simulation study. *Energies* **2020**, *13*, 5715. [CrossRef]

19. Devaux, P.; Farid, M.M. Benefits of PCM underfloor heating with PCM wallboards for space heating in winter. *Appl. Energy* **2017**, *191*, 593–602. [CrossRef]

20. Yun, B.Y.; Yang, S.; Cho, H.M.; Chang, S.J.; Kim, S. Design and analysis of phase change material based floor heating system for thermal energy storage. *Environ. Res.* **2019**, *173*, 480–488. [CrossRef]

21. Elarga, H.; Fantucci, S.; Serra, V.; Zecchin, R.; Benini, E. Experimental and numerical analyses on thermal performance of different typologies of PCMs integrated in the roof space. *Energy Build.* **2017**, *150*, 546–557. [CrossRef]

22. Sun, W.; Zhang, Y.; Ling, Z.; Fang, X.; Zhang, Z. Experimental investigation on the thermal performance of double-layer PCM radiant floor system containing two types of inorganic composite PCMs. *Energy Build.* **2020**, *211*, 109806. [CrossRef]

23. Kuznik, F.; David, D.; Johannes, K.; Roux, J.-J. A review on phase change materials integrated in building walls. *Renew. Sustain. Energy Rev.* **2011**, *15*, 379–391. [CrossRef]

24. Sun, W.; Zhang, Z.; Wu, Z.; Xu, Y. Numerical modeling and optimization of annual thermal characteristics of an office room with PCM active–passive coupling system. *Energy Build.* **2022**, *254*, 111629. [CrossRef]

25. Xu, X.; Zhang, Y.; Lin, K.; Di, H.; Yang, R. Modeling and simulation on the thermal performance of shape-stabilized phase change material floor used in passive solar buildings. *Energy Build.* **2005**, *37*, 1084–1091. [CrossRef]

26. Kośny, J.; Fallahi, A.; Shukla, N.; Kossecka, E.; Ahbari, R. Thermal load mitigation and passive cooling in residential attics containing PCM-enhanced insulations. *Sol. Energy* **2014**, *108*, 164–177. [CrossRef]

27. Soares, N.; Gaspar, A.R.; Santos, P.; Costa, J.J. Multi-dimensional optimization of the incorporation of PCM-drywalls in lightweight steel-framed residential buildings in different climates. *Energy Build.* **2014**, *70*, 411–421. [CrossRef]

28. Santos, P.; Simões da Silva, L.; Ungureanu, V. *Energy Efficiemcy of Light-Weight Steel-Framed Buildings*; European Convention for Constructional Steelwork (ECCS): Mem Martins, Portugal, 2012.

29. Peck, J.H.; Kim, J.J.; Kang, C.; Hong, H. A study of accurate latent heat measurement for a PCM with a low melting temperature using T-history method. *Int. J. Refrig.* **2006**, *29*, 1225–1232. [CrossRef]

30. Solé, A.; Miró, L.; Barreneche, C.; Martorell, I.; Cabeza, L.F. Review of the T-history method to determine thermophysical properties of phase change materials (PCM). *Renew. Sustain. Energy Rev.* **2013**, *26*, 425–436. [CrossRef]

31. Mazo, J.; Delgado, M.; Lázaro, A.; Dolado, P.; Peñalosa, C.; Marín, J.M.M.; Zalba, B.; D'Avignon, K.; Kummert, M.; Lázaro, A.; et al. Verification of a T-history installation to measure enthalpy versus temperature curves of phase change materials. *Meas. Sci. Technol.* **2016**, *17*, 2168–2174.

32. Amaral, C.; Vicente, R.; Eisenblätter, J.; Marques, P.A.A.P. Thermal characterization of polyurethane foams with phase change material. *Ciência Tecnol. Mater.* **2017**, *29*, 1–7. [CrossRef]

Article

Current Practice and Potential Associated with Timber-Based Solutions for Buildings Retrofitting

Cláudio Meireis [1], Filipa S. Serino [1], Carlos Maia [1], André C. Fontes [1] and Jorge M. Branco [2,*]

[1]   Lab2PT, School of Architecture, Art and Design, University of Minho, 4800-58 Guimarães, Portugal; a81783@alunos.uminho.pt (C.M.); a80896@alunos.uminho.pt (F.S.S.); cmaia@eaad.uminho.pt (C.M.); afontes@eaad.uminho.pt (A.C.F.)
[2]   ISISE, Department of Civil Engineering, University of Minho, 4800-058 Guimarães, Portugal
*   Correspondence: jbranco@civil.uminho.pt

Abstract: Current buildings are responsible for the highest energy consumption, exceeding polluting sectors such as industry and transports. In Portugal, a large part of the building stock was built in the 1970s and 1980s, but buildings dated from the 1960s and 1970s are the ones with the most anomalies and worst quality of construction and, therefore, worst energy performance. The renovation of those buildings can represent an excellent opportunity to correct and improve their energy deficiency and, with that, to promote a more sustainable building stock. The ETICS system is the most used for the renovation of buildings in Portugal due to its lower cost, quick application and thermal efficiency, but it doesn't solve other problems that may exist, such as structural safety and interior organization of the existing building. The application of prefabricated systems in the envelope has proved to be successful in improving energy efficiency, allowing new volumes and extra areas while contributing to the structural resilience of existing buildings. This paper aims to describe the current situation of the buildings renovation in Portugal and to discuss the potential of innovative envelope retrofitting solutions, using natural materials like timber, and is more concerned with the problems of existing buildings and the need for comfort and space for the occupants.

Keywords: building stock; retrofitting; energy efficiency; architectural transformation; structural resilience; timber

1. Introduction

According to "Instituto Nacional de Estatística" [1], in 2019, the Portuguese building stock was composed of almost 3.6 million buildings and 5.9 million dwellings. About 63.1% of the building stock was built in the 1970s and 1980s, but buildings dated from the 1960s and 1970s are the ones showing more pathologies with less comfort and lower energy performance. In developed countries, the energy consumption in residential and commercial buildings is between 20% and 40% of the total energy consumption, exceeding the sectors of industry and transport [2]. In the case of Portugal, both high energy consumption and significant energy losses through the envelope are consequences of the lack of regulation and thermal requirements when buildings were built. Studies show that, to reduce buildings' energy consumption, it is necessary to act mainly in its envelope, where the energy losses are higher. For example, the addition of thermal insulation can lead to reductions in heating needs by up to 70% [3,4]. In practice, ETICS (External Thermal Insulation Composite System) is the most common retrofitting system used in Portugal; however, although it has a high energy efficiency and quick and simple application, it doesn't solve other problems that may exist. The cost-benefit assessments of retrofit actions in this sector show excessive payback times, creating a strong and generalized lack of confidence by investors and final users. Regarding the energy retrofit, [5] showed that it is possible to overcome the barriers of high costs and long technological solutions using prefabricated

Infrastructures 2022, 7, 25. https://doi.org/10.3390/infrastructures7020025   https://www.mdpi.com/journal/infrastructures

systems for low energy renovation. Most of these solutions are generally founded on the load bearing capacity of the existing buildings, a condition that is rarely applicable in the highly seismic areas of Mediterranean countries. Thus, in many EU regions, it became imperative to couple energy retrofit with structural safety improvement, to make visible that higher initial investments of retrofit are more interesting in the long term than lower investments with higher paybacks. On the other hand, the confinement derived from the present pandemic caused by the SARS-CoV-2 virus has highlighted the need to incorporate new functions and uses into housing. The post-pandemic housing model should incorporate flexible and new programmatic areas: for teleworking, differentiated spaces for video conferencing, leisure separated from the living areas, outdoor areas, garden, etc. In this regard, the strategies for the renovation of existing buildings should improve three main areas: energy efficiency, structural stability and architectural renovation.

2. Current Practice for Buildings Renovation in Portugal

In Portugal, the current strategy to reduce energy consumption consists of the improvement or replacement of existing window frames (high-performing windows) and in the application of thermal insulation on walls and roofs. The most common thermal insulation solution is the ETICS system (External Thermal Insulation Composite System) composed of a thermal insulation board, generally EPS (Expanded Polystyrene insulation), with a thin plaster reinforced with fiberglass or synthetic mesh and an appropriate coating which can be painted or coated to give a traditional appearance [6]. This system became popular due to its high thermal efficiency, the correction of thermal bridges that can be achieved and consequent reduction of the risk of condensation, and the preservation of thermal inertia since it is placed on the external façade, while representing a low investment cost. Moreover, the quick and simple application in façades with few architectural features, and the convenience of the occupants during the execution (the inner area remains intact), are the features that contributed to the dissemination of this technique. However, the ETICS system does not allow the aesthetical preservation of buildings with architectural or heritage value, the edge finishing execution is complex due to architectural constraints, it has vulnerability to mechanical stresses (impacts) and no fire resistance due to the combustibility of the EPS insulation board, the execution exposed to weather conditions may compromise the performance of the thermal retrofitting solution, and it is not appropriate for façades with ascending humidity or façades composed of very porous materials [7]. Moreover, the appearance of anomalies and durability problems with the system's coating is common, such as material rupture anomalies (oriented cracking, non-oriented cracking, deterioration of the covering of reinforcement, detachment of the finishing coat, partial or total loss of adherence and material gap), color/aesthetic anomalies (efflorescence, runoff marks, corrosion stains, graffiti, biological growth and other color changes) and flatness anomalies (flatness deficiency, surface irregularities, joints between plates visibility, swelling of the finishing coat and swelling of the insulation plates) [8].

In addition to the ETICS system, solutions like "thermal insulation injection in the cavity of double-leaf walls", "internal thermal insulation" and "mortar with improved thermal performance" are also used but in more specific cases. The thermal insulation injection in the cavity of double-leaf walls can be made through the injection of insulation products in granules or foam (expanded on-site). This solution is mainly used when the façade is composed by double-leaf walls, and it is intended to preserve the original internal and external appearance of the façades. However, this solution does not protect the façade from outside actions caused by atmospheric agents, does not eliminate thermal bridges, the execution might have some complexity depending on the façade features and the efficiency of its implementation depends on the existing conditions in the cavity. The internal thermal insulation solution can be made through the ITICS system (Internal Thermal Insulation Composite System) or counter-wall of light brick masonry or gypsum plasterboards. This solution can be applied when the façade is composed of a single leaf wall, and it is intended to preserve the appearance of old buildings with architectural or heritage value. However, with this solution, there are some disadvantages, such as the reduction of the inner area, the constraints for the occupants during its execution, the elimination of thermal inertia of the existing wall and the permanence of thermal bridges. The mortar with improved thermal performance solution can be applied in the external or internal cladding of the façade. Although this solution increases the acoustic properties of the façades, and has easier execution and permeability to water vapor, it also has less thermal efficiency when compared with other solutions [7].

3. Innovative and Integrated Solutions

In the last years, some research and case studies, in particular, within European projects, have been addressing the development and the promotion of retrofitting solutions able to integrate more than just the thermal insulation. Attempts have been made to incorporate architectural and structural demands. This section aims to summarize the ones that have presented higher potential.

3.1. Prefabricated Cladding Solutions

The application of prefabricated claddings in the envelope of existing buildings has been addressed in recent European projects, such as the RetroKit and the BRESAER. Within the Retrokit project [9], a multifunctional façade based on prefabricated modules used on the façade and roof has been developed. These modules integrate solutions that deal with the aspects of heating, ventilation, cooling and electricity in a flexible way. The overall life cycle cost is reduced due to easy installation, simple maintenance since the pipes on façades are easily accessible from the outside, and convenient recycling. Since the prefabricated modules are applied on the exterior, it is possible to solve the problem with the thermal bridges, corners and connections. Moreover, this system improves the aesthetics, comfort, energy performance and property value of the existing building.

The European Project BRESAER [10] developed a prefabricated retrofitting system adaptable to different climate zones through a variable choice of highly efficient energy technologies and intelligent controls. This system is composed of a series of structural and technological envelope elements that are placed on the outer side of the façade and roof and can be adapted to the particular needs of each project. Besides the insulation layer and the support structure, this system consists of solar thermal air heating panels that can be placed on façades and roofs, ventilated façade panels with a lightweight concrete exterior, multifunctional insulating panels with lightweight concrete support, dynamic window replacement modules with shading control, and photovoltaic panels that can be placed on envelope elements (Figure 1).

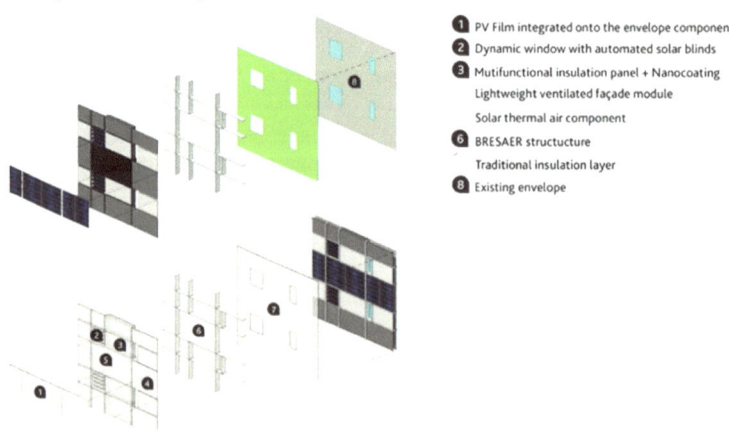

1. PV Film integrated onto the envelope components
2. Dynamic window with automated solar blinds
3. Mutifunctional insulation panel + Nanocoating
   Lightweight ventilated façade module
   Solar thermal air component
6. BRESAER structure
   Traditional insulation layer
8. Existing envelope

Figure 1. Schematic representation of the BRESAER system for façades [10].

The combination of active and passive prefabricated solutions allows the system to reduce the primary energy and greenhouse emissions while improving indoor environment quality. Currently, the passive solutions used are the sun protection devices for windows, Trombe walls and the maximization of natural ventilation. An example of passive solutions is the ventilated façade retrofitting system E2VENT [11] that, besides integrating thermal insulation, also introduces PCM (Phase Change Materials), which, when it changes the physical state, absorbs or releases heat, allowing it to passively control the room temperature and reduce 50% of primary energy needs. Although these systems allow multifunctional interventions and adaptability to different climate zones, they don't take full advantage of the existing buildings, such as spatial organization. In other words, it does not qualify the pre-existing interior spaces, maintaining a static and rigid organization.

3.2. Double Skin and Exoskeleton Solutions

The double-skin façade consists of an external glazing, an intermediate thermal buffer zone and an inner façade. With this solution, it is possible to reduce the energy consumption and enhance the thermal comfort through the renovation of the building's envelope and combination of different typologies and adjustable systems, such as climate conditions, ventilation and depth. Moreover, with the addition of a shading system, inside or outside the double-skin façade, adjustable according to the sunlight angles, the glare problems can be avoided, and the natural lighting can be uniformly distributed inside the existing building. The acoustic insulation is also guaranteed, since the outer skin works as a barrier against the noise, obstructing its propagation. In this regard, the introduction of a double-skin façade solution for the renovation of existing buildings allows the enhancement of thermal comfort, control of daylighting and glare, sound insulation, noise mitigation and structure stability [12].

The exoskeleton system consists of a structure that helps to support other elements. This system is generally used to support technical rooms and mechanical systems; however, its adaptation to the renovation of the envelope can result in the extension of the internal space of the building, creating greater flexibility and adaptability to the needs of people, as well as greater structural safety and energy efficiency. The main difference between double-skin façade and exoskeleton is its support. The exoskeleton solution is supported through its foundation, while the double-skin solution is supported by the existing structure, requiring no foundations. In general, in most of the existing buildings, infill walls are one of the most scattering sources in terms of heat loss. Therefore, ref. [13] proposed a double-skin solution with new infilled RC frames externally added and connected to the existing RC structure to satisfy both thermal and seismic requirements (Figure 2). With this solution, it was possible to contribute to the lateral load bearing capacity in terms of strength and stiffness and to reduce the energy consumption. Reference [14] also proposed an external integrated double-skin façade solution to improve the architectural and urban environment quality, the energy efficiency and the structural performance, regarding the minimum environmental impact principles, the minimum rehabilitation cost requirement and the minimum impairment of the occupants. This solution was conceived as an exoskeleton with a double value: on one hand, the structure provides the existing buildings with the necessary seismic resistance and its dry installation does not require prolonged phases of construction, and on the other hand, the external solution guarantees the minimum impact on the occupants during the building rehabilitation and allows future functional and formal variations. Moreover, the enlargement of the existing building structure allows for the creation of new areas, such as new living spaces, balconies and solar greenhouses.

The improvements in terms of energy performance and structural safety of the intervention have been investigated and have proved the high potential of the expandable architecture in a cost-effective analysis. For example, in an ongoing European Project, Pro-GET-onE, an exoskeleton made of a steel frame (two columns and a beam) for each floor with bracings in the transversal direction connected to the column-beam joints of the existing building, has been proposed. The design of adaptable typologies was also considered through different solutions with different façade and room combinations, such as balconies, extra rooms and sunspaces (Figure 3). However, the disadvantages that this system may have are related to the reduction of daylight due to the depth of the system's structure [15].

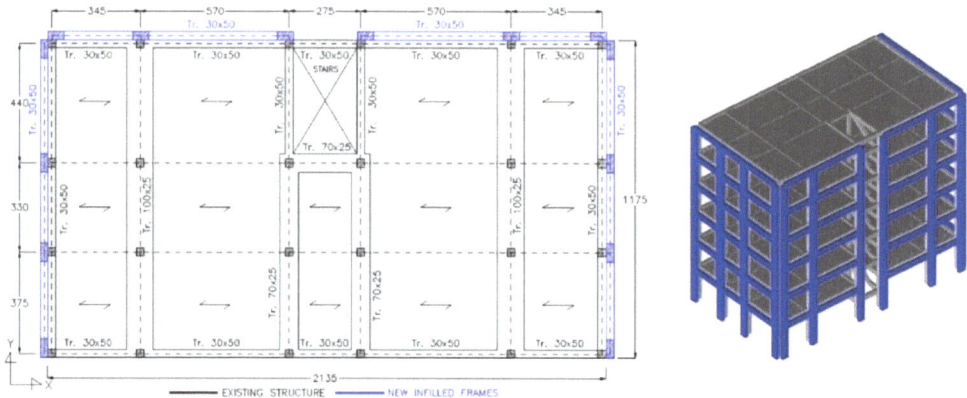

Figure 2. Double-skin solution with new infilled RC frames externally added and connected to the existing RC structure (dimensions in centimeters) [13].

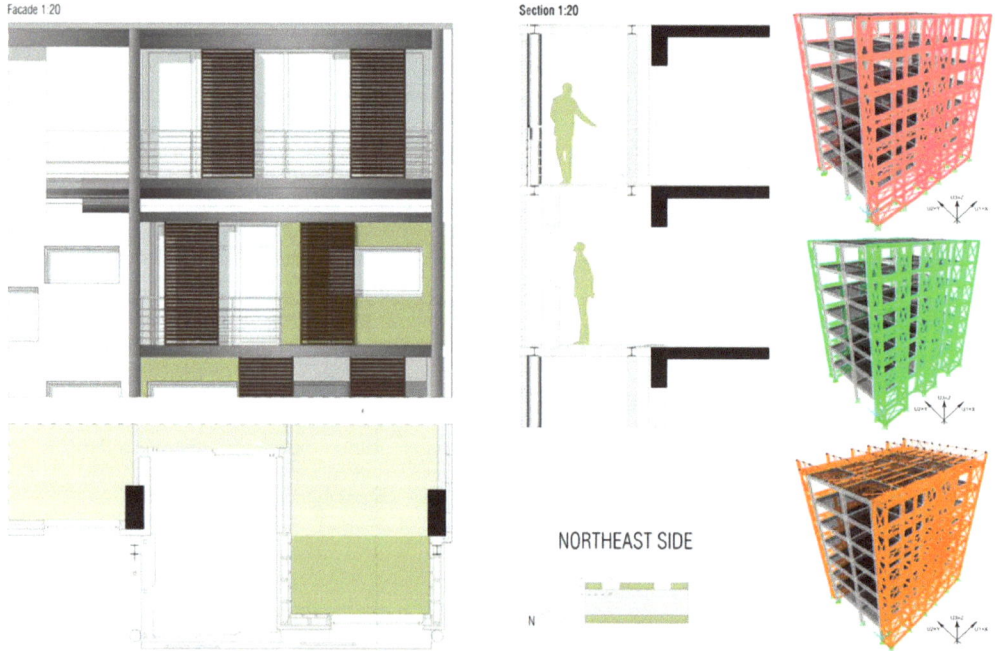

Figure 3. Schematic representation of the Pro-GET-onE system [15].

The use of the exoskeleton allows the system to obtain several architectural solutions, such as the "Five morpho-techno-typological solutions" proposed by [16], which consist of five typologies that can be adapted to the needs of people and the building, and the strategies on interventions on residential heritage proposed by [17], which consist of intervention concepts that can be adopted depending on the architectural ideas and the level of degradation of the building.

An excellent example of the architectural transformation allowed by the exoskeleton solution is the project "Transformation de 530 logements" [18], by Anne Lacaton e Jean Philippe Vassal, that consists of the transformation of three inhabited social buildings. In this project, a metallic exoskeleton was used to extend the interior space and improve the energy efficiency and the quality of the building. With these prefabricated modules, it was possible to add new areas, such as winter gardens and balconies, and redesign the façades of the existing building. The general economy of the project was based on the choice of conserving the existing building without making important interventions on the structure, the stairs and the floors. Furthermore, the project dealt with the global performance of the building envelope, the reconfiguration of vertical circulations and access halls. The existing windows and sills were removed and the concrete walls were opened to introduce the interior thermal curtain and the aluminum frame sliding doors with access to the spaces created. This intervention made it possible to increase the living area, with the addition of the winter garden and balconies, and improve the energy performance of the building by 60%. Although the total cost of the project was lower than the estimated cost of the demolition and reconstruction, it remains relatively high [19]. The volumetric increase of the existing buildings is the main limitation for the exoskeleton-based integrated systems; indeed, it is not always achievable due to lack of available perimetral space and legislative constraints.

3.3. Wood Based Solutions

With the development of new engineered wood products (EWP), such as glulam and the more recent cross-laminated timber (CLT) panels and laminated veneer lumber (LVL), new possibilities for more sustainable interventions and prefabricated solutions have emerged [20]. Those EWP are improved products when compared with solid wood in terms of physical and mechanical performances, while sharing the same sustainable profile, being made of natural and renewable resources with the ability to store CO_2. Moreover, the use of EWP promotes a better knowledge and control on the natural durability, preservation and treatment of the mass timber elements, crucial to develop maintenance plans [21].

There are some projects and systems that explore the energy renovation of existing buildings through the application of timber elements for the structure or cladding. The wood envelope solutions from "Rubner Holzbau" consist of prefabricated wall elements that work as a façade cladding system. In addition to the heat and noise comfort, and fire protection, the prefabrication of wooden elements allows the reduction of construction time as well as cost optimization and quick assembly [22]. The European Projects BERTIM and MORE-CONNECT are examples of systems that explore the renovation of existing buildings through the application of wood prefabricated modules on the façade. The BERTIM system is characterized by the integrated renovation process based on customized mass manufacturing methodologies supported by building information models (BIM). This tool enables the reduction of renovation operation time and makes the renovation process more efficient, through the customization of the mass production, from data gathering, designing, manufacturing and installation [23]. The MORE-CONNECT project focuses on the development of cost-optimal deep renovation solutions towards nearly zero energy buildings (nZEB). To achieve this goal, the introduction of natural materials, such as timber elements, represents an important role since it works as a carbon sponge due to the ability of store carbon dioxide, it is a natural and renewable resource, and it has low embodied energy (total energy used in the building construction process, from production to transportation of materials) [24]. The use of prefabricated panels not only allows the reduction of energy losses through the façade but also eases the maintenance of the buildings. The iNSPiRe project [25] presents an idea of minimal renovation developed through systemic renovation packages that can reduce the primary energy consumption of a building for ventilation, heating/cooling, domestic hot water and lightning. To support the technologies and mechanical systems, a timber frame structure was used. These are some examples of the introduction of wood-based materials for the energy renovation of the existing buildings. However, the use of mass timber solutions is a better option since it increases the energy efficiency, structural safety and architectural renovation of the existing buildings. In this regard, [26] proposed an innovative energy, seismic, and architectural renovation solution for reinforced concrete (RC) framed buildings, based on the addition of CLT panels to the outer walls, in combination with wooden-framed panels. This system is based on the idea of cladding existing RC framed buildings with a new performing skin made of prefabricated and customizable elements. The CLT is an EWP with high strength, stiffness and dimensional stability. Therefore, the CLT structural panels are combined with non-structural pre-assembled panels, which are provided with high-performing windows that will replace the existing ones. This solution uses bio-based insulation materials, such as hemp, cork, wood fiber and cellulose fiber, and in the finishing layer can be used ceramic, wood, stone, glass, photovoltaic modules, etc. The support of the two panels is made through steel profiles connected to the existing RC structure, allowing a quick and easy external installation, which are adaptable to the most common RC framed buildings. With this solution it is possible to reduce the global energy consumption to nearly 60%. The European Project Pro-GET-onE also proposes an exoskeleton made of post-tensioned timber frames and other prefabricated façade elements that increase the energy efficiency and structural safety of the existing buildings (Figure 4). The construction and application of this system can be divided in two parts: firstly, the post-tensioned timber frame is built, and secondly, the insulating façade elements are attached to the structure [27]. The use of CLT, wood-based systems or exoskeletons are good solutions to improve the current environmental and energy efficiency problems and respond to the current renovation requirements of quick installation, cost-effectiveness, use of low-carbon materials and reversibility. However, there are not many studies and systems about integrated wood-based retrofitting renovations; therefore, the potential of these solutions must be further investigated.

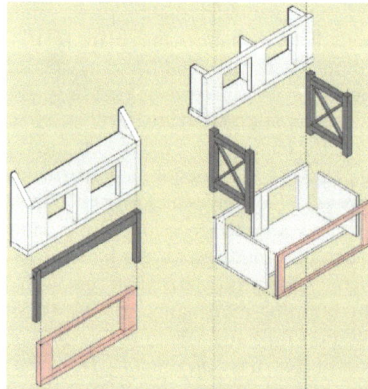

Figure 4. 2D and 3D timber frame systems developed within Pro-GET-onE [27].

4. Discussion

Past design studies and the performed technical–economical evaluation demonstrate that energy efficiency in residential urban complexes can be considered as an extraordinary opportunity to restore environmental, social and urban quality [28]. For example, the possibility to combine add-ons on the top and sides of the buildings (and thus new residential units) with facade solutions have been explored. The need to combine social, safety and energy issues is clear, integrating technical and architectural feasibility of zero energy and low carbon areas with the creation of self-controlled safe environments in emerging new forms of urban communities.

The authors believe that the answer to these new requests could be found in what we call programmatic intermediate zones that can be added to the pre-existing buildings envelope, composed of wood-based systems. In a same holistic and integrated system based on timber pre-assembled components, we should combine the highest performances in terms of energy requirements, safety, social sustainability and market attractiveness. This goal is attained through the application of timber-based solutions for the building envelopes, as well as through an optimum climatic-structural-functional management, grounding on the substantial increase of the real estate value of the buildings through significant energy and architectural transformation. This incremented value will be the result of the development and application of integrated efficient technologies on existing buildings, providing the increase of structural safeness and energy efficiency. The proposal promotes the highest transformation of the existing building's shell with external added volumes, which generate energy efficient buffer zones and, at the same time, increase the building's volume (with balconies, sunspaces and extra rooms). It is carried out from the outside, therefore avoiding building downtime and inhabitant relocation, and it targets eco-efficiency by reducing the environmental impact of the renovation system from the construction to the end-of-use.

The structure of the prefabricated system is composed of glulam columns and beams and CLT slabs. The columns allow the continuity of spaces, and, since there are buildings with an irregular exterior envelope, generally caused by balconies, the use of CLT panels for the slabs will allow it to adapt to any kind and geometry of construction. In fact, in factory, and using the available digital technology of drawing and CNC cuts, it is possible to have a geometry of the CLT panel fitted to the existing building. As wood is a light material (strength/weight ratio), its use in this system allows the absence of additional foundations, with the prefabricated modules being directly supported by the reinforced concrete structure of the existing building.

In Figure 5, the components of the proposed system are represented in axonometry through the decomposition of elements. In addition to identifying the layer and their functions, it is also possible to perceive the relationship between the different elements.

Regarding thermal insulation, mineral wool was chosen to guarantee greater safety against fire and greater thermal and acoustic comfort. As wood has a low thermal conductivity, the insulation is placed in the interstices of the structural layer. Thermal bridges are minimized through the thickness of the thermal insulation and the placement of a wood fiberboard, which acts as additional insulation.

The interior cladding is made of OSB (Oriented Strand Board) panels and the exterior cladding is composed of wooden slat with a surface treatment and protection. The choice of wooden slats as an exterior coating is based on its versatility, since, depending on the distance between the vertical elements, it guarantees privacy for occupants and it controls the sunlight. The wooden substructure, with vertical and horizontal slats, not only supports the exterior cladding but also allows for the creation of a ventilated façade.

Although there are various functions that the building envelope must fulfill, there are layers that can perform several functions at the same time. In this regard, the structure functions as a structural layer and interior cladding; the OSB panel has the function of interior cladding, but also performs the function of airtightness through the placement of single-sided adhesive tapes, and a vapor barrier; the wood fiberboard is pressure resistant and vapor permeable and has the function of additional insulation, protection of structural components, and also a second layer resistant to water and wind.

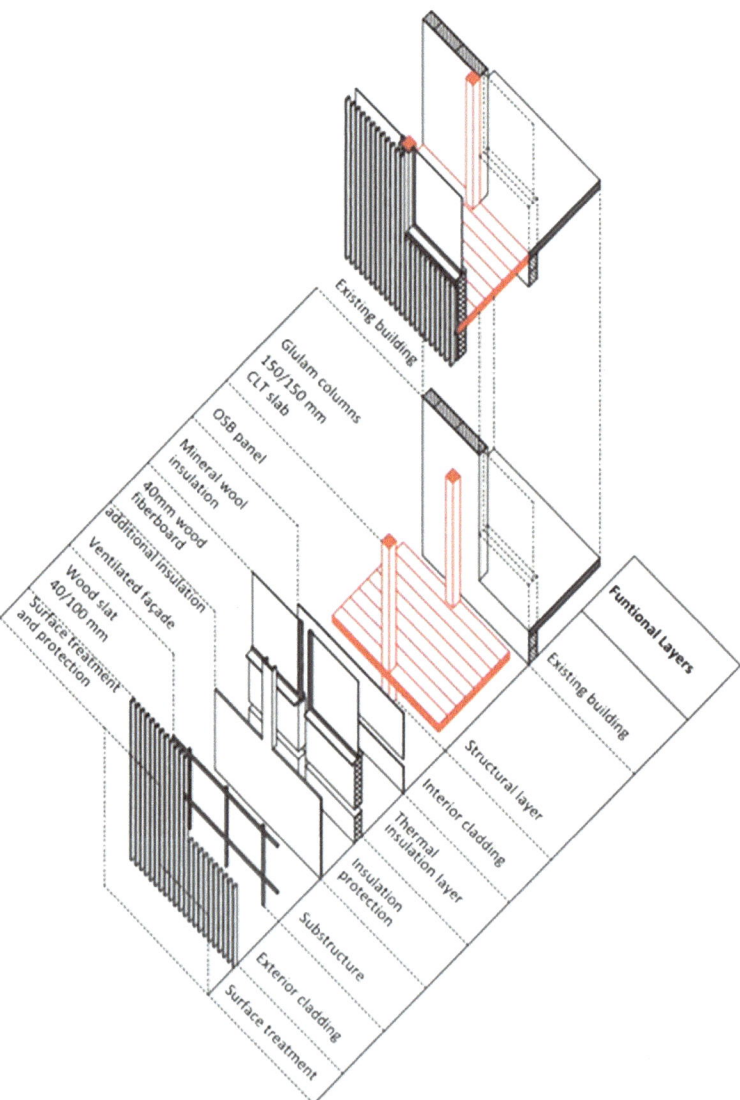

Surface treatment and protection
Wood slat 40/100 mm
Ventilated façade
40mm wood fiberboard additional insulation
Mineral wool insulation
OSB panel
CLT slab
Glulam columns 150/150 mm
Existing building

Surface treatment
Exterior cladding
Substructure
Insulation protection
Thermal insulation layer
Interior cladding
Structural layer
Existing building

Funtional Layers

Figure 5. Structural and functional layers of the proposed prefabricated system.

One of the properties of wood is its combustibility. This is one of the main reasons why people, in general, do not feel safe in buildings with wooden structures, particularly tall buildings [21]. Although wood is a combustible material, there are two distinct approaches that allow a sufficient fire performance of a solid timber structural system: charring and encapsulation. Charring is a process in which, when exposed to fire, the outer layer of wood reaches its point of combustion, creating a layer of charcoal. This outer layer has a low conductivity, reducing fire progression. The inner core of the wood retains its mechanical properties, and only its moisture content is reduced. Therefore, charring is an approach that allows exposing the solid timber structure outside the building, while encapsulation is an approach where the system is coated with fire-resistant materials such as plasterboard panels. In this regard, depending on the height of the buildings in which it will be intervened, it is necessary to be aware of the approach in relation to fire resistance. In other words, the higher the buildings are, the greater the safety requirements must be and, consequently, the covering of its structures.

Next, the case study used as a pilot project will be presented, and the application of the proposed system, previously described, will be discussed.

5. Case Study

Here, a case study is presented with the aim to essay the application of the integrated retrofit strategy based on timber pre-assembled components added to building envelopes. The selected building is part of a social housing complex located in the north of Portugal, more precisely in Viana do Castelo, characterized by its proximity to the Lima River (about 500 m) and by the convergence of two important infrastructures: National Road 13 and the railway line (Figure 6).

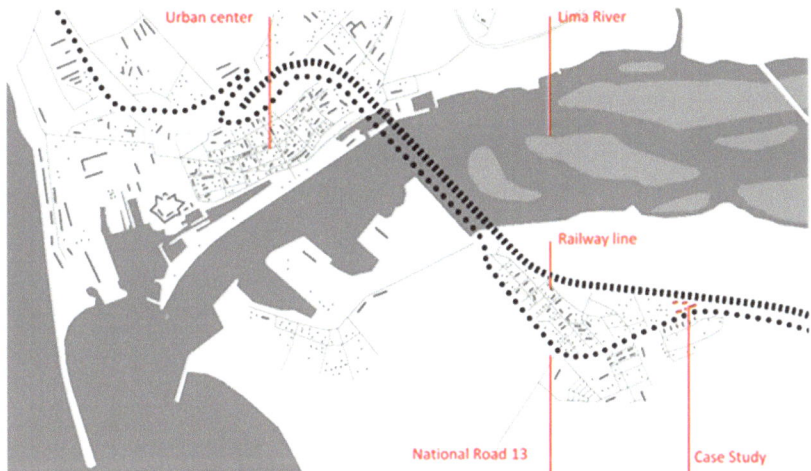

Figure 6. Urban context and location of the case study.

This housing complex is composed of four blocks. The block studied (block 4) was obtained through the conjugation of two distinct modules (Figure 7). Module A has a regular rectangular floor plan with four floors, which corresponds to two duplex typologies, and the access is made through exterior galleries; module B has an irregular plan with three floors. Although this case study was built in the early 1980s, it has several anomalies and low quality of construction. In addition to its poor state of conservation, especially on the north façades, the rehabilitation project for blocks 1 and 2 through the application of the ETICS system, which is currently being finalized, made it possible to compare this system with the proposal here presented.

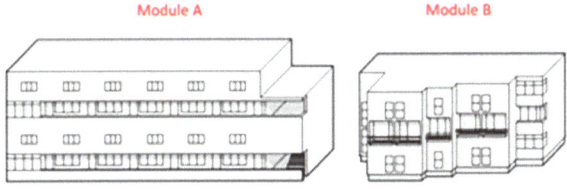

Figure 7. Modules that make up block 4.

5.1. Existing Building's Structure

From the façade, it is possible to understand the structural mesh of the building, as well as the distribution of housing typologies. Module A is composed of a structural frame of about 4.9 m, and the structural frame of module B varies between 6.10 and 2.85 m (Figure 8).

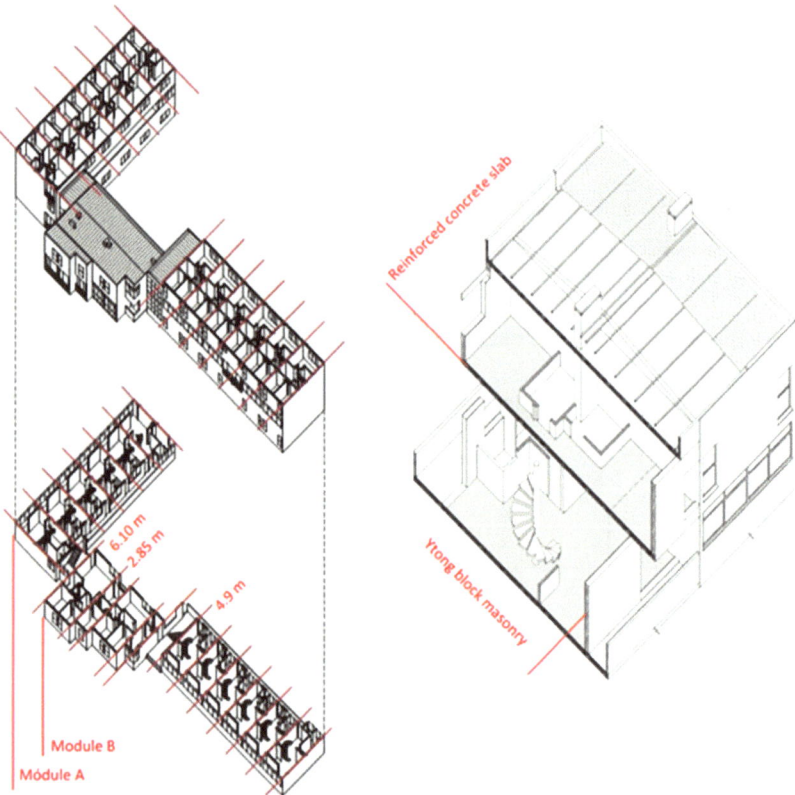

Figure 8. Representation of the structural frame (**left**) and the structure elements (**right**).

The main structure of both buildings, modules A and B, is made of reinforced concrete columns and beams with masonry infills. The slabs are also in reinforced concrete. All filling walls, both exterior and interior ones, are built with Ytong autoclaved aerated concrete blocks, plastered and painted with plastic paint. Exterior walls have a thickness of 20 cm while the interior ones are 10 cm thick.

Ytong blocks are obtained by mixing several elements, namely, Portland cement, silica sand, aluminum powder and water. Subsequently, this mixture is placed in molds with pre-placed reinforcement bars and cut to the desired dimensions. Furthermore, it is placed in an autoclave where it will be hardened. One of the characteristics of aerated concrete is its ability to insulate against cold and heat, allowing the construction of simple and solid walls without the need for additional insulation. This is why, in the context of the know-how and experience of the 1980s when the building was built, no additional thermal insulation was applied in this selected case study. However, it should be noted that the thickness of the Ytong blocks used on the exterior walls is not adequate for the current thermal needs and codes.

The current conservation state of the buildings is mainly the consequence of the proximity of the Lima River and the sea. A homogeneous crack pattern of the outer coating is visible, with some local signs of corroded steel rebars with concrete spalling. The northern façades are the ones more degraded, with a very evident presence of mold and efflorescence.

5.2. Proposed Intervention

Any intervention on the selected case study must solve the thermal inefficiency of the building. Moreover, the intervention shall improve the appearance of the building, degraded by the aging of the materials and by the presence of different degradation agents. On the other hand, since the confinement derived from the pandemic caused by the SARS-CoV-2 virus, it became important to increase the interior living space to accommodate the current needs of the families.

In this context, it is proposed to use a prefabricated wood-based system capable of acting in three distinct areas: energy efficiency, structural safety and spatial organization. As an example, it is proposed to intervene in the exterior of block 4 by placing an exoskeleton, turning it into a habitable envelope (Figures 9 and 10).

In terms of energy, the characteristics of the proposed prefabricated system make it possible to increase thermal and acoustic comfort through the placement of insulation in the surroundings and the installation of high performing windows, with double glazing and a sealing system; improve indoor air quality, with the addition of outdoor spaces (balconies) that allow for indoor ventilation; and create intermediate thermal buffer zones (winter gardens), which allow the interior temperature of the dwellings to be controlled throughout the year. The structural resilience is guaranteed through the structure of the proposed system, which is fixed to the reinforced concrete structure, ensuring greater strength and rigidity. Thus, it allows the distribution and reduction of lateral loads and the increase in structural resilience. Regarding the spatial organization of each apartment, we worked in interior spaces and exterior spaces. Private interior spaces are characterized by their versatility and ability to adapt to the needs of the occupants. In the bedrooms, spaces have been created that can function as an office for teleworking or videoconferencing, a reading area, or even a closet (giving more space to the rest of the room). In the social areas, it was decided to add a winter garden. In addition to being able to be used for leisure, socializing and cultivation of plant species, it also works as a thermal buffer zone. It is worth mentioning the cooperation between the winter garden and the balcony, since these spaces can obtain different configurations throughout the year, according to the functional and thermal needs. In winter, the window frames are closed, creating a thermal buffer zone and protecting the interior spaces from low outside temperatures, while in summer, the window frames are open, in order to increase air circulation and prevent overheating of the winter garden. With this, it is possible to merge the balcony and the winter garden and create an outdoor space with greater dimensions. The modules added to the existing building can interact with the outside through windows and doors. Its position and dimensioning are flexible and can be adjusted to each building, depending on ventilation and lighting requirements. Moreover, the windows and doors are not fixed and can be adjusted to the needs of each resident and even to the regulations of different countries in which the system is being applied.

Whenever possible, we created private outdoor spaces as it allows occupants to enjoy the outside air without having to leave their homes. Such spaces are found on the balconies present in all apartments and in the courtyard on the lower floor of module A. The balconies function as an extension of the interior space, where it is possible to develop various activities related to leisure and rest or even dry clothes naturally. In addition, it allows ventilation of the interior of the building, improving the indoor air quality, and it plays an important role if there is a need for the occupants to remain in prophylactic isolation. On the lower floor of the exterior access galleries, it was decided to create a courtyard entrance for each dwelling, ensuring privacy for residents. This covered courtyard, in addition to allowing direct access to the dwellings, also functions as a transition space between the exterior and interior of the house.

Figure 9. Plan of the added spaces.

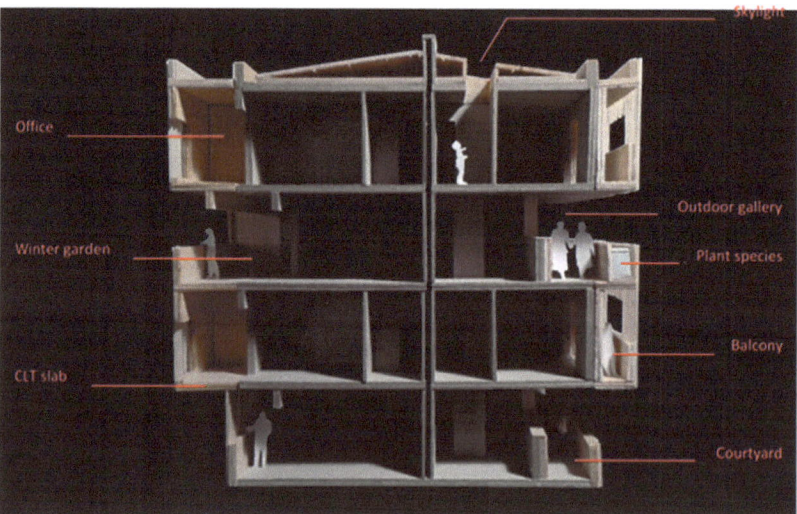

Figure 10. Model of the proposal section.

The public spaces created are the exterior galleries and the roof of module B. On the upper floor, the objective was to make the exterior gallery an extension of the surrounding urban space by enlarging it and placing plant species. This allows residents and local people to enjoy the spaces created and enables the creation of a community environment. In module B, we decided to make the roof accessible, in order to consolidate the interaction between people and take advantage of its location to create a viewpoint over the Lima River. This space works as an open garden through the placement of green spaces for the cultivation of small plants (Figure 11).

Figure 11. Section of module B.

In addition, the placement of skylights makes it possible to light and ventilate the interior spaces, such as bathrooms and vertical accesses (spiral stairs). Unlike module B, the roof of module A is not accessible; however, it was decided to introduce skylights and photovoltaic panels. The façade is composed of wooden slats in which the distance between vertical elements varies according to the spaces. On the ground floor, a smaller distance is used to ensure greater privacy for the occupants. Moreover, it allows controlling the incidence of sunlight. In outdoor spaces, such as balconies and outdoor galleries, the wooden slat is interrupted occasionally, in order to represent the geometry of the original window frames while maintaining the design characteristics. Over time, the vegetation located on the roof and in the outer gallery may extend through the wooden slats, creating a green façade (Figure 12).

Figure 12. Model of the north elevation (**left**) and south elevation (**right**). Representation of three stages: current building, structure and final result.

5.3. Materials

The proposed intervention is composed of glulam elements for the columns and CLT panels for the slabs in order to allow continuity of spaces and because it is possible to adapt to any construction due to the factory cut of the existing building's geometry. Moreover, the interior cladding is made of OSB panels, and the exterior cladding is composed of a wooden slat with a surface protection treatment. The choice of wooden slats as an exterior covering is based on its versatility, since, depending on the distance between the vertical elements, they guarantee greater privacy for residents and greater control of sunlight. The wooden substructure, with vertical and horizontal slats, not only supports the exterior cladding but also allows for the creation of a ventilated façade.

The choice of these materials is due to the fact that they have a high degree of pre-fabrication. Therefore, the normalization and standardization of the dimensions of these elements and their production in the factory reduces the construction and assembly time and reduces the life cycle cost. Furthermore, as the composition of these materials is based on wood, it makes this solution, and, consequently, the case study building, more efficient and sustainable, since wood is characterized by its ability to store carbon dioxide and for being a natural, renewable and ecological material.

The introduction of mineral wool insulation not only allows for greater thermal and acoustic comfort but also guarantees fire resistance. Moreover, the charring approach also contributes to greater fire safety, as the outer layer of wood, when exposed to fire, reaches its point of combustion. In this chemical reaction, heat removes hydrogen and oxygen from the solid wood, leaving a layer of coal, composed mainly of carbon. This outer layer has a low conductivity, reducing fire progression. In addition to the coal layer, a pyrolysis zone is also formed, where the decomposition of wood occurs due to the increase in temperature of the outer layer. The inner core of the wood retains its mechanical properties, and only its moisture content is reduced.

6. Conclusions

The current use of ETICS in Portugal to retrofit the existing buildings stock should be questioned since there are other energy-efficient solutions that also improve the structural stability and increase the architectural aesthetics and organization, with the significant advantage of adding new spaces and rooms adequate to the confinement derived from the present pandemic caused by the SARS-CoV-2 virus. The use of prefabricated wood-based elements and/or systems has demonstrated to increase the energy efficiency, interior air quality, acoustic comfort, waterproofing, aesthetics and real estate value of the buildings, through the protection and placement of insulation in the envelope and the redesign of the façades. Moreover, the rationalization and optimization of the modular constructive elements will reduce the renovation operation time and increase the speed of manufacturing and assembly. As defended by [29], there is still a long way for building scientists and professionals to go in order to make existing building stock more energy efficient and environmentally sustainable.

A holistic and integrated intervention based in the use of prefabricated wooden systems attached to the existing structure was presented and applied to a selected reinforced concrete building from the 1980s. It was possible to improve the energy efficiency of the building while adding volumes and living spaces. More studies are certainly needed but the essay was promising.

Author Contributions: C.M. (Cláudio Meireis) and F.S.S., methodology, formal analysis, investigation, writing—original draft preparation; C.M. (Carlos Maia), A.C.F. and J.M.B., conceptualization, methodology, formal analysis, writing—review and editing, supervision. All authors have read and agreed to the published version of the manuscript.

Funding: This research received no external funding.

Informed Consent Statement: Not applicable.

Conflicts of Interest: The authors declare no conflict of interest.

References

1. Instituto Nacional de Estatística. Estatísticas da Construção e Habitação: 2019. 2020. Available online: https://www.ine.pt/xurl/pub/443821545 (accessed on 31 March 2021). (In Portuguese)
2. Pérez-Lombard, L.; Ortiz, J.; Pout, C. A review on buildings energy consumption information. *Energy Build.* **2008**, *40*, 394–398. [CrossRef]

3. Salvalai, G.; Sesana, M.M.; Iannaccone, G. Deep renovation of multi-storey multi-owner existing residential buildings: A pilot case study in Italy. *Energy Build.* **2017**, *148*, 23–36. [CrossRef]
4. Corrado, V.; Ballarini, I. Refurbishment trends of the residential building stock: Analysis of a regional pilot case in Italy. *Energy Build.* **2016**, *132*, 91–106. [CrossRef]
5. Pohoryles, D.A.; Maduta, C.; Bournas, D.A.; Kouris, L.A. Energy performance of existing residential buildings in Europe: A novel approach combining energy with seismic retrofitting. *Energy Build.* **2020**, *223*, 110024. [CrossRef]
6. Silva, P.M. Avaliação e Caraterização de Medidas de Melhoria Energética na Reabilitação de Edifícios Numa Perspetiva Custo-Benefício. Seleção e Caraterização de Medidas de Melhoria da Envolvente de Edifícios. Master's Thesis, University of Minho, Guimarães, Portugal, 2013. (In Portuguese)
7. Corrêa, D.M. Thermal Rehabilitation of the Facades of Old Buildings. Master's Thesis, Instituto Superior Técnico da Universidade de Lisboa, Lisbon, Portugal, 2016.
8. Amaro, B.; Saraiva, D.; de Brito, J.; Flores-Colen, I. Inspection and diagnosis system of ETICS on walls. *Constr. Build. Mater.* **2013**, *47*, 1257–1267. [CrossRef]
9. European Commission. RetroKit—Toolboxes for Systemic Retrofitting. 2017. Available online: https://cordis.europa.eu/project/id/314229/reporting (accessed on 31 March 2021).
10. Capeluto, G. Adaptability in envelope energy retrofits through addition of intelligence features. *Archit. Sci. Rev.* **2019**, *62*, 216–229. [CrossRef]
11. Dugué, A.; Raji, S.; Bonnamy, P.; Bruneau, D. E2VENT: An Energy Efficient Ventilated Façade Retrofitting System. Presentation of the Embedded LHTES System. *Procedia Environ. Sci.* **2017**, *38*, 121–129. [CrossRef]
12. Lops, C. Integrated Solutions for the Energy and Seismic Retrofit of Existing Buildings. Ph.D. Thesis, Polytechnic University of Catalonia, Barcelona, Spain, 2020.
13. Manfredi, V.; Masi, A. Seismic Strengthening and Energy Efficiency: Towards an Integrated Approach for the Rehabilitation of Existing RC Buildings. *Buildings* **2018**, *8*, 36. [CrossRef]
14. Feroldi, F.; Marini, A.; Badiani, B.; Plizzari, G.A.; Giuriani, E.; Riva, P.; Belleri, A. Energy efficiency upgrading, architectural restyling and structural retrofit of modern buildings by means of engineered double skin façade. In *Structures and Architecture: Concepts, Applications and Challenges, Proceedings of the 2nd International Conference on Structures & Architecture—ICSA2013*; Guimaraes, Portugal, 24–26 July 2013, Cruz, P., Ed.; Taylor & Francis Group: London, Portugal, 2013; pp. 1859–1866.
15. Ferrante, A.; Mochi, G.; Predari, G.; Badini, L.; Fotopoulou, A.; Gulli, R.; Semprini, G. A European Project for Safer and Energy Efficient Buildings: Pro-GET-onE (Proactive Synergy of inteGrated Efficient Technologies on Buildings Envelopes). *Sustainability* **2018**, *10*, 812. [CrossRef]
16. Bellini, O.E. Adaptive Exoskeleton Systems: Remodelage for Social Housing on Piazzale Visconti (BG). In *Regeneration of the Built Environment from a Circular Economy Perspective*; Della Torre, S., Cattaneo, S., Lenzi, C., Zanelli, A., Eds.; Springer: Cham, Switzerland, 2020; pp. 363–374.
17. Scuderi, G. Adaptive Exoskeleton for the Integrated Retrofit of Social Housing Buildings. Ph.D. Thesis, University of Trento, Trento, Italy, 2016.
18. LACATON & VASSAL. Transformation de 530 Logements. 2017. Available online: www.lacatonvassal.com/index.php?idp=80 (accessed on 31 March 2021).
19. Renovate Europe. Grand Parc Apartment Building, Bordeaux—France. Available online: https://www.renovate-europe.eu/reday/reday-2019/online-resources/grand-parc-france-e12 (accessed on 31 March 2021).
20. Think Wood. Designing Sustainable, Prefabricated Wood Buildings. Available online: https://www.thinkwood.com/wp-content/uploads/2018/07/Designing-Sustainable-Prefabricated-Wood-Buildings_Think-Wood-CEU.pdf (accessed on 31 March 2021).
21. Wimmers, G. Wood: A construction material for tall buildings. *Nat. Rev. Mater.* **2017**, *2*, 17051. [CrossRef]
22. Rubner Holzbau. Wood Culture 21: Construction Expertise for Architects, Designers and Building Owners, Rubner Ingenieurholzbau. 2016. Available online: https://www.rubner.com/fileadmin/marken/holzbau/Infomaterial/2020-10_Wood_Culture_21.pdf (accessed on 14 December 2021).
23. European Commission. Building Energy Renovation through Timber Prefabricated Modules. 2019. Available online: https://cordis.europa.eu/project/id/636984/reporting (accessed on 31 March 2021).
24. Europe Commission. Development and Advanced Prefabrication of Innovative, Multifunctional Building Envelope Elements for Modular Retrofitting and Connections. Available online: https://cordis.europa.eu/project/id/633477/reporting (accessed on 31 March 2021).
25. Ochs, F.; Siegele, D.; Dermentzis, G.; Feist, W. Prefabricated Timber Frame Façade with Integrated Active Components for Minimal Invasive Renovations. *Energy Procedia* **2015**, *78*, 61–66. [CrossRef]
26. Margani, G.; Evola, G.; Tardo, C.; Marino, E.M. Energy, Seismic, and Architectural Renovation of RC Framed Buildings with Prefabricated Timber Panels. *Sustainability* **2020**, *12*, 4845. [CrossRef]
27. Ott, S.; Krechel, M. Construction principles of seismic and energy renovation systems for existing buildings. *Technol. Eng. Mater. Archit.* **2018**, *4*, 66–80.

28. Ferrante, A. Energy retrofit to nearly zero and socio-oriented urban environments in the Mediterranean climate. *Sustain. Cities Soc.* **2014**, *13*, 237–253. [CrossRef]
29. Ma, Z.; Cooper, P.; Daly, D.; Ledo, L. Existing building retrofits: Methodology and state-of-the-art. *Energy Build.* **2012**, *55*, 889–902. [CrossRef]

 *infrastructures*

Article

Sustainable Human Development at the Municipal Level: A Data Envelopment Analysis Index

Pedro A. B. Lima [1,*], Gilberto D. Paião Júnior [1], Thalita L. Santos [2], Marcelo Furlan [3], Rosane A. G. Battistelle [2], Gustavo H. R. Silva [2], Diogo Ferraz [1,4,5] and Enzo B. Mariano [1]

[1]   Department of Production Engineering, School of Engineering of Bauru, Campus Bauru, São Paulo State University (UNESP), Bauru 17033-360, Brazil; gilberto.paiao@unesp.br (G.D.P.J.); diogoferraz@alumni.usp.br (D.F.); enzo.mariano@unesp.br (E.B.M.)
[2]   Department of Civil and Environmental Engineering, School of Engineering of Bauru, Campus Bauru, São Paulo University (UNESP), Bauru 17033-360, Brazil; thalita.lacerda@unesp.br (T.L.S.); rosane.battistelle@unesp.br (R.A.G.B.); gustavo.ribeiro@unesp.br (G.H.R.S.)
[3]   Department of Production Engineering, Campus Nova Andradina, Federal University of Mato Grosso do Sul (UFMS), Nova Andradina 79750-000, Brazil; marcelo.furlan@ufms.br
[4]   Innovation Economics, Institute of Economics, University of Hohenheim, 70599 Stuttgart, Germany
[5]   Department of Economics, Institute of Social and Applied Sciences, Federal University of Ouro Preto (UFOP), Mariana 35420-000, Brazil
*   Correspondence: pedro.ab.lima@unesp.br

Abstract: The development of indexes for human development and environmental sustainability issues are an emerging topic in the current literature. However, the literature has put less emphasis on municipal indexes, which is the focus of this research. In this paper, we considered municipal environmental management as the adoption of environmental activities and the development of infrastructural and technical capacities in municipalities. This article aims to create a sustainable human development index with municipal data from the state of São Paulo in Brazil. Using information from the Municipal Human Development Index (IDHm) and the GreenBlue Municipal Program (PMVA), we applied the data envelopment analysis (DEA) technique to connect human development and environmental sustainability in 645 Brazilian municipalities. Our findings show that regions with higher human development present better DEA scores on the Sustainable Human Development Index. In contrast, regions with a low or a middle level of human development do not present significant change considering both dimensions. Moreover, our findings reveal that PMVA certification has a different and statistically significant impact on the DEA score considering certified, qualified, or not qualified regions. We found similar results for urbanized and service-oriented municipalities. Our indicator is an essential and straightforward tool for regional policymakers, helping to allocate resources and to find human development and environmental sustainability benchmarks among developing regions.

Keywords: human development; sustainability; environmental program; environmental management; data envelopment analysis (DEA); index; infrastructure; urban management

1. Introduction

Development indexes that only measure economic aspects, such as gross domestic product (GDP), are increasingly being considered inadequate to measure the development of a region [1]. In this way, other important dimensions for human life were incorporated in development indexes, such as health and education, which are present in the Human Development Index (HDI) [2,3]. In the last two decades, however, besides the incorporation of social indicators, there was also the recommendation to consider environmental indicators in development analysis [2,4,5].

In this context, some authors have been proposing adaptations and new ways of measuring the HDI, including environmental sustainability indicators, in what can be called the Sustainable Human Development Index (SDHI) [2]. In addition, Furlan and Mariano [6] have developed a national environmental justice index by using data development analysis (DEA) with human development and environmental data.

Local governments are important for the achievement of sustainable development and require appropriate sustainability indicators [7]. Some initiatives have been considered at the local level, in different parts of the world, to improve environmental public policies and, therefore, environmental quality [8,9]. One important case is voluntary and regional initiatives that aim to increase the autonomy and responsibility of local governments towards aspects of public environmental management [8].

Within this context, in 2007, the Secretariat of Environment of the state of São Paulo, Brazil, created the Município Verde (Green Municipality) Initiative [10], currently named Programa Município VerdeAzul (GreenBlue Municipality Program (PMVA)). The program aims to stimulate the city halls of São Paulo to adopt environmental management practices, including the development of actions and infrastructure provisioning. The municipalities may receive certification for achieving the goals described in the program's guidelines, which facilitates access to financial resources from the state budget of São Paulo [11].

Sustainability is an important issue to be addressed by municipalities, which need to consider social, environmental, and economical aspects in order to be considered truly sustainable [12]. Discussions about sustainability should not disregard the social justice premises in environmental management programs. Although these programs are important, they are not sufficient to guarantee the sustainable development of the regions implementing them [13]. Therefore, there is the problem of how to better measure the sustainable development of municipalities that adopt environmental management programs.

The aim of this paper is to create an index that considers both human development and environmental indicators at the municipality level, named the Sustainable Human Development Index. To achieve this goal, this research relied on data envelopment analysis (DEA) to create an index using data from the Municipality Human Development Index (HDIm)—a Brazilian internal adaptation of the HDI to evaluate human development in the municipalities—and the grades from the PMVA. In this way, it is possible to increase social justice aspects in the PMVA, creating higher coverage for the index. As already highlighted by Sena et al. [14], social and environmental aspects need to be considered in order to achieve sustainable development in a region.

Aside from the importance of the theme from the practical perspective, this study also contributes to the literature by analyzing a Latin American country, which has fewer studies in the human development literature than more developed regions [4]. Other countries, that have environmental initiatives, can use the approach present in this research in order to develop an index that includes more aspects related to sustainable development in the local context. Moreno-Pires and Fidélis [7] highlighted how municipal sustainable indicators should consider a broad range of dimensions. According to the authors, composite indicators might consider several dimensions to represent social, economic, demographic, and environmental aspects.

Another important aspect of this research is that it is related to some of the Sustainable Development Goals (SDGs) promoted by the United Nations [15], especially goal 11—Sustainable Cities and Communities. The SDGs are an important instrument to promote the three sustainable development pillars (economics, environment, and social) to be achieved in the long term [16]. According to Moyer and Bohl [17], several of the SDGs are closely related to human development. This might indicate a tendency of developing programs to consider both human development and environmental elements together [18,19].

This study is structured as follows: Section 1 presents the introduction with the research problem and objective. Section 2 presents a theoretical background concerning sustainable human development and municipal environmental management. Section 3 presents the material and methods, describing the data used and how the index was developed. Section 4 presents the results and discussion. Section 5 presents the conclusions of the research.

2. Conceptual Framework

In this section, we present the research framework (Figure 1), where we describe the relationship between human development and environmental action (here represented by municipal environmental management) in order to generate sustainable human development.

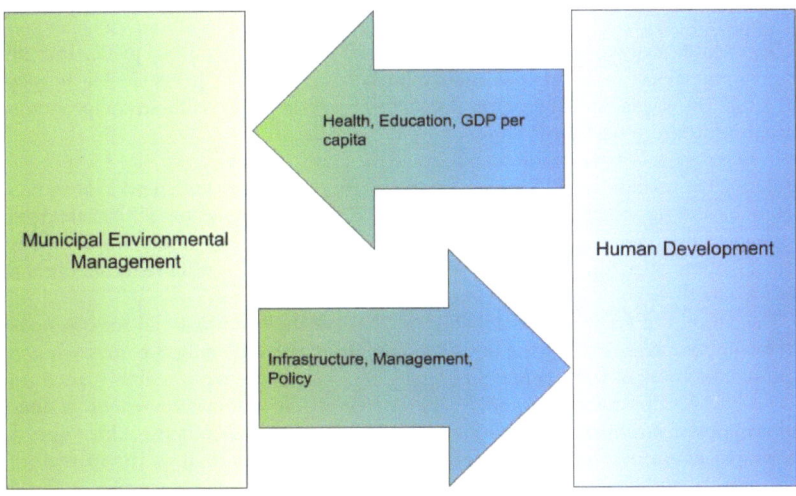

Figure 1. Conceptual framework.

Some studies posit that better levels of human development can increase the number of sustainable development actions, which, in turn, can support human development [6,20–22]. Furlan and Mariano [6] applied this idea to mitigation and adaptation strategies in the climate change context. Lima et al. [22] incorporated this idea in circular economy initiatives. Therefore, in this research, we suggest that the increase in human development, including better levels of health, education, and resources, positively affects municipal environmental management, which supports the development of better infrastructure, management practices, and policies, which in turn supports the increase in human development. This cyclical relationship can lead to the achievement of sustainable human development.

In this context, it would be important that environmental programs consider human development issues in its metrics. Next, we present the human development concept and its relationship with sustainability and the notion of sustainable human development. Then, we present the importance of municipal environmental management and briefly describe the PMVA, which was used as a proxy for the municipal environmental management in Brazil.

2.1. Sustainable Human Development

The idea of human development emerged as a way to complement the purely economic notions of development, such as the gross domestic product (GDP) [3]. "Human development is about enlarging freedoms so that all human beings can pursue choices that they value" [23], p.1. This definition is grounded in the capability approach, which is the main concept in the human development field [24]; according to this theory, development should be seen as the increase in the individual's freedoms in order to have and be whatever they value [24]. For the capability approach, freedom is both the means and the ends of development [3,24].

Sustainable development incorporates aspects of intergenerational justice into the intragenerational justice already present in human development [25]. Sustainable development is the "development that prompts the needs of present people without compromising the needs of future generations" [26].

In this way, it is not possible to minimize the privations currently faced, especially considering the poorest, to the detriment of the future generations; both need to have their capabilities and freedoms ensured [13,25,27]. According to Haughton [13], sustainable development does not require only the adaptation of human behavior, but also the adaptation of the infrastructures that influence these behaviors, which includes economic and social aspects.

The concept of environmental justice emphasizes the need to avoid the ones who have fewer resources, exactly the ones who pollute the least, being the ones who are the most affected by environmental problems [28]. Therefore, environmental justice also has a human development connotation [20]. Therefore, human development has a direct relationship with sustainable development, since the individuals' quality of life depends on a proper environment [27]. A feedback effect also occurs, that is, the increase in individuals' capabilities tends to increase the development of a better environment, due to the application of better behaviors, practices, and technologies that improve environmental quality [22]. Nagy, Benedek, and Ivan [29] found a strong correlation between local HDI in a Romanian region with the indexes of the SDGs achievement, which may indicate a positive relationship between investments in human development and the achievement of sustainable aspects. This may be related to sustainable human development, which is the relationship between human development and sustainable development [2].

The HDI is the most used approach to measure human development in the world. It was developed by Mahbub ul Haq, who had the capability approach as one of the main inspirations. The HDI has three dimensions (economic, education, and health) divided into four indicators (gross national capital per capita, school life expectancy, average years of schooling, and life expectancy at birth), being disclosed annually by the United Nations Development Programme (UNDP) [3,30–32].

According to Dalberto et al. [33], by incorporating these dimensions, the HDI kept the capability approach notion of the development of focusing not only on monetary aspects but also on the social one. As pointed out by Assa [2], the educational and health dimensions measure capabilities, while the monetary measure is a commodity.

The HDI has undergone a "natural selection" process of the indexes, that is, its indicators and manners of calculation have been adapted when necessary, in such a way that it continues to be used even years after its creation [34]. However, the HDI is not exempt from criticism, such as the simplicity of its dimensions; lack of qualitative analysis (for example, quality of education); and the lack of elements directly related to the environment [3,32,33].

Considering the limitations of the global HDI, some countries have been adapting the indicators to better represent the national context. The UNDP encourages this initiative for these countries to increase, substitute, or create new approaches to the HDI's indicators in order to develop more adequate measures for their realities. In Brazil, this index is called the Municipality Human Development Index (HDIm), and it has been applied at the municipality level since 1998 [35].

In 2013, the HDIm began to use the Demographic Census database from 2010, adapting the indicators of the global HDI for the indicators collected by the Brazilian Institute of Geography and Statistics (IBGE). The HDIm presents the same dimensions as the traditional HDI, although it uses different variables and measures to represent human development in Brazil. While the HDIm uses data collected by the IBGE, the HDI uses data from several agencies from the United Nations and other international agencies [35,36].

In the HDIm, the indicator for health is life expectancy at birth, the income is represented by the municipality income per capita, and education is measured by two indicators: (1) the population that is 18 years old or more that completed elementary school, with a weight of 1, and represents the schooling of the adult population; and (2) the population between 5 and 6 years old attending school, the population between 11 and 13 years old attending the last years of elementary education, the population between 15 and 17 years old that completed elementary school, and the population between 18 and 20 years old that completed high school; this indicator has a weight of 2 and represents the school flow of the young population. Therefore, the educational dimension is calculated by the geometric mean of indicators 1 and 2. The complete index is also calculated by the geometric mean of the three dimensions mentioned [35].

Considering the aforementioned indicators, São Paulo has the second largest Brazilian HDIm (0.783), only behind the Federal District (0.824) [33]. The HDI also has the importance of providing information to support development policies, which helps policymakers to map human development and decide how to allocate public resources to boost human development in Brazil [33].

2.2. Municipal Environmental Management

Municipal environmental management is the environmental activities performed by local authorities in the municipalities [37]. In this study, the actions developed by local governments to increase their environmental performance are considered, which include: urban management, infrastructure provision, waste management, development of policies, and environmental education and communication. All these actions are important to support sustainable human development [22,38–42].

Almost all countries face difficulties in achieving better levels of sustainable development, which is particularly difficult for developing countries, such as Brazil, that need to reconcile economic development with environmental preservation. This is hampered by the smaller amount of resources compared to developed countries and greater demand from society for aspects of infrastructures and essential services [43,44]. Tortajada [41] pointed out that developing countries still need to increase their investment in infrastructures in order to support human development.

One way to mitigate these challenges is not to concentrate all the responsibility on a single government entity, but to share responsibility among different administrative spheres, including local, regional, and national government participation [13,29,45,46]. Municipalities are key actors in fostering sustainable development [7,12]. Among possible advantages, local administrations have greater knowledge about their peculiarities and capabilities, while regional and national spheres can help with technical and/or financial support [8,47–49].

It is important to have ways to measure the progress in this kind of activity [49]. Indicators to measure municipality sustainability offer more information for decision makers; Moreno-Pires and Fidélis [7] suggest that these indicators should cover a broad range of dimensions, in order to fully consider sustainable development.

The PMVA is a municipal environmental management program in which the São Paulo State Government (regional sphere) encourages municipal governments (local spheres) to adopt environmental management measures [50]. The program is voluntary, so this flexibility in its adoption requires the program to be credible and have a performance measurement mechanism [9]. This point is present in the PMVA, considering that a database was created with the indicators of each municipality and supported by the presence of a team that upholds and helps to train municipalities to develop environmental management actions and planning [11]. Thus, in addition to the generation of local data [8] that may reflect greater interest by the local population in matters related to the environment [43]; the municipality also does not see itself as alone in achieving the program's goals, since it receives support from the state sphere [46].

Currently, the PMVA has 10 dimensions, called directives: sustainable municipality, structure and environmental education, environmental council, biodiversity, water management, air quality, land use, urban forestation, treated sewage, and solid waste. Each directive has a number of tasks related to: development of municipal legislation to support the environmental management and practices, infrastructure and technical capabilities, and quality presented [11]. Table 1 presents a summary of the directives.

Table 1. Description of the PMVA directives.

Directive	Tasks
Sustainable municipality	Incentive indicators for the generation and consumption of renewable energy sources, inspection of the commercialization of forest products, and incentives for the production and purchase of food from sustainable systems.
Structure and environmental education	Implementation of a minimum organizational structure within the administration that includes a specialized staff and specific legislation. It includes the creation of spaces and actions to promote environmental education among the population.
Environmental council	Implementation, through specific legislation, of the Municipal Environmental Council. The administration must prove the council's activities by means of meeting minutes, the year's goal plan, topics discussed, participation in PMVA events, and actions developed during the period.
Biodiversity	Actions for the conservation of fauna and flora through plans and municipal laws (institution of Payments for Environmental Services *). The resources for these actions must be inserted in the annual budget law. * Mechanism that remunerates rural producers for environmental services that benefit the whole society, for example: conservation and restoration of forests.
Water management	Actions to protect and recover springs, educational actions regarding the conscious use of water, and measures to ensure the quality of the water distributed to the population through laboratory analysis.
Air quality	Actions to reduce air pollution generated by vehicles and fires. In the first case, the indicators focus on controlling vehicle emissions as well as encouraging the use of renewable fuels and public transport. For the second case, the actions involve the mitigation of urban and rural fires and the creation of a fire brigade.
Land use	Tasks related to erosion control in urban and rural areas, as well as the establishment of a Contingency Plan, through civil defense, to map regions susceptible to dangerous geodynamic processes. It also establishes the management and recovery of areas that are contaminated or at risk of contamination, and the management of areas showing exploitation or potential exploitation of minerals.
Urban forestation	Development of municipal legislation aimed at the process of afforestation and urban forestry, establishing norms, standards, and adequacy of road infrastructure. It also requires the municipality to carry out an inventory and diagnosis of the trees on the urban perimeter, calculation of the urban vegetation cover (in percentages), and publicity and environmental education actions related to urban afforestation.
Treated sewage	The directive considers both the coverage of the collection network and the percentage of treatment of the generated sewage. There are also indicators focused on the quality and efficiency of the treatment.
Solid waste	Actions for the correct disposal of solid waste generated in landfills, waste reduction or reuse programs, implementation of selective waste collection, and programs to institute composting (biodigestion) projects. There are also environmental education actions to promote and encourage the population to participate in selective waste collection.

It is important to note that even if the directive did not explicitly mention the necessity for infrastructure, in order to accomplish its tasks it is necessary to develop proper infrastructure, especially in the directives related to sanitation [42]. For example, proper infrastructure is needed to provide appropriate water for the population as required in the water management directive. These kinds of directives not only impact the environment, but also exert influence on socio-economic systems [40]. Although the number of directives has not changed, the number of tasks has increased. In the beginning of the program, it ranged from two to three tasks per directive, now it is common to exceed seven tasks that cover action, management, and results related to the directive [11].

Annually, each municipality receives a final score, called the Environmental Assessment Index (EAI), which is the sum of the points for all tasks of each directive. There are also extra points for proactive actions and a reduction in the score if there are some pending issues or environmental liabilities. The municipalities deliver the documentation to prove and assess the grades, however, 13.73% of the total grades are automatically computed from data measured by other state agencies [50].

The certification is granted to municipalities that achieve an EAI score of 80 or more and facilitates the access to resources from the state Environment Secretariat [11]. There is also an intermediate classification for municipalities that reach an EAI score between 40 and 80, called qualification, in which the PMVA allocates special attention to ascertain whether they are "on the right track" to achieve the certification [11]. Thus, it is possible to classify the municipalities into: non-qualified (EAI score of 0.0 to 39.9), qualified (EAI score of 40.0 to 79.9), and certified (EAI score of 80.0 to 100.0).

The scoring method has undergone some changes over the years, making the requirements for certified municipalities more stringent. In addition to obtaining an EAI score of 80, a score of zero is not allowed in any directive and it is mandatory to implement a minimum municipal environmental legislation.

3. Method

The analyses were performed using DEA, as it is an appropriate method to develop an index ranging from 0 to 1 [6]. DEA is a non-parametric technique developed by Charnes, Cooper, and Rhodes [51], being a mathematical model based on linear programming capable of allocating the set of optimal weights to maximize the efficiency of a decision-making unit (DMU) [1], which is the DEA unit of analysis. Table 2 summarizes the research method that was based on the three steps proposed by Golany and Roll [52] to apply DEA, and in more three statistical tests.

Table 2. Method summary.

Method	Step	Explanation
DEA	1. DMU selection	• 645 municipalities from São Paulo, Brazil

	2. Inputs and outputs definition	• Partial Index HDIm_PMVA:
		  ○ Input: HDIm;
		  ○ Output: PMVA EAI.
		• Partial Index PMVA_HDIm:
		  ○ Input: PMVA EAI;
		  ○ Output: HDIm.

	3. DEA application	• Variable returns of scale • Oriented toward the output • Multiplication of the two partial indexes to develop the Sustainable Human Development Index

Table 2. *Cont.*

Method	Step	Explanation
Statistical tests	4. Normality check tests	• Kolmogorov–Smirnov and Shapiro–Wilk
	5. DMU classifications and hypothesis development	• HDIm level (low, medium, and high), H1; • PMVA (non-qualified, qualified, and certified), H2; • Urbanization level (rural, intermediate, and urban), H3; • Economic sector (agriculture, industrial, and services), H4.
	6. Non-parametric test	• Jonckheere–Terpstra

The first step of Golany and Roll [52] consists of choosing the DMUs, which were all the 645 municipalities of São Paulo, Brazil (Figure 2). The estimated population of the 645 municipalities is 44.7 million inhabitants, being the most populous Brazilian state, representing 21% of Brazil's population. The life expectancy is 79.5 years for women and 73.2 years for men. In the economic aspect, the state presented a GDP of approximately USD 582,18 billion in 2019, representing 31% of the national GDP. Considering the education indicator, the population's average years of schooling were 9.97 years in 2016 [53]. Regional initiatives, even if located in only one state, are important to be studied, since they can contribute to other locations or sectors with lessons and experiences [9].

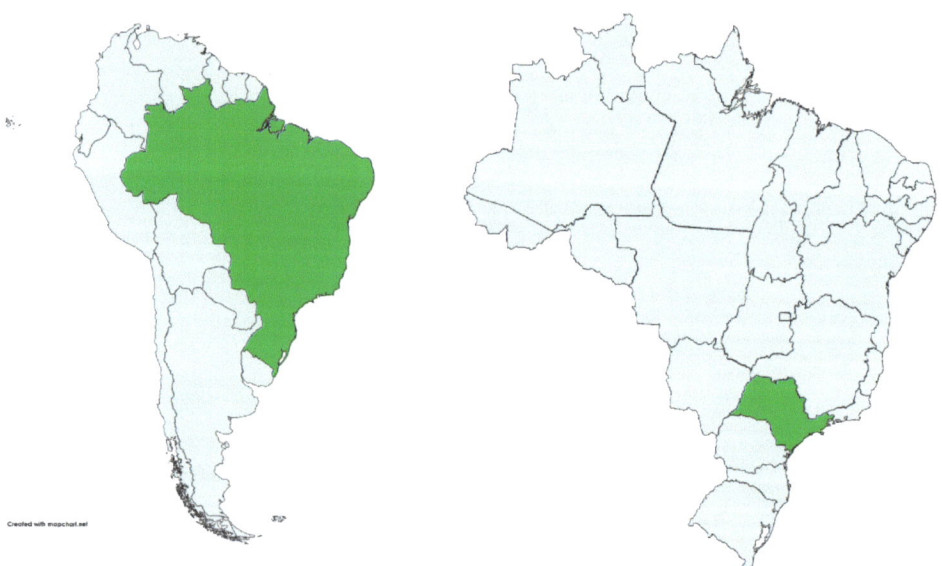

Figure 2. São Paulo location.

Socioeconomic analyses in specific regions of a country, such as the municipalities of São Paulo, are advantageous for having more homogeneous DMUs [4], which is considered an important aspect for DEA [8]. DEA has already been used in other studies that evaluated the efficiency in transforming economic and development-related resources into sustainable development [5,54], and has also been applied with HDI data [1,33].

The second step of Golany and Roll [52] is the definition of inputs and outputs suitable for the analyses. For human development, the three dimensions of the HDIm were used, and we used the 2010 version because it is the most up to date. The HDI is the main reference for this type of study in the field of human development [4]. The data were collected from the official website of the Institute for Applied Economic Research [55].

For municipal environmental management, we used data from the 10 dimensions of the PMVA. We decided to use the 2019 data instead of those from 2020 (most recent) since the pandemic caused by COVID-19 was an extreme and unexpected event that significantly affected society's way of life [56]. This phenomenon created several challenges in the environmental management of municipalities [57] that could affect the intended analyses in this study. The data were collected from the PMVA's official platform [58].

For the third and last stage presented by Golany and Roll [52], the application of the DEA and the subsequent analysis of the results were carried out. We chose the output-oriented model, called BCC, since it presents variable returns to scale, that is, the increase in the input does not interfere proportionally in the output. Considering that the objective is to maximize the output and not to minimize the input, the model was applied with the output orientation, as it is not the objective of any municipality to reduce its output (human development or municipal environmental management), but to increase its input (human development or municipal environmental management) [4–6]. Equations (1)–(3) show the output-oriented BCC model.

$$E = Min \sum_{j=1}^{n} v_j \cdot x_{j0} - w \tag{1}$$

Subject to:

$$\sum_{i=1}^{m} u_i \cdot y_{i0} = 1 \tag{2}$$

$$\sum_{i=1}^{m} u_i \cdot y_{ik} - \sum_{j=1}^{n} v_j \cdot x_{jk} + w \leq 0, \, to \, k = 1, 2, \ldots, \, hw \, no \, signal \, restriction \tag{3}$$

where: x_{jk} is the amount of the input j of the DMU k;
y_{ik} is the amount of the output i of the DMU k;
x_{j0} is the amount of the input j of the DMU under analysis;
y_{i0} is the amount of the output i of the DMU under analysis;
v_j is the weight of the input j for the DMU under analysis;
u_i is the weight of the output i for the DMU under analysis;
w is the scale factor;
m is the number of analyzed outputs;
n is the number of analyzed inputs; and
h is the number of DMU.

Since human development supports the adoption of environmental actions, and a better environment supports the increase in human development in a cyclical relationship [20,21], in this research, HDIm was the first input and PMVA EAI was the output. Then, we also considered the dimensions of PMVA EAI as the input, with the output being the dimensions of HDIm, similarly to what was carried out by Furlan and Mariano [6]. In this way, this research has two partial indexes: HDIm_PMVA and PMVA_HDIm. In both cases the 3 dimensions of the HDIm and the 10 dimensions of the PMVA were considered. Afterwards, the two partial indexes were multiplied to achieve the Sustainable Human Development Index (Equation (4)). Multiplication was chosen because it penalizes possible low results in one of the partial indexes [6].

$$SDHI = SDHI^{HDIm\_PMVA} \cdot SDHI^{PMVA\_HDIm} \tag{4}$$

where:

SHDI is the Sustainable Human Development Index;

$SDHI^{HDIm\_PMVA}$ is the Partial Sustainable Human Development Index (HDIm_PMVA direction);

$SDHI^{PMVA\_HDIm}$ is the Partial Sustainable Human Development Index (PMVA_HDIm direction).

Initially, the DEA index considered all 645 municipalities, generating an efficiency ranking of them. The normality test of the index (step 4) was performed using the Kolmogorov–Smirnov and Shapiro–Wilk methods. As in both tests the significance level was less than 5%, the index could not be considered to follow the normal distribution, so it was necessary to perform non-parametric tests [59].

After the normality test, we created some groups of municipalities in order to compare them and analyze specific variables (step 5). We considered four independent features: (1) classification in the PMVA, (2) level of HDIm, (3) degree of urbanization, and 4) sectoral participation in the municipal GDP.

This group's analyses were inspired by previous work in the area [6,60]. Next, the Jonckheere–Terpstra test (step 6), which is a test for ordered alternatives within independent samples, was applied in order to test the hypothesis created for each one of these features. This test is considered non-parametric and aims to verify differences between analysis groups and identify trends [61,62]. Thus, it was possible to verify whether or not there was a difference between the groups tested regarding the increasing order of analysis (low, medium, and high).

1. The classification of the municipality according to the three PMVA groups (non-qualified, qualified, and certified). From this, we develop the first hypothesis H1: municipalities with different classifications in the PMVA have different performances in the Sustainable Human Development Index.
2. The HDIm and its dimensions (HDIi, DHIh, and HDIe) were divided into three quartiles (low HDIm, up to 0.725; medium HDIm, between 0.725 and 0.753; and high HDIm, above 0.753). This does not mean that the HDIm itself is low or medium according to the UN classification, but that it is a relative measure among the municipalities of São Paulo. From this, we develop the second hypothesis H2: municipalities with different levels of human development have different performances in the Sustainable Human Development Index.
3. The degree of urbanization was divided into urban, intermediate, and rural according to the classification proposed by the Brazilian Institute of Geography and Statistics that depends on both the number of inhabitants and the rate of those living in urban areas [63]. From this, we develop the third hypothesis H3: municipalities with different degrees of urbanization have different performances in the Sustainable Human Development Index.
4. The sectoral participation in the economy considered which sector (agriculture, industry, or service) has more than 33% of participation in the municipalities' economy [64]. From this, we develop the fourth hypothesis H4: municipalities with different levels of sectoral participation in the economy have different performances in the Sustainable Human Development Index.

4. Results

4.1. Descriptive Analysis

First, we present the results from the descriptive statistics of the Sustainable Human Development Index. The index ranges from 0 to 1 and the study samples are composed of the 645 municipalities from São Paulo, with the highest value being 0.996 and the lowest 0.168. In this way, it is noticeable that none of the municipalities achieved 100% efficiency considering the final index. This happened because of the multiplication of the two partial indexes, as when using DEA there is always at least one DMU with 100% efficiency, and in the HDIm_PMVA there were 114 municipalities with 100% efficiency and in the PMVA_HDIm there were 83. The complete rank is available in the Supplementary Material (Table S1).

It is important to highlight that achieving 100% efficiency or something close to it does not mean that the DMU should not improve its indicators, since the DMU can present a low output and be considered efficient by having a low input too. That is, the DMU can be efficient in transforming its low input into output and, in this case, it needs conditions to increase its input in order to increase its output, keeping the same level of efficiency [33]. In this way, the index will allow the municipality to track its value and compare it with other municipalities with similar demographics and human development conditions.

It is possible to notice this aspect regarding the two partial indexes (Table 3), considering that the municipalities with low EAI in the PMVA and with relatively high levels in the HDIm achieve high levels in the partial PMVA_HDIm, but in the inverse relationship of inputs and outputs, the partial HDIm_PMVA, these municipalities presented low levels in the index. The municipality of Nova Europa represents this case well, considering that it is one of the municipalities in the first position with a value of 1.000 in the partial PMVA_HDIm, but it is placed in position 643 with a value of 0.185 in the partial HDIm_PMVA. This aspect highlights the importance of applying the multiplication of the two partial indexes to achieve the final index, considering that this approach allows the development of indexes that better suit the municipalities' reality. In this scenario, the municipality of Nova Europa is only in position 641 with a value of 0.185 in the Sustainable Human Development Index.

Table 3. First and last places in the partial and final indexes.

Municipality	Partial IDHm_PMVA		Partial PMVA_IDHm		Sustainable Human Development Index	
	Position	Score	Position	Score	Position	Score
Águas da Prata	1	1.000	92	0.996	1	0.996
Andradina	1	1.000	98	0.994	2	0.994
Taubaté	1	1.000	104	0.992	3	0.992
Santos	1	1.000	125	0.987	4	0.987
Vinhedo	1	1.000	125	0.987	4	0.987
Nova Europa	643	0.185	1	1.000	641	0.185
Igaraçu do Tietê	641	0.189	173	0.977	641	0.185
Paranapanema	639	0.190	307	0.957	643	0.181
Guaraci	644	0.182	182	0.975	644	0.178
Álvares Florence	645	0.179	450	0.940	645	0.168

Regarding the Sustainable Human Development Index, the first five ranked municipalities were (with the respective values): Águas da Prata (0.996), Andradina (0.994), Taubaté (0.992), Santos (0.987), and Vinhedo (0.987). All these municipalities have the PMVA certification. The municipalities with the PMVA certification tend to be in the first positions of the index, and the worst ranked in this case is the municipality of São Miguel Arcanjo (0.898), in position 140. The last five ranked municipalities were: Nova Europa (0.185), Igaraçu do Tietê (0.185), Paranapanema (0.181), Guaraci (0.178), and Álvares Florence (0.168). All of them are non-qualified according to the PMVA classification. The last 360 ranked in the index are non-qualified municipalities.

The Sustainable Human Development Index proposed increases the social aspects that are barely present in the PMVA, in such a way that it makes it closer to sustainable development rather than only environmental sustainability. The index can be an important tool to support local governments to achieve the Sustainable Development Goals. Besides working as an improvement opportunity for the PMVA, the index has been shown to be feasible to be used in other regions with some adaptations.

4.2. Comparative Analyses of the Sustainable Human Development Index

A summary of the results found in this section is presented in Table 4, and each one of the hypotheses is further discussed.

Table 4. Summary of the hypothesis test.

Hypothesis	Null Hypothesis	Test	Sig. [a,b]	Decision
H1	Municipalities with different classifications in the PMVA have different performances in the Sustainable Human Development Index	Jonckheere–Terpstra	0.000	Accepted
H2	Municipalities with different levels of human development have different performances in the Sustainable Human Development Index	Jonckheere–Terpstra	0.000	Accepted
H3	Municipalities with different degrees of urbanization have different performances in the Sustainable Human Development Index	Jonckheere–Terpstra	0.000	Accepted
H4	Municipalities with different levels of sectoral participation in the economy have different performances in the Sustainable Human Development Index	Jonckheere–Terpstra	0.001	Accepted

[a] The significance level is 0.50; [b] the asymptotic significance is displayed.

4.2.1. PMVA Analyses

The first analysis regarding the created groups considers the classifications of the PMVA: non-qualified, qualified, and certified. The non-parametric test of Jonckheere-Terpstra was applied, which is indicated for analyses of ordinal increscent and decrescent categories (Table 5). The results indicated that there were differences between the groups, with asymptotic significance (two-sided test) equal to 0.000 and, therefore, hypothesis 1 was accepted.

Table 5. PMVA independent-samples Jonckheere–Terpstra test for ordered alternatives summary.

Total n	645
Test Statistic	101,580.500
Standard Error	2285.779
Standardized Test Statistic	21.516
Asymptotic Sig. (2-sided test)	0.000

Then, it was possible to perform the pairwise comparison (Table 6) and the construction of the error bar graphs (Figure 3), in which all the three classifications are statistically different. The non-qualified municipalities present the lowest values in the Sustainable Human Development Index, the qualified municipalities present intermediate values, and the certified municipalities present the highest values of the index. It is noticeable that the mean values of the non-qualified municipalities are much lower than the mean values of the qualified and certified municipalities.

Table 6. Pairwise comparisons of the PMVA classification.

Sample 1 vs. Sample 2	Statistical Test	Std. Error	Std. Test Statistic	Sig.	Adj. Sig. [a]
Non-qualified vs. Qualified	50,313.000	1545.184	15.704	0.000	0.000
Non-qualified vs. Certified	40,760.000	1337.886	15.146	0.000	0.000
Qualified vs. Certified	10,507.500	462.302	10.062	0.000	0.000

Each line tests the null hypothesis that the distributions of the Sample 1 and Sample 2 are the same. Asymptotic significance (1-sided tests) is displayed. The significance level is 0.050. [a] The significance values were adjusted with Bonferroni correction for multiple tests.

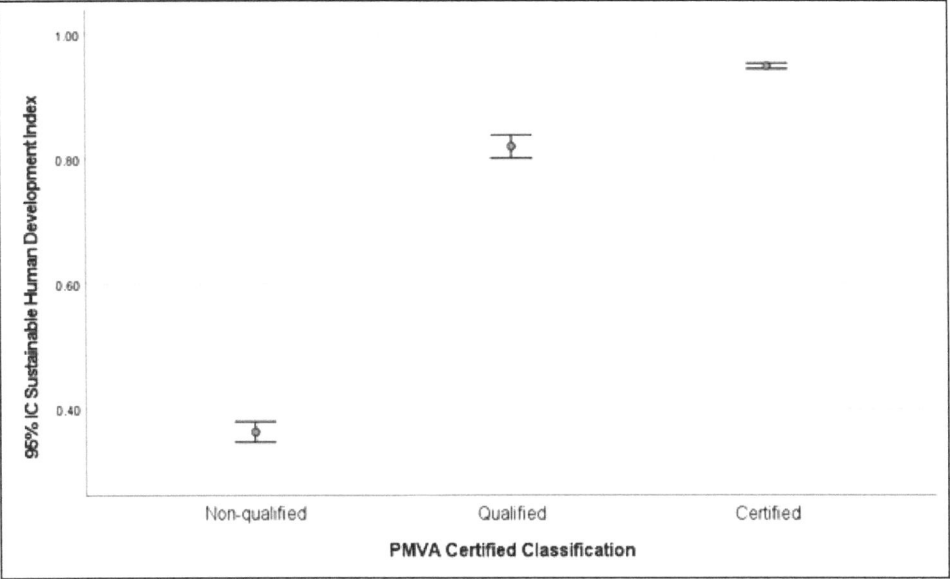

Figure 3. Error bar graph of the municipalities by classification of the PMVA.

Another important aspect regarding this analysis is that the municipalities in the same group present a very low variation between them, especially the certified municipalities (Figure 3).

Regarding the classification of the PMVA, the following maps were developed in order to illustrate the scenario of each group. To accomplish this, we created three stratification levels, with the values in the Sustainable Human Development Index ranging from 0.00 to 0.44, 0.44 to 0.72, and 0.72 to 1.00. The first map shows the municipality in the lower stratification (Figure 4). Only non-qualified municipalities appear in this context.

However, not all municipalities in the non-qualified group follow this trend. Porangaba is an interesting case in this group: the municipality has an EAI score of 31.79 in the PMVA and a value of 0.971 in the Sustainable Human Development Index (17th position), in such a way that Porangaba is the most highly ranked non-qualified municipality in the index. Porongaba features in the group of municipalities with a low level of HDIm (0.703), other municipalities in a similar condition are: Sete Barras (EAI score of 21.35 and HDIm score of 0.673) and Itobi (EAI score of 35.6 HDIm score of 0.717), with a value of 0.940 (74th position) and 0.934 (79th position), respectively, in the Sustainable Human Development Index. Since these municipalities present this peculiar feature, they can be used as benchmarks for municipalities in a similar situation, and future studies should analyze these municipalities more deeply in order to understand the reasons for their performance.

The best positions in the ranking are of the certified municipalities, followed by the qualified ones. However, some non-qualified municipalities also figure in the highest levels. Figure 5 illustrates all municipalities that have the highest stratification value of the Sustainable Human Development Index.

Figure 4. Municipalities in the lower part of the stratification.

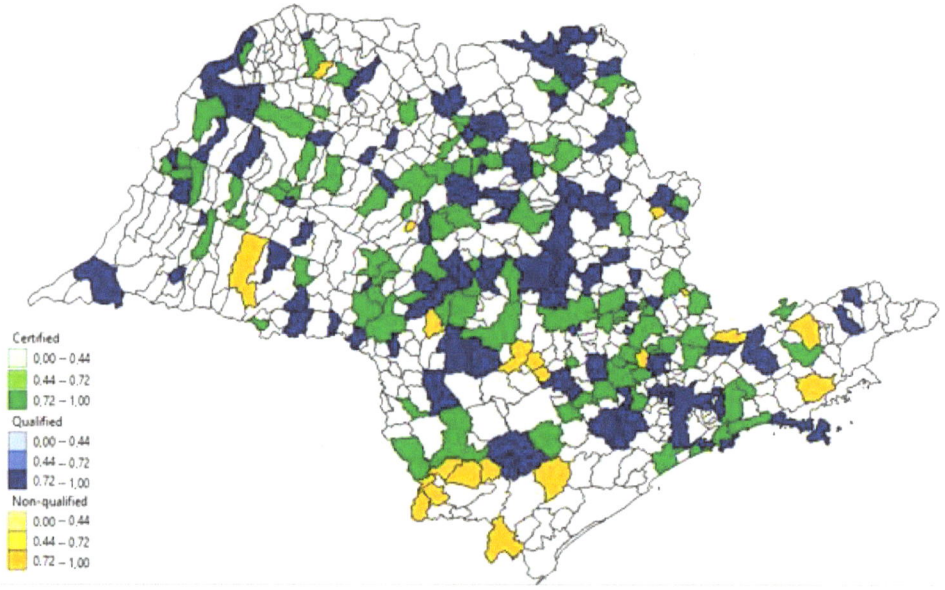

Figure 5. Municipalities in the highest stratification of the Sustainable Human Development Index.

Regarding the intermediate stratification of the index, Figure 6 presents how there are relatively few municipalities in this level, with a balance between the non-qualified and qualified municipalities. It is also noticeable that there are no certified municipalities in this scenario.

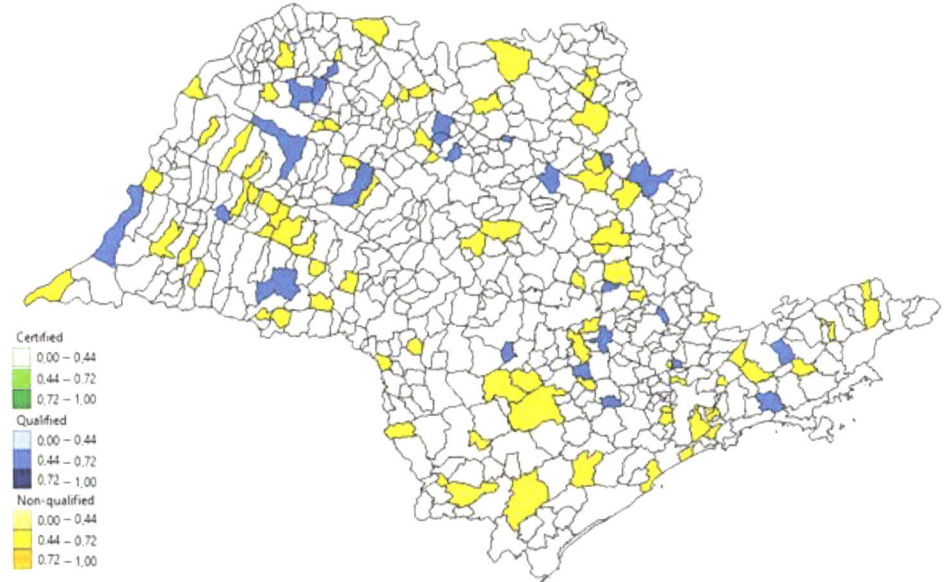

Figure 6. Municipalities in the intermediate range of the Sustainable Human Development Index.

In this way, all the certified municipalities present results in the highest level of the index, while the qualified municipalities are located in the intermediate and high levels, and the non-qualified municipalities have representatives in all levels of the index, with a higher number of municipalities in the lowest level (Figure 7).

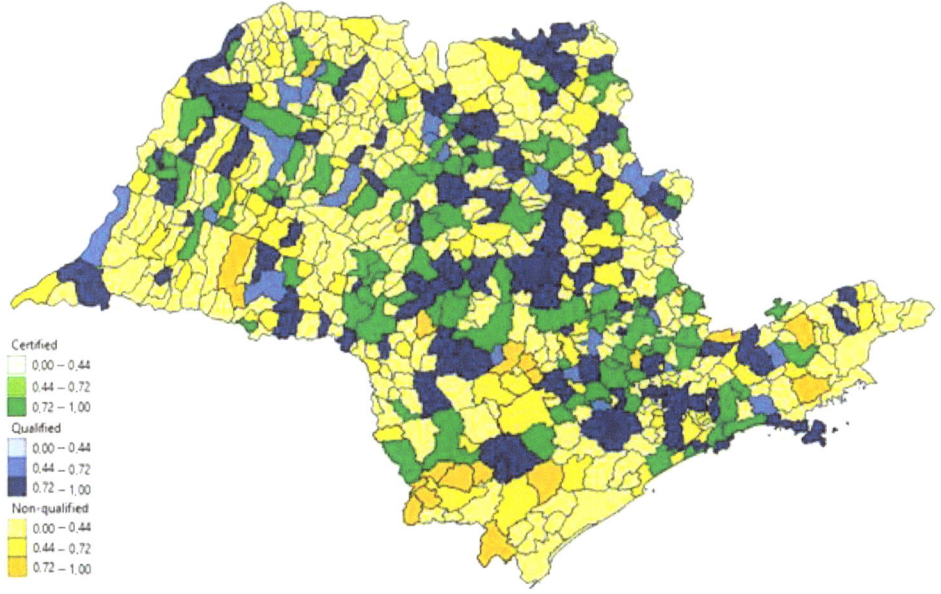

Figure 7. Sustainable Human Development Index.

Considering the geographical distribution of the municipalities in the index, the central and southeast regions of the state concentrate the municipalities with the highest values of the Sustainable Human Development Index. The west and northwest regions, on the other hand, present the highest concentration of municipalities with the lowest values in the index (Figure 7). Considering the two biggest metropolitan areas of São Paulo, it is interesting to note that from the 39 municipalities that comprise the São Paulo metropolitan area, only eight (21.51%) municipalities (Barueri, Guararema, Itaquaquecetuba, Mogi das Cruzes, Osasco, Santana de Parnaíba, São Paulo, and Suzano) are above the value of 0.72 in the developed index, and only Guararema, Mogi das Cruzes, and Osasco are certified by the PMVA. In the Campinas metropolitan area, on the other hand, from the 20 municipalities that comprise it, 12 (66.67%) municipalities (Americana, Campinas, Cosmópolis, Holambra, Hortolândia, Indaiatuba, Itatiba, Jaguariúna, Nova Odessa, Santa Bárbara d'Oeste, Santo Antônio de Posse, and Vinhedo) present values higher than 0.72 in the index, and only three of them are not certified, but qualified by the PMVA (Cosmópolis, Hortolândia, and Santo Antônio de Posse).

4.2.2. HDIm Analyses

Regarding the HDIm classification, the created groups are: low, medium, and high. The results of the Jonckheere–Terpstra test (Table 7) indicated that there were differences between the groups, with asymptotic significance (two-sided test) equal to 0.000 and, therefore, hypothesis 2 was accepted.

Table 7. HDIm independent-samples Jonckheere–Terpstra test for ordered alternatives summary.

Total n	645
Test Statistic	80,188.000
Standard Error	2568.902
Standardized Test Statistic	4.224
Asymptotic Sig. (2-sided test)	0.000

In this way, the pairwise comparison represented in Table 8 demonstrates that the municipalities in the high HDIm group are different from the other HDIm groups. This indicates that when categorizing the municipalities according to their human development, municipalities that achieve a higher HDIm (above 0.753) ensure a certain level of environmental justice when compared to other municipalities. In this way, there might be a threshold point where a certain level of HDIm matches with better results in the proposed index, in such a way that the municipality may have surpassed basic barriers to development, such as low levels of education and health.

Table 8. Pairwise comparisons of Human_Development_Classification.

Sample 1 vs. Sample 2	Statistical Test	Std. Error	Std. Test Statistic	Sig.	Adj. Sig. [a]
Medium HDIm vs. Low HDIm	21,228.500	1282.327	−1.385	0.083	0.0249
Medium HDIm vs. High HDIm	29,978.500	1284.158	5.347	0.000	0.000
Low HDIm vs. High HDIm	28,981.000	1287.089	4.476	0.000	0.000

Each line tests the null hypothesis that the distributions of Sample 1 and Sample 2 are the same. Asymptotic significance (1-sided tests) is displayed. The significance level is 0.050. [a] The significance values were adjusted with Bonferroni correction for multiple tests.

The literature [18,21,65] presents cases of this threshold point of development for environmental performance in some countries, which may occur due to the level of priority given to different areas. Economic growth and political and social stabilization, for example, are usually preferred over environmental aspects.

The error bar graph (Figure 8) illustrates the difference between the performance of the municipalities when categorized for their human development. From the graph, it is possible to notice that there is a growing tendency toward the performance in the Sustainable Human Development Index from the increase in the human development of the municipality. It is also interesting to note that the differences between the mean values of the municipalities in the same group are higher than in the case of the groups from the PMVA classification (Figure 3). Municipalities in the same HDIm group presented scattered values related to the index.

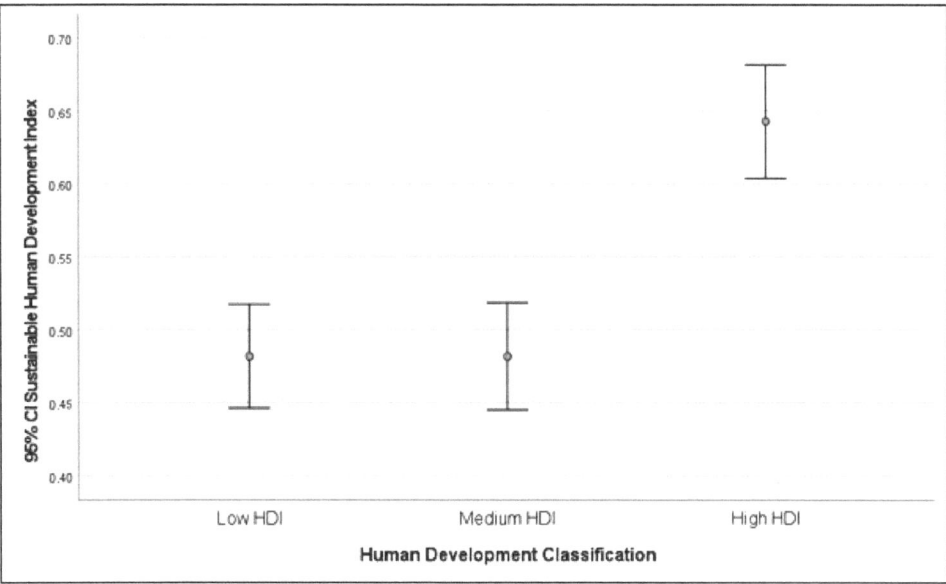

Figure 8. Error bar graph of the municipalities by classification of the HDIm.

Similar to some municipalities with a low level in the HDIm, as already mentioned, that presented good results in the Sustainable Human Development Index, other municipalities with high HDIm presented relatively low values in the index, such as São Caetano do Sul and Águas de São Pedro, which are the two municipalities with the highest HDIm in São Paulo, of 0.862 and 0.854, respectively, but that are only classified as non-qualified in the PMVA (37.11 EAI and 11.00 EAI, respectively). This resulted in low values in the proposed index: 0.679 (231st position) and 0.225 (574th position), respectively.

Municipalities that present good results in the index with low HDIm may be useful benchmarks for municipalities in a similar condition, and they can also be better analyzed by the PMVA. Special attention should be given to these municipalities with high HDIm but low performance in the index, in order to understand the reasons for the performance, for example, if it is due to lack of interest in the program or another specific difficulty in its implementation.

4.2.3. Urbanization Analyses

Considering the urbanization degree, the created groups are: rural, intermediate, and urban. The results of the Jonckheere–Terpstra test (Table 9) indicated that there were differences between the groups, with asymptotic significance (two-sided test) equal to 0.000 and, therefore, hypothesis 3 was accepted.

Table 9. Urbanization degree independent-samples Jonckheere–Terpstra test for ordered alternatives summary.

Total n	645
Test Statistic	71,630.000
Standard Error	2434.793
Standardized Test Statistic	5.208
Asymptotic Sig. (2-sided test)	0.000

In this way, the pairwise comparison represented in Table 10 demonstrates that urban municipalities are different from the other groups.

Table 10. Pairwise comparisons of urbanization degree.

Sample 1 vs. Sample 2	Statistical Test	Std. Error	Std. Test Statistic	Sig.	Adj. Sig. [a]
Intermediate vs. Rural	6665.000	600.509	−0.891	0.186	0.559
Intermediate vs. Urban	52,418.000	2010.023	5.482	0.000	0.000
Rural vs. Urban	12,547.000	836.602	2.626	0.004	0.013

Each line tests the null hypothesis that the distributions of Sample 1 and Sample 2 are the same. Asymptotic significance (1-sided tests) is displayed. The significance level is 0.050. [a] The significance values were adjusted with Bonferroni correction for multiple tests.

Considering the urbanization degree of the municipalities, it is noticeable that the ones considered urban have a better performance in the Sustainable Human Development Index, while the municipalities considered rural or intermediate did not present statistical differences between them (Figure 9). This result could be related to the different sets of opportunities and access to basic infrastructures that the urbanization process offers for sustainable human development, such as sanitation coverage and easier access to education and health facilities [66]. It is also possible that more urbanized municipalities have more infrastructural and technical capacities to develop more municipal environmental management actions.

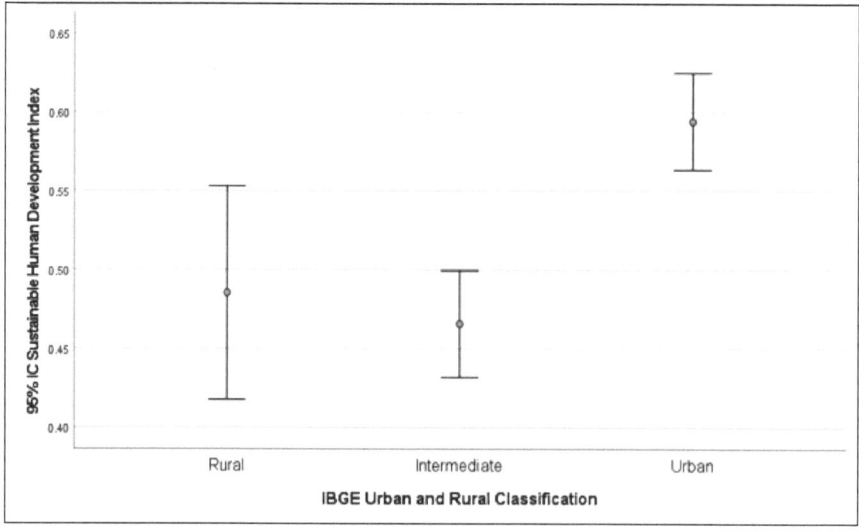

Figure 9. Error bar graph of the municipalities by urbanization degree.

Considering the classification of the municipality in the PMVA with its degree of urbanization, it is noticeable that municipalities with certification present similar values among the three degrees of urbanization. Regarding the qualified municipalities, the intermediate and urban municipalities present similar values, while the disproportion presented by the rural municipalities is due to the small sample of municipalities with this combination of features. An interesting aspect is that there is a difference among the non-qualified municipalities, as the rural ones have better performance in the index compared to non-qualified intermediate and urban municipalities (Figure 10).

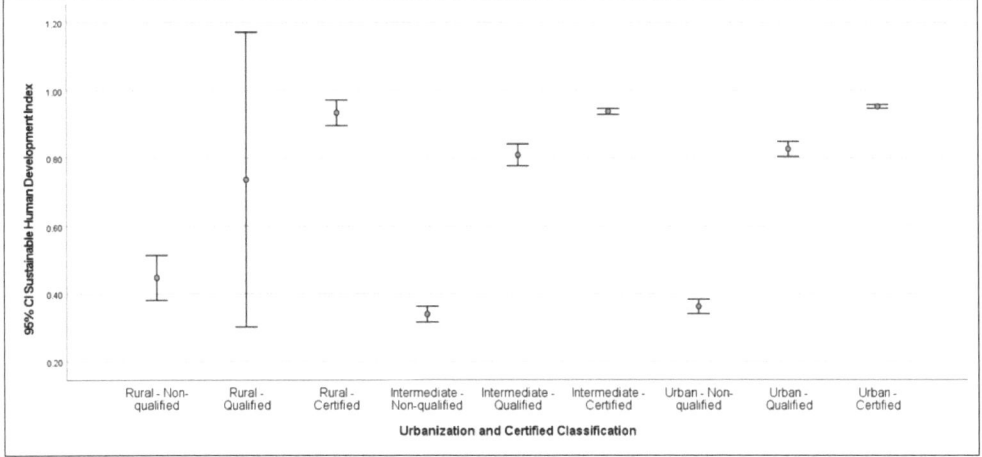

Figure 10. Error bar graph of the municipalities by degree of urbanization and classification of the PMVA.

4.2.4. Sectoral Economic Participation Analyses

Considering the sectoral economic participation, the created groups are: agriculture, industrial, and services. These results of the Jonckheere–Terpstra test (Table 11) indicated that there were differences between the groups, with asymptotic significance (two-sided test) equal to 0.001 and, therefore, hypothesis 4 was accepted.

Table 11. Sectoral participation in the economy independent-samples Jonckheere–Terpstra test for ordered alternatives summary.

Total *n*	645
Test Statistic	44,118.500
Standard Error	1958.866
Standardized Test Statistic	3.390
Asymptotic Sig. (2-sided test)	0.001

In this way, the pairwise comparison represented in Table 12 demonstrates that municipalities with higher participation of services in the economy are different from the other groups.

Table 12. Pairwise comparisons of sectoral economic participation.

Sample 1 vs. Sample 2	Statistical Test	Std. Error	Std. Test Statistic	Sig.	Adj. Sig. [a]
Industrial vs. Agriculture	2278.500	231.965	−0.136	0.446	1.000
Industrial vs. Service	16,589.500	1141.216	2.344	0.010	0.029
Agriculture vs. Service	25,250.500	1446.306	2.765	0.003	0.019

Each line tests the null hypothesis that the distributions of Sample 1 and Sample 2 are the same. Asymptotic significance (1-sided tests) is displayed. The significance level is 0.050. [a] The significance values were adjusted with Bonferroni correction for multiple tests.

Considering the main economic activity in each municipality, those that present higher participation of services in their economy presented better results in the Sustainable Human Development Index than the others. There were no statistical differences between municipalities with higher participation in agriculture and industry (Figure 11). These results could be related to the importance that the service sector may have in increasing economic growth, reducing poverty, and supporting job creation—including higher rates of women's employment [67].

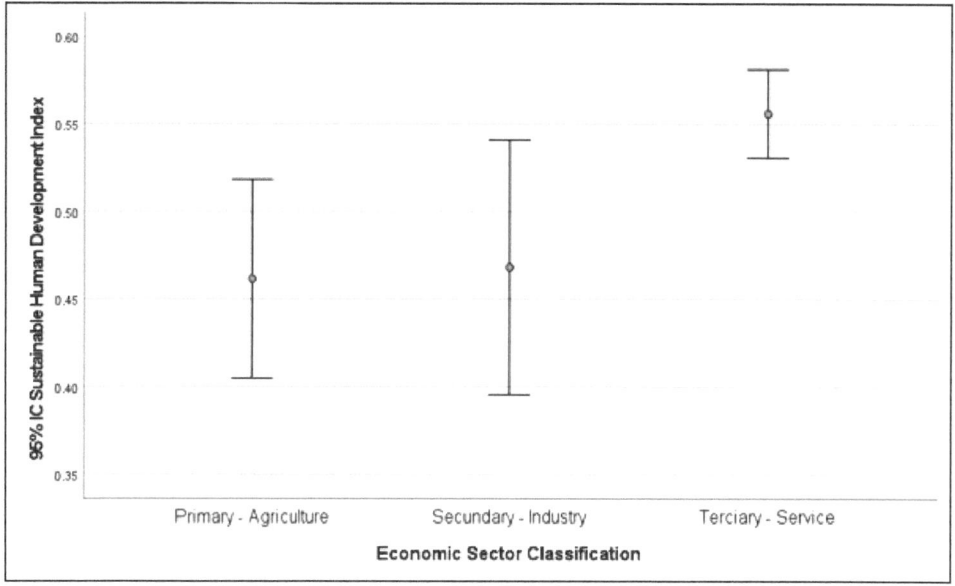

Figure 11. Error bar graph of the municipalities by sectoral economic participation.

5. Conclusions

This research presented the development of a sustainable human development index at a local level that portrays the idea presented in the research framework (Figure 1), that is, human development and municipal environmental management have a cyclical relationship. In this research, the index was developed using data from the HDIm and the PMVA, which are suitable for the Brazilian context. Other countries and regions can use the same method with specific data to cover human development and municipal environmental management—sustainable action—to develop an index suitable for their context.

The results found in this research indicate that municipalities with higher HDI levels obtained better results in the Sustainable Human Development Index. This may have occurred because the municipalities have reached a basic development level, from which more investments began to be made in the environmental area, such as in infrastructure.

The results also indicate that more urbanized municipalities and with higher participation of services in the economy presented a better performance in the index, which may be due to opportunities derived from urbanization and the higher maturity level required for a service economy. It is important to highlight that these considerations are related to the environmental aspects considered in this research, and other environmental elements need to be carefully analyzed; Polloni-Silva et al. [68], for example, found that the service sector is related to considerable CO_2 emissions in São Paulo.

In the results, we also identified differences between the three levels of classification in the PMVA, where certified municipalities tend to show better results than qualified and non-qualified ones. Future studies can analyze whether the fact that a municipality obtains a good sustainability index (or PMVA certification) provides some positive effect on neighboring municipalities.

For environmental justice, when considering that the PMVA certification depends on the score achieved by the municipalities, and that this achievement results in the preference for obtaining resources from the state Secretary of the Environment, it is important to understand if the municipalities that do not achieve this score are not interested in the program or if they do not have sufficient resources to do so. The results of the proposed index indicate that municipalities with high HDIm have the best performances, that is, the municipalities with better levels of human development would receive more resources to improve their environmental performance. Meanehile, the municipalities with fewer resources and lower HDIm—which most need these resources [61]—would continue to face difficulties to develop environmentally and, consequently, improve their HDIm.

The PMVA is an important initiative of the state of São Paulo, unique in Brazil, however, there is still space and opportunity for improvement. The program itself has undergone constant improvement processes. Thus, it is expected that this research can also contribute to the development of the program and others that may arise in other Brazilian states and in other countries. Therefore, it is believed that the contributions of this research are important from an academic and practical point of view. Another positive point is the incorporation of the environmental justice aspect, since, as indicated by Agyeman, Bullard, and Evans [28], many sustainability policies are implemented without incorporating this aspect.

Some limitations of this study are expected to open multiple avenues for future research. First, we proceeded with an empirical analysis by using secondary data. However, this study did not present a detailed analysis of case studies. In this sense, future research might incorporate some relevant case studies to explain the rank position of our indicator. Second, we did not explain the determinants of DEA scores, which is relevant to reveal how regions might increase sustainable human development. Future studies might use econometric models to understand which variables explain DEA scores. Third, we did not use financial resources as inputs in our analysis, which did not consider aspects of social and eco-efficiency. New studies can investigate new DEA rankings considering financial aspects to sustainable human development. Fourth, we considered regions in São Paulo. However, Brazil is a vast and heterogeneous country that allocates important areas for the environment (i.e., Amazonia). For this reason, we encourage future studies to apply our indicator to the whole Brazilian territory.

Finally, it is important to highlight the voluntary nature of the PMVA, so that all municipalities that obtained low values in the index do not necessarily present low sustainability aspects. However, this does not influence the proposal of the index combining human development and environmental management at the municipality level. Moreover, these results can support the improvement of this type of environmental management program, aiming to increase the participation of the municipalities and consequently their levels of sustainability.

Supplementary Materials: The following supporting information can be downloaded at: https://www.mdpi.com/article/10.3390/infrastructures7020012/s1, Table S1: Complete ranking of the Sustainable Human Development Index.

Author Contributions: Conceptualization, P.A.B.L., G.D.P.J. and M.F.; methodology, P.A.B.L., G.D.P.J., M.F. and E.B.M.; software, M.F.; validation, R.A.G.B., G.H.R.S., D.F. and E.B.M.; formal analysis, P.A.B.L., G.D.P.J., T.L.S. and M.F.; writing—original draft preparation, P.A.B.L. and G.D.P.J.; supervision, E.B.M. All authors have read and agreed to the published version of the manuscript.

Funding: The APC was funded by PROAP/CAPES via PROPG/UNESP.

Institutional Review Board Statement: Not applicable.

Informed Consent Statement: Not applicable.

Data Availability Statement: Not applicable.

Conflicts of Interest: The authors declare no conflict of interest. The funders had no role in the design of the study; in the collection, analyses, or interpretation of data; in the writing of the manuscript, or in the decision to publish the results.

References

1. Mariano, E.B.; Rebelatto, D.A.N. Transformation of wealth produced into quality of life: Analysis of the social efficiency of nation-states with the DEA's triple index approach. *J. Oper. Res. Soc.* **2014**, *65*, 1664–1681. [CrossRef]
2. Assa, J. Less is more: The implicit sustainability content of the human development index. *Ecol. Econ.* **2021**, *185*, 107045. [CrossRef]
3. Mariano, E.B. *Progresso e Desenvolvimento Humano: Teorias e Indicadores de Riqueza, Qualidade de Vida, Felicidade e Desigualdade*, 1st ed.; Alta Books: Rio de Janeiro, Brazil, 2019.
4. Mariano, E.B.; Sobreiro, V.A.; Rebelatto, D.A.N. Human development and data envelopment analysis: A structured literature review. *Omega* **2015**, *54*, 33–49. [CrossRef]
5. Santana, N.B.; Rebelatto, D.A.N.; Périco, A.E.; Mariano, E.B. Sustainable development in the BRICS countries: An efficiency analysis by data envelopment. *Int. J. Sustain. Dev. World Ecol.* **2014**, *21*, 259–272. [CrossRef]
6. Furlan, M.; Mariano, E. Guiding the nations through fair low-carbon economy cycles: A climate justice index proposal. *Ecol. Indic.* **2021**, *125*, 107615. [CrossRef]
7. Moreno-Pires, S.; Fidélis, T. A proposal to explore the role of sustainability indicators in local governance contexts: The case of Palmela, Portugal. *Ecol. Indic.* **2012**, *21*, 608–615. [CrossRef]
8. Dantas, M.K.; Passador, C.S. Programa Município VerdeAzul: Uma análise integrada da gestão ambiental no estado de São Paulo. *Organ. Soc.* **2020**, *27*, 820–854. [CrossRef]
9. Hughes, S. Voluntary Environmental Programs in the Public Sector: Evaluating an Urban Water Conservation Program in California. *Policy Stud. J.* **2012**, *40*, 650–673. [CrossRef]
10. São Paulo. Secretaria de Estado do Meio Ambiente. Resolução nº 21, de 16 de maio de 2007. Dispõe Sobre a Instituição dos Projetos Ambientais Estratégicos da Secretaria do Meio Ambiente. Available online: https://www.infraestruturameioambiente.sp.gov.br/legislacao/category/municipio-verde-azul/ (accessed on 16 November 2020).
11. São Paulo. Secretaria de Estado do Meio Ambiente. Resolução nº 33, de 28 de Março de 2018. Estabelece Procedimentos Operacionais e os Parâmetros de Avaliação da Qualificação para a Certificação e Certificação no Âmbito do Programa Município VerdeAzul. Available online: https://www.infraestruturameioambiente.sp.gov.br/legislacao/category/municipio-verde-azul/ (accessed on 16 November 2020).
12. Ahvenniemi, H.; Huovila, A.; Pinto-Seppä, I.; Airaksinen, M. What are the differences between sustainable and smart cities? *Cities* **2017**, *60*, 234–245. [CrossRef]
13. Haughton, G. Environmental justice and the sustainable city. *J. Plan. Educ. Res.* **1999**, *18*, 233–243. [CrossRef]
14. Sena, A.; Ebi, K.L.; Freitas, C.; Corvalan, C.; Barcellos, C. Indicators to measure risk of disaster associated with drought: Implications for the health sector. *PLoS ONE* **2017**, *12*, e0181394. [CrossRef] [PubMed]
15. UN—United Nations. Sustainable Development Goals. Available online: https://sdgs.un.org/goals (accessed on 8 May 2021).
16. Griggs, D.; Stafford-Smith, M.; Gaffney, O.; Rockström, J.; Öhman, M.C.; Shyamsundar, P.; Steffen, W.; Glaser, G.; Kanie, N.; Noble, I. Sustainable development goals for people and planet. *Nature* **2013**, *495*, 305–307. [CrossRef] [PubMed]
17. Moyer, J.D.; Bohl, D.K. Alternative pathways to human development: Assessing trade-offs and synergies in achieving the Sustainable Development Goals. *Futures* **2019**, *105*, 199–210. [CrossRef]
18. Asongu, S.A.; Odhiambo, N.M. Economic development thresholds for a green economy in sub-Saharan Africa. *Energy Explor. Exploit.* **2021**, *38*, 3–17. [CrossRef]
19. Spiliotopoulou, M.; Roseland, M. Urban Sustainability: From Theory Influences to Practical Agendas. *Sustainability* **2020**, *12*, 7245. [CrossRef]
20. Alves, M.W.F.M.; Mariano, E.B. Climate justice and human development: A systematic literature review. *J. Clean. Prod.* **2018**, *202*, 360–375. [CrossRef]
21. Cerqueira, P.A.; Soukiazis, E.; Proença, S. Assessing the linkages between recycling, renewable energy and sustainable development: Evidence from the OECD countries. *Environ. Dev. Sustain.* **2020**, *23*, 1–26. [CrossRef]

22. Lima, P.A.B.; Jesus, G.M.K.; Ortiz, C.R.; Frascareli, F.C.O.; Souza, F.B.; Mariano, E.B. Sustainable Development as Freedom: Trends and Opportunities for the Circular Economy in the Human Development Literature. *Sustainability* **2021**, *13*, 13407. [CrossRef]
23. UNDP—United Nations Development Programme. Human Development Report 2016: Human Development for Everyone, United Nations Development Programme. Available online: http://hdr.undp.org/sites/default/files/2016_human_development_report.pdf (accessed on 7 January 2022).
24. Sen, A. *Development as Freedom*; Oxford Paperbacks: Oxford, UK, 2010.
25. Anand, S.; Sen, A. Human development and economic sustainability. *World Dev.* **2000**, *28*, 2029–2049. [CrossRef]
26. Brundtland, G.H.; Khalid, M.; Agnelli, S.; Al-Athel, S.; Chidzero, B.J. *Our Common Future*; World Commission on Environment and Development: New York, NY, USA, 1987.
27. Sen, A. The ends and means of sustainability. *J. Hum. Dev. Capab.* **2013**, *14*, 6–20. [CrossRef]
28. Agyeman, J.; Bullard, R.D.; Evans, B. Exploring the nexus: Bringing together sustainability, environmental justice and equity. *Space Polity* **2002**, *6*, 77–90. [CrossRef]
29. Nagy, J.A.; Benedek, J.; Ivan, K. Measuring sustainable development goals at a local level: A case of a metropolitan area in Romania. *Sustainability* **2018**, *10*, 3962. [CrossRef]
30. Frugoli, P.A.; Almeida, C.M.V.B.; Agostinho, F.; Giannetti, B.F.; Huisingh, D. Can measures of well-being and progress help societies to achieve sustainable development? *J. Clean. Prod.* **2015**, *90*, 370–380. [CrossRef]
31. Gasper, D. Is Sen's capability approach an adequate basis for considering human development? *Rev. Political Econ.* **2002**, *14*, 435–461. [CrossRef]
32. Hickel, J. The sustainable development index: Measuring the ecological efficiency of human development in the anthropocene. *Ecol. Econ.* **2020**, *167*, 106331. [CrossRef]
33. Dalberto, C.R.; Ervilha, G.T.; Bohn, L.; Gomes, A.P. Índice de desenvolvimento humano eficiente: Uma mensuração alternativa do bem-estar das nações. *Pesqui. Planej. Econ.* **2015**, *45*, 337–363.
34. Morse, S. Stirring the pot. Influence of changes in methodology of the Human Development Index on reporting by the press. *Ecol. Indic.* **2014**, *45*, 245–254. [CrossRef]
35. Programa Das Nações Unidas Para O Desenvolvimento (PNUD); Instituto de Pesquisa Econômica Aplicada (IPEA); Fundação João Pinheiro (FJP). Available online: http://www.atlasbrasil.org.br/acervo/biblioteca (accessed on 15 January 2021).
36. Martins, P.C.R.; Pontes, E.R.J.C.; Higa, L.T. Convergência entre as Taxas de Mortalidade Infantil e os Índices de Desenvolvimento Humano no Brasil no período de 2000 a 2010. *Interações* **2018**, *19*, 291–303. [CrossRef]
37. Mostovoy, N.; Romano, G.H.C.; Rabinowitz, D.; Soroker, S.; Carmi, N. The municipal council, my neighbors and me: Social environmental influences in the city. *J. Environ. Manag.* **2021**, *288*, 112393. [CrossRef]
38. Boni, A.; Lopez-Fogues, A.; Walker, M. Higher education and the post-2015 agenda: A contribution from the human development approach. *J. Glob. Ethics* **2016**, *12*, 17–28. [CrossRef]
39. Fowler, A.R., III; Close, A.G. It ain't easy being green: Macro, meso, and micro green advertising agendas. *J. Advert.* **2012**, *41*, 119–132. [CrossRef]
40. Pandit, A.; Minné, E.A.; Li, F.; Brown, H.; Jeong, H.; James, J.-A.C.; Newell, J.P.; Weissburg, M.; Chang, M.E.; Xu, M.; et al. Infrastructure ecology: An evolving paradigm for sustainable urban development. *J. Clean. Prod.* **2017**, *163*, S19–S27. [CrossRef]
41. Tortajada, C. Water infrastructure as an essential element for human development. *Int. J. Water Resour. Dev.* **2014**, *30*, 8–19. [CrossRef]
42. Delanka-Pedige, H.M.K.; Munasinghe-Arachchige, S.P.; Abeysiriwardana-Arachchige, I.S.A.; Nirmalakhandan, N. Wastewater infrastructure for sustainable cities: Assessment based on UN sustainable development goals (SDGs). *Int. J. Sustain. Dev. World Ecol.* **2021**, *28*, 203–209. [CrossRef]
43. De Oliveira, J.A.P. Implementing environmental policies in developing countries through decentralization: The case of protected areas in Bahia, Brazil. *World Dev.* **2002**, *30*, 1713–1736. [CrossRef]
44. Jakob, M.; Steckel, J.C.; Klasen, S.; Lay, J.; Grunewald, N.; Martinez-Zarzoso, I.; Renner, S.; Etdenhofer, O. Feasible mitigation actions in developing countries. *Nat. Clim. Chang.* **2014**, *4*, 961–968. [CrossRef]
45. Roy, K.C.; Tisdell, C.A. Good governance in sustainable development: The impact of institutions. *Int. J. Soc. Econ.* **1998**, *25*, 1310–1325. [CrossRef]
46. Button, K. City management and urban environmental indicators. *Ecol. Econ.* **2002**, *40*, 217–233. [CrossRef]
47. Mancini, R.M.O.M. Política Ambiental Local: A Influência do Programa Município VerdeAzul. Doctoral Thesis, University of São Paulo, Sao Paulo, Brazil, 2016.
48. Lodi, D.C.R. Ação Ambiental Voluntária nos Municípios: Um Estudo Sobre os Fatores que Influenciam a Participação Voluntária dos Municípios do Estado de São Paulo no Programa Município VerdeAzul. Doctoral Thesis, University of São Paulo, Sao Paulo, Brazil, 2017.
49. Bruzzi, L.; Boragno, V.; Serrano-Bernardo, F.A.; Verità, S.; Rosúa-Campos, J.L. Environmental management policy in a coastal tourism municipality: The case study of Cervia (Italy). *Local Environ.* **2011**, *16*, 93–113. [CrossRef]
50. *Programa Município VerdeAzul: Relatório Gerencial 2018–2019*; Secretaria de Infraestrutura e Meio Ambiente: São Paulo, Brazil, 2020.
51. Charnes, A.; Cooper, W.W.; Rhodes, E. Measuring the efficiency of decision making units. *Eur. J. Oper. Res.* **1978**, *2*, 429–444. [CrossRef]
52. Golany, B.; Roll, Y. An application procedure for DEA. *Omega* **1989**, *17*, 237–250. [CrossRef]

53. SEADE—Fundação Sistema Estadual de Análise de Dados Home Page. Available online: https://www.seade.gov.br/# (accessed on 15 January 2021).
54. Rosano-Peña, C.; Guarnieri, P.; Sobreiro, V.A.; Serrano, A.L.M.; Kimura, H. A measure of sustainability of Brazilian agribusiness using directional distance functions and data envelopment analysis. *Int. J. Sustain. Dev. World Ecol.* **2014**, *21*, 210–222. [CrossRef]
55. IPEA—Instituto de Pesquisa Econômica Aplicada Atlas do Desenvolvimento Humano no Brasil. Available online: http://www.atlasbrasil.org.br/consulta/planilha (accessed on 15 March 2021).
56. WHO—World Health Organization. Impact of COVID-19 on People's Livelihoods Their Health and Our food Systems. Available online: https://www.who.int/news/item/13-10-2020-impact-of-covid-19-on-people\T1\textquoterights-livelihoods-their-health-and-our-food-systems (accessed on 17 January 2021).
57. Kulkarni, B.N.; Anantharama, V. Repercussions of COVID-19 pandemic on municipal solid waste management: Challenges and opportunities. *Sci. Total. Environ.* **2020**, *743*, 140693. [CrossRef] [PubMed]
58. Secretaria de Infraestrutura e Meio Ambiente PMVA. Available online: https://www.infraestruturameioambiente.sp.gov.br/verdeazuldigital/pontuacoes/ (accessed on 9 November 2020).
59. Rossoni, H.A.V.; Faria, M.T.D.S.; Heller, L. Aspectos socioeconômicos e de desenvolvimento humano municipal determinantes na ausência de prestadores de serviços de esgotamento sanitário no Brasil. *Eng. Sanit. Ambient.* **2020**, *25*, 393–402. [CrossRef]
60. Lo, S.-F. The differing capabilities to respond to the challenge of climate change across Annex Parties under the Kyoto Protocol. *Environ. Sci. Policy* **2010**, *13*, 42–54. [CrossRef]
61. Bougara, H.; Hamed, K.B.; Borgemeister, C.; Tischbein, B.; Kumar, N. Analyzing trend and variability of rainfall in the Tafna basin (Northwestern Algeria). *Atmosphere* **2020**, *11*, 347. [CrossRef]
62. Mambrey, V.; Rakete, S.; Tobollik, M.; Shoko, D.; Moyo, D.; Schutzmeier, P.; Steckling-Muschack, N.; Muteti-Fana, S.; Bose-O'reilly, S. Artisanal and small-scale gold mining: A cross-sectional assessment of occupational mercury exposure and exposure risk factors in Kadoma and Shurugwi, Zimbabwe. *Environ. Res.* **2020**, *184*, 109379. [CrossRef]
63. IBGE—Instituto Brasileiro de Geografia e Estatística. Classificação e Caracterização dos Espaços Urbanos e Rurais do Brasil. Available online: https://biblioteca.ibge.gov.br/visualizacao/livros/liv100643.pdf (accessed on 4 November 2021).
64. SEADE—Agência de Estatísticas do Estado de São Paulo. Repositório, Tabela—PIB 2018. Available online: http://repositorio.seade.gov.br/dataset/pib-municipal-2002-2018/resource/ce96b862-f3d0-4bea-95fa-5ad7e85c4c06 (accessed on 20 November 2021).
65. Caniato, M.; Tudor, T.; Vaccari, M. International governance structures for health-care waste management: A systematic review of scientific literature. *J. Environ. Manag.* **2015**, *153*, 93–107. [CrossRef] [PubMed]
66. Seto, K.C.; Golden, J.S.; Alberti, M.; Turner, B.L., II. Sustainability in an urbanizing planet. *Proc. Natl. Acad. Sci. USA* **2017**, *114*, 8935–8938. [CrossRef]
67. Ghani, E.; Kharas, H. The service revolution. *World Bank Econ. Premise* **2010**, *14*, 1–15.
68. Polloni-Silva, E.; Ferraz, D.; Camioto, F.D.C.; Rebelatto, D.A.D.N.; Moralles, H.F. Environmental kuznets curve and the pollution-halo/haven hypotheses: An investigation in Brazilian Municipalities. *Sustainability* **2021**, *13*, 4114. [CrossRef]

MDPI AG
Grosspeteranlage 5
4052 Basel
Switzerland
Tel.: +41 61 683 77 34

Infrastructures Editorial Office
E-mail: infrastructures@mdpi.com
www.mdpi.com/journal/infrastructures

www.ingramcontent.com/pod-product-compliance
Lightning Source LLC
LaVergne TN
LVHW072341090526
838202LV00019B/2454